TENNYSON:

HIS ART AND RELATION TO
MODERN LIFE

BY

STOPFORD A. BROOKE

LONDON
ISBISTER AND COMPANY Limited
15 & 16 TAVISTOCK STREET COVENT GARDEN
1902

Printed by BALLANTYNE, HANSON & Co.
London & Edinburgh

CONTENTS

INTRODUCTION

THE death of Tennyson was worthy of his life. He died with the simplicity which marked his life, and yet with a certain conscious stateliness which was all his own ; and these two, simplicity and stateliness, were also vital in the texture of his poetry. But his dying hour, though it has left a noble picture on the mind of England, is not the important thing. His life and poetry are the real matter of use and interest, and his death gains its best import from its being the beautiful and fitting end of all the work that had gone before it. It became an artist, it became a Christian, it became a man. To these three points this Introduction is dedicated—to his relation to beauty, to his relation to the Christian faith, and to his relation to the movement of humanity. The art of his poems, his work on nature and his work on human life, as far as this immense subject can be compressed into a few hundred pages, will be treated of in the rest of this book. For more than sixty years he practised his art, and his practice of it, being original and extraordinarily careful and self-respecting, suggests and comments on almost every question that concerns the art of poetry. For more than sixty years he lived close to the present life

of England, as far as he was capable of compre-
hending and sympathising with its movements; and
he inwove what he felt concerning it into his poetry.
For many years to come that poetry—so close to
modern life—will open a vast storehouse of subjects
to those writers who are interested in the application of imaginative emotion to the problems and
pleasures of life. Half at least of those problems
and pleasures eluded Tennyson, or he did not see
them. But he felt the other half all the more
strongly, and he felt it for this long period of sixty
years. He then who writes on Tennyson has so
wide a country over which to travel, that he
cannot do much more than visit it here and there.
When he has finished his journey, he knows how
much he has left unseen, untouched; how much
more of pleasure and good he will gain in many
more journeys over this varied, home-like, and
romantic land.

I

The first characteristic of Tennyson's art—that
is, of his shaping of the beauty which he saw in
Nature and Humanity—was simplicity, and this
came directly out of his character. The way in
which he worked, his choice of subjects, his
style, were all the revelation of a character drawn
on large and uncomplicated lines; and in this
sense, in the complete sincerity to his inner being
of all he did and in the manner of its doing, he was
simple in the truest sense of the word. Nothing
was ever done for effect; no subject in which he
was not veritably involved was taken up. Nothing

was even tried, save a few metrical exercises, for experiment's sake alone, much less to please the popular moment. The thing shaped was the legitimate child of natural thought and natural feeling. Vital sincerity or living correspondence between idea and form, that absolute necessity for all fine art as for all noble life, was his, and it is contained in what I have called his simplicity.

His clearness is also contained in this simplicity —clearness in thought, in expression, and in representation of the outward world, one of the first and greatest things an artist can attain. It is true that Tennyson never went down into the obscure and thorny depths of metaphysics and theology; it is true that he did not attempt to express the more dreadful and involved passions of mankind, such as Shakespeare in his Tragic worked upon, nor the subtle and distant analogies and phases of human nature in which Browning had his pleasure. It was easy, then, it may be said, for him to be clear. But I think it was not from inability to try these subjects that he did not write about them, but from deliberate choice not to write about that which he could not express with lucidity of thought and form. He determined to be clear. He chose plain and easy lines of thought in philosophy and theology, but he expressed them with art—that is, in beautiful form proceeding outwards from impassioned feeling; and a poem like *The Two Voices* or *Out of the Deep* is an instance of the way this was done. The same choice of the easy to be understood presided over his human subjects. For the most part he wrote of the everyday loves and duties of men and women;

of the primal pains and joys of humanity; of
the aspirations and trials which are common to
all ages and all classes and independent even of
the disease of civilisation; but he made them new
and surprising by the art which he added to them
—by beauty of thought, tenderness of feeling, and
exquisiteness of shaping. The main lines of the
subjects, even of the classical subjects, are few, are
simple, are clear.

And I think all the more that this choice of
clearness (of clearness as a part of simplicity) was
deliberate, because of his representation of Nature.
It is plain that he might have entered into infinite
and involuted description; that he could, if he
pleased, have expressed the stranger and remoter
aspects of Nature, for he had an eye to see everything from small to large. But he selected the
simple, the main lines of a landscape or an event
of Nature, and rejected the minuter detail or the
obscurer relations between the parts of that which he
described. What was done was done in the fewest
words possible, and with luminous fitness of phrase.

English literature owes him gratitude for this
clearness. At a time when we are running close
to the edge of all the errors of the later Elizabethans, Tennyson never allowed himself to drift
into obscurity of thought or obscurity of expression, and showed (as those did not who restored
clearness to English song in the time of Dryden)
that simplicity of words, as well as jewelled
brightness of thought and description, might
be also compact of imagination. The lamp
of language which he held in his hand burnt
with a bright, keen, and glowing flame. The

debt we owe Tennyson for this is not owed by English literature alone; it is personal also. Every writer should acknowledge the debt and follow the example. Clearness in thought and words ought to be a part of a writer's religion; it is certainly a necessary part of his morality. Nay, to follow clearness like a star, clearness of thought, clearness of phrase, in every kind of life, is the duty of all. But the poets are most bound to feel and fulfil that duty, and it is not one of the least which belong to their art and their influence. Tennyson felt it and fulfilled it.

One other thing I may briefly add to these judgments concerning his simplicity. It is that (after his very earliest work) his stuff is of almost an equal quality throughout. I do not mean that all the poems are equally good, but that the web on which their pattern was woven kept, with but a few exceptions, the same closeness and fineness throughout. The invention, the pictures, the arrangement, and the colouring of the things wrought on the web were variable in excellence, but the stuff was uniform. This is an excessively rare excellence in a poet, and it continued to the close. The workmanship is curiously level from youth to age; and that kind of simplicity has also its root in character.

Mingled with this simplicity, which was due to the unconscious entrance of his character into his art, there was also in all his poetry, as I have said with regard to his death, a certain stateliness entirely conscious of itself, and arising out of a reverence for his own individuality. The personality of Tennyson, vividly conscious of itself and respecting itself, pervades his poetry, is part of his art, and gives it part of its power. I have called it self-respecting to distinguish it from the personality of those poets who, like Byron, spread out their personality before us, but whom we cannot suspect of reverencing themselves. " Reverencing themselves" seems an invidious term, but in the case of poets like Tennyson, and there is a distinct class of such poets, it means that they look upon themselves as prophets, as endowed with power to proclaim truth and beauty, as consecrated to do work which will delight, console, and exalt mankind. It is, then, rather their high vocation which they reverence than anything in themselves ; and this bestows on all their work that stateliness which is self-conscious, as it were, in all their poems. They are never seen in undress, never without their singing and prophetic robes, never unattended by one or other of the graver Muses.

We have had two great examples of this type of poet in the past. Milton was one, Wordsworth was another. Milton never moved his verse unconscious of Urania by his side. Wordsworth never lost the sense that he was a consecrated spirit. And Tennyson never forgot that the poet's work was to convince the world of love and beauty ; that he was born to do that work, and to do it worthily. This is an egotism (if we choose to give it that term) which is charged with power and with fire. Any individuality, conscious of itself, respecting itself because of its faith in a sacred mission entrusted to it and beneath which it may not fall without dishonour, lifts and kindles other individualities, and exalts their views of human life.

It does this work with tenfold greater force when it is in a poet, that is, in one who adds to its moral force the all-subduing power of beauty.

This conviction, which cannot belong to a weak poet, but does (when it is consistent throughout life) belong to poets whose nature is hewn out of the living rock, enters as stateliness into all their verse, gives it a moral virtue, a spiritual strength, and emerges in a certain grandeur or splendour of style, more or less fine as the character is more or less nobly mixed. This sense of the relation the poet bears to mankind, this sense he has of his office and of the duty it imposes on him, was profoundly felt by Tennyson, became a part of him as an artist, and was an element in every line he wrote. Personal it was, but it was personal for the sake of humanity; and dignity, stateliness in subjects, in thoughts and in style, issued naturally from that conviction.

These are things which belong to a poet's art, but by themselves they would not, of course, make him an artist. The essential difference of an artist is love of beauty and the power of shaping it. The greatness of an artist is proportionate to the depth and truth of his love of beauty; to his faithfulness to it, and to his unremitting effort to train his natural gift of shaping it into fuller ease, power, and permanence. As to beauty itself, men talk of natural beauty, of physical, moral, and spiritual beauty, and these term-divisions have their use; but at root all beauty is one, and these divided forms of it are modes only of one energy, conditioned by the elements through which it passes. They can all pass into one another, and they can all be expressed in terms of one another.

To define, then, what beauty is in itself is beyond our power, but we can approach a definition of it by marking out clearly its results on us. What is always true of beauty is this, that, wherever it appears, it awakens love of it which has no return on self, but which bears us out of ourselves; it stirs either joy or reverence in the heart without bringing with it any self-admiration or vanity; and it kindles the desire of reproducing it, not that we may exult in our own skill in forming it, but that our reproduction of it may awaken emotions in others similar to those which the original sight of beauty stirred in our own heart— that is, it more or less forces the seer of it into creation. This creation, this representation of the beautiful, is art; and the most skilful representation of the ugly—that is, of anything which awakens either repulsion, or base pleasure, or horror which does not set free and purify the soul, or scorn instead of reverence, or which does not kindle in us the desire of reproduction of it that we may stir in others similar emotions to our own—is not art at all. It is clever imitation, it is skill, it is artifice, it is not art. It is characteristic of an age which is writhing under the frivolous despotism of positive science that the accurate and skilful representation of things and facts which are not beautiful is called art; and it belongs to all persons who care for the growth of humanity, not to denounce this error, for denunciation is barren of results, but to live and labour for the opposite truth. Far more rests on that effort than men imagine. A third at least of the future betterment of mankind, to which we now look forward with more hope than we have done for years, depends on this effort, on all that it involves, on all that it will create in the imaginative and spiritual life of the human race.

With a few exceptions, into which this tendency to scientific representation carried him—poems of dissection and denunciation, like *Despair*, and worse still, *The Promise of May*, Tennyson was faithful through his whole life to beauty, writing always of what was worthy of love, of joy, of solemn or happy reverence ; and by this, and in this sphere, was the steady artist. The manifestation of these things, his creation of them, for the love and pleasure and veneration of himself and men, was his unbroken delight.

How much we owe to him for this, especially at this time, only the future will fully know. It is true, this faithfulness to beauty is the foremost characteristic of all great artists, the very quintessence of their genius, that which makes them permanent ; but he deserves perhaps more praise for it than many others, for he was tempted by the tendency of his time to swerve from it, as Wordsworth, Shelley and Keats were not tempted. Once or twice he yielded, as I said, but these instances only show how much he resisted, and how faithfully. This, then, it was which kept him always fresh, even to advanced age. He whose eyes are steadily fixed on the beautiful, always loves, and is always young.

Moreover, the true artist has written on his heart, "Love not the world, nor the things of the world," and this, in spite of many foolish things said of him, was true of Tennyson. If what I said of his love of beauty be true, he could not have bent his art to the world, and he never did. For the artist knows that absolute beauty is a perfection which he never can fully grasp, which always becomes before him a greater ocean, which therefore invites and kindles an incessant pursuit. He can never furl his sail in this pursuit ; he can never turn aside, while he is full of its ardour, to any lower or meaner love, to any selfish strife. The passion it makes glow is one which devours all other passions. The desire to reveal beauty, to make it clear, so far as he has seen it, is a desire which makes all merely personal desires common and unclean.

Whatever vulgar folk have said of Tennyson, his whole work breathes with that desire. I do not believe, and I cannot trace in one line of his poetry, that he ever wrote for the sake of money, or place, or to catch the popular ear, or to win a transient praise. He wrote only that of which he loved to write, that which moved him to joy or reverence, that which he thought of good report for its loveliness. Even the things he did as Poet Laureate, where, if ever, he might have been untrue to this, have no tinge of the world about them. They speak to royalties of the things of eternal beauty, of the natural sorrows and joys of faithful motherhood and wifehood, of duties and sacrifice performed in high places—the same duties and sacrifice which might be done by the labourer and the slave—of love and honour and faith, of those ideals of humanity which are as capable of being pursued and fulfilled in the cottage as in the palace. The Laureate Odes are more lessons to royal folk than celebrations of them.

He was, then, faithful to loveliness. It is not too much to say that he saw all the universe of man and Nature and of God in their relation to ineffable beauty, and that the getting of this pervading essence out of all things, the shaping of it, and the crying of—"Look there ; love and worship, rejoice and reverence," was the one supreme thing in his art for which he cared. This may be said of all true poets, and it is here said of him. It is the mightiest debt we owe to the faithful artists, and we feel it all the more deeply at a time when art yields more than is seemly to the temptations of the world.

But the power of seeing beauty, and the love of beauty, are not all that makes the great artist. He must also have the power of shaping the beauty which he sees, and in a way peculiarly his own. There must be in the work the personal touch, the individual surprise, the unique way, the unimitated shaping which provokes imitation. We ought to feel in every artist's work the immediate pressure of an original, personal creator, who has his own special manner with things and words. This is one of the main tests of genius. Of every great poet it is true, and it is plainly true of Tennyson. Every line is alive with his own distinction.

On his natural gift of creating, and on his careful training of it, I need not dwell, nor yet on his practice and love of the skilfulnesses of his art, of the careful study of words and their powers in verse, of his mingled strength and daintiness and

B

weakness, of all that belongs to Form. These things and their like in him have been for years the food of critics. No one disputes that he touched excellence in them, or that he had the power of creation. But I maintain that all his technique was not for its own sake, but was first urged by his love of beauty. It was necessary, for the sake of his faithfulness to her, that the shape he gave to what he loved should be as perfect, as strong, as gracious, and as full of delightful surprises as he could make it; and not one of our poets has striven with a more unfailing intensity to do this honour to all the beauty he saw in Nature and in man ; as eager in this at eighty as at thirty years. It is a great lesson to all artists; it is a lesson to us all.

Power, then, to see beauty, power to shape it, these were his. How far he saw it, with what degrees of excellence he shaped it, how great an artist he was—is not now the question. The question is, Did he always see it with love and joy ; did he always shape it with faithfulness ? And I answer that his fidelity to beauty, whenever he saw it, was unbroken.

II

The next subject I treat of in this Introduction is Tennyson's relation to Christianity.

When Tennyson passed from school to the university, religious life in England had very much decayed. The spirit which animated Wesley, and which had fallen like the prophet's mantle on the earlier Evangelicals, had now become cold.

English religion, in and out of the Church, was like the valley Ezekiel described, full of bones, and the bones were dry. And in the midst of the valley one figure, now old, who had seen the fire of religious sacrifice rise high to God in the past, who had welcomed its descent and directed it into new channels but who had outlived his enthusiasms, went to and fro, chilled at heart, and wailing for what had been. It was the soul of Coleridge, and if the voice of the Spirit asked him: " Son of Man, can these bones live ? " he answered, but not in hope, " O Lord God, Thou knowest." He died before he saw the resurrection which Tennyson saw, the blowing of the wind of God, and the bones coming together, and the slain breathed upon, so that they lived and stood upon their feet, an exceeding great army. Nevertheless, the old prophet did his work, and his power moved in the two men, though in a very different fashion, who, in the same years which saw a political and poetic resurrection, awakened into a new spring, with all the promise of summer, the religious life of England. The true beginning of Tennyson's as of Browning's poetical life was coincident with the birth of the movements afterwards called the High Church and the Broad Church movements, and with the birth of a new political and social era.

> Never alone
> Come the immortals.

This religious awakening was felt and seized by two distinct types of character, or of human tendency, and crystallised by two representative men, by J. H. Newman and Frederick Maurice ;

and it is curious for those who care for analogies to the evolution of species to trace how the one was the child of the University of Oxford and the other of the University of Cambridge. The main difference which lay between their method of presenting the faith was a time-difference, if I may be allowed to invent that term. In the matter of religion the past was the foremost thing to Newman, to Maurice the present. Newman looked back to the past (the nearer to the Apostles the nearer to truth) for the highest point to which religious life, but not doctrine, had attained, and his immense reverence for the past became part of the mind of Tennyson. But it was balanced in Tennyson by even a greater reverence for the present as containing in it an immediate inspiration and revelation from God. This foundation for poetic thought and emotion was given to him by the religious work of Maurice. The deepest thought in the mind of Maurice was that God was moving in the present as fully as He had moved in the past ; and the incessant representation of this, in every form of it, was his great contribution to Theology. Of course, others before him had said similar things, but he said this in a new way, and under new conditions. Maurice could not, however, quite escape from the web of the past, and his struggle to combine the past and the present entangled him, entangled his mind, and entangled his followers. When he clung, as he did, to the ancient intellectual formulas as laid down in the Creeds and Services of the Church, and tried to weave them into harmony with his main faith, he damaged his position, and, up to a certain point, his work.

Tennyson, as a poet, did not fall into this ill-fortuned position. What his personal views were concerning the creed of Christendom is not the question here. It would be an impertinence to discuss them. That is a private matter, and we shall hear what his family choose to disclose to us at the fitting time. But his poetry is a public possession, and in that poetry there is naturally no doctrinal confession, no intellectual propositions which define his faith. I say *naturally*, because art has to do with the illimitable, with that which is for ever incapable of definition, with the things that belong to love and beauty, joy and hope and veneration—the shapes, degrees, powers, and glory of which are for ever building, un-building, and rebuilding themselves in each man's soul and in the soul of the whole world. Art not only rejects, it abhors all attempts to bind down into unchanging forms the thoughts and emotions which play like lightning round the infinite horizons towards which the imagination sails, piloted by love, and hope, and faith. It has no creeds, no articles of faith, no schemes of salvation, no confessions ; it cannot have them by its very nature. The unknowable, but the believable, is its country, its native land, its home.

Whatever then, in this matter of religion, the man as thinker may confess, the man as poet keeps in the realm of the undefined, beyond analysis, beyond reasoning. When he does not, when he is tempted into analytic discussion, into doctrinal definition, he ceases to be a poet for the time and

the trouble into which he gets is pitiable. When
Milton argues like a school divine, when Wordsworth draws out a plan of education, when Byron
explains his view of original sin, how sad it is,
how the Muses cover their faces, how angrily
Apollo frowns! Even Dante, who was obliged
to do something of this kind of work, does it only
as a means by which he may launch himself forward into the infinite. And Tennyson rarely in
this way lost his position as an artist. There is
no formulated creed in his work.

But the main faiths of Maurice, which were
assertions of what he conceived to be " eternal
verities" concerning the relations of God to man
and to the universe, and concerning the end to
which God was leading them—assertions backed
up by no proof, for the matters insisted on could
neither be proved nor disproved—were naturally in
the realm of the imagination, of faith and hope, in
the infinite realm of love, and were brought to
receive acceptance or dismissal before the tribunal
of human emotion, not before the tribunal of the
understanding. As such they were proper subjects
of poetry ; and the ever-working immanence of
God in man and in the universe as Will and Love,
as King and Father ; the necessary brotherhood of
man, and the necessary practice of love one to
another, if all were in God ; the necessary evolution (if this vital union between God and man
existed) of the human race into perfect love and
righteousness, and the necessary continuance on
the same hypothesis of each man's personal consciousness in a life to be ; the necessary vitality
of the present—that deep need for high poetic

work—man alive and Nature alive and alive with
the life of God—these faiths (I will not call them
doctrines, for their definition changes incessantly
with the progress of human thought and feeling)
lay at the root of the religion we find in the poetry
of Tennyson and influenced that poetry from 1830
to 1892. They were part of the elements of the
soil out of which his poetry grew, and by them,
and by the way in which he held them, carefully
keeping them apart from all intellectual definition
and in the realm of faith alone, he is separated on
the one side from all those poets who either ignore
these things like Keats or profess disbelief in them
like Shelley, and on the other side from all those
poets who like Milton, Byron or Browning have a
definite theology in their poetry.

These things, then, may justly be said with
regard to the religious elements in the poetry
of Tennyson, and they are all contained in *In
Memoriam ;* nay more, they are the very basis
of that poem. But the assertion of them does not
answer the question : What relation does Tennyson's poetry bear to Christianity ? For all these
beliefs might be held by a Theist—even by one
who ignored or depreciated the teaching of Jesus.
If Tennyson is then to be claimed as a Christian
poet it must be shown that he considered Jesus to
be the great proclaimer of these truths, the one who
concentrated into Himself the religious truths which
before Him had been in man, re-formed them in His
own thought, and issued them with new power and
charged with new love, to claim the belief of men.
This certainly was Tennyson's position.* So far

* *In Memoriam*, xxxvi.

as that goes, Tennyson was distinctly Christian, and this is the position of a great number of persons at the present day. But if that be all, then a great number of persons will deny him the right to call himself a Christian. In their mind a Christian man must have a distinct faith in Jesus as God, as the unique Saviour of man, and as a revealer of God in a way different in kind from that in which we can call any other person a saviour or revealer. Is that view contained in Tennyson's poetry? We cannot take the phrases concerning Christ used in the *Idylls of the King,* or such phrases as " Him who died for me " in *The May Queen,* as any proof of his views, for these might be said to be only local colour; but when we come to *In Memoriam* we have before us a poem exceedingly personal and distinctly theological; and Christ is called there " The Life indeed "; His power to raise the dead is confessed; He is the receiver of the souls of the dead into the world beyond this world; He is the Word of God that breathed human breath and wrought out the faith with human deeds. This is not enough to make Tennyson, as a poet, an orthodox Christian in the doctrinal sense, but it is enough to place him among those who confess Jesus as the Light of the world, as their spiritual Master, their Life; and that with a distinctness which does not belong to any other of the great poets of this century, so far as their poetry is concerned. This position becomes a certainty if the introduction to *In Memoriam*—beginning " Strong Son of God, immortal Love"—be an address to Jesus. I think it is, and that this is the most natural explanation; but nevertheless it is left vague. On the whole,

there is no clear doctrinal definition of the person
or the work of Christ. What is *not* left vague,
what is quite clear, is that Tennyson is more Christian than Theist; that no mere Theist could have
said the things that he has said in *In Memoriam*.

This absence of definite doctrine, which is the
reason many persons say that Tennyson was not a
Christian (holding the amusing theory that the
Nicene Creed rather than the teaching of Jesus
is the test of Christianity) is, first of all, neces-
sitated by his art; secondly, it is in itself Christian. Definite doctrinal statements are, as I said,
abhorrent to poetry. They belong to the world of
the understanding, to the world of analysis—a
world in which the artist cannot breathe at ease,
and in which, if he continue, his art decays and
dies. They take him out of the illimitable sky in
which the imagination flies towards the unknown,
the yet unconceived, and the ever-varying un-
changeable. Had Tennyson defined his view of
Jesus, he would never have said " Ring in the
Christ which is to be." In that line the idea of
Christ and His Gospel in mankind is given an infinite extension. We may give the phrase fifty
meanings, and we shall not exhaust it; and a
hundred years hence it will have totally different
meanings allotted to it by the gentlemen who wish
to define.

Secondly, this absence of propositions invented
by the intellect, in which ideas like the immanence
of God in man are limited to one meaning, in
which the Fatherhood of God or the brotherhood of
man is rendered particular instead of being left
universal, is in harmony with the teaching of

Jesus.   He proclaimed truths which He believed to
be universal—God's Fatherhood, man's brotherhood, love as the absolute life of God and of man,
personal immortality in God, the forgiveness of sin
—but He never put these into any fixed intellectual
form ; He never attempted to prove them by argument ; He never limited them by a prosaic statement of their import ; He never took them out of
the realm of love and faith ; He never gave them
a special shape or organised them into a body of
belief.   He left them free, left them as spirit and
life ; and as to their form, every nation and
kindred and tongue, every kind of society, nay,
every person, could give them whatever intellectual
shape each of them pleased.   If they were loved
and felt, and the love at the root of them expressed
in the action of a life, I do not believe that Jesus
cared at all what form they took in the understanding, or how they were organised into ritual and
creed—provided only the form or the organisation
did not contradict the universality of the love of
God, or the universality of the love between man
and man which was contained in them.   Theological creeds were nothing to Jesus, but their
limitations which produced hatreds and cruelties
and quarrels, these, to this hour, He looks upon
with the pity and the indignation of love.   The
absence then of definite opinions about infinite
truths, which is the necessary position of the poet,
which was the position of Tennyson in his poetry,
is the position of Christ Himself.

Again, Christianity does not take the same ground
as ethics, nor was Christ, primarily, a moral teacher.
"This do and thou shalt live," the moralist says,

and it is a good thing to say. "When you have done all," says Jesus, carrying the whole matter of life into boundless aspiration, "say, We are unprofitable servants, we have done only what it was our duty to do." "Lord, how oft shall I forgive my brother? Unto seven times? Surely there must be some definition." "Unto seven times?" answered Christ, in astonishment at any limit to forgiveness—"nay, any number of times—to seventy times seven!" "All these things," cried the young moralist, "all these duties, I have kept from my youth up. What lack I yet?" That was the cry of the ideal in him : the inward longing for something more than conduct—for the unknown perfection. And Jesus, answering this aspiration to the ideal, to those unreached summits of love which transcend duty—said, "Sell what thou hast, and give to the poor, and come and follow me." "Whom shall I love," they asked ; "my relations, my friends, my own nation, the members of my Church? Where is the limit?" There is no limit, was the teaching of Jesus ; the infinitude of God's love is your true aim. "Love your enemies, do good to them that hate you ; so will you be like your Father in heaven, whose sun shines on the evil and good alike." "Shall I be content with the duties which I can do, with the love I can certainly give to my fellow-men, with the plain things which lie before me in this world, with the possible in conduct?" No, thought Jesus, that is not my teaching, nor the ground I take. You must aspire to the impossible, strive to be equal to the infinite love, love far beyond anything you can understand. It is not the possible, but the perfect, for which you must live. "Be ye perfect in love, even as your Father is perfect in love." Union with the infinite Love by loving; that is the aim of man, an illimitable aim.

At every point this position of Christ is in the strictest analogy to that which the artist takes up with regard to beauty. Love, not duty, is the first thing with Jesus; the teaching of loving, not the teaching of morality. If love be secured, morality is secured. If a man love God, that is, if he love the living source of love, righteousness, justice and truth; he is absolutely certain to secure noble conduct. Morality then is not neglected, it is taken in the stride of love. And that is the root of Jesus. Love fulfils the law; and all the poets, and every artist (whether nominally a Christian or not), take a similar position. Love, in its tireless outgoings towards infinite beauty— the seen suggesting for ever the unseen beauty, and that which is conceived of it opening out a vision of new loveliness as yet unconceived—is the artists' root; and whatever morality they teach is the secondary matter, comes as a necessary result of love having its perfect work—love which, when we have reached the farthest horizon we first saw of it, opens out another equally far, and when we have attained that, another, and again another, always and for ever.

This is the Christian position, and it is the position Tennyson preserves all through his poetry. There is no one, it is true, from whose work better lessons can be drawn for the conduct of life, for morals in their higher ranges, than can be drawn from Tennyson. But below all conduct, as its foundation impulse, lies in this poet's work the love of the infinite Love, the passion of unending effort for it, and the conviction of an eternity of life in which to pursue after it. This eternal continuance in us of the conscious life of love; in other words, of incessant action towards greater nearness to the illimitable Love which is God, is the position of Christ; and it is the position of one who believes in a personal immortality. One of the foundation faiths of Jesus was that every man and woman was as unbrokenly connected with the Eternal God as a child is with a father. God was our nearest relation; the relationship was a personal one, and could never be untied. In that, our immortal continuance, our immortal personality, our immortal goodness, were necessarily contained. The declaration of immortality was not in itself new, but this ground of it—the Fatherhood of God and the childhood to Him of every man so that each soul was felt by God, in Himself, as a special person to whom He was in a special relation—this, and the universality of its application, were new.

This was Tennyson's position. It might be proved up to the hilt from his poetry, and it makes him clearly Christian. Owing to the circumstances of his time, it was especially round this question of immortality that Tennyson, in his relation to Christianity, concentrated himself. Its truth held in it for him the Fatherhood of God, the salvation of man, the brotherhood of man, the worth of human life. If it were not true, Christianity in his eyes was not true—there was no God in the universe for man; there was no true union possible between man and man ; there was no religion—nothing to bind men together ; there was no explanation of the pain of earth, and the whole history of man was a dreadful tragedy. That was his view, and he maintained it with all a poet's fervour.

But it would not be true to say that Tennyson had not to fight for it against thoughts within which endeavoured to betray it, and against doubts which besieged it from without. He did not always *repose* in it ; he had to fight for it sword in hand, and many a troublous wound he took. He was a poet, sensitive to all the movements of the world around him, and it fell to his lot to live at a time when the faith in immortality has had to run the gauntlet between foes or seeming friends, of a greater variety and of a greater skill than ever before in the history of man. He felt every form of this attack in himself ; he battled with himself as he felt them ; he battled with them outside himself ; and he won his personal victory, having sympathised thus, throughout the course of sixty years, with those who have had to fight the same battle. Of what worth his contribution is to the problem is not the question here. I only state the fact, and the manner in which it was done. It was done in the manner of a poet—never by argument as such, rarely from the intellectual point of view—but by an appeal to the emotions, by an appeal to the necessities of love. Had he done otherwise, he would have, at that point, ceased to be the poet, ceased to rest the truth of immortality on faith in that unprovable conviction that there was a

God and that He was indissolubly bound up with the personality of all of His children.

The trouble began early with him. The religious change I have noted in the thirties disturbed, no doubt, his early faith, and the result is written for us in the *Confessions of a Sensitive Mind*. Vacillation of faith is the basis of that poem ; and no answer is given to the questions proposed therein. Again, the whole question—on the basis of " Is life worth living ? Is it not better not to be ?"—is taken up in *The Two Voices*. The answer is—" Life is not worth living if it does not continue, if love is not immortal in God and in us." Then *The Vision of Sin* asks the same question in another form. Sensual pleasure in youth has ended in cynicism in age. What hope ? There is an answer, the poet says, but it is in a tongue no man can understand ; nevertheless it comes out of a horizon where God shows like a rose of dawn.

The same question forms the basis of *In Memoriam*. What is the proper answer to the problem of sorrow, of the loss of those we love —to the cry of the breaking heart all over the world ? Immortal life in God who is immortal Love, and therefore immortal Life, is the answer ; immortal development—immortal union with all we love ; the never-ending evolution of all into more and more of perfection.

> One God—one law—one element,
> And one far-off divine event,
> To which the whole creation moves.

A number of questions arising out of the matter are

proposed, many speculations are made, but the answers suggested are all founded, in the necessary manner of a poet, on an appeal to love in us, and to the love which, if there be a supreme goodness, must be at the very root of His being.

Lastly, it is plain that Tennyson had, when he finished *In Memoriam*, settled down into quiet on this matter. He had fought his doubts and laid them. But the time in which he lived did not let him rest. He had again to put on his armour and to draw his sword. The argument of Darwin that our conscience and our emotions came by descent from the brutes was used as an argument against immortality. The great development of physiological science tended to increase among persons of a certain set of mind a naked materialism, more or less cynical; and especially went against all beliefs, like that of immortality, which could not be tested by experiment. Then, all the outward authority on which the Christian faith had long reposed, the grey-haired authority of the Church, the younger authority of the infallibility of the Bible, was shaken to its foundations by the application of the science of historical criticism to the New Testament stories and to the history of the Early Church, so that the outward authority for immortality passed away from the minds of multitudes, and with it that which is bound up with it —the belief in a Divine Father of mankind.

And, now, among those—the greater number, it is true—who still clung to these faiths, there was no longer peace. Doubts, incessant questions troubled them; faith veiled her face for long periods. Men and women fought and still fight for the truths dearest to them, as Arthur fought with his foes in that dim, weird battle of the West, in a chill and blinding vapour, and looking up to heaven only see the mist.

Then it was that Tennyson—and it is from his poetry alone that I gather this—shaken out of his certainty in *In Memoriam*, feeling all the new trouble of the world, took up again the sword against his own questionings and against the scepticism of the world in which he lived. The mystery of the pains of life, side by side with a God of love, deepened around him. No creed, no faith, seemed to completely answer it. But all the more, he felt that the only chance of an answer was in clinging to the conviction of a life to come in which all shall be wrought into union with God. Once or twice he was carried beyond tolerance into hot indignation with those who took away what he believed to be the only reply to the problem of pain and evil.

In his poem of *Despair* he denounced the " know-nothings," as he called them, as well as the liars who held eternal punishment, and with equal wrath and vigour. In *The Promise of May* he painted, and unfairly, the materialist as almost necessarily immoral. He need not have been so angry, and he did no good by the passages of attack in those poems. Had he believed more at the time he wrote them he would not have been so violent. He would have felt that, if all men were God's children, it mattered little whether these persons denied immortality or not. They would find out the truth in the end, and their disbelief could do no final harm to them or to

C

mankind. However, as his life went on, his anger
seemed to pass away. He resumed his old method
of warfare—the method of the artist—the appeal to
love, the appeal to the heart of man, the appeal to
the incredibility of all the glory and all the growth
of man, of all the dreadfulness of his fate, being
alike closed in universal death. Many are the
poems in his later volumes, poems like *Vastness*, for
example, which take up this artist-position. At
last, as it seems, all his distress ceased in quiet, in
a faith even more settled than that of *In Memoriam*.
Some trouble still lives in the last volume, published
while he was yet alive. *Vastness* still strikes a
wavering note. He says in another poem that,
" In spite of every creed and faith, Life is the
Mystery." In the poem, *By an Evolutionist*, the
end seems a matter of hope rather than of certainty. The last poem in the book, *Crossing the
Bar*, is the first clear cry of happy faith—all
doubt and trouble past ; and it is a quiet faith
that persists through a new volume which contains
his last words to the people of England. *The
Making of Man*, while it accepts evolution, carries
it onward to the perfect accomplishment of all
humanity in God :

> Hallelujah to the Maker. It is finished. Man is made.

The Dreamer has no uncertainty. *Doubt and
Prayer* and *Faith*, the one following the other,
assert that " Love is his Father, Brother, and his
God," and that Death flings open the gates of all
that we desire in the heart. *God and the Universe*,
written on the threshold of death, reveals that all
fear of dissolution has gone for ever. " The face of

Death is toward the Sun of Life—his truer name is ' Onward,'" so the poet speaks again to the mourners in the last poem of his last book.

This faithful fighter then, who stood, like Horatius, for sixty years defending the strait bridge of faith in immortal life, defending it against his own doubts and those of his time, laid down his arms at last, conscious of his victory. Time will tell whether it is a victory also for us. For my part, I have no shadow of doubt as to the conclusion the world will finally come to on this matter ; and when that conclusion is reached, the long battle of Tennyson for the Christian faith, for God as the Father of all, and for the necessary inference of immortality from that primary declaration of Christ Jesus, will be acknowledged by the steady gratitude of mankind.

III

I now turn, in this Introduction, to Tennyson's relation to the movement of Humanity.

In literature as in Nature there is continuity of development, and the germs of the subjects which the new poetry of any generation develops into full-foliaged trees are to be found in the poetry which preceded that new poetry. The poetry of Nature, as fully written by Wordsworth, Shelley, and Keats, had, as it were, a child-life before their time. The theological poetry of Browning, of Tennyson, of a host of minor poets, arose out of certain tendencies of thought and emotion which were expressed, in opposition to the orthodox theology of their time, by Byron and Shelley.

The various forms of the poetry of human life, and especially of the poetry of human progress, which the poets embodied from the year 1830 to the year 1870, were outlined, as it were, in the poetry of the first thirty years of this century. In what manner Tennyson developed the poetry of Nature is a fascinating subject; but it will best be treated in connection with his poems. What he did with regard to the theological shapes which emerged in his time has already received notice. What did he say of the subjects which belong to the growth of humanity towards a better society? What relation did he bear to social politics, if I may use that term?

With the impulse given by Reform in 1832, a number of questions belonging to social progress were reawakened into a fuller life, and took new forms. Was the power of government best placed in the hands of the whole people, or in the hands of great men? It is plain that Tennyson answered with Carlyle that great men (provided they had, like Wellington, a supreme sense of duty, a proviso Carlyle did not always insert) were those in whose hands power should dwell. Freedom, in his conception of it, was safer with them. The voice of the people, he thought, was a babbling voice, for the people were led by mere orators. Tennyson was never democratic at heart. He never understood what democracy in its reality meant, much less did he ever conceive its ideal. He was always an aristocrat, though he would have said, with justice, that it was a government of the best men that he desired, and not a government of rank and birth alone. Rank and birth, when they were

unworthy of their privileged position, he despised
and denounced, because they were inhuman. But
I do not think that he ever wished that rank
should be dissolved, or privileges overthrown, or
that he even conceived the idea that the people of
themselves were to choose the best men. He saw
(from his poetic point of view) that all men were
equal in their relations to the common feelings and
duties of the race ; that in suffering, in love, in the
desire of right and justice, in the visions and long-
ings of youth and age, there was an eternal
equality ; and, like all the great poets, his work
in this realm of thought has drawn men and
women of all ranks and classes into a closer sympathy with one another, and placed them hand in
hand on a common ground of humanity ; but when
it came to extending that community of human
relationship into the political or the social sphere,
he not only drew back, he did not understand
what this meant. The Republicanism with which
Wordsworth and Coleridge were at first enchanted,
and from which they afterwards retreated ; the
revolutionary spirit of Byron and his crusade
against respectability ; the more deliberate wrath
of Shelley with the whole of the idols and
oppression of a society founded as he believed
on caste and force and not on equality and
love, were one and all wholly unrepresented by
Tennyson, nay, they were implicitly attacked by
him. His whole conception of law and government, and of freedom, excluded them from its circle.
Not in his hands, then, lay the development of
the seeds which Shelley had scattered in his manhood. No, nor even those which Wordsworth

had sown in his youth. He was much more, on
this side, the true successor of Keats, to whom
all these political and social questions were, because of their apparent ugliness, repulsive; and
who took refuge from them in the stories of the
Greeks and of the Renaissance out of which time
had withdrawn the coarse and left the beautiful.
But Keats lived at a time when there was no
national emotion, when men were really weary of the
democratic ideas, and he represents that weariness.
Tennyson, on the contrary, did live in a time of
national emotion, and though he partly followed
Keats in a retreat to the past, yet he could not
altogether, even had he desired it, loosen himself
from the excitement which encompassed him. His
age was vividly with him, and he wrote of patriotism, of the proper conception of freedom, of the
sad condition of the poor, of the woman's position
in the onward movement of the world, of the place
of commerce and science in that movement, of war
as the remedy for the selfishness and evils of
commerce, and of the future of the race. These
are the main things he touched, and of them all
it is true that they were questions which had been
outlined in the previous poetic period, and outlined
in the new forms they took after 1832.

The first of these is Patriotism.

I have said that he felt strongly the vitality of
the present in which he lived. But he also brought
into the present an immense reverence for the past,
and that is one of the strongest foundations of his
patriotism. The poem, which begins

Love thou thy land, with love far-brought
From out the storied Past,

is but one of a hundred utterances, the note of
which remained the same clear sound from the
beginning to the end. It was a pity that the
emotion was chiefly given to the warlike glories of
England by land and sea, and but little bestowed
on the long and more glorious though fameless
struggle of people and towns for civic liberty;
but we may well excuse the poet's preference for
valour and for death in behalf of the honour of
the land in the striking circumstance of war.
This is more vivid for verse, and *The Revenge :
A Ballad of the Fleet*, and *The Defence of Lucknow*,
and *The Charge of the Light Brigade*, will always
stir English hearts.

Moreover, no one has better dwelt on the noble
elements of English character, their long descent
to us from the past, and the sacred reverence
that we owe to them, than Tennyson. He has
strengthened, by the expression of this reverence,
love of country among this people, and the strength
he has thus added to it will endure as a power
in England. It will be more than a power. It will
be a voice to recall us to reverence when, in the
push onwards to a future liberty and in the heated
atmosphere of that strife, we tend to forget how
much we owe to the ancient forms and to the bygone men, the results of whose work we may put
aside as unfitted for the present time. For if in
our excitement for the future we lose reverence
for the past, the loss of reverence will so injure
the soul of the nation that when we gain our
objects in the time to come, we shall not be able
to keep them nobly or to use them rightly. No
splendid future, splendid in that just feeling for

righteousness and love which hinders the despotism that so often succeeds a wholly irreverent revolution, can be won by a nation which has forgotten veneration for its magnanimous past. The work of Tennyson, in this point of patriotism, is altogether fine and true.

Nevertheless, it had its extreme. It ran sometimes into an English *Chauvinism*, and in this extreme Tennyson became, with a curious reversion to the type of the Englishmen of Nelson's time, the natural opponent, even the mocker of France and the French character. The words which, at the end of *The Princess*, he puts into the mouth of the Tory member's son, represent a part of his own point of view, though they are modified in the reply that follows. Phrases like

The red fool-fury of the Seine,

show how he looked on the passionate forms which political ideas had received in France, and the one-sided view he took of our neighbours' character. He saw only the evil of these things, just because he was so exclusively of the solid English type. Now and again the natural variety of a poet made him attempt to see the other side, as in the answer to the Tory member's son. But it was against the grain. He saw but little of what France has done for us ; he had no gratitude to her for her audacity, her swiftness, her logical expansion into form of the thoughts of progress ; he did not see or feel that much of the freedom we have lately won was owing to England's calm contemplation, with a certain amount of pleasurable but base contempt, of the mistakes which France alone had the boldness and the self-sacrifice to make for the world. He did not see our cool acceptance of the results for liberty which emerged after the mistakes of France had run their course. She bore the consequences of her mistakes, but in exhausting these she set the true form of certain ideas of liberty clear. We take the ideas she has set free, but we forget that she revealed them. There has been no ingratitude so great in the history of humanity as the ingratitude of Europe to France, and Tennyson represented with great vividness this ingratitude in England.

Hence, or rather along with this, he did not, except now and then in vague suggestions, carry the love of country forward into the love of mankind. He had but little sympathy in his poetry with other nations. At this point he is far behind Coleridge, Wordsworth, Byron, and Shelley. The only struggles for freedom with which he openly sympathises were those of Poland in his youth, and of Montenegro in his age. The battle of Italy for liberty is scarcely mentioned. The struggle of the North against slavery in the United States is never touched. Nor could he write, and this illustrates still further his insulation, as Browning wrote, of Italy, of Spain, of France, of modern Greece, of men and women's lives away from England. He never became international. The higher conception to which love of our own nation is to lead—the love of all nations as contained in one nation, the nation of Man—did not shine in the mind of Tennyson. It arose into clear form with the French Revolution ; it has taken a new and a better form in modern times, but none of its

developments were sympathised with, were even
conceived by Tennyson. He was at this point
over-English. He is, at this point, out of sympathy with the progress of Man. He is not, at this
point, our poet or the poet of the future.

Again, take the idea of human freedom ; which,
thrown as it was by Shelley into the arena where
the young emotions of the present contend with
grey-haired theories of the past, became a much
more actual consideration in all national life after
1832. That idea is not only freedom to speak the
thing we will, or freedom of act or contract, or such
national liberty only as all Englishmen enjoy—but
the setting free of all members of the State by the
State from all that hinders the full development of
every citizen. That is what it has now become
within the last thirty years. But it was nothing
like that in 1832. It was a bourgeois, not a
popular, reform which was then initiated ; and the
poor were as much neglected by it, as the middle
class had been before it. But the disturbance
it caused extended downwards to the labouring
classes, then quite uneducated ; and the riots and
excesses that arose made short-sighted persons
doubt the expediency of even the measure of Reform given in 1832. These riots and violences
were caused by the misery and by the neglect of
the poor, and they seemed mere mob-furies to men
of a quiet type, like Tennyson. Such men felt
themselves forced to consider over again the idea
of freedom ; and the reaction from what seemed
revolutionary action on the one side, and on the
other side from Utopias like Shelley's, was extreme.

One would have thought that a poet, touched by
the reality of misery and its exceeding bitter cry,
would have held the balance equally poised at
least, and not yielded too far to the reaction ; that
he would have had indignation at the state of
society, and been inwardly urged to give, in the
manner of a prophet, some prediction of a hope
near at hand for the woes and weakness of the oppressed. But though there are many passages
where Tennyson does try to hold an equal balance,
and to excuse or even to advocate the impassioned
rising of the oppressed in speech or act against
their fate, these passages are short, are tentative ;
he is, as it were, forced into them ; and the main
line he takes is the line of careful protection of the
old against the onset of the new, of steady but very
prudent advance through obedience to existing law,
of protest against that which he calls " raw haste,"
of discouraging of indignant speech and act on the
part of the people, of distrust, even of contempt,
for what seemed to him the mob and for their
"lawless din " ; and, in consequence of all this,
he puts off the regeneration of society to a
period so far away that it may be counted by thousands and thousands of years. It is with almost a
scientific analysis of the whole question of the
future society, and with arguments drawn from
geology (as if humanity were in close analogy to
Nature), that he predicts the enormous time in
which the betterment or the perfection of society
will be wrought. He had really little or no
faith in man as man, but he had faith in man
as conducted, in reasonable obedience, to the
final restitution by an entity which he called

law, and which was, in reality, his own conception of the Constitution of England built up
into power, not by the people, but by a few great
men and by the bulk of the educated and landed
classes who alone were fit to direct the blind forces
of the people.   I do not say that he did not slide
out of this position here and there in his poetry.
He could scarcely help it as a poet, but nevertheless this was his main position, and on the
whole he kept to it all his life.   It was not altogether his standing-place when he was young.   A
different spirit inflames the lines which begin :

> And Freedom rear'd in that august sunrise
> Her beautiful bold brow,
> When rites and forms before his burning eyes
> Melted like snow.

That, and the rest of them, smack of the passionate poet.   But this vague fire did not last.   A
batch of poems : *You ask me why tho' ill at ease
—Of old sat Freedom on the heights—Love thou
thy land*—mark his new position—that of a man
who, like the constitution of a land

> Where Freedom slowly broadens down
> From precedent to precedent,

" regards gradation, lest the soul of Discord race
the rising wind," and sits (distrusting all that is
not accurately balanced, all that shares in political
emotion whether of wrath or eager love) apart
from those stormier miseries of man which seem
to double whenever men eagerly desire for their
lives a greater freedom of development.   I do not
presume to blame him for this.   On the contrary,

this position towards the progress of man in freedom, this "nor swift, nor slow to change, but firm"; this quiet maturing, in self-control, of liberty ; make this close respect for law a standing-place necessary to be preserved. It is, in fact, that of the sturdy good sense of England, led to this conclusion by careful reasoning on the past, and by an intellectual analysis of the course of its history. I should be very sorry to lose the ballast of the boat.

But when it is the *only* position taken up by the army of freedom, it ends in the overwhelming of freedom for a time. It becomes blind and deaf to the woes of man. And it is always a position in which it is surprising to find a poet. One would think that *he* would naturally be in the other great division of the army of freedom—on the side of the inarticulate emotions of the people —supporting that struggle for freedom of growth which is inspired by indignation against oppression, or by impulsive pity which rushes into act ; which is driven on by faiths which do not argue ; by hopes which have little ground in experience ; by aspirations towards all that at present seems impossible ; by the fire of the greater passions whose speech and deeds seem madness to the steady world. This is the side which the poet, when he thinks of freedom for man, naturally takes. Wordsworth took it, Coleridge took it, Byron took it, Shelley took it, Browning took it, but —Tennyson did not! His was the view of the common-sense, well-ordered Englishman—of Whiggism in her carriage with a very gracious smile and salute for Conservatism in hers—and he tried, unhappily as I think, to get this view into poetry.

Through the whole of Tennyson's poetry about the problem of man's progress, this view of his does damage to the poetry ; lowers the note of beauty, of aspiration, of fire, of passion ; and lessens the use of his poetry to the cause of freedom. If the poet take the unpoetic side of any question, he gives no help to mankind, so far as the question concerns mankind. The same things said in prose are very good sense, and in harmony with their vehicle. But, said in poetry, they sound wrong ; they seem unnatural ; and they harm the cause they intend to support. It had been far more right and natural, had Tennyson taken up the other side—a side just as necessary, even more necessary, for the advance of human freedom than the side of cautious and lawful development of liberty—the side of the rushers, of the enthusiastic seekers, of the wild warriors, of the sacrificers whom the world calls insane, of the indignant men whose speech and action Tennyson thought were "the blind hysterics of the Celt." That way poetry lies : and that way lies the permanent influence of a poet on humanity, *so far* as this question is concerned.

This unfortunate position—not in itself, for I have maintained it as quite a true position for one-half of the army of freedom to support, but unfortunate for a poet—threw his poetry on matters related to the full and free development of mankind out of gear. He sometimes got curiously in the wrong, as on the subject of war. He became unpoetically hopeless with regard to the future, wavering to and fro without any fixed or luminous faith in progress; having a distant and half *laissez-faire* sympathy with the sorrows of the people, and seeing—and this is the strangest of all—a remedy for their sorrows in the greater growth of commerce as it exists at present, and in the further development of practical science hand in hand with commerce. When we read these things in poetry we say: " Why, this is wondrous strange! "

When he does express indignation for the miseries of the poor and against the cause of them—the unbridled competition of commerce—he puts that indignation into the mouth of the half-hysterical and morbid lover of Maud, or into the mouth of the lover in *Locksley Hall*, when he has grown old. Moreover, he does not speak from himself, but in the voice of the characters he draws, men wanting in " self-reverence, self-knowledge, self-control." A false light is thus thrown on the sorrows of the poor. It is as if half of them existed only in the morbid fancies of men. At least, there is no vital sympathy expressed for them; and, indeed, Tennyson lived apart from this suffering world and knew nothing about it. He vaguely sees that ruthless competition is at the bottom of these evils, but he looks for the extension of that system of commerce which is based on and makes competition as one of the main elements in the fully developed happiness of mankind. He vaguely sees that mechanical science has been made the slave of competition, and has increased, through this unhappy union, the troubles at the bottom of society, but he looks for the fuller development of

the present system by science as one of the means
of redeeming these evils. He sees plainly that the
world is wrong, but he seems to think that it is to
be cured by the slow and steady improvement of
the present social and commercial system, tempered, when it gets too bad, by wars. He sees,
or Maud's lover sees, that this system leads to
organised selfishness ; that men become, under it,
materialised ; that the higher qualities of the heart
and soul are crushed by it——and this is the subject
of the beginning of *Maud*, and of a few other
poems. What is his remedy ? Not the abandonment of the system, not a crusade against the
causes of these evils, not even any legislative
attempt to lessen them, but a war, in which " commerce should not be all in all, and noble thought
be freer under the sun," in which men should " feel
with their native land, and be one with their kind,"
in which the desire of self-sacrifice should again
awake in the country. Of all means of cure suggested for the evils of competition, war is the most
foolish, and it doubles the misfortunes of the poor.
Those who are sacrificed the most in battle, and
tortured to death by thousands, and who get none
of the personal glory, are the poor. The taxes are
doubled, and the doubling falls heaviest on the poor.
The competition and the cheating of those capitalists
who happen to desire to increase their store at any
cost are increased in war-time. The selfish are
made more selfish ; the troubles of the poor work-
men are trebled ; the army suffers and starves, and
dies of cold and misery—as we found out, only too
well, in the Crimean war. A costly medicine it
was !

This is not the way to remedy the ills of the people, nor is it the best way to develop self-sacrifice, noble thought, civic honour or justice in a people. There is another way in which the call for civic self-sacrifice enters into the daily and hourly life of every citizen; but that way, which forms now the basis of all action and prophecy towards a nobler society, did not enter into the poetry of Tennyson at all, and its absence left him no expedient for curing a selfish society but the clumsy expedient of war.

I make no complaint against Tennyson for all this. I only state the case. If he was of this temper, it was because it was mainly the temper of the time in which he grew to his maturity, the thirty years from his first volume to the end of the sixties. He represented the political and social opinions of that time very fairly, but not as a poet who had much prophetic fire and pity in him would be expected to write. Nor did he make any impetuous casts into the future when he wrote of these things, save once in *Locksley Hall*. In these matters, he was not before his age, nor when the age changed did he change with it. He remained for another thirty years in precisely the same position, while the world changed round him. His poetry on other matters continued to exalt and console the world, to illuminate it with beauty and grace and tender thought. He has been a blessing to us all in a thousand ways in these last thirty years. But on the matters which I treat of here, he was either silent or in opposition to the ideas of a higher liberty. Collectivism, for example, which began to grow up about 1866

D

(which, while it was in opposition to the individualism which so rapidly developed after 1832, yet holds in it a much greater opportunity for complete individuality than we have even conceived as yet) does not seem to have even dawned on the mind of Tennyson. He is behind the whole of this movement—the master movement of our time. In matters then of this kind he is not the poet of the people. He *is* our poet in the things which he treated poetically; and in those which have to do with Nature and God and the sweet honest and tender life of men and women, he will remain our poet as long as the language lasts, but in these social matters not. One only subject of this kind he treated well and as a poet, and that was the question of woman and her relation to modern life; a question which was started by Shelley, and which occupied a great place in poetry after 1832. As far as he saw into that matter, he saw it with freedom and clearness and love, and *The Princess* is a real contribution to that subject. But that stands alone. In all other matters belonging to the progress of society, he does not belong to the last thirty years, to our time, our hopes, or our faith; nor does he think and feel in them as a poet.

Look, in conclusion, at the faith he had concerning the future of mankind, at the hopes he entertained for it. Was he swept away, as the poets are, into high prediction? Did he realise by faith that a better time might be near at hand? No, embayed in these conservative doctrines, unable to loosen himself from their ice, he had enough of the logic of a poet to see that, supposing they were all true, the progress of society towards a better and a perfect life must be of almost an infinite slowness ; so very slow, so very far away, that man in the present is left all but hopeless. There is nothing in Tennyson in this matter of the rush or the faith of the prophet. The impulse he gives is faint, and his hope is only too like despair. The young man of *Locksley Hall* repents when he is old of almost all the enthusiasms of his youth :

Forward far and far from here is all the hope of eighty years.

In the very last book, the "Ghost of the Brute" in men may be laid, but only in a hundred thousand years, or in a million summers away. Before the crowning age arrive in the making of man, æon after æon shall pass. "We are far from the noon of man, there is time for the race to grow."

Time ! when half the world and more are in torture ! It ought not to be in a poet to take things so easily. It is true that Tennyson looks beyond this world, and sees the sorrowful made blessed there, and, indeed, I hold that to be the truest of consolations. But if it is to make us take evils easily here—we especially who are comfortable—I hold that it is not unwise to put it out of our minds for a time ; and it may be that the general disbelief in immortality has its deepest ground in that feeling, and perhaps its reason. For my part, I do not think we have any right to think of a heaven for others, much less of a heaven for ourselves in the world to come, until we are wholly determined to make this world a heaven for our fellow-men, and are hoping, believing, loving, and working for that, and for its realisation not in a thousand or a million years, but in a nearer and a nearer future. That is what a poet should feel and write for nowadays. That should be the passion in his heart and the fire in his verse.

CHAPTER I

THE POEMS OF 1830

IT is fortunate for the historian of poetry in this century that the close of each school of poetry is so clearly divided from the rise of its successor. Shelley, Byron and Keats died within a few years of each other, between 1821 and 1824. Wordsworth, Coleridge, Southey, Landor and Walter Scott (though they lived beyond 1824), belonged to a school which preceded that of Byron, Shelley and Keats. They overlapped the lives of these three poets, but all the three had arisen when Wordsworth and the rest had done their best work. They represent other spheres of thought, and embody other worlds of emotion. Byron, enamoured of his own powerful personality, and rejoicing in his isolation from the crowd while he was angry with its attack upon him, proud and vain at the same time, laughed to scorn the peaceful, proper, prim and comfortable life into which the English middle class had subsided after the peace of 1815, and held up himself as its poetic contrast—the lonely, soul-shattered wanderer whom a quiet home-life revolted, who preferred, for choice, to live like the Giaour or the Corsair—and who finally attacked all the respectable hypocrisy of England in the revolutionary mockery of *Don Juan*. He did this needful work with exaggeration, but had it not been done with exaggeration, it would not perhaps have rescued England's poetry from the ideal of George III. No temper can be a greater contrast than Byron's on the one side to that of his predecessor, Wordsworth, and on the other to that of his successor, Tennyson. Byron did not like —and I put it mildly—the philosophic gentlemen of *The Excursion;* he would have disliked still more the Arthur of the *Idylls of the King.* Indeed, it was high time, when poetry in the hands of Tennyson had dwelt so much on the conservative, law-abiding, and regular elements of life as to make us fear that the more audacious and freer elements beyond conventional society would be lost to poetry, that Swinburne should again, like Byron, bring in the revolutionary spirit, and attack that temper in poetry which, in weaker hands than Tennyson's, might again degenerate into Pharisaism and put the imagination into a coop like a goose at Strasburg. The way Swinburne did it in his youth was open to objections—poets, by their very nature, sweep into wild exaggeration of their revolts—but it was well that it was done. Byron did the same thing in his time. He was at this point the child of the literature which preceded the Revolution. His movement of mind and emotion is part of the storm which began to blow in the eighteenth century.

Shelley was also its child, but he represented his parent in a very different manner from Byron. He was not personal; he did not attack the existing society with mockery. He did not praise the isolated or the corsair life, nor the immoral life. He lived as he pleased, it is true, and he left English society severely alone. But he was concerned chiefly with ideas, and what he attacked were the evil things which hindered the progress of mankind. He hated despotisms; he hated those religious views which enslaved the soul, and those persons who used these views for the sake of power. As such, he went back, when the political aim of the Revolution was dead in England, to the original ideas of the Revolution. He took up their all but extinguished torch, and waved it round and round his head, till in his hands it took fire again. It was only for a time. He had not power enough to keep it kindled, and finally he left behind him all hope of realising in his own time the ideas of equality. What he did do, was to conceive in his own mind the regeneration of society and the overthrow of its evils; and to sing of what humanity would be in the future; and it is his undying hope in this regeneration of man, his faith and love of it, and the power with which he has infused it into men, for which we owe him an endless gratitude.

This was the last effort of this school of poetry applied to the conditions of the world of its own time, the last recognition these poets gave to their present. It was also the last breath for the time of the impulse given to song by the early ideas of the Revolution. The poetry of this century, up to this point, had been frequently concerned with the social and political movement, with the European struggle, with ethical or theological forms of thought, with the life and feelings of the poor, with the glory of the past, with humanity at large, with philosophies and theories of the race and its destiny. But now poetry ceased to speak of these matters. And no wonder! The poets received no impulse from without. There was no care for an ideal life left in England, no interest in the future condition of man, no enthusiasm of humanity. England was sick of social, political, and theological matters, of theories of life. "Let me alone," it said, "torment me not;" and it fell into a materialism which stopped its ears to every voice likely to disturb its dull repose. Words-worth felt this even in 1806, ten years before its fulness, when he wrote that sonnet on the besotted state of the country—

> The world is too much with us: late and soon,
> Getting and spending, we lay waste our powers:
> Little we see in Nature that is ours;
> We have given our hearts away—a sordid boon!

a sonnet which ends, having declared that man-kind was out of tune with natural beauty, in one of his rare outbursts of passion—a cry for deliver-ance from a stagnant world—

> Great God! I'd rather be
> A Pagan suckled in a creed outworn;
> So might I, standing on this pleasant lea,
> Have glimpses that would make me less forlorn
> Have sight of Proteus rising from the sea;
> Or hear old Triton blow his wreathèd horn.

Keats felt the same loss of joy and life in the world with a shock of misery, and expressed it. "Glory and loveliness," he cried, "have passed

away." What did he do? The present said
nothing to his imagination. No wind from it blew
upon his soul and awakened the flowers in its
garden. He had no care for theologies, for social
theories, for humanity at large, for its future destiny. Living alongside of Byron and Shelley, he
had nothing to do with their interests. He was,
practically, living after them, in a world which did
not share in a single one of their emotions. But
emotions are necessary to a poet, and if he cannot
get them in the present, and if the future be
nothing to him, as it is nothing to the man who is
not excited by the present, he must seek for his
emotions in the past. There, in that bygone world,
is the beauty, or the romance, which he cannot find
beside him; or there, at least, he sees and feels it.
It was in the past that Keats chose to live, quite
away from England. The Pagan world to which
Wordsworth wished to return in his temporary
passion, Keats always desired to have with him. He
sang of Endymion in the woods and caves of Latmos.
He sang of young life at Athens; he sang of a
more ancient world and of the primeval gods. He
sang of Lorenzo and Isabella in mediæval Florence;
he sang of Porphyro and Madeline in a world which
has no history. And the only thing he saw in the
present which was worth a song was the doings of
Nature, whose youth is everlastingly lovely, and
who has nothing to do with man.

His poetry, therefore, represents the complete
exhaustion of the fire of the Revolution, the complete abandonment of the present as able to give
any impulse to the poet; and if no new impulse
had come to stir England to her depths, to place

all the old problems in a new light which light also brought with it a kindling fire, to awaken new interest in the life of the present and in the strife of humanity to its goal, poetry would have altogether ceased after Keats. The past alone does not supply enough fuel to keep up the fires of the imagination.

And, indeed, we see that plainly enough in the history of the time. No poet of any vivid eagerness, much less of any originality, appeared now for some years. The poetry which was produced, with the single exceptions of Landor, and of Wordsworth (whose work, though it had lost youth, was still weighty with power and grave sentiment), was either an imitation of past models, or pale, pretty, washed-out work like that of Mrs. Hemans, with an easy melody and a slipshod sentiment. Every one knew the methods, the images, the very rhymes that were used. All was convention, naught was art.

The *Poems of Two Brothers*, written by Alfred Tennyson and his brother, and published in 1827 —a collection of their very youthful efforts—illustrate this point. They are without one trace of originality, force, or freshness—faded imitations of previous poets, chiefly of Byron ; or, where not imitative, full of the futile modesty of boyhood, which would fain be vain but does not dare ; made up partly of bold noise and partly of sentimentality, accurately true to the type of the English poetry between the death of Shelley and the publication of Tennyson's volume of 1830. It is one of the literary puzzles of the world that certain great poets, as, for example, Shelley and here Tennyson, write

trash in their boyhood ; and within a year or two
step on to a level of original power. What happens
in the meantime to make the change ? It is not
as if these boyish poems were only poor work.
Shelley's verses before *Queen Mab* were detestable.
Tennyson's verses in the *Poems of Two Brothers*
were only not quite so bad. But they were in
complete harmony with the poetry of the time.

Along with this dishevelled work there was
a wonderful flourishing of criticism. Reviews
and weekly papers explained what poetry was,
and slashed and praised the poets past, present,
and even to come. The more poetry decayed,
the more eagerly the critics dissected her body,
till, when any living poetry really appeared, they
(having been accustomed to the lifeless poetry)
cried out at the living thing as something too
horrible to be endured. This is the fate and the
punishment of criticism of the Arts done for the
sake of criticism. The more, then, the critics think
they see, the blinder they become. Along with this
there was necessarily a highly cultured literary
class, who were indeed chiefly made up of the
critics, and who wrote incessantly about literature,
but rarely created any—just such a class as exists
to-day revelling in their academic excellence ; who
do two things, both equally foolish, overblame what
is new, or overpraise it; having special enmities or
special affections, and equally damaging those they
abuse and those they praise. The one thing of
which, as a body, they are almost incapable, is the
recognition of that which is really good, which has
in it life, continuance, and power. As only one or
two men (and those poets themselves) saw what

was in Wordsworth, Shelley or Keats when they published their second volumes, so only one or two saw what was in the earlier volumes of Tennyson and Browning.

Tennyson's poems of 1830 were, with the exception of about a dozen, very much like the other poetry of the time. But those new things set Tennyson apart. He who wrote them was quite certain to write better and better poetry, They were original in their metre (which was poor), in word-painting, in the use of words, in thought, and in the way in which emotion was reached and seized and shaped. The same originality, but to a greater degree, belongs to Browning's first poem. My business, however, is Tennyson, and I will now place, in connection with what I have said, his earliest emergence as an original poet. That emergence is first seen in the Cambridge Prize Poem—1829—of *Timbuctoo*, and in *The Lover's Tale*, written the year before, when he was nineteen years old. Tennyson withdrew *The Lover's Tale* from publication after he had printed it in 1833, but on its being pirated in 1879, published it with its continuation *The Golden Supper* in 1879. The poem tells of a boy and a girl who are brought up together. The boy falls into passionate love with the girl; the girl cares for him only as a sister and tells him in her innocent confidence that she loves his friend Lionel. The misery of this to the boy is the whole subject of the poem. It is full of the metaphysics of sorrow, and of the fantastic play of words and thoughts with which the Elizabethans described the poetry of unhappy love. It seems plain from many passages that Tennyson had read at this time the Sonnets of the Amourists, and the work of the love-poets of the age of James the First. Here is one of these passages :

> It was ill-done to part you, Sisters fair ;
> Love's arms were wreath'd about the neck of Hope,
> And Hope kissed Love, and Love drew in her breath
> In that close kiss, and drank her whisper'd tales.
> They said that Love would die when Hope was gone,
> And Love mourn'd long, and sorrow'd after Hope ;
> At last she sought out Memory, and they trod
> The same old paths where Love had walk'd with Hope,
> And Memory fed the soul of Love with tears.

This metaphysic of fantasy—an embroidery of the personified passions as on a tapestry, and represented in successive pictures—does not stand alone. It is frequent in this early poem, and it became in after-times, but greatly improved in its usage, a habit of the poet. Many instances of it occur in *In Memoriam*.

The lover's sorrow is also mingled up with Nature. Every natural description illustrates and reflects the changing moods of the characters : so early did Tennyson begin this consistent habit of his art. Two or three vivid descriptions and a few happy single lines that isolate natural phenomena, prove how far he had left behind him the aimless looseness of the *Poems of Two Brothers*, but do not prophesy the distinctive power which Tennyson had afterwards over Nature. The one charm of the poem is its youthfulness. The lavishness, the want of temperance, the inability to stop when enough has been said, the welling-over of words, the boyishness of sentiment, the playing at sorrow

—while they prove that Tennyson was right in withdrawing the poem from publication—nevertheless give us pleasure, the pleasure of touching youth.

Next year he wrote *Timbuctoo*. It is not at all like a prize poem, and to be original in a prize poem was so audacious that it is a clear proof that Tennyson had become conscious of his proper power. He imitated no more. Some lines in it are fine, but its main interest is that his conception of the subject proves that he had now seen that Fable was a great storehouse of poetic material. He builds the Timbuctoo of fable ; a vision like that of El Dorado. He weaves it through and through with spiritual thought. The excitement and the method are the same as those he felt and used when he began take up the legend of Arthur. Neither of these poems, however, had anything to do with English life, or was influenced by the movements of the time. Nor did the poet appeal in them to the public. That step was made by the volume of 1830, and of what kind it was, and moved by what impulses, is now the matter in hand.

I have maintained that when Keats died there was no national excitement in England, no emotional movement towards either a social or political betterment of life, no care for ideas such as will make a poet feel the thrill of humanity in the present. Without that, he may write, like Keats, for a time about the past, but he will not produce a new poetic world. Well, this excitement of the nation was supplied to Tennyson and to Browning. The Reform movement had now begun

and was coming to its height. A new religious
movement also began, and had taken two forms
before three years passed by; one towards a greater
freedom of religious thought, and another towards
a vitalising of Church doctrine and ritual. Both
contained a greater intensity of self-sacrifice than
had been known for years, and a greater development of practical work for the poor and the sorrowful. Both were an extension of the love of man,
and carried with them an emotion which ran rapidly
through England. Along with these two opposite
tendencies of religious thought there was, of course,
and owing to their clashing, an awakening of
spiritual doubt, questioning and trouble which made
a host of men interested in or tormented by religion.
Traces of this are everywhere found in Tennyson. " What am I ? Whence have I come ?
Whither am I going ? What authority have I
for any faith ? What has God to do with me, or
I with God ? What are my duties to man, and
what is their foundation ?" These were the kind
of questions which stirred in England, like leaven
in meal. Excitement then in politics, in social
questions, in religious questions, was rife in this
country when Tennyson and Browning began to
write. Their youth was stirred by a series of
national impulses. This was the atmosphere
in which they wrote their first poems ; and their
after-poems were filled with it. Thus poetry
again began, like Pygmalion's marble, to move
and speak, stepped down from its pedestal and
took its share in the life of men and women.
The blood grew warm and quick within its veins.

And now the question is : Of what kind will

the first poems be—or, rather, of what kind
were Tennyson's—under these conditions? They
will not be directly written on the special
national excitements. The poet is kindled by
these excitements, but he does not write on
them. The stirring in his heart which he receives
from the nation he applies to his own subjects,
those which are personal to him. The primary
emotion is national, the secondary emotions are
personal, but it is on the secondary that he writes.
Even when he makes a poem upon that which was
affecting all thoughtful men in the nation—on the
religious problem—the poem is not written to express the national feeling, but to express his own.
And this is the case in that quasi-religious poem
in the volume of 1830, which Tennyson calls the
Confessions of a Sensitive Mind, and which ends

> O weary life! O weary death!
> O spirit and heart made desolate!
> O damnèd vacillating state!

Keats could not, for one moment, have got into
the condition in which this conclusion and the
poem which precedes it were possible. When
Tennyson in 1830 wrote his sonnet to J. M. K., in
excitement about the work this friend of his was
to do as a preacher among mankind; when he
said that his friend would be a "soldier-priest, no
sabbath-drawler of old saws," but spurred at heart
with fieriest energy to embattell and to wall about
his cause

> With iron-worded proof, hating to hark
> The humming of the drowsy pulpit-drone
> Half God's good sabbath, while the worn-out clerk
> Brow-beats his desk below,

he was moved by the emotion of the religious
revival which had begun in England. Such an
emotion could not have been felt by Keats.
Had Keats, indeed, lived longer it would have
been different, for he began before he died to
step out of his isolation in beauty and to wish to
be a soldier of humanity ; and he would have been
profoundly moved by the new impulses in English
life. Nor would it have been possible for Keats, in
his time, to write the *English War Song*, or the
National Song at the end of the volume of 1830,
which are filled with a young man's patriotic pride,
and with a contempt of the French people. They
are not fine things, but they illustrate my contention—that the poets had again taken interest in the
present ; that the nation, being new-born into fresh
emotion, was making a new ground for poetry.

That is one thing to say. Another is that
the poet will not altogether get rid of the condition of things in which he has lived since he
was a boy. He will write a number of poems
in his first books which will be of the same
class as those written by the men and women
of the exhausted time, pretty, graceful, powerless
poems, without any forward outlook. And of
these a good deal of this first volume of Tennyson's is made up. The first poem, entitled *Claribel*,
is of this quality. So are most of the poems
addressed to various imagined women—such as
Lilian, Madeline, Adeline. So also are the Songs,
which do not even vaguely prophesy the excellence
Tennyson afterwards reached in this kind of poetry.
It is true, the refined choice of words in these
poems, their over-wrought phrasing, are better than

E

the conventional grace and slippered wording cf
the contemporary verse ; but they are still of that
mould into which Mrs. Hemans and the rest cast
their poetry. The poet, even though he is to
become a leader of fresh song, is then like one of
those figures we see in the mediæval pictures of
the Resurrection at the Last Judgment, half risen
from the earth, their heads and arms uplifted to
the new light of life, their legs still clasped by
the encumbering earth.

This was exactly the case with Tennyson. He
is partly sunk in the old clay, but he is partly risen.
There are poems in this book of 1830 in which the
fresh utterance of a new Maker of song is ringing
clear, in which he has got free altogether of the
past. And one of the earliest things he wrote
(" written very early in life " is his own addition
to the title) is one of these prophetic things.
This is the *Ode to Memory*. We hear in it faint
echoes of Coleridge, or of Milton ; but we also hear
a clear, original and dominant note of his own,
belonging to none; self-felt, self-invented ; thought
and emotion unknown before; music and phrasing
new. No wonder, having done this as a boy, he
felt himself a man apart, with the laurel of Apollo
within his reach. When we hear a verse like this :

> Listening the lordly music flowing from
> The illimitable years,*

we know that he who wrote it has begun work
which has the power to continue.

And when we read this description of a natural
landscape, we know that we are listening to one

---

* This is also used in *Timbuctoo*.

who will reveal to us Nature under a new light, and new worlds of Nature. He is still speaking to Memory:

> Thou wert not nursed by the waterfall
>   Which ever sounds and shines
> A pillar of white light upon the wall
>   Of purple cliffs, aloof descried:
>
> Come from the woods that belt the gray hillside,
> The seven elms, the poplars four,
> That stand beside my father's door,
> And chiefly from the brook that loves
> To purl o'er matted cress and ribbèd sand,
> Or dimple in the dark of rushy coves,
>   Drawing into his narrow earthen urn,
>   In every elbow and turn,
>   The filter'd tribute of the rough woodland,
>   O hither lead thy feet
> Pour round mine ears the livelong bleat
> Of the thick fleecèd sheep from wattled folds,
>   Upon the ridgèd wolds.

The metrical movement is untrained, there is not sufficient rejection of the superfluous; but there is the original thing. The sight of Nature and its expression owe something to Wordsworth and Keats. But beyond the echoes there is the sounding of a new horn on Apollo's hill. Nor does this stand alone. There are at least twelve poems in this first book which are like the gates into a fresh world, and better work at every point than this *Ode to Memory*. Among these are *Mariana*, *Recollections of the Arabian Nights*, *The Poet*, *The Dying Swan*, *Love and Death*, *Oriana*, *The Sleeping Beauty*, *The Sea Fairies*.

In these Tennyson's picture-poetry begins in a number of elaborate studies of Nature, with one figure in them to give them human interest; and

these studies are of two kinds.   Some are carried
through a poem of many verses, like *Mariana*,
where the one landscape is described *at various
times* of day and night, where birds and animals
correspondent to the emotion are introduced, and
where all are led up to one lonely figure.   Others
are in short single verses—a whole landscape set
in the frame of a quatrain—like those composed in
1833 for *The Palace of Art*.   This was, on both its
sides, a new method.   The previous poets had not
invented it.   Here is a passage from *Mariana* of
pure landscape.   I quote from the volume of 1830:

> About a stone-cast from the wall,
>   A sluice with blacken'd waters slept,
> And o'er it many, round and small,
>   The cluster'd marish-mosses crept.
> Hard by a poplar shook alway,
>   All silver-green with gnarlèd bark ;
>   For leagues no other tree did dark
> The level waste, the rounding gray.

The last two lines illustrate his homelike love
for a land of wide horizons and low skies, fringed
with humble hills, such as he saw continually in the
fen country; such as he pencils out in one rapid
sketch in *Oriana*, where in only two lines we see
and hear the wintry world with equal vividness—

> When the long dun wolds are ribb'd with snow,
> And loud the Norland whirlwinds blow.

There is already the full-mouthed vowel-music of
Tennyson ; one of the characteristics of his careful
art in words, of which no one before, except
Milton, was so skilled, so conscious, or so continuous a master.   A whole essay might be written

on this part of his technic art; and it is worth a reader's while, for once at least, to collect together these great vowel-passages from his poems.

The *Recollections of the Arabian Nights* is another of these landscape poems. Every verse is a picture of a new reach of the river Tigris; the sound of every word is studied in them, so that the words in their varied sound should do the same office for the poetry that the various tones of colour do for a painting. And to accomplish this the better, he now invented, but far too much and with a luxuriance which he afterwards pruned away, a number of double adjectives, chosen as much for their sound as for their images. All the poems about women are filled with these—sudden-curved, golden-netted, forward-flowing, silver-chiming, fountain-fragrant, shadow-chequered, hollow-vaulted, sable-sheeny— and very many more: a dangerous trick to gain, and one from which it is difficult to escape. Tennyson loved these double-shotted words, but he had power enough afterwards to bring their use into moderation.

There is another poem, *The Sea Fairies*, not much in itself, but also prophetic of a new world in poetry. The first three lines in the song of the Sirens is the first true note of the singing quality, both in metre and in unity of theme, which afterwards made the songs of Tennyson so distinguished. The other songs in this book might have been written by half a dozen other men—they belong to the merely graceful—but this is his own, and its quality is altogether of a new kind. It begins:

Whither away, whither away, whither away? Fly no more:
Whither away with the swinging sail? whither away with the
  oar?
Whither away from the high green field and the happy
  blossoming shore?

This is the easy movement of a metrist's wing
in an early flight, singing all the time. I say
an early flight, for his metrical movement, as most
of the poems in this book declare, was at this
time broken, halting, and unmusical. Coleridge
said, when he read these poems, that Tennyson
had "begun to write verses without very well
understanding what metre is"; and indeed he
arrived at the excellence he did attain in metre
more by study than by natural gift. But the
capability of fine artistic song is as clearly
shadowed forth in *The Sea Fairies*, as the full
sunlight is by the colours of the dawn. What
it was to become, after some years of training,
any one may read in the song in *The Lotos-Eaters*,
of which this poem is, as it were, the first sketch.

Moreover, there is another characteristic of
Tennyson's future poetry in *The Sea Fairies*. It
is the first of the small classical studies in which
he excelled, and it is built on the same foundation
as the rest of them. When he takes a classical
subject he builds it up with one underlying
thought which, running through the whole of the
poem, gives it unity. He chooses a simple
thought, common to all mankind; felt by the
ancients, but to which he gives continual touches
and variations which grow out of modern life, and
out of his own soul. This is the case with *Ulysses*,
Œnone, *Tithonus*, and the rest. But the unity

and simplicity of the thought, its mingled ancient and modern air, and its careful inweaving into the whole body of the story, make these classical things of his unique. No one has ever done them in the same fashion, and the fashion is extraordinarily interesting.

In *The Sea Fairies* the thought is the weariness of the ceaseless labour of the world. " Why toil so much for so little ? Take the joy of rest and love. Sleep, before the great sleep." We shall see how this excessively simple thought is splendidly wrought out in *The Lotos-Eaters*. It is enough now to say that this is the first of these classical poems, and, so far as method is concerned, it is similar to them all. This, then, is also a new thing.

Once more, on this poem, we have in it and *The Mystic* the first clear sound of the blank verse of Tennyson. These lines from *The Mystic* belong to him :

> He, often lying broad awake, and yet
> Remaining in the body, and apart
> In intellect and power and will, hath heard
> Time flowing in the middle of the night,
> And all things creeping to a day of doom.

Still more prophetic of a new blank verse are the lines at the beginning of *The Sea Fairies :*

> Slow sail'd the weary mariners and saw,
> Between the green brink and the running foam,
> White limbs unrobèd in a crystal air,
> Sweet faces, rounded arms, and bosoms prest
> To little harps of gold ; and, while they mused,
> Whispering to each other half in fear,
> Shrill music reach'd them on the middle sea.

No one, with an ear, can mistake the novelty of

the verse. It is plainly done by one who had read Milton, but it is not Milton's way; it is Tennyson's own; and it is charming to hear the first note of a music which has delighted us so long in two lines like these:

> Slow sailed the weary mariners and saw,
> Between the green brink and the running foam.

These, then, are the new things in the poems of 1830. It remains to speak of his conception of what a poet was, and of himself as poet.

I have said that Tennyson was conscious all his life of being set apart as a prophet, and of the duties which he owed to humanity. His life, in his own mind, was weighted with the sense of these duties. He would have quoted for himself that noble passage in which Milton pictures himself and realises what sort of character the lofty poet must possess. He would have felt with that equally noble passage in *The Prelude*, where Wordsworth describes himself as consecrated to his work by Nature and by God. And it marks that change in the temper of England of which I wrote at the beginning, that Tennyson could not conceive, like Keats, of his work as done for beauty's sake alone, but also for the sake of humankind. The new earnestness and excitement of the world compelled him to conceive of his work with the same intensity as Wordsworth when, writing under the enrapturing and fresh enthusiasm of humanity and buoyant with youthful vigour, he came at first to Grasmere. Wordsworth paints his soul, its outlook and its energy, in undying lines at the end of *The Recluse;* and the comparison of these (which

I commend to my readers) with Tennyson's verses on *The Poet* is full of delightful interest.

In that poem, Tennyson lays down, and out of his own inward experience, what he conceived himself to be, and how he conceived his work ; and he never abandoned, betrayed, or enfeebled his conception. It is a remarkable utterance for so young a man, weighty with that steadiness of temper which, if it diminished spontaneity in his art, yet gave it a lasting power.

> The poet in a golden clime was born,
>   With golden stars above;
> Dower'd with the hate of hate, the scorn of scorn,
>   The love of love.

That is the beginning, and the first needs of the poet's nature could scarcely be better expressed. Then he speaks of the clear insight into God and man which is the best gift of the poet.

> He saw thro' life and death, thro' good and ill,
>   He saw thro' his own soul.
> The marvel of the everlasting will,
>   An open scroll,
> Before him lay.

Then his thoughts, blown like arrow-seeds over the whole world with melodies and light, take root, and become flowers in the hearts of men, till high desires are born, and truth is multiplied on truth,

> And thro' the wreaths of floating dark upcurl d
>   Rare sunrise flow'd.

And in that sunrise, Freedom clothed in wisdom came upon Man, and shook his spirit, and ruined anarchies and oppressions. This was Tennyson's youthful conception of his work, and we should never forget it when we read his poetry, though we are tempted sometimes to think that he forgot this last part of it himself. I quote the final verses, and from the book of 1830. Their note is new. Their power, in contrast with the light verse that was contemporary with them, is the revelation of a poetic resurrection :

> And Freedom rear'd in that august sunrise
>   Her beautiful bold brow,
> When rites and forms before his burning eyes
>   Melted like snow.
>
> There was no blood upon her maiden robes
>   Sunn'd by those orient skies ;
> But round about the circles of the globes
>   Of her keen eyes
>
> * And in the bordure of her robe was writ
>   Wisdom—a name to shake
> Hoar anarchies, as with a thunder-fit.
>   And when she spake,
>
> Her words did gather thunder as they ran,
>   And as the lightning to the thunder
> Which follows it, riving the spirit of man,
>   Making earth wonder,
>
> So was their meaning to her words.   No sword
>   Of wrath her right arm hurl'd,
> But one poor poet's scroll, and with *his* word
>   She shook the world.

> * Recast in 1842.

> And in her raiment's hem was traced in flame
>   Wisdom, a name to shake
> All evil dreams of power—a sacred name.

CHAPTER II

THE POEMS OF 1833

THREE years after the volume of 1830,
Tennyson published the little book of 1833,
containing thirty new poems. In this second
volume he wrought still further at the new veins
he had struck, and turned their ore into finer
shapes. But he not only developed work he had
already begun ; he found fresh and different veins
of poetry, opened these also, and made out of
their gold new creations full of the spirit of youth
hastening to a greater excellence. Evolution then
of the subjects discovered in 1830—creation of
new subjects in 1833—these are the matter of
this chapter.

But first, it is well to mark how the artist, as
artist, grows. He cannot cease inventing ; new
things, new forms spring up under his hand ; ever
uncontent because the unattainable of Beauty lures
him on. " If thou givest me," cries Beauty in his
heart, " a thousand shapes, there are yet a million
more which thou mayest invent for me, and yet
I shall not be exhausted." He who feels that
allurement and hears that cry has the artist's
temper ; he who can embody what he feels and
hears, in ever varying forms, till old age touch him

with inability, is the artist. He moves "from well
to better, daily self-surpast," till he has no more
power. We know when his power is lessening, for
then he begins to repeat himself. We know that
it still exists, however feebly, when, in the midst
of repetitions, new things now and then appear.

And it is one of the happy things in Tennyson's career, that even till he was past eighty
years of age, this creativeness—that is, this power
of being inflamed with the love of Beauty and
animated by her into creation—did not altogether
die. In the very last volume he published there
appeared a poem called *The Gleam*, which, if it was
written shortly before the book was issued, was a
new and beautiful blossom on his ancient tree.
Those who, walking in an English park, have
come upon an oak, broken off short by age or
storm and hollow within, but whose rugged
gnarls send forth leaves as delicate as those of
its childhood, must have often thought, "There is
the image of the great artist in his old age, of the
great musician, the great painter, the great poet;"
and though Tennyson does not stand among the
very mightiest, yet he had this singular and noble
power of fresh creation in old age.

We are sure to find this creativeness in his
youth. It appeared, as we have seen, in 1830, and
I have discussed some forms of it in the previous
chapter. Two forms of it, however, I omitted—
one, the drawing of "characters"; the other, the
drawing of Nature. Both of these were more fully
worked out in the volume of 1833. Both are new
in manner, and interesting beyond themselves.

The types of character were drawn, each apart,

like solitary statues.   As a young man, he chose women on whom to try his prentice hand, and we have a series of these pictures, with fanciful names written underneath them.   They are lifeless as women, lay figures with elaborate dresses ; word-painted, nothing but words.   There are no surprises in these characters, nothing inexplicable, nothing unexpected, nothing veiled, no profound simplicity, nothing which recalls a woman.   They are, above all, logically worked out ; one verse opens into another in an intellectual order.   We can predict what is coming—as if their subjects moved in accordance to law.   It was like a young man to try this, but it was a pity he did not prefer to draw his college companions, for the one man's character that he does outline is a fairly-painted type.   Here are two verses of it :

> Most delicately hour by hour
> He canvass'd human mysteries ;
> And trod on silk, as if the winds
> Blew his own praises in his eyes,
> And stood aloof from other minds
> In impotence of fancied power.
>
> With lips depress'd as he were meek,
> Himself unto himself he sold ;
> Upon himself himself did feed :
> Quiet, dispassionate and cold,
> And other than his form of creed,
> With chisell'd features clear and sleek.

But even that is more like an exercise in the description of a type than like the picture of a living man.   Character is shown by clashing with character.   It may " form itself in silence," but it is ignorant of itself till it can speak to others and answer their speech.   Hence the Maker, who is bound to paint men and women, almost always paints them in movement with or against one another. Tennyson did that fairly afterwards, but never superbly. The effort to make a type was always too much with him. The men and women in the *Idylls of the King* want life. The personal edges and angles have been worn away in order to establish the type. Enid, Tristram, Vivien, Arthur, even Lancelot who is the most living, are often like those photographs which are made by photographing the faces of a series of politicians or philosophers or artists one on the top of another. We get the general type—or they say we get it—but we do not get a man. The men and women who are most actual in Tennyson's poetry are those whom he painted out of every-day life, and in the sphere of the common affections and troubles of mankind— in stories like *Enoch Arden*, in country idylls like *The Gardener's Daughter*, *Dora*, *The Brook;* in the Lincolnshire dialect poems, which bring before us the most living persons in his books.

Nevertheless, the attempt Tennyson made at this time to draw separate characters is in harmony with the age in which he began to write. Character-making was once a favourite species of poetry, but it had not been done well since the time of Pope. None of the greater poets from Wordsworth to Keats took up this special form of art. But Tennyson, and with greater power Browning, deliberately insulated and painted a number of characters, and of generalised types of character, as if a certain driving force from without, a tendency of popular thought, urged them to make much of the

individual, as if society had concluded that it
was to find its betterment in the support of strong
individualities. And indeed this was the case in
England in 1833. As great as the tendency is at
present to collectivism, so great was the tendency
then to individualism. It grew steadily in politics,
even in art and religion, for thirty years, and
then it began to abate. Large crowds of men
laid all their lives in the hands of great leaders
of thought ; and thus, while they maintained the
necessity for strong individualities, lessened
individualism by collecting in mass under the
banner of one man ; so curiously and so certainly
do extremes cut their own throat. The individual,
the powerful character, is everything, said Carlyle,
and said it for more than forty years. This
was partly a protest against the past dulness
of society, it was still more the protest of the
fear of the cultivated man that in the coming
democracy all men would be levelled and a dull
monotony rule supreme. Every valley, they cried,
will be exalted and every mountain and hill
brought low; there will be no varied scenery in
humanity. We hear that dread expressed by
Tennyson in *Locksley Hall :*

Knowledge comes, but wisdom lingers, and I linger on the
    shore,
And the individual withers, and the world is more and more,

The verses which follow; the hero's desire to
break all links of habit, to escape to summer
isles, "where the passions, cramped no longer,
shall have scope and breathing space "; where
men shall be free to make themselves, continue

the same thought. He had then in 1842, when *Locksley Hall* was published, realised fully the desire for individualism which was then rife in England. It was this force which pressed him in 1830 and 1833 into the writing of characters.

Secondly, I have drawn attention to the new way of painting Nature which Tennyson developed, and to the new world of Nature to which he introduced us. He composed his Nature into pictures, a thing not done by Byron, Shelley, or Keats, or at least not so deliberately, not so consciously. This picture-composing of Nature is carried to much greater excellence in the volume of 1833. I might contrast *Mariana in the South*, a poem of 1833, with the *Mariana* of 1830, but it would not prove my point—that his power of nature-painting had increased. It suggests, however, another point with regard to Tennyson's natural description. *Mariana in the South* is not so good as its predecessor ; and I believe that the reason of its comparative failure is that the scene is laid in the South, and Tennyson was so English, and so much the child of long habit, that when he got outside of this country, even outside of the landscape which surrounded him year after year, he did not choose so happily as in England the right thing to say in order to give the sentiment of the landscape. This is, however, subject to exception. What I say is true concerning his foreign land-scapes, whenever he is working direct from Nature, or composing out of things he has seen. It is not true when he is deliberately inventing his landscape out of his own head, and with reference to his subject—as he is in *Œnone* or *The Lotos-*

Eaters. There he paints the inward vision ; and he does it with a noble clearness. But we understand that the landscape is imagined, that it has never been seen.

With this exception, it is only the accustomed landscape of his own land, studied from the life, that he sees clearly and describes well ; and this belongs to his character as well as to his art. He was a homelike person, and it was not till Nature had for many years slowly "crept into the study of his imagination" that he could paint her with the affectionate finish he desired. Rapid impressions received in travel he could not, like Byron or Shelley, record with excellence. The poem called *The Daisy*, in which he attempts this work, is, with the exception of one verse, a failure. But that which had endeared itself to him for years, which amid a thousand varieties of aspect had unity of sentiment, the landscape of Lincolnshire, the fens and the meres and sea ; the landscape of Surrey, Kent, Hampshire and the Isle of Wight—of the chalk and the sandstone—this he did to perfection. In *The Palace of Art*, the landscapes are on the tapestry, and of course are themselves pictures. All the more then they illustrate his way of looking at Nature—his turn for composing her like a painter. Each landscape is done in four lines, and with the exception of two, they might all be in Lincolnshire. I quote from the poem as altered in 1842 :

> One seem'd all dark and red—a tract of sand,
> And some one pacing there alone,
> Who paced for ever in a glimmering land,
> Lit with a low large moon.

F

The second is not Lincolnshire :

> One show'd an iron coast and angry waves.
>   You seem'd to hear them climb and fall,
> And roar rock-thwarted under bellowing caves,
>   Beneath the windy wall.

That seems to be a piece of the coast of Yorkshire, outside of his own country. It is good, but if he had belonged to the Yorkshire coast, and loved it like the glimmering lands of Lincoln with the low-hung moon, the second line would have been better done. The next is full Lincolnshire, and might be a motto for the art of De Wint :

> And one, a full fed river winding slow
>   By herds upon an endless plain,
> The ragged rims of thunder brooding low,
>   With shadow-streaks of rain.

The next is from the South. "Hoary in the wind" is the vision of the grey underside of the olive-leaf tossed upwards over a whole hillside by the gust into the sunlight.

> And one, the reapers at their sultry toil.
>   In front they bound the sheaves. Behind
> Were realms of upland, prodigal in oil,
>   And hoary to the wind.

The whole is, however, not clear ; he does not see it as vividly as the rest, and there is little sentiment in it.

But the next—could it be better ? And how drenched it is in the sentiment of England !

> And one, an English home—gray twilight pour'd
>   On dewy pastures, dewy trees,
> Softer than sleep—all things in order stored,
>   A haunt of ancient Peace.

This is Tennyson in love with his subject, and
the quality of the poetry rises with his love. Moreover, it is delightful to see him stretch out his hand
to Virgil, who was as fond of his country as Tennyson of England——" Softer than sleep."

Again, we stand on the long shallow sands of the
sea-coast near his early home, and there is no better,
briefer, yet more finished picture in all his work :

> A still salt pool, lock'd in with bars of sand,
>   Left on the shore; that hears all night
> The plunging seas draw backward from the land
>   Their moon-led waters white.

These are properly pictures, but the immense
improvement in the description of Nature which
took place between 1830 and 1833 is more
fully seen in poems where Nature and human affections are woven together, as in *The May Queen*
and better still in *The Miller's Daughter*, both of this
year. The girl's cottage is on the hillside, above
the valley and the meadowy stream. The land is
full of flowers and grass. The cowslip and the
crowfoot are all over the hill, the honeysuckle is
round the porch, the faint sweet cuckoo-flowers
grow beside the meadow trenches ; "And the wild
marsh-marigold shines like fire in swamps and
hollows gray." Where in the world can we place
this except in England——half in Lincoln, half in
Kent ?

Fond as he was of the common flowers, he was
even fonder of the birds. The red cock crows, in
this poem, from the farm upon the hill :

> The building rook 'll caw from the windy tall elm-tree,
> And the tufted plover pipe along the fallow lea,
> And the swallow 'ill come again with summer o'er the wave.

Every line is a picture in a new style of art, something which had not been done before in this fashion and finish; no, not even by Wordsworth whose love of flowers and birds is less pictorial, but more instinct with the spirit of the thing he describes.   Nor could Wordsworth, who is the mountain poet, have made us feel the landscape of the lower English lands as Tennyson does—with our pity for the dying girl woven through it all—in these four lines, so clear and fine :

> When the flowers come again, mother, beneath the waning
>   light
> You'll never see me more in the long gray fields at night;
> When from the dry dark wold the summer airs blow cool,
> On the oat-grass and the sword-grass, and the bulrush in
>   the pool.

Still more of England and of the scenery of the chalk-lands, which whosoever loves, loves well, is all the landscape in *The Miller's Daughter*. In this poem, as in the last, there is no special picture made of the landscape, for the human interest is first.   But we might, culling from verse to verse our indications, paint the whole of the country-side round the mill, so careful is Tennyson in his drawing, so deeply has the scene sunk into his imagination.   It is owing to this full digestion, in contemplation, of the landscape, that the human figures—the miller, the lover, the maiden—are so much felt, as we read, to be at union with the natural world round them, even to be partly made into what they are by dwelling with it for so long. Tennyson, who himself, with regard to the Nature he described, was in part a product of that Nature, knew how to do this

artistic thing, and it gives an extraordinary
unity to a great number of his poems. Had
he not absorbed his scenery in this fashion, he
could not have had the capacity, not only to see
the minuter things, as the colour of ash-buds in
March, a capacity which was not fully developed
till ten years after this volume, but to give, in a
line or two, the very image of the whole country
its essential marks :

> The white chalk-quarry from the hill
> Gleam'd to the flying moon by fits—
> *   *   *   *
> On the chalk-hill the bearded grass
> Is dry and dewless. Let us go.

Night and day, the whole country lies before us.
This is one of the great art-powers, the power of
choosing out of a multitude of impressions that
single thing which will awaken all the rest of the
landscape, with its sentiment, before the eyes. It is
partly natural gift, but it is also the result of long
indrinking of the special landscape, and years of
inward contemplation of it. And in this matter of
living with Nature in one place for years, and out of
the incessant observation of love of actually creating
in poetry a portion of England, with its birds and
flowers, its skies, woodland, meadows and streams,
and so vividly and truly that every touch tells ; every
adjective, the sound of the words, the pauses in the
line, enhancing the life of the whole description—for
this reproduction of a whole land and of the final
impression made by it after many years upon the
soul, and for the power of making us feel the land
as the poet felt it—we must get back, if we would
find a comparison, to Wordsworth. Wordsworth

did for the Lake country what Tennyson did for southern England and the Fenland. But Wordsworth did not do this part of his work with as much specialised power as Tennyson.

This is the first thing to say of his landscape. The second concerns his invented landscape, but this will be more fitly treated of in the chapter on the Classical poems.

Meanwhile, Tennyson began two new kinds of poetry in this book of 1833. The first was the treatment of moral questions under the symbolism of poetry. Of this symbolic poetry he afterwards produced a few examples. *The Vision of Sin*, made in 1842, is one. There is a dream in *In Memoriam* which may be said to be another example. Within the main allegory of the *Idylls of the King* there are other examples to be found. The dream in *Sea Dreams* is another. Of these there are not many, for this species of poetry, which embodies a moral problem in a highly ornamented vision, is as exceedingly difficult to do well, as it is exceedingly easy to do badly. When Tennyson did it, he gave all his powers to it, and was not content till he had wrought it, by change after change, into the most careful and skilful finish. There is only one poem in this volume of 1833 which is in this manner. It is *The Palace of Art*, and it stands out clear—a new thing, a fresh effort.

As we read it in the volume of 1833, it has many weak lines. So far as composition goes, it is often all awry. Often we say to ourselves, "Would this were better." But as we read it in the volume of 1842, when it had received eight years of recasting and polishing, it is one of the most perfect of Tennyson's poems. To compare the first draft of this poem with the second, or to compare the first draft of *Œnone* with the second, is not only to receive a useful lesson in the art of poetry—it is also to understand, far better than by any analysis of his life, a great part of Tennyson's character; his impatience for perfection, his steadiness in pursuit of it, his power of taking pains, the long intellectual consideration he gave to matters which originated in the emotions, his love of balancing this and that form of his thought against one another, and when the balancing was done, the unchangeableness of his acceptance of one form, and of his rejection of another; and finally, correlative with these qualities, his want of impulse and rush in song, as in life—English, not Celtic at all. These qualities appear in his elaborate recasts of his poems, and when we compare the recasts with their originals, the man, as well as the artist, seems to grow before us into actual being.

But, returning to the poem, it marks the first rising in his mind of thought on the graver questions of life; not thought on the world around him, or on any question as it affects humanity, but on a question concerning himself and his duty as an artist. "Shall I love art and beauty which I shape in art for the sake of art alone, beauty for beauty only; knowledge only for the sake of the beauty it brings to me? Shall I live, apart from the world of men, and work with no desire to help, exalt or console the blind and ugly herd of men?" This is a question that we ask in the present day, and some answer, "Yes, beauty only, beauty

for its own sake—art without any aim of love in
it—art in isolation from mankind!" And they
retire to a sheltered solitude and sing their song
alone, refusing to hear, behind their hushed tapes-
tries, the cry of human sorrow for human love.
What is their fate? They lose love, for love is
only gained by loving ; and they lose the beauty
they desired to grasp, for beauty is the child of
love. Outside the power of loving man, no beauty
lasts. And finally, having none to love, and therefore nothing to take them out of themselves,
they are wholly thrown on themselves. Their
only companion is their self, and this is absolute
horror and dismay.

This, then, was his subject, and he puts it in
the Introduction. I write, he says, a sort of
allegory of a soul that loved beauty only, and good
and knowledge only for their beauty, and who shut
out Love :

> And he that shuts out Love, in turn shall be
> Shut out from Love, and on her threshold lie
> Howling in outer darkness.

It is a good subject for an essay or a sermon,
but when an artist seizes it as the subject of a
poem it must first be filled with human passion ;
and secondly it must be ornamented with lovely
images. Passion is given to it by Tennyson by
making the soul a person who goes through pride
to dreadful pain, and through pain into repentance.
Beauty is given to it by the description of the
palace which embodies all the various arts and
wisdom of the world in imaginative symbolism.
And surely no more superb and lovely house was

ever built by the wit of man. Take two verses
out of many : *

> Four courts I made—east, west, and south and north,
>   In each a squarèd lawn, wherefrom
> The golden gorge of dragons spouted forth
>   A flood of fountain-foam.

> And round the cool green courts there ran a row
>   Of cloisters, branch'd like mighty woods,
> Echoing all night to that sonorous flow
>   Of spouted fountain-floods.

The vowels roll and ring, and the ornament is
lovely—ornament which Tennyson takes care to
introduce between his successive representations
of the state of the soul. The whole palace is
dedicated to loveliness. The rooms are filled with
the great painters' art ; all fair landscape is there,
and pictures of great romance from Christian
history, from Arabia, India, Greece, and Rome ;
portraits of the great poets ; and on the floors,
in choicely planned mosaic, is wrought the human
tale of the wide world's history ; while all philosophy and knowledge—in the chiming bells, and
in melodies and in the lights that lit the domes
—were heard and realised. There lived the soul
alone unto herself.

> And "while the world runs round and round," I said,
> "Reign thou apart, a quiet king—"
>   *   *   *   *
>   She took her throne :
> She sat betwixt the shining Oriels,
>   To sing her songs alone.
>   *   *   *   *

* I have quoted the passages in this poem from the revised
version of 1842. No poem of Tennyson's underwent more
revision.

> Communing with herself: " All these are mine,
> 　And let the world have peace or wars,
> 'Tis one to me."
> 　　*　　　　*　　　　*　　　　*
> " I take possession of man's mind and deed,
> 　I care not what the sects may brawl.
> I sit as God, holding no form of creed,
> 　But contemplating all."
> 　　*　　　　*　　　　*　　　　*
> Full oft the riddle of the painful earth
> 　Flash'd thro' her as she sat alone,
> Yet not the less held she her solemn mirth,
> 　And intellectual throne.

Then comes the punishment, full of human interest, and wrought with an emotion which lifts it above the level of mere symbolism. Despair, confusion of mind, fear and hatred of solitude, self-scorn, terrible silence, hatred of life and death, entombment in fire within, fell on her. At last she cried :

> " What is it that will take away my sin
> 　And save me lest I die ? "

And out of the repentant cry came escape from the dread comradeship of her self. " I will return to humility and to love, to lowly life with men and women.

> ' Make me a cottage, in the vale,' she said,
> ' Where I may mourn and pray ; '

for ' love is of the valley,' and when love is learned I will return to my palace ; for when I love, and return with others there, bringing all I love with me to enjoy with me—the beauty which turned to corruption when I was alone will live again in glory."

This is Tennyson's confession of the duties of

his art, and of the law of its practice; and it is
characteristic of this conclusion that now for the
first time he begins that poetry of common human
life, of the daily love of child and lover and wife
and father and mother, of the ordinary sorrows
and joys of men and women, which he wove all his
life long with so much sweetness, tenderness, and
power, in homespun thread and colour, that there
is no class, of whatever rank and knowledge, who
will not take pleasure in it for all time, who will
not love him for it. What Wordsworth had done
for the beginning of this century, Tennyson has
done for the midst of it. He brought us into
touch with the general human heart in the midst
of common life. Shelley, Keats, and Byron had
not done this, nor Southey, Coleridge or Scott.
Since the waters of the *Lyrical Ballads* had
streamed into the heart of man, this simple,
fruitful subject had been neglected by other poets
than Wordsworth; this subject which lies among
the roots of the tree of all the arts, and which,
when other subjects of a more grand or fantastic kind are exhausted, sends its ever youthful
life into the tree, and renews the arts. Its
essence, pure and faithful love, is eternal in the
human heart, and beyond it, in all spirits, and in
God Himself. It takes in every true sorrow and
true joy. It is universal, and yet its forms are
infinite. It is everywhere, like the grass that we
love so well, and of which we never weary. All
men, women, and children feel and understand it.
It varies from the lowest note of the commonplace
to the highest note of imaginative passion, and
the artist can choose whatever note he pleases to

strike. There are many other subjects for the poet; but if he wish to initiate a new world of song, this is one of the subjects to which he must devote a part of his work; and we shall find, when we are out of this transition period of poetry in which we live at present and are fully wearied with its fantasies of Nature and passion and words, that the poet who will recreate our song will take up again the common love and life of men. He will drink of the wayside fountains of humanity.

It was thus now with Tennyson. He began this vein with *The May Queen*, to which the galloping verse has sometimes given an air of sentimentalism. The same things would have made a different impression had the verse been shorter in line, and a little statelier in form. But it is sweet and gracious enough, and the mother, the poor pretty child and Robin her lover are our friends. He began it also with *The Miller's Daughter*, a simple story of true sweethearting and married love; but raised by the loveliness of the scenery which is inwoven with charm and grace into the tale, and by the simplicity of the expression, into a steady and grave emotion, worthy of a love built to last for life betwixt a man and woman. This was the sort of love for which Tennyson cared, for which Byron and Shelley did not care, which was not in the world where Keats lived at all—but which was in Wordsworth's world, and which, after all our excursions into phases of passion, is not only the deepest and highest of the affections, but the father and mother of all the other loves of earth. It was first in Tennyson's mind, but it had many companions. Love of many kinds, joy and sorrow of many kinds, as they were felt by the common human heart, not only by the great, but by the lowly upon earth, were now his interest, and many and lovely were the poems he dedicated to them. Who is likely to forget *Dora*, *The Gardener's Daughter*, *Sea Dreams*, *The Brook*, *Enoch Arden*, and a host of others? This is the democratic element in Tennyson. It is, in all its phases, the democracy of the artist.

CHAPTER III

THE POEMS OF 1842

I DO not think that since the time of Shakspere there have been in England any poets so close to the life of their own time as Tennyson and Browning; no, not even Wordsworth. Other men, like Pope, have got as close, or even closer, to distinct phases of thought or classes of society, but Tennyson and Browning settled themselves down to paint as far as they could all classes and their interests. They did this in different ways, but they both had a more universal aim than their predecessors, and covered a much larger and more various extent of ground. Of course they had more opportunities, more means. The steam-road, with its rapid travelling, extended literature to the country and brought the country into contact with the towns. The poet in London or the poet in the Isle of Wight touched a great number of different types of men which would have remained unknown to him fifty years before. In the same way the manifold forms of natural scenery in England or abroad were much more easily brought to his knowledge. Moreover Tennyson and Browning were lucky in their time. Their present was full of aspiration, of ideals, of questioning, of excitement. They

were like ships floating into a great sea-loch, on a
brimming tide and with a favouring wind.

Tennyson's interest in the humanity of his own
day now grew continuously.   I shall show in the
next chapter how he could not help modernising
the Greek and the romantic subjects of which he
treated.   Keats went away to Athens or Florence,
and living in an alien age forgot his own time.
Tennyson said to Ulysses or Arthur, "Come down
from the ancient days, and live with me, here
in England."   And they came ; and did their best
to wear the modern dress.   When we turn from
these Greek subjects, we find him altogether
English and modern.   A series of poems entered
into various phases of youthful love. *The Gardener's
Daughter* painted with beauty and simplicity the
upspringing of the fountain of love in a young
artist's soul, and carried it on to marriage.   And
the love was set in a framework of soft and
flower-haunted English scenery, every touch of
which, in Tennyson's way, was woven into the
feelings of the two young hearts.   Moreover,
though I think that the collecting of the story
round two pictures is awkward, it enables Tennyson to throw over this tale of first love the
glamour and tenderness of memory.   The man
who tells it has lost the wife of his youth, whose
picture he shows to his friend.   The loveliness of
unselfish sorrow, which makes remembrance joyful
in regret, veils the story with the delicate vapour
of spiritual love.   At first reading, there is a want
of closeness, of reality in the feeling described.
But when we know that it is a mature man recalling what has been when she whom he loved of

old has long since been in the heavenly life, we understand how the clear edges of passion melt into ideal mist ; and then we read the poem from the poet's point of view.

The Talking Oak is another poem of youthful love. The lover to whom the tree speaks of his maiden and who tells the tree of her, is a motive which has been often used, but never with greater skill and charm. There is a youthful animation, and a happy chivalry in rivalry of praise between the lover and the tree, which are full of natural grace, that quality somewhat rare in Tennyson, who was frequently too academic, too careful in his work to attain it. In this poem, also, his inweaving of Nature's heart with the heart of man is more than plain. The oak talks to the lover. Nay, the oak itself is in love with the maiden. His very sap is stirred by her kiss. He drops an acorn on her breast ; and the half-jealous lover knows that he need not be jealous. Above all, there is no poem more English in all the poems of Tennyson. We see the park, the Chase that Englishmen of all ranks love so well ; the roofs of the great house above the trees ; the wild woodland deep in fern, the deer, the mighty trees, the oak which has watched so many English generations, so much of English history—bluff Harry who turned the monks adrift—the Roundhead humming his surly hymn—the modish beauties of the Court of Anne—the English girl of to-day who leaves her novel and piano to race singing through the park. This is Tennyson close down to his own land, vitally interested in modern life, and the thing and its method are new in English poetry.

The same springtide of love is described in *Locksley Hall* and in the gay delightfulness of *The Day-Dream*, with its modern applications; but in *Locksley Hall* we pass on into one of those graver phases of love which Tennyson now treated. The hero's love suffers a mean disillusion, and he is angry like a boy; but in *Love and Duty* the matter is more serious. Two love one another, whom duty forbids to fulfil their love. Was the love fruitless, did it turn to dust? Because passion was denied, were two lives ruined? No, is the answer of Tennyson. Because duty was lord over passion and drove their lives apart, love itself, honoured more in giving up than in taking an earthly joy contrary to righteousness, lasted in both hearts, unstained and lovely, and bettered both their lives. The man, emerging from himself, gained the higher love, and never knew

> The set gray life, and apathetic end.

The woman knew, when the parting was over, that all

> Life needs for life is possible to will.

And happiness came to her, and freedom, and the distant light was pure.

There was a conviction in Tennyson's mind that the sanctity of the marriage tie was one of the eternal foundations of all true personal, social, and national life; that no amount of passionate love excused its breakage. This is not the view of the artists in general, but it is the view which prevails in the English nation. And Tennyson felt and represented it all through his poetry. It is a sin

G

against that, with all its excuses also stated which, in his recast of the Arthurian story, overthrows the whole life-work of the king and brings about the last great battle and the death. It is to establish the true idea of marriage as he conceived it that *The Princess* was written ; and a number of other poems, enshrining his reverence for long-continued faithfulness through all the troubles of domestic life, and culminating in the honour he gave to the Crown, chiefly for this reason, make him, even more than Wordsworth, the poet of the sanctity of marriage. *Love and Duty* seems to be the first of these poems.

Two things are, however, curious in this poem. One is the passionate meeting of the lovers. From Tennyson's steady point of view, married faith which permitted what he relates is not faith at all. And if it was not marriage, but some other duty which stood in the way, then the intensity of the piece is overdone. That is the first curious thing, and the second is the predominance of the man in the matter. It is he that feels the most ; it is he that directs the whole business of duty. It is he that expresses passion, or allows it to be expressed. It is he alone who is strong, who alone resists ; and when both retire into steady life, he alone does work ; " he is most Godlike, being most a man," and he uses his self-conquest to improve the world ; but the woman tends her flowers, is sadly happy, dreams a little by day, dreams more at night, and does no human work at all. In *The Princess*, Tennyson expands another view, being somewhat forced into it by his subject. But, on the whole, this subordinate position of woman, or rather this instinctive dominance of the man, is a weakness, at least from our modern point of view, in his work. He never conceives womanhood quite clearly. The masculine is too strong in him for that, and its preponderance is the cause why few of his women have the weight, the worth, or the character some other poets give them. Wordsworth's picture of his sister, his short poem to his wife, his *Affliction of Margaret,** his *Highland Girl*, any of his women, are of more reality than the women of Tennyson. It seems—and it is a fault in a poet—as if at the bottom of his mind, and in spite of his *Princess*, he tended to the view of woman which his angry boy expresses in *Locksley Hall :*

> Woman is the lesser man, and all thy passions, match'd with
> mine,
> Are as moonlight unto sunlight, and as water unto wine.

This is, of course, continually modified. He is always trying to conceive women as higher than

---

* Compare the passion of motherhood as expressed in this magnificent poem with that of Psyche in *The Princess* in the lines beginning

> Ah me, my babe, my blossom, ah, my child,
> My one sweet child, whom I shall see no more.

There is no comparison. Indeed, the motherhood in Wordsworth's *The Complaint* and in *Her eyes are wild* is closer, more intimate to this primal passion, than anything in Tennyson, save always the intense penetration of *Rizpah*.

> My baby, the bones that had suck'd me, the bones that had
> laughed and cried—
> Theirs? O, no! they are mine—not theirs—they had moved
> in my side.

That is as great as Nature herself.

this, and he succeeds ; but a blind pull in his mind,
growing out of his nature, appears to draw him back
to this lower conception.   He cannot get his women
of equal worth with his men.   One of the results of
this is that there is no vital or supreme passion
between the sexes expressed by Tennyson.   There
is always a certain element of condescension in the
man, and where there is a shred of condescension
there is no supreme passion.   The nearest he gets
to it is in the expression of the longing for lost
love, and this is expressed by the man rather than
by the woman.*   It is the man who utters in
Maud that most sorrowful and lovely of all
Tennyson's cries :

> O that 'twere possible
> After long grief and pain
> To find the arms of my true love
> Round me once again !

But of the longing for lost love there are two
poems, one in this book, and one included in it little
later, which record the wild love-sorrow of men.
One is a kind of ballad, *Edward Gray*, and the greater
part of it attains power through its simplicity, but
Tennyson was led away at the end, and the poem

---

 * There are always exceptions to be found to general statements of this kind, and they are frequently strong exceptions.
Elaine draws near to such an exception, and the song in *The
Princess*—" Tears, idle tears "—is sung by a girl, and she sings it
in her own person.   The lines :

> Dear as remember'd kisses after death,
> And sweet as those by hopeless fancy feign'd
> On lips that are for others ;

are intimate with a passion elsewhere almost unknown in
Tennyson.

passes into weakness. Fancy and reflection come in when the passion is over, and we are left a little disenchanted. I wish the last three verses were expunged. The other is a poem of much greater force, fully conceived, and sounding its way through deeper waters than we often try to fathom in Tennyson. Its motive, while uncommon, is adequate to the emotion expressed. Here it is:

> Come not, when I am dead,
>   To drop thy foolish tears upon my grave,
> To trample round my fallen head,
>   And vex the unhappy dust thou wouldst not save.
> There let the wind sweep and the plover cry;
>   But thou, go by.
>
> Child, if it were thine error or thy crime,
>   I care no longer, being all unblest;
> Wed whom thou wilt, but I am sick of Time,
>   And I desire to rest.
> Pass on, weak heart, and leave me where I lie;
>   Go by, go by.

Weariness of love after long anger of love, weariness of life from weariness of love, and, beneath both, unforgetful tenderness, were rarely better expressed. But, to close these notes on the love poems in this volume, it is somewhat strange, but illustrative of what I have said about the dominance of the man in Tennyson, that the poem of fullest regret for love drowned in death is written in memory of a man. Every one knows it; it is a piece of perfect work, fully felt, and fully finished, simple and profound—and with what fine art Nature is inwoven with its passion!

> Break, break, break,
>   On thy cold gray stones, O Sea,
> And I would that my tongue could utter
>   The thoughts that arise in me.

There is no need to quote the rest : it lives in the memory of man.

Along with these poems of love arose poems of modern life, half dramatic, half idyllic; dramatic idylls—some of a serious, even a stately simplicity, quite close to common human life, like *Dora*, which is a little masterpiece ; others of a homespun humour mingled with imaginative thought, like *Audley Court* and *The Golden Year;* and others full of that honest University humour which characterises the talk of Englishmen when they are on a vacation tour, like *Walking to the Mail* and *Edwin Morris.* These are pure modernism ; they also are new in English poetry; they have opened a vein which many others may work at, and they have opened it in an excellent and varied way. The very similes Tennyson uses in them are in harmony with the character of the poems, similes drawn from every-day sounds and sights, and so vital with observation of common English life and things that they seem to illuminate the page with England.

> A body slight and round, and like a pear
> In growing, modest eyes, a hand, a foot
> Lessening in perfect cadence, and a skin
> As clean and white as privet when it flowers.

> James—you know him—old, but full
> Of force and choler, and firm upon his feet,
> And like an oaken stock in winter woods,
> O'erflourish'd by the hoary clematis.

> He laugh'd, and I, though sleepy, like a horse
> That hears the corn-bin open, prick'd my ears.

Scattered through these poems, and in accordance with all I have said of Tennyson's incorporation of Nature and the heart of man, are lovely, true, and intimate descriptions of Nature in England, done with an art which never forgot itself, and which seemed sometimes too elaborate in skill. Indeed, we should often feel this, were it not that the full product gives so complete a pleasure.

The Gardener's Daughter is alive with such descriptions ; and it would be worth while to read that of the entrance into the garden. Step by step, as we move on, the changing scene is painted. We walk through the landscape with Tennyson. This garden-passage begins :

> We reach'd a meadow slanting to the north.

When the last line strikes the ear,

> The twinkling laurel scatter'd silver lights,

it is meant to paint the very thing by words ; but a far finer instance of this, where the line is so arranged in sound as to be itself what he describes, is towards the end of the poem :

> Or as once we met
> Unheedful, tho', beneath a whispering rain
> *Night slid down one long stream of sighing wind,*
> And in her bosom bore the baby, Sleep.

Nor can I pass by that description of the Lincoln meadows, near the town, lush in thick grass and in broad waters, and deep in wind-washed trees—

> Not wholly in the busy world, nor quite
> Beyond it, blooms the garden that I love.
> News from the humming city comes to it
> In sound of funeral or of marriage bells ;
> And, sitting muffled in dark leaves, you hear
> The windy clanging of the minster clock ;

> Although between it and the garden lies
> A league of grass, wash'd by a slow broad stream,
> That, stirr'd with languid pulses of the oar,
> Waves all its lazy lilies, and creeps on,
> Barge-laden, to three arches of a bridge
> Crown'd with the minster-towers.
>   The fields between
> Are dewy-fresh, browsed by deep-udder'd kine,
> And all about the large lime feathers low,
> The lime a summer home of murmurous wings.

The close of *Audley Court* is as near to truth :

> The town was hush'd beneath us: lower down
> The bay was oily-calm ; the harbour buoy,
> With one green sparkle ever and anon
> Dipt by itself, and we were glad at heart.

That is evening, when the moon is high : here is morning lifting herself in exultation :

> Then when the first low matin-chirp hath grown
> Full quire, and morning driv'n her plow of pearl,*
> Far furrowing into light the mounded rack,
> Beyond the fair green field and eastern lea.

This has that classic note of Milton, but it is quite original.   There are many touches of Nature as fine as this in *Locksley Hall*, but that poem has far more to do with man than with Nature.   It is, however, set in landscape which reflects the temper of the hero—sandy tracts on which the ocean thunders and the curlews cry—the sea-shore on one side, and the moorland on the other ; and at the last, the vapour blackening from the moor with the blast in its breast to fall on Locksley Hall.

* Compare the lines in *The Princess* :

> Morn in the white wake of the morning star
> Came furrowing all the orient into gold.

Every one knows this poem. Its form is good, its divisions clear. It passes from one division to another with ease and imagination. Every one knows the hero, with his hour of happy love, his rage of disillusion, his hope at the end that the living present may excite him by its science, and give him back his youthful inspiration. I never thought that this blustering youth, " weak as is a breaking wave," whom Tennyson invented so well, and who is so true to a common type—a type he lowers much further in the hero of *Maud*—would find any inspiration in science or the march of commerce ; and the second *Locksley Hall*, where Tennyson draws the same personage after he had settled on his lees, proves that he got no good out of science or the British carrying trade. But how modern it all is ; how kindled Tennyson is by the time in which he was living, how alive to its wants, its strife, its faults, its good ! We are miles and miles away from the temper in which Keats or Shelley regarded their world.

Three other poems in this volume may be called theological, and grouped together : *St. Simeon Stylites*, *The Two Voices*, and *The Vision of Sin*. The first is a study of the type of the ascetic in its extreme. Nevertheless, so ably, so robustly, and yet so delicately is it done that its spirit and its qualities belong to the whole range of ascetics, from Stylites down to the slightest subduer of the flesh. The conviction that all evil lies in matter and all good in its subjugation ; that the more the flesh is punished, the more certain is salvation, and the greater the power of the punisher over matter, so that miracles are wrought ; the claim, the right established over God, from whom self-inflicted penance wrenches privilege; the incessant assertion of sin in apparent or real humility, lest God should catch him tripping; the steady underlying vanity and boastfulness; his contempt of the flesh-ridden people; his isolation—all these and far more are given in this admirable study, filled with thought and insight. Rarely has Tennyson thrown himself more completely out of himself. Moreover, and this is perhaps the best and most poetic thing in the piece, he does not make us dislike or despise the Saint. We touch the human soul of one whom we can pity, and even admire. Nearly forty years of that mad existence had not unmanned the ascetic altogether. To convey that impression was an excellent trait of art.

I cannot find a like pleasure in *The Two Voices*. As much as Tennyson has gone outside himself in *Simeon Stylites*, so much has he gone into himself in *The Two Voices*. A man may do that and be still poetic, and the poem proves this. It is full of a poet's power, especially in the illustrations taken from Nature, like that of the dragon-fly and the mountain-angle jutting clear from the mist; but the self-involution of the poem places it on a lower level than poetry which loses self-thought in the creation of a being beyond the self of the poet. Moreover, the argumentative form lowers still more the power of making excellent poetry. The best part is where the disputing voices have ceased to talk, where the poet throws open the window, and sees every one going to church in the summer morning.

The Vision of Sin is, on the contrary, one of the

very good things in this book.   It is allegorical, but
not too allegorical.   The youth who rides to the
palace and who rides away into the waste, a ruined
cynic, dominates the allegory by his personality ;
and our interest in him and his fate is greater than
that we feel in the meaning of the poem.   Nevertheless, both the thoughts and the allegory are of a
quality as original as they are just.   Tennyson has
never done better thinking.   The youth who rides
the horse of the soul, winged with aspiration and
imagination, weighs the horse down, for he has
already been mastered by the flesh.   He is led
into the palace of sensual pleasure, not coarse
but refined pleasure, slipping incessantly, however,
into coarser forms.   The main contention of the
allegory is that subtilised sensuality is finally
driven, in order to capture fresh pleasure, into
wilder, fiercer, and baser forms, till all pleasure dies.
Then the mist of satiety,

<blockquote>A vapour heavy, hueless, formless, cold,</blockquote>

creeps slowly on from where Eternal Law, sitting
beyond the darkness and the cataract and annexing
the punishment of exhaustion to unbroken indulgence, makes himself an awful rose of dawn.

The end of the youth is shamelessness and
malice, disbelief in love and goodness, scorn of
self and scorn of man, sour cynicism—and the
picture of this state of mind is admirably drawn
in the jumping verses that follow.   But Tennyson does not leave him to utter loss.   The mystic
mountain range arises again.   In the gulf below,
the sensual who in their youth were half divine
are devoured by worms, and quicken into lower

forms ; but three Spirits apart, three Spirits of
judgment, speak of the youth who has ruined his
life.   The world beyond takes interest in him.

The first says :

> Behold ! it was a crime
> Of sense avenged by sense that wore with time.

The truth could not be more briefly or better put.
Every lust of sense is driven, in order to retake the
original pleasure, to increase the stimulant, to make
it fiercer and more brutal.   At last no stimulation
awakens the sense, for the stimulation has para-
lysed it.   This is sense avenged by sense.   But
the man is forced to go on with the sensual
effort, as a drunkard is forced to go on drinking,
while at the same time no pleasure attends the
effort.   The sense has worn with time.   Justice is
done.

But the loss of all pleasure has made him hate
happiness, call it vile, and scorn both God and
man.   So another Spirit cries :

> The crime of sense became
> The crime of malice, and is equal blame.

Nevertheless, the man is not wholly lost.   Were
he absolutely evil, he would have had no feeling,
no scorn, no mockery; he could not even see
the love and goodness at which he grins.   So
another Spirit answers :

> He had not wholly quenched his power.
> A little grain of conscience made him sour.

Then a voice cries, Is there any hope ? and the
close of the poem is majestic.

> To which an answer peal'd from that high land,
> But in a tongue no man could understand;
> And on the glimmering limit far withdrawn
> God made Himself an awful rose of dawn.

Moreover, this poem, with the *Ulysses*, marks
with great clearness what an advance Tennyson
had made in his art since 1833. It was plain now
that he deserved his audience, and that he was
determined to be more and more master of his
art. He had laboured at perfecting its powers.
Metre is no more a difficulty. The rush of the
lines of *Locksley Hall* is like the incoming of billows
on the beach. The thing to be said is always
given a poetic turn; there is not a line of prose
in the whole book. The subjects are worthy, are
human, are at our doors. They are still evolved
out of his own consciousness, out of his own life
and feeling; but they are moving on to the time
when the subjects will come from without, when
the thought and feeling of universal man will press
on him, and demand that he should express it.
Not only the present, but the future is beginning
to interest him,

> For he sings of what the world will be
> When the years have died away.

CHAPTER IV

THE CLASSICAL AND ROMANTIC POEMS OF 1842
WITH THE LATER CLASSICAL POEMS

THE classical poems in the volume of 1833
were two, *Œnone* and *The Lotos-Eaters*. I
have kept them for separate treatment, because in
1842, when they reappeared, they were so largely
recast, and their landscape so changed, that it
would have been unfair to Tennyson to consider them save in the finished form he gave
them in 1842. In that year also he added
another classical poem to these, the *Ulysses*.
These are the three, and the first thing to think
of is their landscape, which is distinct and invented.

I have said that Tennyson, when he worked on
natural scenery outside of his own land, was
not a good landscapist. Not only had he little
sympathy with southern Nature, but he also
required to assimilate during long years of companionship the scenery he described, before he
could, with his full power, embody it in verse. But
the impressions he received in travel were brief.
They did not soak into him, and he could not
reproduce them well. This, I said, was the case
when he painted direct from Nature.

But it is not the case when he invented, when
he painted from the vision he had of a landscape
in his own soul. He saw it, rising like an exhala-
tion into form around his figures. He took the
cloud-shapes, and composed them slowly ; rejecting
this, accepting that, till he had got the background
which he needed for Œnone, or Ulysses, or the
mild-eyed Lotos-eaters. Then his Nature-painting, wherever the scene is placed, is fine in itself,
and necessarily fits the subject. Of course, he
does not stand alone in such invention. Every
poet, as every painter, practises, more or less, this
part of his art. Wordsworth and Walter Scott
are almost solitary in their habit, rarely infringed,
of painting all their landscape on the spot, direct
from Nature. But then, they did not take subjects
outside of their own country and their own time, or,
if they did, as when Wordsworth took a classical subject like *Laodamia,* they did not put in a landscape.

But the greater number of the poets invent ;
and there is no more fascinating subject in literature,
or one as yet more untouched, than this invented
landscape of the poets. In what way each of them
did it ; their favourite tricks in doing it ; the
different way each of them uses Nature for his
purpose or his figures ; the limits of invented
landscape ; its analogies to landscape painting—
these are all branches of the subject, and when
we have little to do and want amusement, we
could not find happier entertainment than the study
of this kind of Nature-painting in Shelley or Keats
or Spenser ; or, when we have done such a study
of two or three poets' work, than a comparison
of their separate methods of invention.

Such invented landscape is sometimes done from a previous study from Nature which is worked up afterwards into a picture, and of this the landscape in the *Œnone* of 1833 is an instance. At other times, it is a picture composed out of various impressions of diverse places brought together into one landscape, and this is the case with a number of the landscapes in *The Revolt of Islam*, and in the *Prometheus Unbound*. It is sometimes used to illustrate the human passions treated of in the poem, the landscape echoing as it were the feelings of the persons, even the progress of their thoughts. Spenser does this echoing landscape with great directness, as in the description of the bower of Acrasia, or of the Cave of Mammon, or of the haunt of Despair. Tennyson does it with great deliberation in *The Lotos-Eaters*. Shelley, in the latter part of *Alastor*, makes the whole scene—and especially the course of the river down the glen, the narrowing of the glen, and the sudden opening out of its jaws on a vast landscape lying far below in the dying sunlight—image, step by step, the thoughts of his poet wandering to his death. Sometimes this invented landscape is simply a background, without any purpose in it, only that the tones are kept in harmony with the human action; and sometimes it is done for pure pleasure in composing Nature, but in that case, when there are human beings in the foreground of the poem, there is a great danger lest Nature overwhelm humanity in the poem, or lest the poem lack unity ; and both these pitfalls, for example, are fallen into by Keats in *Endymion*.

In classical poems, the landscape must of course be invented, unless, like the Pre-Raphaelite Brotherhood, the poet should go to Troy or Ithaca, and describe things as they are now, in order to gain local colour. Since the days of Pre-Raphaelitism, some poets have used this way, but for the most part they invent ; and Tennyson saw his Lotos Island and the Mount of Ida only " with the intellectual eye." In *Œnone*, however, he began with direct description, with his eye upon the scene. It was a valley in the Pyrenees, we are told, which he chose as background for his betrayed maiden, for Paris and the goddesses, when he wrote of them in 1833 ; and here is this first landscape :

> There is a dale in Ida, lovelier
> Than any in old Ionia, beautiful
> With emerald slopes of sunny sward, that lean
> Above the loud glenriver, which hath worn
> A path thro' steepdown granite walls below
> Mantled with flowering tendriltwine. In front
> The cedar-shadowy valleys open wide.
> Far seen, high over all the Godbuilt wall
> And many a snowycolumned range divine,
> Mounted with awful sculptures—men and Gods,
> The work of Gods—bright on the dark blue sky
> The windy citadel of Ilion
> Shone, like the crown of Troas.

As Tennyson thought of this, he saw how poor it was in comparison with what he might do if he chose. The blank verse halts ; a hurly-burly of vowels like " Than any in old Ionia " is a sorrowful thing ; there is no careful composition of the picture ; the things described have not that vital connection one with the other which should

H

enable the imaginative eye to follow them step by step down the valley till it opens on the plain where Troy stands white, below its citadel.

Now observe what an artist who has trained his powers can make of his first rough sketch, when, neglecting what he has seen, he invents and composes with imaginative care.   Here is the picture of 1842 made out of the sketch of 1833 :

> There lies a vale in Ida, lovelier
> Than all the valleys of Ionian hills.
> The swimming vapour slopes athwart the glen,
> Puts forth an arm, and creeps from pine to pine,
> And loiters, slowly drawn.   On either hand
> The lawns and meadow-ledges midway down
> Hang rich in flowers, and far below them roars
> The long brook falling thro' the clov'n ravine
> In cataract after cataract to the sea.
> Behind the valley topmost Gargarus
> Stands up and takes the morning: but in front
> The gorges, opening wide apart, reveal
> Troas and Ilion's column'd citadel,
> The crown of Troas.

The verse is now weighty and poised and nobly paused—yet it moves swiftly enough.   The landscape now is absolutely clear, and it is partly done by cautious additions to the original sketch.   Moreover, being seen by the imagination in an hour of joy, it is far truer in its details to Nature than the previous sketch.   In any invented landscape, though the whole has not been seen in Nature, the parts must be true to her ways ;   and nothing can image better the actual thing than that phrase concerning a lonely peak at dawn, that it "takes the morning" ; nor the lifting and slow absorption of the mists of night when the sun slants warm into the pines of the glen, than those slow-wrought, concentrated lines about the mountain vapour.

That is one illustration of my point, and in this instance the original has been expanded. I will now compare another piece of the *Œnone* of 1833 with its new form in 1842. Here there is no expansion, there is contraction. The original was too diffuse : it is now concised with admirable force. This is the original description of the coming of the goddesses :

> It was the deep midnoon ; one silvery cloud
> Had lost his way among the piney hills.
> They came—all three—the Olympian goddesses :
> Naked they came to the smoothswarded bower,
> Lustrous with lily flower, violeteyed
> Both white and blue, with lotetree-fruit thickset,
> Shadowed with singing pine ; and all the while,
> Above, the overwandering ivy and vine
> This way and that in many a wild festoon
> Ran riot, garlanding the gnarlèd boughs
> With bunch and berry and flower thro' and thro'.

And this is the new thing, with its one line—

> "And at their feet the crocus brake like fire,"

which is the centre light and passion of the whole, which fills the scene, not only with golden glory, but with the immortal power of the gods, before whose deity Nature blossoms into worship :

> It was the deep mid-noon : one silvery cloud
> Had lost his way between the piney sides
> Of this long glen.   Then to the bower they came,
> Naked they came to the smooth-swarded bower,
> And at their feet the crocus brake like fire,
> Violet, amaracus, and asphodel,
> Lotos and lilies : and a wind arose,

And overhead the wandering ivy and vine,
This way and that, in many a wild festoon
Ran riot, garlanding the gnarlèd boughs
With bunch and berry and flower thro' and thro'.

Nothing can be more careful than the composition of this background for the goddesses. Some
have said that it is a little too pictorial for poetry ;
but we will be thankful that we have a piece of
work of a kind which was then new in poetry,
and that it is splendidly done.*

But there is something more to say. In the
original cast, the scenery of the poem was not fully
inwoven with Œnone's mind. It did not fit her
or feel with her as subtly and intimately as he
wished ; she did not seem to have lived with it
in long association——a thing Tennyson felt was
necessary for himself if he were to describe
a landscape perfectly. Nor were the mountains or the woods or the gorge in the first draft
deep enough or high enough for her passion or for
the fateful meeting of the goddesses, or sombre
enough for her misery or for the fate of Troy,
which lies beyond the poem and yet is contained
within its action.

To fulfil and embody in the landscape these

---

* See how Tennyson has left out the thoroughly bad line—
"They came—all three—the Olympian goddesses"—how he has
made melodious the halting lines, such as "Both white and blue,
with lotetree-fruit thickset " ; and how the confusion of colour
and flowers, the over-description of the flowers, and the addition
of the pine-groves above the bower, all of which take our eyes
away from the goddesses, are omitted or reduced to simplicity.
Moreover he knew clearly the good things in his original verses
and did not touch those admirable four last lines. He may have
had in his ear Milton's "with the gadding vine o'ergrown," but
if so—how delightfully he has fulfilled that which Milton only
touched with a single adjective.

various hues of passion, to make the landscape more absolutely one with them, Tennyson set himself to work in the new poem, and he did it by adding a touch here and a touch there, by describing the landscape—a trick of his which he first used in *Mariana*—at different times of the day with a greater fulness than before, until at last we can no more divide Œnone from the Nature in which she is placed than we can separate the soul from the body of a friend. She is involved in the Nature which surrounds her, and the Nature in which she lives has mixed itself with her thought and her passion. Her constant cry, even in the first draft, proves this:

> O mother Ida, harken ere I die!

This power of forging together Nature and the heart of man adds emotion to the skill with which the occasional figures are placed in the landscape, and to the vividness with which they are suddenly, almost flamingly, struck upon the sight. I need not quote the splendid image of Aphrodite in this poem, but here is Paris issuing from the wood:

> Beautiful Paris, evil-hearted Paris,
> Leading a jet-black goat white-horned, white-hooved,
> Came up from reedy Simois all alone.
> .   .   .   .   White-breasted like a star
> Fronting the dawn he moved; a leopard skin
> Droop'd from his shoulder, but his sunny hair
> Cluster'd about his temples like a god's;
> And his cheek brighten'd as the foam-bow brightens
> When the wind blows the foam.

From end to end the *Idylls of the King* is full of figure-painting, as illuminated and illuminating the scene, as that of Paris here on Ida. Another example, from *The Lady of Shalott*, where Sir Lancelot comes riding down by the river side, is too well known to quote. These are the first five lines of it:

> A bow-shot from her bower-eaves,
>   He rode between the barley-sheaves;
>   The sun came dazzling thro' the leaves
>   And flamed upon the brazen greaves
>   Of bold Sir Lancelot.

The rest of it is equally brilliant. Horse and man, sunlight and scenery, gleaming river and glancing armour—how they fit together, into what unity of impression they are knit! The verse flashes and scintillates like the armour, like the eyes of Lancelot in the sunlight. The passage is perhaps almost over-sparkled, and it might be chastened a little, shortened by at least one verse, and improved; but it is a wonderful piece of gold and jewel-work, and only Milton can excel it in its own sphere. We might compare it with the description of Raphael and his dress in *Paradise Lost*. Of course the Miltonic work is the more dignified, for the figure is that of the Angel of the Earth. Milton's verse too is stately—blank verse, not the jingling trot of the light metre Tennyson chose for his lightly-imagined subject—but the colour, the clearness, the presentation of the dress and the figure, the many-hued sculpture, and the glorious gleaming of Milton's Archangel, make clear to us on what master Tennyson, even in these pictorial matters, now modelled his technical work.

Such, to return from this excursion on figure-drawing, is the invented landscape in *Œnone*. But fine landscape and fine figure-drawing are not enough to make a fine poem. Human interest, human passion, must be greater than Nature and dominate the subject. Indeed, all this lovely scenery is nothing in comparison with the sorrow and love of Œnone, recalling her lost love in the places where once she lived in joy. This is the main humanity of the poem. But there is more. Her common sorrow is lifted almost into the proportions of Greek tragedy by its cause and by its results. It is caused by a quarrel in Olympus, and the mountain nymph is sacrificed without a thought to the vanity of the careless gods. That is an ever recurring tragedy in human history. Moreover, the personal tragedy deepens when we see the fateful dread in Œnone's heart that she will far away in time hold her lover's life in her hands, and refuse to give it back to him—a fatality that Tennyson treated before he died. And secondly, Œnone's sorrow is lifted into dignity by the vast results which flowed from its cause. Behind it were the mighty fates of Troy, the ten years' battle, the anger of Achilles, the wanderings of Ulysses, the tragedy of Agamemnon, the founding of Rome, and the three great epics of the ancient world.

This was then a subject well chosen, holding in it mighty human thoughts and destinies, and these are living in the poem. But there is something more to say. Tennyson, in the way I have already explained, makes all these classic poems fit in with modern times and instruct the conscience or enhance the aspiration of those who read his work. Wordsworth did this in his *Laodamia* and *Dion*. Keats did not do it, Greek as were his subjects. He loved their beauty, not their lessons to mankind. Tennyson does give what Wordsworth does not—their sensuous beauty —but he also gives their universal lesson. And in *Œnone* he lays down that which in all his poetry and in his character also was one of the first of thoughts to him, not only the foundation of life, and government, of true power, and, in the end, of beauty, but also the root of the glory and strength of England as he wished her to be. This is held in the speech of Pallas, and is the centre of the poem :

> Self-reverence, self-knowledge, self-control,
> These three alone lead life to sovereign power.
> Yet not for power (power of herself
> Would come uncall'd for) but to live by law,
> Acting the law we live by without fear ;
> And, because right is right, to follow right
> Were wisdom in the scorn of consequence.
>   I woo thee not with gifts.
> Sequel of guerdon could not alter me
> To fairer.   Judge thou me by what I am,
> So shalt thou find me fairest.
>
> *   *   *   *   *
>
>   Oh, rest thee sure
> That I shall love thee well and cleave to thee,
> So that my vigour, wedded to thy blood,
> Shall strike within thy pulses, like a god's,
> To push thee forward thro' a life of shocks,
> Dangers, and deeds, until endurance grow
> Sinew'd with action, and the full-grown will,
> Circled thro' all experiences, pure law,
> Commeasure perfect freedom.

In these thoughts we pierce down to one of the roots of Tennyson. On those thoughts he built his patriotic poetry. In order to enhance those thoughts, he built as their contrast and opposite the character of the hero in the two *Locksley Halls.* On those lines he draws the character of King

Arthur. On those lines, in a hundred poems, he lays down what he considers to be the greatness of England, the greatness of mankind. Athena in the heart, to use Ruskin's phrase, is a universal need; and the expression of this thought of Tennyson's makes *Œnone* not only a classic but a modern poem.

In *The Lotos-Eaters* the landscape is also invented. There is no description in the *Odyssey* of the land of "the Lotos-eaters, who eat a flowery food." It is only said that "whoso ate the honey-sweet fruit of the lotos had no desire to bring tidings to the ship, or to come back to it, but chose to dwell among the lotos-eating folk, and, forgetful of returning, fed upon the lotos." This is the source of Tennyson's poem. But in a Nature-loving world like ours and midst of that modern poetic temper which makes Nature reflect humanity, so simple a treatment is not enough for Tennyson. He drives the bark of Ulysses into a shallow bay opening up shoreward into a deep valley bordered with cliffs, down whose sides thin streams of silken mist are falling, and at the head of the valley three snow-crowned mountain-peaks are rosy in the sunset. The vale is filled with the soft murmur of a river which glides at last through the yellow sand of the seashore into the sea over which the sun is setting. This is his landscape, and everywhere below the pines, in every creek and alley, on every lawn, beside every stream, the lotos blooms and sheds its yellow dust upon the weary wind.

But the landscape itself is not enough. It must be put into harmony with the soft oblivion which the lotos brings, with the rest and slumber of life dreaming that it dreams. So the air is languid, and

the moon has completed its waxing and is full-faced;
and the streams fall in slow-dropping veils of thin-
nest lawn, and their sheets of foam are slumbrous,
and the snow on the rosy peaks is very old, and the
amber light dreams, and the waves curve tenderly
upon the land, and the leaf and the apple on the trees
round to fulness and fall, full ripe, and all the winds
and sounds are low. Nature, like the indwellers of
the land, has eaten of the indolent forgetfulness of
the flower. This is the poet's way, and he had his
examples of this kind of work in Spenser's Cave of
Sleep and in Thomson's *Castle of Indolence;* but I
think he has excelled them both.

As to the main thought of the poem, it is, like
that of these classical poems in general, of great
simplicity, and its feeling felt at all times of human
life. "Why should we only toil, the roof and
crown of things? Death is the end of life, why
then should life be labour?

> Let us alone. What pleasure can we have
> To war with evil? Is there any peace
> In ever climbing up the climbing wave?

Enough of action, of trouble on trouble, pain on
pain. No more of pursuit, of mending what is
broken, of the strife of love. To dream, to sleep:

> Oh rest ye, brother mariners, we will not wander more.

The first sketch of this thought was in the *Sea-
Fairies* of 1830, and a lightly treated thing it was.
Then that was made into *The Lotos-Eaters* of 1833,
the first part of which is kept in the recast of the
poem of 1842. But in the latter part, a great and
vital change was made. First, the passage,

Dear is the memory of our wedded lives, &c.,

was added, and it is a passage which doubles
the human interest of the poem ; and, secondly,
instead of the jingling, unintellectual, merely fanciful ending of the poem of 1833, every image of which
wanders hither and thither without clear purpose
and weakens the impression of the previous part,
the poem thus closing in a feeble anti-climax, we
have the weighty, solemn, thoughtful, classic close,
embodying the Epicurean conception of the gods,
bringing all Olympus down into harmony with the
indifferent dreaming of the Lotos-eaters, but leaving
in our minds the sense of a dreadful woe tending
on those that dream ; for what the gods do with
impunity, man may not do.   Yet, even the Lotos-
eating Gods inevitable fate awaits.

This is the work of a great artist, and in this
steady improvement of his poems Tennyson stands
almost alone.   Other poets, Wordsworth, Shelley,
Keats, did not recast their poems in this wholesale
fashion, and the additions or changes which they
made were by no means always improvements.
Tennyson, working with his clear sense of what
was artistic, and with the stately steadiness which
belonged to his character, not only improved
but doubled the value of the poems he altered.*

* It would be an excellent thing if Lord Tennyson would
permit Messrs. Macmillan to reprint the volumes of 1830 and
1833. In most cases it is a mistake to issue the earliest forms
of a great poet's works—forms which he has rejected as in-
adequate. But in this case it would not be a mistake. It
would be a lesson to all artists, and still more to all critics,
to study the noble changes Tennyson here made; and it would
not diminish, but greatly enhance, our admiration of his art and
character.

Many persons would like another kind of artist—
one who does at a rush what he desires to do,
or one who could not go back on what he had
done, because new things occur to him incessantly;
and this our liking is a matter of temperament.
But Tennyson was built in another fashion. What
he did was wholly in harmony with the man, and
our business is not to wish the artist different, but
to find out what he is, and to love him within
the necessary limits of his sphere. In that way
we get his good, and are not troubled by his weak-
nesses.

The last of the classical poems in the volume of
1842 is, from contemplation's point of view, the best.
This is the *Ulysses*. The scene is set on the shore
of Ithaca, at the port. The time is evening. The
moon is rising and the sea is gloomed by the
shadows of the coming night. There is no description of the landscape, but enough is given
to make us feel the time and place. Yet when
Tennyson touches Nature in this poem it is done
with even more mastery than in *Œnone*; with
extraordinary brevity and force. A whole world
of ocean weather and of sea experience is in the
last two lines of this:

> All times I have enjoy'd
> Greatly, have suffer'd greatly, both with those
> That loved me, and alone: on shore, and when
> Thro' scudding drifts the rainy Hyades
> Vext the dim sea:

And I quote the three lines which follow, not only
because the Nature in them strikes the note of that
profound melancholy which lay underneath the

intense and hopeless curiosity of the Renaissance
—the same kind of curiosity which Ulysses feels
in this poem—but also because the second line is
one of Tennyson's finest examples of sound echoing
the sense :

> The lights begin to twinkle from the rocks :
> The long day wanes : the slow moon climbs ; the deep
> Moans round with many voices.

But the dominant interest here, more than in
Œnone and *The Lotos-Eaters*, is the human interest
—the soul that cannot rest, whom the unknown
always allures to action—the image of the exact
opposite of the temper of mind of the Lotos-eaters.

> Yet all experience is an arch wherethro'
> Gleams that untravell'd world, whose margin fades
> For ever and for ever when I move.
> How dull it is to pause, to make an end,
> To rust unburnish'd, not to shine in use !
> As tho' to breathe were life.   Life piled on life
> Were all too little,—and of one to me
> Little remains: but every hour is saved
> From that eternal silence, something more,
> A bringer of new things ; and vile it were
> For some three suns to store and hoard myself,
> And this gray spirit yearning in desire
> To follow knowledge like a sinking star,
> Beyond the utmost bound of human thought

There never was a better description of the
temper of the higher spirits of the Renaissance in
Italy. We listen to the very soul of Leonardo
da Vinci.

This too is Tennyson. I have heard it said
that, in this poem, he drew the portrait of his own
mind. I can well believe it, and it is a noble
temper with which to step into the fuller manhood

of middle life. Indeed, he never thought it too
late to seek in his own art a newer world. Even
at eighty years he took new subjects and tried new
ways in poetry. The cry of his Ulysses was the
cry of his old age :

> Tho' much is taken, much abides : and tho'
> We are not now that strength which in old days
> Moved earth and heaven ; that which we are, we are ;
> One equal temper of heroic hearts,
> Made weak by time and fate, but strong in will
> To strive, to seek, to find, and not to yield.

Thus he returned to the Greek, as Keats had
done ; but not as Keats, only for the sake of the
beauty of Greece, but also for the sake of the ethic
power of her stories ; not like Keats, that he might
find in ancient times a refuge from the baseness
of the present, but that he might bring thoughts
out of the past to rejoice and illuminate the present.
The speech of Pallas to Paris is spoken to England :
the song of the Lotos-eater is a warning to the
drifters and dreamers of our world ; in the thoughts
of Ulysses is held the power and the glory of
England. Nevertheless, though these poem shave
an ethical direction, it is subordinate to their first
direction, which is to represent the beauty in
their subjects. No one who has any sense of
art will presume to accuse them of being didactic
rather than artistic.

It was, however, not only in Greek story that in
these years he sought his subjects. He turned to
that great romantic cycle which has for eight centuries at least kindled the imagination of England
and been the darling of her poets. He turned to
the tale of Arthur and his knights.

It may be that his study of Milton, which now appears so clearly in his blank verse, had made him think, quite early in life, of an Arthurian epic, which, if Milton swerved from, he might himself fulfil ; but it is probable that his interest was at first only a slight and glancing interest, such as every poetic person takes in the tale with all its Celtic allurement. The small fragment of *Launcelot and Guinevere* is only a charming piece of glittering grace. *The Lady of Shalott* is a pleasant piece of play with his readers—simplicity in a mask of mysticism. *Sir Galahad* is graver, but still only an occasional piece, such as a poet makes " to try his hand."

Of these *The Lady of Shalott* is the best, as it is intended to be. No poem is more brilliant in words, but it does not attempt so much as *Sir Galahad* to make the sound of the verse describe the thing. It has no lines so imitative as

<blockquote>The shattering trumpet shrilleth high,</blockquote>

but it has that amazing piece of diamond description which I have already quoted. As to its meaning, folk have exhausted themselves to find it, and fruitlessly. It was never intended to have any special meaning. Tennyson was playing with his own imagination when he wrote it. He saw the island and the girl in the tower, and then the loom and web and mirror crept into the tower ; and then he saw the pictures in the mirror, and was pleased to describe them ; and then he thought of the curse, and then of Lancelot, and then of death. The poem grew without intention like a flower which had not been on earth

before.   Yet out of all the fancy arose one touch
of reality.   What a secluded maid sees are but
pictures, but the hour comes when she says,
" I am half sick of shadows."   To know that the
pictures of the mind are shadows is to be wild to
seek reality.   Then if love come, hopeless love,
all the world of mere phantasy breaks up, and
the actual kills :

> Out flew the web and floated wide ;
> The mirror crack'd from side to side ;
> " The curse is come upon me," cried
> The Lady of Shalott.

If there be meaning at all in this piece of gos-
samer fancy, that is it, and, like all Tennyson's
meanings, it is as simple as the day.

As to the *Sir Galahad*, the true romantic note
which, in the creation of Galahad, is made to
thrill more high and clear by the addition of the
keener note of virginity, fills that poem.   The
conception of the total conquest of the evil of
matter, of the total indifference to all appetite and
sense, so that life on earth was lived in a supersensuous realm wherein all things and beings
thought to be invisible were visible—was a conception of pure art, I might even say of pure
romance.   In that conception religious passion was
added to romance, and asceticism clothed with
spiritual beauty.   Art, therefore, found in it one of
its natural subjects.   Tennyson, even more than
in the Galahad of the *Idylls of the King*, seized in
this poem the beauty of celestial purity, and of the
supernatural world it opened to his virgin knight.

No one can speak too highly of verses like that beginning :

> When down the stormy crescent goes,

or the two that follow it. It is not only Galahad who is represented in them as above Nature, but it is that Nature herself, while she is seen and heard, is spiritualised. In their high-ringing clang we feel the world which is the substance of the shadow-world we see.

When we come to the *Morte d'Arthur*, we come to that which is more serious than these tentative flights over a great subject. We come to the love of a lifetime. The poem itself belongs to the *Idylls of the King*, and I shall speak of it in its place. But the prologue and epilogue belong to the history of 1842, and to the whole subject of this chapter. The prologue, with its types of modern social life, the parson, the poet, and the man of the day— each giving and taking as in a dinner-conversation —each in their way maintaining that poetry must sit close to the life of the present—shows how vivid modern society was now to Tennyson. " A truth looks freshest in the fashion of the day." The phrase embodies his method in these poems. Nor must we miss his description of himself. No one who has ever heard him read his own poetry can mistake the portrait :

> . . . . And the poet, little urged,
> But with some prelude of disparagement,
> Read, mouthing out his hollow oes and aes,
> Deep-chested music.

It could not be more truly done.

I

As to the epilogue, it illustrates all I have been saying about Tennyson's method with subjects drawn from Greek or romantic times. He filled and sustained those subjects with thoughts which were as modern as they were ancient. While he placed his readers in Camelot, Ithaca, or Ida, he made them feel also that they were standing in London, Oxford, or an English woodland. When the *Morte d'Arthur* is finished, the hearer of it sits rapt. There were "modern touches here and there," he says, and when he sleeps, he dreams of

> King Arthur, like a modern gentleman
> Of stateliest port; and all the people cried,
> "Arthur is come again; he cannot die."
> Then those that stood upon the hills behind
> Repeated—"Come again, and thrice as fair:"
> And, further inland, voices echoed—"Come
> With all good things, and war shall be no more."

The old tale, thus modernised in an epilogue, does not lose its dignity; for now the recoming of Arthur is the recoming of Christ in a wider and fairer Christianity. We feel here how the new movement of religion and theology had sent its full and exciting wave into Tennyson. Arthur's death in the battle and the mist is the death of a form of Christianity which, exhausted, died in doubt and darkness. His advent as a modern gentleman is the coming of a brighter and more loving Christ into the hearts of men. For so ends the epilogue. When the voices cry, "Come again, with all good things,"

> At this a hundred bells began to peal,
> That with the sound I woke, and heard indeed
> The clear church-bells ring in the Christmas-morn.

This inoculation of ancient stories with modern thought, while the tales themselves were kept either classic or romantic, received its fullest development in the *Idylls of the King*. But it was less and less used in the classic poems written after 1842. They still retained the use of one simple thought around which each poem gathered itself, but this thought ceased to be so plainly modernised as before. Tennyson did not bring Tithonus or Lucretius or Tiresias into England. He went to them and he stayed with their personality and in their time. This change shows, I think, that as his years went by he felt that, having done so much for modern life, he was licensed to live in these poems, if he liked, wholly among the ancients. It seems fitting to treat of them in this chapter, even though I transgress the chronological order in which I generally speak of his poetry.

So many writers have written on the knowledge of classic thought displayed in these poems and on their nearness to classic feeling, that I need not dwell upon these matters. It has been a favourite subject of reviews. Many also have drawn attention to Tennyson's frequent use of phrases from the classic writers, and sometimes in such a way as to suggest that he was a plagiarist. This is an absurd suggestion. He had a perfect right to transfer to his poems expressions and even lines from the classic poets, provided he gave them a new setting, or a novel phrasing, in his translation. All the great poets have done this when their subject was classical, or their poem heroic. Virgil did it, Dante did it; so did Spenser, Tasso, Ariosto, Racine, Corneille, and

Milton ; and it did not occur to their contempo-
raries to accuse them of borrowing without acknowledgment.　There was no acknowledgment needed.
The poets thought that every one who read their
classic phrases would know whence they came, and
would understand that they did not insert their
original in a note, just because to do so would
insult the culture of their readers.　I do not suppose it occurred to Tennyson to explain that something in his *Ulysses* was owed to Dante, or that
" Softer than sleep," or

> This way and that dividing the swift mind,

and a hundred other lines and phrases, were from
Virgil or Homer, Sophocles or Pindar, Catullus
or Horace.　He thought that every one would
know these things, and he used them as we use,
in writing, phrases from the Bible or Shakespeare
without taking the trouble of putting them. in
inverted commas.　Moreover, he may have thought
that the world would be pleased to find lovely
phrases which were the common property of all
writers beautifully translated and delightfully
reset.　Of all the half-suggested accusations made
against Tennyson, this of plagiarism from the
classic poets is, under the circumstances, the most
futile and the most invidious.

Among these later classic poems, the first, in
order of date, is *Tithonus.*　I suppose from internal
evidence that this poem, published in 1860, was
written not very long after the *Ulysses*.　It has the
same atmosphere of youthful feeling and the same
technical maturity.　It seems even finer than the
Ulysses as a piece of art.　Indeed, nothing of its

kind approaches it in modern poetry, nor anything in which the imagination of Tennyson is at work with greater creativeness, insight, pathetic power, passion, noble sensuousness and simplicity. The subject was also one of extraordinary difficulty. It was easy, in comparison, for Tennyson to write the *Ulysses*. That poem was built out of his own character, and embodied a type with which he had the strongest sympathy. But when he wrote of Tithonus he was obliged to get out of himself altogether, or, at least, to use up for his work not a constant but a temporary attitude of his soul. Moreover, the scene was laid in a dim, unknown country, on the outskirts of the heaven and the earth, below the visible, where there was no landscape. This had to be realised, and it is done with full imagination, not only in the lines which describe the quiet limit of the world—

> The ever-silent spaces of the East,
> Far-folded mists, and gleaming halls of morn,

but also in the impression made by the whole of the poem. Its world is not a world of night or day, but of the transitory dawn. Aurora herself seems to die at sunrise, and the description of her wakening —the glimmer on her brow, her sweet eyes slowly brightening before they blind the stars, her wild team shaking the darkness from their loosened manes, and her departure, weeping for her chilly lover— is of the very finest quality. Yet, remote as the place is from humanity, Tennyson has filled his poem with pathetic emotion. Immortal age tied to immortal youth, immortal youth pained for immortal age; the gift love gave of immortality the

curse of him to whom it was given, the memory, in
decay, of youth and of love once passionate, the
dreadful inability to love, the dreadful inability to
die—all is subtly, beautifully and firmly realised.
The very movement of the blank verse is tender
with the irreparable woe of Tithonus.

The main thought of the poem has often been
used. Immortality for men, without youth, and
with its memories, is an accursed gift. Swift
exposed the horror of it in his own savage fashion,
lacerating himself and man with self-tormenting
scorn. Tennyson has done it with exquisite
tenderness for man ; and made the victim think
gently of his own race, and truly of their fate :

> Why should a man desire in any way
> To vary from the kindly race of men—
> Of happy men that have the power to die ?

Nor does he forget to touch the story with one of
those ancient thoughts which in all ages have
expressed part of the tragic of our destiny :

> The gods themselves cannot recall their gifts.

The next of these classic poems is *Lucretius*.
It is Roman, not Greek, and it bears the impress
of the Roman race. In Tennyson's Greek poems,
the Greek's grave beauty shines through the
modern thought, through the modern description
of Nature. Even in speeches like those of
Athena and of Ulysses, beauty sits hand in
hand with the experience of life. But in *Lucretius*, stern, robust, rigid duty to self - chosen,
self-approved law is first ; the sense of the
beautiful as a part of life does not appear in

the poem. Lucretius has no religion save that of acceptance of Nature, but to that he is faithful. He has no duty to the gods, but he has duty to his own philosophic honour. He dies rather than be mastered by lustful visions which a Greek, even in the noble time when beauty meant pure harmony, would have gone through, smiled at, and forgotten.

The philosophy also is a Greek philosophy, but Lucretius has made it Roman in temper; and one of the noble excellences of this poem is that Tennyson has never deviated in a single word from the Roman basis of the soul. Moreover, it takes a great poet to assimilate, as Tennyson has done, the essence of Lucretius as a thinker and a poet in the space of about three hundred lines, and to combine this with the representation of a man in an hour of doom and madness, such as an inferior poet, overloading it with frenzied ornament, would have made intemperate. Tennyson's masterly reticence, rigid restraint only to the absolutely necessary, are supreme in this poem. Only one passage, that about the breasts of Helen and the sword, seems to me awkward in conception.

The introduction is a little masterpiece of statement. In the rest of the poem, independent of the superb setting forth of the Epicurean philosophy as grasped and dignified by Lucretius, two things belonging to the conduct of the subject are remarkable. First, Tennyson has seized on the spasmodic action of a poison to enable him to represent Lucretius as having lucid intervals. A lesser artist would have kept him always in

insanity. But Lucretius, whom the poet wishes
us to respect while we pity him, is for the most
part sane. The influence of the philtre comes on
him only in recurring attacks, and between the
attacks his mind is clear. Even his moral
power, that is, his truth to his own nature,
maintains its mastery. Not for an instant does
Tennyson's Lucretius ever truly think that he is
the same person as the man who sees the
visions of lust. Not for a moment does he
confuse his own Alma Venus, the ambrosial,
warm and generative power in Nature, with the
Cyprian goddess of desire whose dreams invade
his soul. Lucretius is, in more than half this
poem, the clear thinker, the noble poet, and the
lover of passionless tranquillity who abhors the
storm within him.

Secondly, Tennyson invents, with the greatest
skill, a storm in the night to illustrate the tempest
in the soul of Lucretius, and at the same time to
supply him with a ground for speaking of his
Nature-philosophy. The storm suggests the dream
of the flaring atom streams,

<blockquote>Ruining along the illimitable inane—</blockquote>

a line that Milton might have praised. The returning calm of the morning suggests the description of the eternal tranquillity of the gods and
their dwelling-place, and to Lucretius, the hope
that he may win back his own calm—

<blockquote>Seeing with how great ease Nature can smile,
Balmier and nobler from her bath of storm,
At random ravage.</blockquote>

These are the methods of a great artist; but how the whole poem is wrought, how nobly the character of Lucretius emerges line after line, with what poetic strength and sculpturing power his masculine passion clears its way to death till the brief close shuts up the tragedy, is for every reader to grasp as he has capacity.

Tiresias, though published in 1885, is a much earlier poem, perhaps of the same period as *Lucretius*. I class it here, because the subject, except in the universal thought of sacrifice of life for the good of the State, is not modernised at all. The lines about the gods being slower to forgive than human kings, and those describing the yearning of Tiresias,

> For larger glimpses of that more than man
> Which rolls the heavens, and lifts, and lays the deep,
> Yet loves and hates with mortal hates and loves,

are fully classical; and the way Tiresias thinks and feels throughout is not modern, save perhaps in one passage about the tyranny of all, and the tyranny of one.

The poem is said by Tennyson himself to "date many a year ago." We may suppose then that he did not think it good enough to publish alongside of *Tithonus* or *Ulysses;* and indeed it falls far below these poems. It repeats itself, and the conclusion ought not to be so long; though Tiresias, believed for the first time in his life, might well be excused a little garrulity. But any one may be glad to have a poem which contains that dazzling description of the landscape of the mountain-side in the blaze of the sun, and the royal image of Pallas Athene climbing from the bath in the secret olive

glade, and the blinding light of her virgin eyes.
Nor is the close less splendid in words and in the
huge thought of the last line where the Prophet
pictures his final rest among the happy vales that

> Wind, clouded with the grateful incense-fume
> Of those who mix all odour to the gods
> On one far height in one far-shining fire.

Ir *Demeter and Persephone* was written about the
time at which it was published, in 1889, it is a
wonderful proof of the persistence of mature power
in old age.   Tennyson was eighty years of age
when this poem was issued.   It bears no traces
of failing strength, or of outworn imagination.
Lines like

> The shrilly whinnyings of the team of Hell,

or,

> The sun
> Burst from a swimming fleece of winter gray,

are as clean-ringing and clear-eyed as any written
in 1842.   The introduction, with the slow dawning
of Persephone's recognition of the earth, and of her
mother who is the Earth-mother, is as good as the
introduction to *Lucretius*, as delicate and tender as
that is strong and austere.   The imaginative thought
which kept the solemn, unhuman darkness of Hades
still in the eyes of Persephone—

> Child, those imperial, disimpassioned eyes
> Awed even me at first, thy mother—

the rapid picture of the lonely Fates,

> And, following out
> A league of labyrinthine darkness, came
> On three gray heads beneath a gleaming rift,

who " know not what they spin," and cry

"There is a Fate beyond us;" the dream of
Demeter, which this cry originates, of a race of
younger and kindlier gods whose reign and
worship will be love, and who will subdue even
Hades to their light; the sense Tennyson infuses
into his readers that this dream is born out of the
heart of the kindly earth itself—not a Christian
thought but an anticipation of that thought; the
ill-content of the Earth-goddess with the highest
gods who are old in their careless tyranny,
and the founding of this ill-content with them,
on the ground that she is naturally nearer than
they to men and fonder than they of the works
of men—is she not the mother of them all?—
the deep sympathy of Demeter with the earth-
dwellers, and naturally her greater share in
human passion—especially the most human of all
passions, that of motherhood—all these ideas,
in subtle, half-suggested images, passed through
the fire of imagination and made lucid and crys-
talline thereby, are wrought into the poem with
a power which seems almost incredible in a poet
of eighty years.

The poem smells of the fruitful rain-washed
earth; the earth breathes and is pregnant and
gives birth in it; all her motherhood loves all
her children from line to line of it. Motherhood,
first of the Earth, and then of Humanity, is the
innermost being of the poem—the "deathless heart
of motherhood." At last, in order to make this
universal more particular and more at home with
us, the personal motherhood of Demeter, the
motherhood of one heart for one child, is driven
home to our imagination. When she loses her

child, she implores heaven for her, she wanders over all lands to find her, she forgets her own Earth ; but the loveliest thing she does—and it is imagined with infinite tenderness—is to console all the troubled mothers of the world. She gives to failing children the same breast which nurtured Persephone—

> Thy breast to wailing infants in the night.

The Death of Œnone, the last of these poems, recalls the earliest of them, and the landscape is much the same, only as it is winter in Œnone's heart, it is now winter by the cave and in the glade, where formerly, at the coming of the goddesses, the greensward of spring burst into fire. And Paris comes to see her as of old, but now

> Lame, crooked, reeling, livid, thro' the mist,

to beg her to heal him of his grievous wound. She refuses ; a woman after ten years of brooding wrath and pain was not likely to forgive. He passes away into the mist, dies, and is burnt on a pyre by the shepherds. She flings herself on the pyre. I do not know the date of this poem—there can never be any proper study of Tennyson until all these late-published poems are accurately dated— but it is quite plain that the mind which grasped *Ulysses*, *Lucretius*, or even *Tiresias*, has here lost much of its power. It is well put together as a little tale ; but the subject is not seized by the right handles. I cannot guess to what idea or emotion in Tennyson's mind the story has been sacrificed, but it is sacrificed. It is too improbable that Paris should walk up Ida to call for Œnone, considering where and how he was wounded; or stagger down the hill from her.   If the art of the piece were made better by this change in the tale, this criticism would be nought ; but it is not made better, and the improbability is impossibility.   Nor do I understand the husband and wife and widow business, unless it be that Tennyson desired to express over again his devotion to the eternity and sanctity of the marriage relation.   This is wholly out of place in the story.   The union between Paris and the nymph Œnone was not a marriage nor anything that resembled it.   When we come to

> Her husband in the flush of youth and dawn,

we do not know where we are.   We are certainly not on Ida.   When we hear Œnone's answer to the cry of Paris for help, we are in the midst, not of the light unions between Greek mortals and the nymphs, but of the social moralities of England.

> Adulterer,
> Go back to thine adulteress and die!

This is not credible on the lips of Œnone.   Still more strange is that which follows, still more distant from Greek thought.   Œnone, the mountain nymph, dreams that Paris calls to her from the other world to come to him, and has repented his unfaithfulness :

> Come to me,
> Œnone!   I can wrong thee now no more,
> Œnone, my Œnone.

Christian, it maybe, but not Greek ; and, still more, not possible for a nymph to dream.   And the end is equally out of the question. It is a pretty thought in itself, and might well belong to a mortal woman, even to an Oriental pagan, but it does not belong to a mountain nymph of the Greek imagination who never dreamt of marriage and would have smiled at any union of the kind :

> And all at once
> The morning light of happy marriage broke
> Thro' all the clouded years of widowhood,
> And muffling up her comely head, and crying
> "Husband!" she leapt upon the funeral pile,
> And mixt herself with *him* and past in fire.

CHAPTER V

THE PRINCESS

IN MEMORIAM is the most complete, most
rounded to a polished sphere, of the larger
poems of Tennyson ; the *Idylls of the King* is the
most ambitious ; *Maud* is the loveliest, most
rememberable ; and *The Princess* is the most
delightful. Holiday-hearted, amazingly varied,
charming our leisured ease from page to page,
it is a poem to read on a sunny day in one of
those rare places in the world where "there is no
clock in the forest," where the weight and worry
of the past, the present, or the future, do not make
us conscious of their care. There is no sorrow
or sense of the sorrow of the world in it. The
man who wrote it had reached maturity, but there
is none of the heaviness of maturity in its light
movement. It is really gay, as young as the Prince
himself who is its hero ; and the dreams and desires
of youth flit and linger in it as summer bees around
the honied flowers. A great charm is thus given
to the poem. We feel for it the affection which
is bestowed on youthfulness by those who have
passed by youthfulness, that half-regret, half-ten-
derness, and sweet memory in both, the sadness of
which is not too much, and the pleasure of which
is not too little.

Mingled with the youthfulness in the poem is the serious thought of manhood. There is enough of gravity to dignify the subject-matter, and enough of play to take dulness out of the gravity. The poem is like the gray statue of Sir Ralph robed with Lilia's orange scarf and rosy silk. Of course, this twofold element adds to that variety which stirs new pleasure and new thinking from page to page. But beyond that, the scheme of the poem enabled Tennyson to invent all kinds of fantastic events that follow one another as thickly as they do in a romantic tale ; and he is up to the level of the invention required. One scarcely expects him to do this with ease. Inventiveness of incident lags somewhat in Tennyson's work. The invention of the greater number of the episodes in the *Idylls of the King* is excellent. The invention of the events which carry on the story is not so good, and it is certainly not opulent. Moreover, we see in the dramas how slow-moving his inventiveness is ; their movement continually drags from the want of that which the dramatists call business. Here, however, the story runs along with a lively variety both of characters and events glancing and charming through it.

This variety is still more increased by the mingling of ancient and modern in the poem—modern science jostling with ancient manners modern dress with ancient arms, girls' colleges with tournaments ; the woman-question of to-day with the woman-ideal of the days of chivalry ; Joan of Arc with the Cambridge girl ; and rising out of both—out of the old and the new—first, Tennyson's own view of womanhood, and secondly, that which is always old and new, the eternal feminine face to face with the eternal masculine. Moreover, this variety is kindled and brightened with the steady fire of Tennyson's imagination—not, in this poem, the imagination which pierces to the depths of the human heart (for the half-serious, half-grotesque form precluded that), but the imagination which illustrates human life by analogies drawn from Nature. Each comparison fits at every point; and the things in Nature which are used as comparisons are not only described with extraordinary accuracy, choice, and truth, but are also seen with such love that their inmost heart is touched. When King Gama is sketched, his voice is cracked and small :

> But bland the smile that like a wrinkling wind
> On glassy water drove his cheek in lines.

Cyril, the Prince's friend, " has a solid base of temperament," but is on the surface lightly blown by impulse. He is like the water-lily, which starts and slides

> Upon the level in little puffs of wind,
> Tho' anchor'd to the bottom—such is he.

The eyes of Lady Blanche, full of malice, are like "the green malignant light of coming storm," and the line is charged with the very colour and rage of tempest on the horizon. There are two similes of the Princess in wrath, one in which the jewel on her brow is like " the mystic fire on a masthead, prophet of storm," and the other where she stands above the tossing crowd of rebellious girls like a beacon-tower above the waves

K

of tempest, which are as absolutely fitted to the
emotions they illustrate as the glove to the hand.
Her angry and scornful smile is compared—and the
Nature picture is superb—to

> A stroke of cruel sunshine on the cliff,
> When all the glens are drown'd in azure gloom
> Of thunder-shower.

When she is compassed by two armies and the
noise of arms, she stands like a stately pine on an
island, on each side of which a great cataract
divides, " when storm is on the heights," and the
torrents roll,

> Suck'd from the dark heart of the long hills—

a splendid concentration of natural truth.   When
she knows that all her purpose is overthrown,
Tennyson uses what he must often have himself
seen from the downs of Freshwater to express
her pain :

> As one that climbs a peak to gaze
> O'er land and main, and sees a great black cloud
> Drag inward from the deeps, a wall of night,
> Blot out the slope of sea from verge to shore,
> And suck the blinding splendour from the sand,
> And quenching lake by lake and tarn by tarn,
> Expunge the world.

This and the equally fine description of the whirlwind tell of Nature in giant effort.   But he can
see the delicate, minute things of Nature just as
clearly and describe them with equal force.   There
is an image of a maiden's thoughts and ways
which is as new as it is lovely.   Not a thought, a
touch,

> But pure as lines of green that streak the white
> Of the first snow-drop's inner leaves.

And when he wishes to reveal how two young hearts slid into love, he says it was no more strange

> Than when two dew-drops on the petal shake
> To the same sweet air, and tremble deeper down,
> And slip at last all-fragrant into one.

A perfect image—but to what minute observation it bears witness! In these examples alone what a range of vision! How many things and sights were noted and stored up before these were chosen to use! In what a lucid light they were seen! With what truth, and, more difficult still to do, with what clearness, fitness, finish, and choice expressed! This is the artist's keen eye, observant love and trained capacity, working together, and it is a pleasure to be led by it to observe more lovingly the world of Nature. From point to point this method of illustrating—a method he learned from Homer— enlightens and expands the poem.

These belong to the qualities of Tennyson's mind, but in the prologue and epilogue of *The Princess*, as well as in the poem itself, we have a picture of some points in his character. He feels that he is of the North rather than of the South.

> And dark and true and tender is the North,

is a line in which he paints what he wished to be. His Prince is of the North, and has that special mysticism of the North which appears in the dreams so constantly told in the Icelandic Sagas. He frequently loses consciousness of

the outward, or rather he loses the consciousness of its reality. All around him becomes
visionary, or the visionary world becomes the real
world, till he is not able to distinguish between
both.

> On a sudden in the midst of men and day,
> And while I walk'd and talk'd as heretofore,
> I seem'd to move among a world of ghosts,
> And feel myself the shadow of a dream—

That is Tennyson. He talks of it as a " weird
seizure," but it is a common experience. The
sudden unsubstantialising of the outward world, of
all events and places, was Wordsworth's frequent
feeling. It is not, indeed, the unique property of
the poets, but it brings before us the half-pantheistic
idealism which dwelt in Tennyson's nature side
by side with his sturdy realism. The same
experience is alluded to in *The Holy Grail*, and
is put in the mouth of Arthur :

> Let visions of the night or of the day
> Come, as they will, and many a time they come,
> Until this earth he walks on seems not earth,
> The light that strikes his eyeball is not light,
> This air that smites his forehead is not air,
> But vision—yea, his very hand and foot—

Right opposite to this is that rough forcibleness, that
downright squareness which in him called a spade
a spade, and which is at the root of so many of the
poems. Both opposites were well represented in his
figure—the great-boned, loose-limbed, gigantesque
man, with his domed head—and the soft dark hair,
the gentle eyes, and the white, smooth, fine-
lined brow, covered with delicate skin through
which the blue veins shone. Force and fineness

were married in his face and form as well as in his verse.

Then in this prologue and epilogue there are other characteristics of what he had become. His fancy for science, and for the age in which he lived being made great by science, which springs to light in *Locksley Hall*, has grown in this poem. His Princess's favourite study is the Natural Sciences. She thinks that learning and philosophy will be the salvation of women. The holiday-makers in the prologue are taught by facts ; electricity, steam, hydraulics go hand-in-hand with the rustic sports. We have somewhat too much of this. An artist cannot introduce Physical Science into his art-work without introducing trouble into it. Now and again he may play with its results, but it must be play. Tennyson did not always play with it, and he sometimes seemed to feel that Science was more important than Art. Whenever he did, his poetry suffered. However, there are traces enough, especially in his later poems, that he was weary of the claim of Science to be greater than Art, and that he feared it might stifle poetry :

> Let Science prove we are, and then,
> What matters Science unto men,
> At least to me ?

And he speaks still more particularly in a poem, the *Parnassus* of 1889 :

> What be those two shapes high over the sacred fountain,
> Taller than all the Muses, and huger than all the mountain ?
> On those two known peaks they stand ever spreading and
> heightening ;
> Poet, that evergreen laurel is blasted by more than lightning !

Look. in their deep double shadow the crown'd ones all
    disappearing !
Sing like a bird and be happy, nor hope for a deathless
    hearing !
" Sounding for ever and ever " ?　Pass on ! the sight con-
    fuses—
These are Astronomy and Geology, terrible Muses !

It makes me happier to read that poem, for I know
then that he was saved from the impertinent
despotism which claims that the reasoning intellect
is higher than the imagination, and the work of
Science of more importance to man than the work
of Art.　We see then, that, in his old age,
Tennyson felt that beauty and the representation
of it were being crowded out of the world by
Science.　But we also see in the end of that poem
how he consoles himself.　" If the poets," he
answers, " are crushed here, they need not greatly
care.　They sing their songs for ever, and other
worlds listen."

Then, too, his political judgments appear ; and
though I have already alluded to them in the
introduction to this book, it seems needful to
touch on them again in connection with this prologue.　We find the honest Whig views of 1840,
modified from their universal aims by a cherished
insularity ; a fancy for the squirearchy as the backbone of England ; a sense that the English temper,
of which he knew nothing below the middle class,
is the only temper in which freedom grows straight.
With this there is a steady contempt for France,
modified by the thought which seems at some
odd moments to have made a lodgment in his
mind, that social theories and dreams and the wild
popular storms that follow them may be of more

use than we think. It occurs to him at times
that the world does not always move as England
moves, by broadening slowly down from precedent
to precedent. It may be there is some use and
need, he thinks, for revolutions. The passage I
mean begins :

> "Look there, a garden!" said my college friend,
> The Tory member's elder son,

and he points to the coast of France, and contrasts
" our Britain whole within herself, a nation yet,"
having a sense of duty, reverence for law, some
civic manhood firm against the crowd, with France
and the mock heroics of France. And the whole
speech and the reply to it are replete with Tennyson, of the same mint as the poem, " Love thou
thy land with love far brought," in the volume
of 1842. " Have patience," answers another
friend, "ourselves are full of social wrong." It
is Tennyson's modification of the insular view.
And indeed, in 1847, the state of the agricultural
labourer, here pictured on one day of holiday and
feasting in the year, under the generosity of Sir
Walter,

> A great, broad-shoulder'd, genial Englishman,

was scarcely an inch better than it was in the
year 1830, when all rural England was a cry of
misery. One of the similes in *The Princess* is
derived from the rick-burning into which the
horrors of starvation and disease had driven the
people. Of all this, Tennyson had either little
conception—only a few cared then, and he was
of his time—or he was absorbed in the glory of
that English country life in hall and park and

comfortable farm which he paints so well, as if
that included more than a tenth of the rural popu-
lation. What of the rest ? The time thought little
of them, neither did Tennyson ; and the crowd
around the abbey where *The Princess* is invented
are content to cry, and Tennyson seems to think it
is enough for them to ask—

> Why should not these great Sirs
> Give up their parks some dozen times a year
> To let the people breathe ?

This is Tennyson in the prologue. As to the poem
itself, it enshrines the woman's question as it
appeared nearly fifty years ago, and considering all
that has been done since then, it is a prophetic
utterance. A good deal which is here suggested
under a mock-heroic mask has actually been put
into practical form. Moreover, he has touched,
with grace and clearness, a number of the phases
of opinion which now prevail, and which then had
only begun to prevail ; embodying each phase in
one of his characters. The woman's question
owes a great deal to *The Princess*. It has been
objected to it by the women who want humour
(that want so strange and yet so common in women)
and who have the faith that science solves all
questions (that faith so unexpected by those who
have the traditional conception of a special spirituality in women), " that the poem is not serious, not
argumentative, not set on a foundation of facts.
The question can only be solved by knowledge,
argument, and action."

This objection would be valid if this were a
treatise, and not a poem. But here the question

is brought into the sphere of art, and it must
be treated in the manner of art. If it is to be
made the subject of a poem, it must not be argumentative, it must not be scientific, and it must
not be serious except when emotion intervenes.
The moment it argues, it loses its place in the world
of art. Every point then which would naturally be
argued by the understanding in a treatise, must
here be worked by the imagination ; and lest the
poem should by any chance slide into reasoning,
a gamesome element is added to it, to protect
it from becoming scientific. Tennyson, who was
an artist, understood this clearly, and wrought
out his method with care before he began. He
is never serious in *The Princess*, except when the
deep affections of humanity enter into the movement of the piece ; and the affections, in spite of
all the wiseacres, are not subject to logic. Science,
if it have the insolence to ascend the steps of
their palace, falls dead upon its threshold. When,
then, the affections come in, Tennyson steps into
seriousness, but when he has to put opinions, he is
light and gay ; and art obliged him, on such a subject, to be serious and gay by turns. The result
was, that he was compelled to choose a mock-heroic
form in which to build his poem. This would enable
him to be sometimes lively and sometimes grave,
sometimes grotesque and sometimes noble, sometimes
chivalrous and sometimes full of raillery, and sometimes mingling both these opposites ; and the choice
of this mode of building his poem gave him great
room for ranging, and varied opportunities for
imagination. " What style would suit ? " he
asks.

The men required that I should give throughout
The sort of mock-heroic gigantesque,
With which we banter'd little Lilia first:
The women—and perhaps they felt their power,
For something in the ballads which they sang,
Or in their silent influence as they sat,
Had ever seem'd to wrestle with burlesque,
And drove us, last, to quite a solemn close—
They hated banter, wish'd for something real,
A gallant fight, a noble princess—why
Not make her true-heroic—true sublime?
Or all, they said, as earnest as the close?
Which yet with such a framework scarce could be.
Then rose a little feud betwixt the two,
Betwixt the mockers and the realists:
And I, betwixt them both, to please them both,
And yet to give the story as it rose,
I moved as in a strange diagonal,
  And maybe neither pleased myself nor them.

It is not often that an artist explains the way
in which he came to choose the form of his architecture, but, given his subject, he could not have
chosen it better. The Prince has been betrothed
to a Princess in the South, and made her his ideal,
loving her from her portrait. His father sends an
embassage to claim her for his son. His claim is
put off; the Princess refuses to marry. She,
enthralled with the idea of rescuing women from
the slavery of man, has founded a college for girls
into which no man shall enter on pain of death. The
Prince with two college friends goes on adventure
to find the Princess. They disguise themselves as
girls and penetrate into the college, betray themselves, are discovered, and would have been slain,
had not the Prince saved the life of the Princess.
The three men are thrust out of gates with con-
tumely. The Princess refuses all overtures of
marriage, and summons her three brothers, huge

warriors, to support her cause. Both sides agree to settle the question by a tournament of fifty against fifty knights, and the Prince and his party are wounded and overthrown. Ida, the Princess, moved by the fate of a child who is the pivot of the action here, admits all the wounded to the college, dissolves the college, and, in tending the wounded Prince, finds love at her heart, and they are knit together. These are the main lines of the story. Each of these male characters has his own opinion about womanhood and its sphere, the Prince and his father, Cyril and Florian the two friends of the Prince, the King, the father of the Princess, and Arac her brother. Six men then deliver six views of womanhood, embodying six phases of the question. Then the women have also their say. We hear the view of the mother of the Prince who is dead ; we have the view of Lady Blanche who educated the Princess to despise love and set women against men ; of the Princess's friend, Lady Psyche, who is the child's mother ; of Melissa, a young maiden, and of the mob of girls at college; finally, of the Princess herself ; so that through the piece almost every phase of opinion on the matter is delivered by both men and women. This is done with great skill and charming art. In the midst, the various offices of womanhood are brought forward by the events of the story, and become part of the question to be solved. Moreover, what motherhood is, is shown in two instances ; what maidenhood is, is also displayed. And woman's friendship with woman is introduced. All these, both those which belong to the men and those which belong to the

women, run up at last into the Princess and are
bound around her, so that she stands forth alone,
the centre of the poem. They also run up into
the Prince, but he is kept subordinate, as the
poem demanded, even when, at the end, he gets
his way. His opinion prevails, but his personality
is less than that of the Princess. This is all
admirable art.

The scenery, too, of the piece is delightful,
full of sunshine, gaiety, and grace. The college,
with its grounds and high-wrought architecture,
courts and gardens, walls and fountains, brightened
with glancing girls and silken clad professors, is
charmingly imagined. We see the view from
its walls. The Prince stands upon the northern
terrace :

> And leaning there on those balusters, high
> Above the empurpled champaign, drank the gale
> That blown about the foliage underneath,
> And sated with the innumerable rose,
> Beat calm upon our eyelids.

We watch the Princess, creator of all this beauty,
in the great hall, in the fountain-splashing courts,
in the gardens, among the hills which border the
park, on the great meadows of the tumbling river,
erect upon the battlements above the gates—and
we see grouped around her, the whole country, as
if with the actual eye. Then we look on the
warrior camps, on the tournament and on the
battle-field ; and then on the women, issuing from
the great bronze valves, and moving through the
trees to tend the wounded. And, last of all, we
see the college again, its building filled with the
wounded, and the girls who stayed flitting through

it from couch to couch, or learning love in its bosky
alleys. So vividly is it all drawn, that a painter
might paint from point to point what the poet has
created. The passage beginning—

> We dropt with evening on a rustic town,
> Set in a gleaming river's crescent-curve,
> Close at the boundary of the liberties,

will illustrate this careful scene-painting—a word
I use without its depreciating note.

Nature is not described for her own sake, but
inwoven in Tennyson's manner with the emotions
of those who are looking upon it. When the
Prince, full of youthful ardour, resolves to follow
his dream, all the woods and wind are with him;
her picture lies

> In the green gleam of dewy-tassell'd trees,

and all the mingled sounds of woods are shaken
into one cry of " Follow, follow." The lines I
quote below exactly express that which is so rarely
observed—the different murmur of differently foli-
aged trees in a faint wind which a fine ear can
distinguish in a wood, but which, when a fuller puff
goes by, are merged into one chorus with the
singing of birds and tossing of boughs :

> A wind arose and rush'd upon the South,
> And shook the songs, the whispers, and the shrieks
> Of the wild woods together; and a Voice
> Went with it, "Follow, follow, thou shalt win."

When the Prince has reached the college where
the Princess lives, this fine picture of the sea at
night is equally descriptive of the fulness of his
heart, and the prophecy it makes and loves.

> Half in doze I seem'd
> To float about a glimmering night, and watch
> A full sea, glazed with muffled moonlight, swell
> On some dark shore just seen that it was rich.

And when the dawn of love in the Princess's heart
is beginning, the early dawn of nature to which he
compares it was never more fully or more tenderly
imagined than in these lines of lovely simplicity—

> Till notice of a change in the dark world
> Was lispt about the acacias, and a bird,
> That early woke to feed her little ones,
> Sent from a dewy breast a cry for light.

In the poem, however, there is no elaborate
description of landscape. The Nature touches are
chiefly in the comparisons ; and this is fitly so,
for the human interest is manifold. In a single-
subject poem like *The Gardener's Daughter* or
Œnone, it is not out of place to have a long
description of Nature. The full scenery then
illustrates and enforces the simple subject. But
long descriptions of Nature in a story with many
characters and events, would divert the interest
from the movement. Like Homer then, and following him, Tennyson keeps his Nature in this
heroic tale chiefly for his similes, to strengthen
from time to time moments of passion in the
tale.

The one piece, moreover, in the poem which is
fully descriptive of Nature, is not in the story.
It is a part of an interlude—the Idyll read by
the Princess while she sits by the bedside of the
Prince. In its midst is a noble and unique
gathering together of the sights and sounds and of

the destroying horror of the deep recesses of the
upper Alpine gorges, followed by a concentration
into three lines of the sweetness and charm of the
pastoral vales of the Alps.   " Come down, sweet
maid," cries the shepherd from the heights, " for
love is of the valley."   Love does not care to
walk

> With Death and Morning on the silver horns.
> Nor wilt thou snare him in the white ravine,
> Nor find him dropt upon the firths of ice,
> That huddling slant in furrow-cloven falls
> To roll the torrent out of dusky doors :
> But follow ; let the torrent dance thee down
> To find him in the valley : let the wild
> Lean-headed eagles yelp alone, and leave
> The monstrous ledges there to slope, and spill
> Their thousand wreaths of dangling water-smoke,
> That like a broken purpose waste in air ;
> So waste not thou : but come ; for all the vales
> Await thee ; azure pillars of the hearth
> Arise to thee ; the children call, and I
> Thy shepherd pipe, and sweet is every sound,
> Sweeter thy voice, but every sound is sweet ;
> Myriads of rivulets hurrying thro' the lawn,
> The moan of doves in immemorial elms,
> And murmuring of innumerable bees.

Finally, with regard to the poem as distinguished
from the social question it speaks of, beauty is kept
in it pre-eminent.

It is first in Tennyson's, as it ought to be in
every artist's heart.   The subject-matter is bent to
the necessity of beauty.   The knowledge displayed
in it, the various theories concerning womanhood,
the choice of scenery, the events, are all chosen
and arranged so as to render it possible to
enshrine them in beautiful shapes.   This general
direction towards loveliness is never lost sight of

by the poet. It is not that moral aims are neglected, or the increase of human good, or the heightening of truth, or the declaring of knowledge; but it is that all these things are made subservient to the manifestation of beauty. It is the artist's way, and it is the highest way. To say this seems to many to say the wrong thing. To put the manifestation of beauty on a higher level than the manifestation of morality or knowledge appears to them to be too bold. It is to say that Art does more for the world, and teaches better things than either Science or Ethics. But the saying does not seem so strange when we define beauty as the form of love, and its innumerably various images as the images of the thoughts of love.

The underlying cause of beauty in all art is this love in the artist's soul, as well as the love which, existing in others and in nature outside of himself, he represents in his art. The greater the artist, the greater his capacity for loving and for seeing and feeling in men and women what is loving. The greater too is his desire for creating its images and the intensity with which he strives to perfect his gift of creation. This was the longing, and this the strife of Tennyson from end to end of his life.

The Princess is only one illustration of these things. The woman's question is not by itself a lovely thing. But it is made beautiful in *The Princess*, because every one of its issues is solved by love, by an appeal to some kind or another of love—to filial love, to motherly love, to the associated love of friendship, to the high and sacred love between a maiden and her lover, to the natural

love which without particular direction arises out
of pity for the helpless, and to the love we feel for
the natural world. Thus the various questions
that issue out of the main question, and the main
question itself, are answered by showing what love
would naturally reply. Now the effects of true
love are always beautiful, and he who represents
them with love and joy embodies beauty.

So Tennyson made the woman's question lovely.
But he was so exalted by this abiding in love
that he could not help at times in the poem breaking out into lyric songs, in which he might
express a keener feeling of beauty, and reach a
higher range of poetry than in the rest of the poem,
where the subject forbade him to rise above a
certain level. So he wrote in the midst of the
poem two love-songs, one of the sorrow of love
past by for ever, of the days that are no more;
another of the joyful hope of love, of the days
that were to come. The first of these, *Tears, idle
tears*, as I have already said, represents more nearly
than any of the songs of Tennyson, but chiefly in
the last verse, one phase, at least, of the passion
of love between man and woman. It does not
represent its enjoyment, but the wild regret of its
continued existence in unfulfilment. The three
verses which lead up to this intense climax with
slow and soft approaches are drenched through and
through, more than any other regretful song I
know, more even than any of Shelley's songs, in
the heavy dew of long and living sorrow for love
just touched but unattained.

The Princess hears the song and calls its tone
to order.

L

If indeed there haunt
About the moulder'd lodges of the past
So sweet a voice and vague, fatal to men,
Well needs it we should cram our ears with wool
And so pass by.

Then rising on a wave of hope and effort, she bids her girls sail on to the great year to come, and in one of the noblest similes in the poem, Tennyson paints the disappearance of the mightiest ideas of the past in the warm life of the future.

While down the streams that float us each and all
To the issue, goes, like glittering bergs of ice,
Throne after throne, and molten on the waste
Becomes a cloud.

At this the Prince, emboldened, sings of hope in love ; a mere love poem the Princess calls it, in her fresh disdain. "Great is song," she says, "used to great ends" ; "duer unto freedom, force and growth of spirit than to junketing and love," phrases which represent Tennyson's own view, in certain moods, of the aim of Poetry. Yet the song is lovely in movement ; its wing-beating and swift-glancing verse is like the flight of the bird that has suggested it.

O Swallow, Swallow, flying, flying south.

Both songs are unrhymed, yet no one needs the rhyme, so harmoniously is their assonance arranged, not so much at the end of each line as in the body of the lines themselves. *Tears, idle tears* is a masterpiece of the careful employment of vowels.

The song of triumph which Ida sings is also

unrhymed. The comparison of the cause of
woman to a tree is too elaborate in detail, and is
not throughout well developed, but the last verse
has its own splendour, and the tree becomes a
Universe-tree.

> Our enemies have fall'n, but this shall grow,
> A night of summer from the heat, a breadth
> Of autumn, dropping fruits of power ; and roll'd
> With music in the growing breeze of Time,
> The tops shall strike from star to star, the fangs
> Shall move the stony bases of the world.

The last song in the body of the poem :

> Now sleeps the crimson petal, now the white :

is still unrhymed, and might be called the palace-
song of love, so full is it with the rich and lovely
things which belong to the royal gardens of the
earth, when night in a clear sky has fallen on
them. But of itself, the song and the love in it
are not of much worth.

When Tennyson, however, had read over what
he had done, the overwhelming mastery of love,
of love of every kind, which fills the poem, urged
him to new creation, and he celebrates love in six
of its various phases—in six delightful and happy
songs, inserted in the third edition between the
main divisions of the poem. They were, he says,
ballads or songs to give the poets breathing
space. So

> The women sang
> Between the rougher voices of the men,
> Like linnets in the pauses of the wind.

They are all of a sweet and gentle humanity, of
a fascinating and concentrated brevity, of common

moods of human love made by the poet's sympathy
and art to shine like the common stars we love so
well. The falling out of wife and husband reconciled
over the grave of their child, the mother singing
to her babe of his father coming home from sea,
the warrior in battle thinking of his home, the
iron grief of the soldier's wife melted at last
into tears by his child laid upon her knee, the
maiden yielding at last to love she had kept at bay—
these are the simple subjects of these songs. They
please this large poet, he was at home in them, and
as long as human nature lasts they will please the
world, because they will endear love to the world.

Among these the cradle song,

> Sweet and low, sweet and low,
> Wind of the western sea,

is the most beautiful and writes, as it were, its
own music, but the song,

> The splendour falls on castle walls,
> And snowy summits old in story,

is the noblest, a clear, uplifted, softly-ringing song.
It sings, in its short compass, of four worlds, of
ancient chivalry, of wild nature, of romance where
the horns of Elfland blow, and of the greater future
of mankind. And in singing of the last, it touches
the main subject of love, love not of person to
person, but of each life to all the lives that follow
it :

> Our echoes roll from soul to soul,
> And grow for ever and for ever.

Yet it is the lover who tells this to his sweetheart,
and the universal element is made delicate by

its union with the personal love of these two happy creatures. It is well that the soul of man should enter into the close of the song, but the greatest poetical beauty has been reached in the second verse, where by a magical employment of words the whole world of Elfland is created, and with it all the romantic tales echo in the ear.

These are the songs of this delightful poem, and it is with some difficulty that we turn away from them to speak of the way in which Tennyson has treated the social side of his subject. It seems necessary, however, to discuss for a little time his views of the woman's question.

CHAPTER VI

THE PRINCESS—THE WOMAN'S QUESTION

WHEN, in *Locksley Hall*, Tennyson makes his
hero, in his anger, cry

> Weakness to be wroth with weakness! woman's pleasure,
>   woman's pain—
> Nature made them blinder motions bounded in a shallower
>   brain :
> Woman is the lesser man,

it appears as if the woman's question had already
occupied his mind. It continued to dwell with
him, for in *Edwin Morris*, a poem published four
years after *The Princess*, the curate, Edward Bull,
who was fatter than his cure, answers his friend,
a poet, to whom his sweetheart's

> least remark was worth
> The experience of the wise,

that this idealising of the woman was all non-
sense.

"I take it," said he,

> " God made the woman for the man,
> And for the good and increase of the world.
> A pretty face is well, and this is well,
> To have a dame indoors, that trims us up,
> And keeps us tight : but these unreal ways

Seem but the theme of writers, and indeed
Worn threadbare. Man is made of solid stuff.
I say, God made the woman for the man,
And for the good and increase of the world.''

This is a more Philistine opinion concerning the object of a woman's life than even those held by the kings in *The Princess.* Tennyson did not agree with that view being exhaustive :

" Parson," said I, " you pitch the pipe too low ! "

At what note he wished the pipe pitched, we hear in *The Princess;* and I write throughout of the poem as it was finished in editions subsequent to that published in 1847.

The subject is introduced in the Prologue. A story is read of a feudal heroine of Sir Walter's house (in whose grounds the company are met who make the poem), who rather than yield to the wild will of a king, took arms and conquered him. " Where lives," asks one, " such a woman now ? " And Lilia, Sir Walter's daughter, replies :

" There are thousands now
Such women, but convention beats them down ;
It is but bringing up ; no more than that :
You men have done it ; how I hate you all.

    *   *   *   *   *

O I wish
That I were some great princess, I would build
Far off from men a college like a man's,
And I would teach them all that men are taught ;
We are twice as quick !

    *   *   *   *   *

But I would make it death
For any male thing but to peep at us.''

The whole question (as Tennyson told it from

the woman's side) is there laid down ; and out of
Lilia's wish grows the tale.   Her view is the same
as that of Ida, the Princess.   When Ida, however,
was young, she dreamt that the man was equal
to the woman, but that each was the half of the
other, that each fulfilled defect in each, and that
together they became the perfect being.   This is
the view of the Prince at the end of the book,
and Ida says the dream was once hers.   But when
we find her at the beginning of the poem, this is
not her view.   Women have been made either
toys or slaves by men !   Their will, their faculties,
their very characters, have been lost in those of
men ; their weakness taken advantage of, their
ignorance encouraged that they may be kept in
subjection.   "Women have been great," she cries
with indignation, " great in war, great in government, great in science, great in the work of the
world.   Why should they not always be as great ?
I will make it so.   They shall be

> living wills, and sphered
> Whole in themselves, and owed to none."

She sees thus both types of womanhood, the
enslaved and the free ; but she sees only one type
of men in their relation to women——those who
treat them " either as vassals to be beaten or
pretty babes to be dandled."   It was not wise for
the sake of her cause to be thus one-sighted.   It
began the battle by taking up a position on half a
truth.   She did wrong to set aside as unworthy, or
to be angry with, the opinions of those men who
either idealised women, or said that they were the
equals of men, but in dissimilar qualities.   It was

part of her theory of isolation to despise all the views of men on her sex, good and bad alike; and this foolish contempt is even now one of the reasons for the failure or the slow advance of the cause of woman.

She makes two more mistakes. What do women need, she asks, to level them with man? They want nothing but knowledge. Equality of knowledge will equalise them with men. And that they may gain this knowledge, even be free to gain it, there is only one way—isolation from man. The thing needed and the way to win it are thus both laid down, and both are mistakes, then and now.

So the college is established. Here, she says, the women shall be moulded to the fuller day; and then, when the girls are trained at all points as men are trained; then, when the secular emancipation of half the world will have been wrought, why then, afterwards, let women marry—and everywhere shall be

> Two heads in council, two beside the hearth,
> Two in the tangled business of the world,
> Two in the liberal offices of life,
> Two plummets dropt from one to sound the abyss
> Of science, and the secrets of the mind ;
> Musician, painter, sculptor, critic, more ;
> And everywhere the broad and bounteous earth
> Shall bear a double growth of those rare souls,
> Poets, whose thoughts enrich the blood of the world.

But at present, till the work be done, death to the man who enters the college gates. " Let there be no love yet between man and maid. For *there* lies our weakness—in our leaning to tenderness, in our personal cry for love. I, for one, will never wed." "What," says the Prince, "have neither

love, children, happiness, what every woman counts
her due ? " " Love ? " she answers, " I have left its
feeble fancy behind me. Children ? Would that
they grew like flowers—and yet, in our love of
them, we lose the higher things. They kill us
with pity, *break us with ourselves !* " She feels
in that phrase her great difficulty—that Nature is
against her—feels it, but does not realise it. She
dreads her own womanhood. Yet, she sees no
other way of action ; isolation from man is necessary to re-establish the just equality of women. This
is her position, and it includes a denial of natural
love which smacks of Lady Blanche, the grim, disap-
pointed woman whom Tennyson creates in order to
motive Ida's exclusion of natural affection from her
plan. We excuse then what was foolish in Ida's
effort ; it is not wholly her fault—but at the same
time we lose some of our respect for her intelligence.
For to deliberately knock her head against the
certainties, to believe that they are not certainties
and can be dodged, is the greatest of follies. To
ignore love between the sexes is one of the little
games some women play in the battle for their
rights. On the contrary, one of the axioms they
ought to lay down in the planning of their struggle
is that this kind of love is certain to arise.

This union made by love is not the only union
which ought to exist between man and woman. All
the work of the world ought to be done by both of the
sexes in harmonious and equal co-operation, each
sex taking what fits best its hand. Without this
union the world's work is only half done. And
with regard to the woman's cause itself, it can
make no progress as long as the law that in all

work both sexes should labour together is dis-
obeyed. In obedience to that law, which Tennyson in this book meant to dwell upon (at least so
far as regards the aim of the Princess), the proper
and successful conduct of the woman's cause is
everywhere contained. Women sometimes deny
this, and try to carry out their aims independent
of men. I do not wonder that they make the
effort, for men have long shut out women from any
active share in a great number of their ends,
isolating women in home alone. None, indeed,
have violated more than men the law which is here
laid down. In that has lain the most crying mistake of civilisation. Owing to that disobedience
the whole progress of humanity has made only half
the way it would otherwise have done. Government, law, religion, literature, art, commerce, science
of all kinds, social order and progress, national
and international union, are all only developed to
half the excellence they would have reached, had
women shared in them as co-workers with men.
But the more women believe that this is true, the
more foolish it would be for them, for the sake
of a petty vengeance or a personal pique, to per-
petrate, even at one single point, the same folly
—to isolate their work from men as men have
isolated their work from women in the past. On
the contrary—always together, as Nature means.
Tennyson saw this up to a certain point, and now
and again in this poem seems to infer the whole
of it. But he did not really go so far. He seems
to keep himself within equality in married life.
But his principle goes beyond that sphere. Day
by day his limits fade away.

This, then, was Ida's first mistake—isolation of woman from man. The second was that she thought knowledge alone was enough to lift woman into equality with man, to rescue her from her position as toy or slave. Knowledge, of course, is good ; the more knowledge women get the better. It is an absolute necessity. But *alone* it injures more than assists their cause. It does part of their work ; it cannot possibly do all. It can destroy the opinions which make women dolls to be played with or vassals to be exploited. It can supply them with the tools necessary to carve their way upwards, to take up the works that men assume as only theirs ; but it cannot supply the spirit which feels the right way to do these things ; it cannot create the imaginative or spiritual powers which illuminate or kindle work ; nor can it enable womanhood to guard her own nature from its excesses or defects. By itself, it is weak, save to destroy ignorance or prejudice. And by itself, it has its own prejudices, its own blindness. Worst of all, it has its own vanity, and the vanity of knowledge is the most successful corrupter and overthrower of the noble causes for which mankind has fought and suffered. If this vanity of knowledge should prevail among women (and they are peculiarly liable to it) their cause will break up, the positions they have won will be lost. One of its tendencies, when women think that knowledge is all they need, is to lead them to deny or minimise the radical difference of sex on which Tennyson dwells so much. It is an astonishing piece of folly. Only women could have the audacity to contradict one of the primeval facts of the universe. It is a case where the vanity of knowledge devours knowledge itself.

Again, when knowledge, full of its self-admiration, neglects or denies the imagination, the affections, the sentiment of life ; when it passes by beauty as of no importance and looks on the ideal faiths of man as folly—there is nothing which is so certain to take the wrong road, and to ruin the cause it boasts that it supports. Any one of the emotional, imaginative, and spiritual powers of nature directs and moves personal and collective human life more than the intellectual power directed to the objects of knowledge. With all their tendency to run into extremes these powers are safer guides than mere knowledge in the affairs of daily life and in the working of great human causes. Each of them—emotional, imaginative, or spiritual—needs knowledge, and to let any one of them act without knowledge is as foolish as to let knowledge act without them. But even when one of them does act alone, it does not do quite as much harm to the progress of humanity as knowledge does, when it isolates itself in its pride as the only master of action or the only guide of thought.

And many women in the present day seem to look with a certain contempt on sentiment, on imagination, on beauty and art, on the affections, on the high passions of the ideal or of the religious life. It is a fatal pride, and a folly for which they will sorely suffer. Women do not want less emotion but larger emotion, nobler and less personal direction of emotion ; more of love and not less, more true passion and not less ; more sense of beauty and not less ; more imagination, more of the energy of faith working by love, more sacrifice of self, that is, more universal, less particular sacrifice. Education in these they want above all, and they want it at present more than men.

These, then, were the two great errors into which the Princess fell, and they defeated her cause. And this is the main meaning of Tennyson.

The college is broken up first by the love of a man to a maid. Death stands before the Prince, but the danger emboldens him.

> Over rocks that are steepest
> Love will find out the way.

What are isolations to that overwhelming conqueror ! Love blows his trumpet, and the walls of the college fall down.

Secondly, it is broken up by feminine jealousy. Ida neglects Lady Blanche for Psyche, a younger friend, one nearer her heart, and the clashing of these two (owing to the Princess following her affections) disintegrates the college. The sketch of this little in-and-out of feeling is no doubt intended by Tennyson to illustrate a danger which does not indeed belong only to the woman's question. Jealousies and personal claims of the sort made by Lady Blanche, personal affections like that of the Princess which neglect some comrades and favour others, personal feelings of any kind pushed athwart the cause—with their envies, their pettinesses, even their malignancies, their party preferences, their claims for office, their dwelling on small points which men or women make into important things in order to fix attention on them-

selves—these are the worms which eat into the
heart of great causes and rot away the finest
plans. Women are even more subject to these
faults than men—not that men are naturally better,
but women have not had that public training which
men have in the repression of the personal and all
its stupidities.

Thirdly, the march of events breaks up the
college. The college has isolated itself from the
general work of the world. Whenever a movement does that, it is certain to be walked over and
crushed by the general movement. Events come
knocking at its doors—and the gates break down
under the pressure. The representation of this is one
of the most skilful things that Tennyson has done in
this poem. And it will never do for the leaders of
the woman's movement to isolate it. It must take
part in affairs other than its own, bring them into
itself, fit itself to events and events to it—harmonise
itself with all the forward forces round about it.
Otherwise it will be dissolved and have to crystal-
lise all over again.

It is not only the college which is dissolved.
The Princess herself is broken down, and at every
point this is done by the recurrence of the natural
emotions from which she has tried to free her
heart lest they should weaken her will. Nature
expelled returns all armed. Ida keeps the child
of Psyche with her in the college—that is, she
keeps with her an impulse to the motherhood she
has abjured. She cannot give up the child to its
mother. True sympathy with her own sex would
not permit her to be guilty of so great a want
of nature ; yet, along with this unnatural hard-

ness, she is softened by the child's silent appeal
to her womanhood :

> " I took it for an hour in mine own bed
> This morning : there the tender orphan hands
> Felt at my heart, and seem'd to charm from thence
> The wrath I nursed against the world."

Her soul, it is plain, is now a kingdom divided
against itself. It cannot stand. But when Cyril
appeals to her to give it back to the mother, all
the woman surges up ; she kisses it, and feels that
" her heart is barren," and we hear in the phrase
the regret of her life for the motherhood she has
abandoned. Then she passes by the wounded
Prince, and his old father, his beard dabbled in
his son's blood, points to her hair and picture on
his heart. She thinks of his love ; and all

> Her iron will was broken in her mind,
> Her noble heart was molten in her breast.

"Give him to me," she cries, "to tend in the
palace." Then she finds her friend Psyche, who
begs forgiveness for her flight from the college.
At first, rapt in the child, she does not answer.
Her brother, who has fought for her, cannot
understand her hardness :

> " Ida—'sdeath ! You blame the man ;
> You wrong yourselves—the woman is so hard
> Upon the woman."

Her father cries out at her : " No heart have
you." The father of the Prince breaks out :

> " Woman, whom we thought woman even now,
> And were half-fool'd to let you tend our son,

> Because he might have wish'd it—but we see
> The accomplice of your madness unforgiven ;
>   the rougher hand
> Is safer : on to the tents; take up the Prince."

Step by step, natural love invades her will, love of children, pity for the man who loves her, love of her friend :

> The touch of that which kills her with herself

drags her from her isolation. Finally, she throws open the whole college in pity of the wounded and in personal indignation with Lady Blanche. Whatever man lies wounded, friend or foe,

> Shall enter, if he will. Let our girls flit
> Till the storm die.

The same action of natural love besets and conquers Psyche. She will not betray her brother to the death, and forgets her oath, and she clung

> About him, and betwixt them blossom'd up
> From out a common vein of memory
> Sweet household talk and phrases of the hearth.

Melissa does not bear that heart within her breast,

> To give three gallant gentlemen to death ;

and all the mob of girls cry, when the hour is stormy, that their May is passing—that love, children, ruling of a house are far from them—that men hate learned women. Theirs is the vulgar cry, but it is forced on them by an isolation which denies nature. And the vulgarity passes away when they tend the wounded, when pity and tenderness are allowed full scope, when love is

M

born in the college glades. Thus, the natural
affections break down the Princess and her plan.

This main contention in the poem is mixed up
with a concise representation of the common prejudices of men concerning the work of women.
Different characters represent different opinions.
The father of the Princess, King Gama, lets things
slide. " I let Ida have her way," he says ; " it
did not matter to me. I wanted peace and no
dispute. Let my daughter play her game." This
indifferent, half-contemptuous treatment of the
earnestness of women by the man, mingled with
an irritating profession of love for them, is not
unknown to the women of the present day.

Then there is the rough old King, the father of
the Prince. He is the image of the savage view
come down to modern times. Ida's opinions of
her sex and its work are rampant heresy to him.
" Look you, sir," he breaks out,

> " Man is the hunter: woman is his game ; "

and the lines which follow put this opinion with
admirable bluntness.

Cyril, bold, reckless and honourable, the lover
of the sex, represents another type. When he
hears the women lecture, and the Prince says
" They do all this as well as we,"

> "They hunt old trails," said Cyril, " very well:
> But when did woman ever yet invent ? "

" What is all this learning to me ? I looked on
Psyche, and she made me wise in another way. I
learnt more from her in a flash than if every Muse
tumbled a science into my empty brain. Love has

come in with me into the college, and I have
thought to roar, to break my chain, and shake
my mane." This is the natural man who thinks
that love is all, who, when he loves, idealises
the woman into the teacher of things which no
knowledge can give him, but who always thinks
that his man's strength is the natural victor over
the woman. Yet, he it is whom Tennyson
chooses to put his main contention. Cyril loves
Psyche, and begs the Princess to give back the
child. He has no theories, no ideal of woman's
future ; but he stands for Nature and for love.

> O fair and strong and terrible ! Lioness
> That with your long locks play the Lion's mane !
> But Love and Nature, these are two more terrible
> And stronger.

These are the main male opinions about women
which Tennyson embodied. That of the Prince
remains, and he represents Tennyson's full thought
upon the matter. After the battle, the Prince and
the Princess are face to face. And the pity of his
long illness, in which she has nursed him tenderly,
" and hatred of her weakness, blent with shame,"
and sight of all the lovers in court and grove, and
constant usage of the charities of life, and softening
sadness, change her whole soul to gentleness and
pity, and both at last to love. And when the Prince
awakes to consciousness, and, thinking her who sits
beside him some sweet dream, calls her to fulfil the
dream to perfection and kiss him ere he die, she
stoops and kisses him, and all

> Her falser self slipt from her like a robe
> And left her woman.

When in the night he wakes again and hears Ida
reading a song that strikes the note of that which is
to be their life, they speak together of all that has
been. " She was wrong," she says, " she had failed,
had sought less for truth than power in knowledge,
but something wild within her breast,

A greater than all knowledge, beat her down."

For the moment, no doubt—the moment of her
passionate yielding—she does not surrender too
much. But she surrenders too much if she speaks
as a woman for women. And the Prince, with
all his views of pure equality, accepts too much
of masterhood. There is a certain lordliness in
his lecture on the woman and the man which
belongs to Tennyson's attitude on the subject,
and which makes me dread that Ida in after years
lost a good deal of her individuality. This might
be a gain for the comfort of the palace, but it
would be a loss to womanhood and to the world.
But what the Prince says, independent of his
attitude of mind, is true, for the most part, to the
heart of the question, and remains true, even
though fifty years have passed away.

But we have now far more data to go upon than
Tennyson possessed. The steady work of women
during these fifty years, and the points they have
so bravely won, have added element after element to
our experience. But all that has been gained has
made more plain that

The woman's cause is man's : they rise or sink
Together.

One is the equal half of the other ; the halves are

diverse for ever, each complements each ; both
united in diversity make the perfect humanity; their
work must be together, in difference. These are
the vital truths which Tennyson expresses in the
famous lines of the Prince's speech, and they
govern, or ought to govern, the whole question
of the future position of womanhood in a better
society than that in which we live. They do *not*
govern the position or the life of womanhood at
present. The prejudices both of men and women
are against their full development. Nor do I
think that Tennyson himself (save on a wind of
prophecy) saw clearly to what conclusions his
own views would lead. We could not expect
he should, but men and women will in the end
grasp with proper largeness of thought what this
means :

> And so these twain, upon the skirts of Time,
> Sit side by side, full summ'd in all their powers,
> Dispensing harvest, sowing the To-be,
> Self-reverent each and reverencing each,
> Distinct in individualities,
> But like each other ev'n as those who love.

These verses assert far more for women than
that they should find their only perfect life in
marriage and in home; their only exercise of sacrifice in motherhood, in nursing the sick, in tending
on the poor, or their only career in personal
devotion to those they love. Tennyson, sometimes
seeing farther, comes back to circle round these
things of home alone ; and most men and women,
even now, think that these exhaust all the womanly
work of women. It is not so. We have gained
a wider view. To be, indeed, a true wife, such as

Tennyson has drawn on the lips of the Prince ; or
to be a sweet and noble mother, one

> Not learned, save in gracious household ways,
> Not perfect, nay, but full of tender wants,
> No angel, but a dearer being, all dipt
> In angel instincts, breathing Paradise,
> Interpreter between the gods and men,
> Who look'd all native to her place, and yet
> On tiptoe seem'd to touch upon a sphere
> Too gross to tread, and all male minds perforce
> Sway'd to her from their orbits as they moved
> And girdled her with music. Happy he,
> With such a mother!

—to be these noble creatures at home, and to build
up children into noble life—this, indeed, is the
work of womanhood done not only at home, but for
the State and for humanity at large. No higher
work in the world exists than that of motherhood
forming children into true and loving men and
women.

But this does not cover all. In our complex
and crowded society, there are thousands of
women who have no home, who are not wives
and mothers, but who are hungry to become
themselves, to realise themselves in work, to live
outside of themselves in the life and movement of
the whole. These scarcely come into Tennyson's
outlook at the end of *The Princess*. For these, the
education in knowledge and the training of their
powers to all kinds of work which Ida established
in her college are necessary, but with a clear
consideration of sexual difference. This work is,
however, to be carried out on other principles than
those which Ida laid down—in union with man,
with as large a training in the just use of the

emotions, in the just expansion of the imagination, in a true sight of the beautiful, and in the wise development of the ideal and the spiritual, as in the accurate knowledge of science and history, of law and literature. And then, the work of the world lies open to woman, to do in a different way from man, but with the same ends, and in the same cause—the cause of the happiness, the goodness, and the love of humanity.

When that is possible—when we shall have applied to all the problems of society the new and as yet unused elements which exist in womanhood—all results will be reached twice as quickly as they are now reached, all human work will be twice as quickly done. And then, perhaps, some new poet will write a new *Princess*.

CHAPTER VII

IN MEMORIAM

THE history of the writing of *In Memoriam* is well known. If an immortal fame can comfort Arthur Hallam, who was so soon bereft of the brightness of the earth, then he is consoled in his high place for the loss of human life; for surely while the language of England lasts, so long will *In Memoriam* be read and Arthur Hallam be remembered. Thirty years ago, I made a pilgrimage to the little church near Clevedon, where the Hallams rest, and saw the graveyard, the yews, and the marble tablet glimmering in the church. It was then a lonely quiet place, in a furrow of the sandy slopes, not a house standing near it; and fifty yards from it, but hidden from view, the broad estuary of the Severn filled with the tide. I heard the water wash the feet of the low cliffs as it passed by. Sorrow and death, peace that passeth understanding, the victory of the soul, seemed present with me; and the murmuring of the Severn became, as I dreamed, the music of eternal love, into whose vast harmonies all our discords are drawn at last.

I felt, it seemed, the impression of the place. I knew afterwards that it was the impression of the poem that I gave to the place. And this indeed is the lasting power of *In Memoriam.* It is a song of victory and life arising out of defeat and death ; of peace which has forgotten doubt ; of joy whose mother was sorrow but who has turned his mother's heart into delight. The conquest of love— the moral triumph of the soul over the worst blows of fate, over the outward forces of Nature, even over its own ill—that is the motive of the poems which endure, which, like the great lighthouses, stand and shine through the storms of time to save and lead into a haven of peace the navies of humanity. We are flooded to-day with poems of despair, with verse which boasts that it describes the real when it describes the base, which takes the vulture's pleasure in feeding on the corruption of society, and prophesies, when it lifts its dripping beak from the offal, that to this carcass-complexion the whole of humanity will come at last. Tennyson himself has painted the class :

> We are men of ruin'd blood,
>   Therefore comes it we are wise !
>   *   *   *   *
> Virtue !—to be good and just—
>   Every heart, when sifted well,
> Is a clot of warmer dust,
>   Mixed with cunning sparks of hell.

The art and the temper that produce the poetry of despair and vileness will not last ; and it is a comfort to think of this when we are greatly troubled with the stenches of what they falsely call the real. The poetry of the soul's defeat withers in the mind of the race. The poet himself who writes it withers away. Had *In Memoriam* been only wailing for loss it would have perished, even if its work

had been better than it is; but since it tells of loss
passing into love, since it describes death entering
into life, it is sure to live, and would do so even
if its work had been less excellent. Of course I
do not mean that inartistic work, if its motive
be a victorious one, will live. I write of artists
and their work, not of those who are not artists.
The poetic work of those that are not artists, of
whatever temper it be, is bound to perish.

But *In Memoriam* is a work of art, done by a man
whose natural gift had been polished by study, and
carefully trained by steady practice till it rejoiced
in its own power. Its subject impassioned its
writer, and the subject was simple, close to the heart
of man. As the poem moved on, the subject expanded, and the sorrow spoken of passed from the
particular into the universal. The victory over the
evil of sorrow made a similar passage. The poet's
personal conquest of pain became the universal
conquest of the human race. This expansion of
the subject ennobled the poem, and the triumphant
close secured and established its nobility. It will
last when all its detractors and their criticisms are
together dust.

It was published in 1850. The collected poems
were published in 1842, *The Princess* in 1847; but
the subject of *In Memoriam* and the writing of the
poem had been kept in Tennyson's mind for seventeen years, from 1833 to 1849, ripening season by
season into the full and perfect fruit. This is the
way in which Tennyson wrought at his natural gift,
and I repeat that it was partly owing to this steady
slowness of his that his poetic genius retained to so
great an age its clearness, its power, and its fire.

It was owing to this also that his gift gained and retained that capacity for beautiful and careful finish which, when the ardour of youth has departed from an artist, is the excellence which makes the work of his maturity delightful. This was in his character. There was that in him from his very birth which made him love to grow and work as slowly as an oak lays fibre to fibre ; as firmly, as steadily, and with as enduring a vitality. His patient work on *In Memoriam* was of the very essence of the man.

And now, how did *In Memoriam* arise into its form ?

When a poet first begins to write, he writes of the motives which have excited his youth, and those motives are born out of his own life, rather than out of the life of the world without him. They are individual, not universal. His boyhood, his youth, his early loves, his pleasures at the university, his classic studies, the charm of the Greek stories ; his first delight in the romantic tale such as that of Arthur, his vacation rambles and the discussions which made them vivid ; the light fancies of youth, the happy pity of sad stories ; the loveliness of Nature round his home, and in the wilder places of the mountain and the glen ; the daily life of country folk, seen through the emotions of youthful love ; and now and then such philosophy of life as belongs to the young man who argues round rather than pierces into the great problems, because they have not as yet smitten him to the heart—these are the motives of a poet's youth. Out of this experience or rather this want of experience, this personal play of only personal

emotion over circumstance and over the working
of his own soul, the first poems of the artist are
born, and they fill his heart to the exclusion of
those greater subjects which concern the whole of
humanity.

The weight and trouble of the world of men,
the cry of the questioning soul of humanity, the
massive problems of the whole race, have not yet
sent their waves of emotion on him with sufficient
force to put his individuality into the second place.
There is no room for these outward and world-
wide emotions until the personal emotions of
youth are expressed and exhausted by expression.
But when these have been expressed (as in the
volumes of 1830 and 1833), then the soul is, as
it were, empty. And on this void soul, waiting
for new thoughts and their emotions, the great
trouble of mankind flows in with a full tide, and
brings with it universal tidings, deeper passions,
greater ranges of thought than the poet has known
as yet. It does more; it has a distinct action
on the soul itself. It not only brings new
things from without, but it also awakens within
the poet powers of his own as yet unknown
by him, as yet asleep. They are the powers by
which the poet is fitted to deal with the great and
universal questions, to answer which constitutes
the struggle of mankind. Now and then they
lift their head, and appear in the verse, but their
time is not yet, and they let fall their head again
in slumber. But now, at the inward rush of the
vast trouble of the world of man, they spring into
full life, and dwell in the place that personal feeling
once occupied alone. The universal has come,

and though the particular is not destroyed, it is absorbed.

Into what shape it will first turn itself—whether it will gather its questions and feelings round religion, or social movements, or war, or womanhood, or liberty, or the existence of evil, or the future advent of good—will depend on circumstance. The circumstance which settled the first direction of Tennyson towards the universal, which brought the world-question into its special shape for him, was the death of his dearest friend. And the death was so tragic, and the circumstances so special, that it was impossible that the questions roused by it should be only personal. Arthur Hallam was as young as Tennyson; his powers seemed so exceptional that his father, who was of all literary men the most sober and balanced in his judgments, imagined him capable of the greatest things. It was thought that a splendid future was before him, and his loss seemed to his friends to be a loss to all mankind. The grief of family, of all who loved him, came, in this fashion, to be representative of the sorrow of the whole world. This touched Tennyson home, and depth and poignancy were given to it because his friend was not only a friend, but a brother artist. Both were poets, both worked together at poetry, both looked forward to a long life of art together. I do not remember anything like it since the death of Girtin and the silent sorrow of Turner; but the parallel is a worthy one, it fits at almost every point.

Thus the outward impulse came on Tennyson's soul, now discharged of all the gathered subjects of youth, relieved of the merely individual. The

vast question of human sorrow for the loss of
those who are loved, sorrow as infinite and as
varied as love, belonging to all the lovers and
friends of the whole world, going back with unremitting force through the whole of time, felt as
keenly by those who chipped out the flake of flint
as by Tennyson himself—this, in all its universal
humanity, was borne in upon him now, and filled
his soul. He felt the loss of his friend; he felt the
loss of all the friends of the whole world. This
was Tennyson's step into manhood as a poet:
and the slow, sustained and yet impassioned march
by which his character forced him to advance, made
it but natural for him to take seventeen years to
realise and embody his progress in a work which is
worthy of the time given to it, and which remains
the weightiest in thought, the best in form, the
most varied in feeling, and the most finished of all
his longer poems.

Such is the psychical history of this poem, as
I conceive it, and I think the poem bears out
the analysis, even in its arrangement. Before,
however, I speak of that arrangement, I wish to
dwell on some characteristics of the poem and on
some accusations made against it. First, it was
begun immediately after the youthful poems, and
youth lingers in it in lovely ways. When young
Imagination rushes forward in it, he does not appear
in his gaiety, in his youthful dress. He is solemnised
somewhat by the subject, and wears the noble
mask of tragedy. The rush is there, but its swiftness is stately. Moreover, it is quite natural that
these passages of youthful fire and glow do not
occur in the first part where the personal grief is

recent and foremost, but in the second, or rather in
the third, when the pain of loss is lessened, and
the sweetness of memory and the soothing of faith
have discharged bitterness from the soul. I do
not know in any of the earlier poems, not even in
Maud, anything on a higher range of passionate
imagination, and breathing more of youthful ardour
weighted with dignity of thought, than a song like
this :

LXXXVIII.

Wild bird, whose warble, liquid sweet,
　　Rings Eden thro' the budded quicks,
　　O tell me where the senses mix,
O tell me where the passions meet,

Whence radiate : fierce extremes employ
　　Thy spirits in the darkening leaf,
　　And in the midmost heart of grief
Thy passion clasps a secret joy :

And I—my harp would prelude woe—
　　I cannot all command the strings ;
　　The glory of the sum of things
Will flash along the chords and go.

Or, take this other, where the loveliness
of Nature is met and received with joy by that
receptive spirit of delight in a sensuous impression
which a young man feels, and where the depth
of the feeling has wrought the short poem into an
intensity of unity ; each verse linked, like bell to
bell in a chime, to the verse before it, and all
swinging into a triumphant close ; swelling as they
go from thought to thought, and finally rising from
the landscape of earth to the landscape of infinite
space—can anything be more impassioned and yet
more solemn ? It has the swiftness of youth, and
the nobleness of manhood's sacred joy:

Sweet after showers, ambrosial air,
　　That rollest from the gorgeous gloom
　　Of evening over brake and bloom
And meadow, slowly breathing bare

The round of space, and rapt below
　　Thro' all the dewy-tassell'd wood,
　　And shadowing down the hornéd flood
In ripples, fan my brows and blow

The fever from my cheek, and sigh
　　The full new life that feeds thy breath
　　Throughout my frame, till Doubt and Death,
Ill brethren, let the fancy fly

From belt to belt of crimson seas
　　On leagues of odour streaming far,
　　To where in yonder orient star
A hundred spirits whisper ' Peace.'

There are many other passages I might quote in this connection, but these are enough to prove that the ardour of youth is not absent from *In Memoriam*. Only one thing I add. The passion is not that of love alone, of personal pain or joy alone. It is felt for all humanity, as well as for himself—nay, his self is drowned in the greater emotion. It is a passion also which is not all feeling ; it is deepened by the universal thoughts which are mingled with it ; and when emotion is charged with thought (as the great waters are with salt), it is then strongest, most living, and most worthy of humanity. Nevertheless, the sweetness and nearness of personal feeling is not wanting. This is also felt as one feels it in youth, when tenderness rather than thoughtfulness is first. The loveliest example of this in the poems of 1833 is :

Break, break, break,
　　On thy cold gray stones, O Sea.

But the little poem which here follows is not unworthy of this predecessor. I do not even know whether its note is not more delicate and tender; the wash of the Severn in it is more home-like, more near to the humanity of sorrow than the desolate dash of the sea.

> The Danube to the Severn gave
> The darken'd heart that beat no more;
> They laid him by the pleasant shore,
> And in the hearing of the wave.
>
> There twice a day the Severn fills;
> The salt sea-water passes by,
> And hushes half the babbling Wye,
> And makes a silence in the hills.
>
> The Wye is hush'd nor moves along,
> And hush'd my deepest grief of all,
> When fill'd with tears that cannot fall,
> I brim with sorrow drowning song.
>
> The tide flows down, the wave again
> Is vocal in its wooded walls;
> My deeper anguish also falls,
> And I can speak a little then.

That is the full pathos of personal sorrow. There is nothing universal in it. It is all youth—and yet how finished is its art! How delicately the work of Nature without is woven together with the labour of pain within, and how unforgetful, is the reader kept, as the verse goes on, of the place where the poet stands, of the grave in which Arthur lies !

Connected with this last, and indeed a part of it which I desire to isolate, is the next point. An objection similar to that made to *Lycidas*, is made to *In Memoriam*. As in *Lycidas* the grief is lost, as some say, in conventional ornament, or,

N

as others say, in the mere making of a poem, so the grief in *In Memoriam* is lost, we are told, in theology and philosophy. There is some apparent truth in the objection. But first and foremost, the grief is not lost. It appears, as it does not appear in *Lycidas*. Secondly, we must remember that the poem is the tale of two years and a half, and that the sorrow for his friend passes through this period, and changes its form as time changes all our sorrows. It is full, close, and even over-sentimental in expression at the beginning. It is mingled, in the middle of the poem, with the doubts that its suffering brings. It passes into peace and victory at the close. But it is never lost, and it becomes more true to human nature, more gentle, as the poem develops. There are few lyrical movements lovelier and tenderer than the great canzone where Tennyson describes his reading late at night the letters of the dead, and the waking vision of thought, when his soul, touched by his friend's power from the other world, is borne with him into the universe of spirit. That is the voice of true love, infinitely tender, and, while regretful, moved by a nobler friendship than had been of old on earth; and every one who has loved and lost, and has not yielded to the selfishness of grief, knows that such an hour is deeper, and more tender than tongue can tell. Moreover, we must also remember that the subject has passed, beyond his sorrow for his friend, into consideration of the sorrow of the whole world; and the universality of the emotion felt increases the intensity of it. We can trace its growth. The first part of the poem which belongs only to his particular sorrow for

This is a first even for United College every line is underlined.

Arthur is weak in comparison with the last. Yet, when he comes to think of the universal sorrow, it is knit up still with his friend, and the triumph of the whole is also the triumph of his friend. When we compare even that fine passage I have quoted, "The Danube to the Severn gave," with this— "Dear friend, far off, my lost desire"—which now I quote, what a change! what a difference in the depth and strength of the feeling! The feeling is still personal, but it is also universal. The love which fills it is not less because it mingles the whole universe with his friend. Nay, it is greater, for the love of the whole world, of God and Nature and man, and the joy of love's victory have been added to it:

CXXIX.

Dear friend, far off, my lost desire,
　　So far, so near in woe and weal;
　　O loved the most, when most I feel
There is a lower and a higher;

Known and unknown; human, divine;
　　Sweet human hand and lips and eye;
　　Dear heavenly friend that canst not die,
Mine, mine, for ever, ever mine;

Strange friend, past, present, and to be;
　　Loved deeplier, darklier understood;
　　Behold, I dream a dream of good,
And mingle all the world with thee.

CXXX.

Thy voice is on the rolling air;
　　I hear thee where the waters run;
　　Thou standest in the rising sun,
And in the setting thou art fair.

What art thou then? I cannot guess,
  But though I seem in star and flower
  To feel thee some diffusive power,
I do not therefore love thee less:

Thy love involves the love before;
  My love is vaster passion now;
  Tho' mix'd with God and Nature thou,
I seem to love thee more and more.

Far off thou art, but ever nigh;
  I have thee still, and I rejoice;
  I prosper, circled with thy voice;
I shall not lose thee tho' I die.

That is one form of the fervent feeling of Tennyson, and it is worth a hundredfold more than our merely personal sorrows, joys, and loves. The deep and ardent emotion which is awakened by the mightiest and best thoughts, gathering round the great and noble realities which belong to all mankind, and stir eternal yearning and high desire in the heart of man, is worthier to feel, and nobler to celebrate in song, than the fleeting ardours of youth which are concerned with ourselves alone, and which imprison us in ourselves.

It has been said that Tennyson fails in passion, and when men say that, they mean the embodiment of the passion of love in verse. It is true that he is not capable of describing the wilder, the more sensuous phases of love. The only poem in which he ever tried it is one called *Fatima*, and it is a great failure. But to say that he is incapable of describing the ardent love of a man for a maid is to forget *Maud*, and *Maud* does not stand alone. Nevertheless, his intenser singing belongs to other spheres. The personal loves of earth fade and die, unless they are taken up into wider and higher loves, unless they are expanded to fit into the love of man and the love of God. And Tennyson always, or almost always, lifts them into those loftier regions. This is the full drift of *In Memoriam.*

Moreover, as age grows on us, and youthful ardours fade, love, which was once engaged with persons, and which, in loving persons, learned to know itself and its powers, is content no longer with persons. It desires to expand, it prunes its wings for a larger flight into regions where self-desire is lost. It loves a country and can die for its honour. It loves the great causes which set forward mankind, and in such devotion it loves the whole race of man. It loves Nature, not in parts as once in youth, not because it is made to reflect our feelings, but as a whole and for itself alone. It loves the great ideas—truth, justice, honour, purity, uprightness, the liberty and duties of man, the union of all mankind in spirit and in truth. It loves, finally, God in whom all Nature and man are contained and loved, in whom all the great ideas and truths are embodied, from whom they flow and to whom they return, bringing with them the men and women to whom they have been given. It loves, thus, the whole universe. And the emotion which these vaster loves awaken is deeper, stronger, and more noble than that which is stirred by the personal loves of youth. It is enduring; it is coeval with God Himself; and man only reaches his true destiny when he is thrilled through and through with its powers. These are

the loves which Tennyson, more than any other
poet of this century, felt and sang. For these he
wrote with a greater depth of feeling than other
men. It is in celebrating these diviner forms of
love, as I might show in poem after poem, that he
writes with the greatest glow and fire; and it is for
this that humanity, as it grows into capacity for
the more immortal affections, will always honour
him. This, too, was in his character. It was one
of the roots of the man. The tendency, the conduct, the upbuilding, the power, and the life of his
poetry find in this their best explanation; nor
is there any better example than *In Memoriam* of
this expansion of love from the particular to the
universal, or of the profound ardour with which he
made its song.

It remains to say something of the manner in
which Tennyson uses and describes Nature in *In
Memoriam*. The scenery of the poem is partly of
the downs and of the sea in the distance; partly
of a woodland country made vocal by a brook;
and sometimes of a garden full of flowers and a
lawn with far-branching trees, elm, beech and
sycamore. Two parts of England contribute their
landscape to the verse, for in the midst of the
poem Tennyson changes his dwelling-place; but
the scenery of the first part is often recollected and
described in the second.

Nature is used in diverse ways. Sometimes the
landscape is taken up by the poet into his own
being, spiritualised therein, and made by stress of
passion to image the movement of his inner life.
Then the outward scene and the inward feeling

are woven together moment by moment with an intensity which makes them one. And this is done in an accumulative fashion. Vision after vision of Nature, each of a greater beauty and sentiment than its predecessor, succeed one another, and each of them is fitted to a corresponding exaltation of the emotions of the soul. There is no better example of this method than the song I have elsewhere quoted :

Sweet after showers, ambrosial air.

Nor is the conclusion of xcv.—that full-throated passage about the growing dawn and the rising wind—inferior in this intense clasping together of Nature and the soul, or in this accumulating power. Another example of the same method is to be found in the Hesper-Phosphor poem (cxxi.). This, the form of which is different from the other examples of the same method, is the most finished piece of conscious art in *In Memoriam.* Two general aspects of Nature under the same star— the evening and the morning star—are taken to represent the two positions of his soul, in the past and in the present. Both these aspects are made alive by the simple doings of human life that naturally belong to the waking of the world from rest, and the going of the world to rest. Then both, since Hesper and Phosphor are the same, since the morning brings the evening in its arms, since the evening bears within it the waking of the dawn, are smitten together, like his past and present, into one.

Another method describes at some length a single aspect of Nature, and then at the end throws back on this special aspect the mood of his mind. In these poems we have the finest descriptions of Nature in *In Memoriam;* and frequently in two adjacent poems two opposed moods of Nature are represented in contrast one with another. The calm of the whole world in the morning hour (xi.) is set over against the tempest which the evening has brought upon the same landscape (xv.). They image his calm despair and wild unrest, and perhaps created them ; for Nature often makes our passions and then mirrors them.

No calm was ever deeper in verse than it is on that high wold in the morning, and no storm wilder than it is on the same wold in the evening ; and Tennyson takes the greatest pains to describe the vastness of the outspread landscape, under both these moods of Nature. In the first he sees the moor at his feet, the dews on the furze, the gossamers that tremble not, so still is the air, but which twinkle in the lifting light of morning. Then he raises his eyes, and that far landscape to which Shelley or Wordsworth would have allotted twenty or thirty lines, is done in four :

> Calm and still light on yon great plain
> That sweeps with all its autumn bowers,
> And crowded farms and lessening towers,
> To mingle with the bounding main.

This is Tennyson's concentrated manner, and the landscape seems all the larger from the previous description of the small space of ground on which he is standing. I do not say that it is better than the expansive landscapes of Shelley or Wordsworth, but it is done in a different way, and with its own distinct emotion. We may set beside it another description of calm in the epilogue where the landscape is equally far and vast—a moonlight vision alive with streaming cloud and with the moving of the moon all the night long—a most beautiful thing, drenched with the silent loveliness of the universe.

> Dumb is that tower that spake so loud,
>   And high in heaven the streaming cloud,
> And on the downs a rising fire :
>
> And rise, O moon, from yonder down,
>   Till over down and over dale
>   All night the shining vapour sail
> And pass the silent-lighted town,
>
> The white-faced halls, the glancing rills,
>   And catch at every mountain head,
>   And o'er the friths that branch and spread
> Their sleeping silver through the hills :

The landscape is as far as it is fair, and it is immediately taken up, in accordance with the first method of which I have spoken, into his own soul, into his blessing on the bridal pair ; and then inwoven with the coming child, and with the race of man. We might now think that this poet of wide distances would not be able to picture the quiet of a narrow and enclosed space ; of a lawn and garden on a summer evening. But he does this with equal force and beauty. The poem (xcv.) beginning—

> By night we linger'd on the lawn,

breathes with the peace of all the country-homes of England, and, even more, with the happy stillness of human hearts, of one another sure.

The storms described in *In Memoriam* are done

in the same way as these images of calm. The
tempest of the fifteenth section begins with what is
close at hand—the wood by which he stands at
sunset—

> The last red leaf is whirl'd away,
> The rooks are blown about the skies.

And then, after that last admirable line which fills
the whole sky with the gale, he lifts his eyes, as
before, and we see with him the whole world
below, painted also in four lines—the forest, the
waters, the meadows, struck out, each in one
word ; and the wildness of the wind and the width
of the landscape given, as Turner would have given
them, by the low shaft of storm-shaken sunlight
dashed from the west right across to the east—

> The forest crack'd, the waters curl'd,
>   The cattle huddled on the lea ;
>   And wildly dash'd on tower and tree
> The sunbeam strikes along the world.

Lastly, to heighten the impression of tempest, to
show the power it will have when the night is
come, to add a far horizon to the solemn world—he
paints the rising wrath of the storm in the cloud
above the ocean rim, all aflame with warlike sunset,

> That rises upwards always higher,
>   And onward drags a labouring breast,
>   And topples round the dreary west,
> A looming bastion fringed with fire.

It is well done, but whosoever reads the whole will
feel that the storm of the human heart is higher
than the storm of Nature.

Tennyson always loved tempestuous days, and
this general description of storm is followed by

many others of fierce weather. In lxxii. the
whole of the day is wild, but here he dwells on
the small and particular effects caused by the
wind. The blasts "blow the poplar white"; the
"rose pulls sideways"; the daisy "closes her
crimson fringes to the shower"; the "burthened
brows" of the day—that is, the looming clouds—
pour forth winds

> That whirl the ungarner'd sheaf afar,
> And sow the sky with flying boughs.

Nor is the winter gale and the wintry world
neglected. Stanza cvii. opens with the sunset
and the "purple-frosty bank of vapour" on the
horizon, and then the north-east wind comes with
the night. Its fierceness, keenness, iron-hearted-
ness, its savage noise, the merciless weather of it,
pass from the woods out to the sea, and the moon
hangs hard-edged over the passing squalls of snow.
The use of rough vowels, of words that hiss and
clang, and smite the ear, heightens the impression.

> Fiercely flies
> The blast of North and East, and ice
> Makes daggers at the sharpen'd eaves,
>
> And bristles all the brakes and thorns
> To yon hard crescent, as she hangs
> Above the wood which grides and clangs
> Its leafless ribs and iron horns
>
> Together, in the drifts that pass
> To darken on the rolling brine
> That breaks the coast.

The hand that wrought this winter landscape is
equally cunning in summer and spring. The
summer garden and the summer lawn of lxxxix.
are steeped in heat and light. The lines "Im-

mantled in ambrosial dark," "The landscape
winking thro' the heat," hold in them alike the
shade and blaze of summer days ; and the joyous
sound of the scythe in early morn is full of the
sentiment of summer——

> O sound to rout the brood of cares,
>   The sweep of scythe in morning dew,
>   The gust that round the garden flew,
> And tumbled half the mellowing pears !

I give one more example for the brief perfection
of the picture :

> When summer's hourly-mellowing change
>   May breathe, with many roses sweet,.
>   Upon the thousand waves of wheat
> That ripple round the lonely grange.

As to spring, the poem is full of its wakeful
charm, of its glad beginnings, "when flower is
feeling after flower." The rosy plumelets that tuft
the larch, the native hazels tassel-hung, the living
smoke of the yew, the little speedwell's darling
blue, the laburnum's dropping-wells of fire, the sea-
blue bird of March flitting underneath the barren
bush, the low love-language of the dove, the rare
piping of the mounted thrush, are all phrases
which tell how closely he watched her wakening ;
and when his heart is happy at the end of his
poem, he breaks into one of the loveliest songs of
spring that English poetry has ever made.

> CXV.
>
> Now fades the last long streak of snow,
>   Now burgeons every maze of quick
>   About the flowering squares, and thick
> By ashen roots the violets blow.

I need not quote the rest, but it is lovely throughout. Almost all the joys of spring, her scenery and its indwellers, her earth, and sky, and sea, and at last the springtide of his own heart, are vocal in its feeling and its art.

Finally, there is the landscape of memory—another method of description, in which many happy and different aspects of Nature are gathered together, some described in two lines, some even flashed forth in half a line, and every one of them humanised by tender feeling—that feeling through recollection of Nature and his friend together which makes for every landscape its own ethereal atmosphere, half of soft air and half of soft emotion. Of this kind of natural description, so difficult, so rarely done well, so exquisite when it is at the same time brief and full, the two poems c. and ci., are most lovely and delicate examples, and every one who cares for poetry should possess them in his soul. Many also are the scattered phrases about the natural world which might be collected for their subtle simplicity, beauty, and truth ; but I close this praise of the poet with only one, in which man and Nature are inwoven, and the way he wrote his poem enshrined :

> Short swallow-flights of song, that dip
> Their wings in tears, and skim away.

CHAPTER VIII

IN MEMORIAM—ITS STRUCTURE

THE question of this Chapter is—How was *In Memoriam* shaped? What is the conduct of the poem?

It was shaped into the continuous story of two years and a half; not a story of events but the story of the voyage of a soul. First, the hurricane of sorrow came; then the fierceness of the storm grew less, but left the sea tormented and the ship of the soul tossing from wave to wave, from question to question. At last there was calm, and the soul rested; and then a clear wind arose in sunny skies, and the ship flew forward, all the sails set to victory, into a harbour of peace. But better words than these to describe the history of *In Memoriam* are those of the Psalm, said of those who go down into the deep: "They go up to the heavens, and down again to the depth; their soul melteth away for very trouble. They reel to and fro and stagger like a drunken man, and are at their wits' end. So they cry unto the Lord in their trouble, and He delivereth them out of their distress. He maketh the storm a calm, so that the waves thereof are still. Then are they glad because they are at rest: so

He bringeth them to the haven where they would be."

The time of this story is well marked, and it is the first thing its reader should understand. It outlines the map of the poem. It begins in September 1833, when Tennyson hears of his friend's death at Vienna. It is autumn; the leaves are reddening to their fall, the chestnut is pattering to the ground, as the poet waits for the body of his friend. This autumn closes with a great storm :

> To-night the winds begin to rise,
> And roar from yonder dripping day,
> The last red leaf is whirl'd away,
> The rooks are blown about the skies.

Then the twenty-eighth, twenty-ninth, and thirtieth sections describe the first Christmas after the death of Arthur. In the thirty-eighth, the spring of 1834 has come, and in the forty-eighth the swallows are flying over the waters. The seventy-second records the anniversary of his friend's death, September 1834. One year has passed by.

The Christmas of 1834 is recorded in the seventy-eighth, and the spring of 1835 arrives in the eighty-third sections. Full summer is with us in the eighty-ninth and the ninety-fifth ; and in the ninety-ninth the day of his friend's death dawns after storm in balm and peace. A second year has gone by, September 1835.

Another Christmas comes with the hundred and third section, and at the hundred and fourteenth these notes of time close with the April of 1836. The poem lasts, then, just two years and seven

months. The epithalamium at the end, the cele-
bration of his sister's marriage-day, belongs to
1842 ; and the prologue to the poem was written
last of all, and is dated 1849.

And now, to illustrate the progress of the soul
from sorrow to peace, I will take the three main
marks of time : the anniversaries of the death
of his friend, the Christmas-tides, the advents of
spring, and dwell on the changes of mind displayed
in the record of them. When Tennyson hears of
Arthur's death (to take the death-days first) grief
is all ; it drowns the world ; Nature seems pur-
poseless, " a hollow form with empty hands" ; the
sullen, changeless yew-tree symbolises the hardness
of his heart. When the anniversary of the death
comes the memory of it is still miserable. That hour

> sicken'd every living bloom
> And blurr'd the splendour of the sun.

It was a

> Day mark'd as with some hideous crime,
> When the dark hand struck down thro' time
> And cancell'd nature's best—

a day "to hide its shame beneath the ground."
Thus even when a year has gone by the wrath-
fulness of sorrow is still deep. As yet there is no
forgiveness of pain and no peace (lxxii.).

When the next anniversary dawns (xcix.) the
tone is changed ; the birds are singing, the
meadows breathe softly of the past, the wood-
lands are holy to the dead ; there has been storm,
but the breath of the day is now balmy, and the
swollen brook murmurs a song "that slights the
coming care." But the greatest change is that

he thinks less of his own pain and more of the pain of mankind. The dim, sweet dawn awakens to myriads on the earth memories of death, and he feels that he is the comrade of all these mourners :

> O wheresoever those may be,
> Betwixt the slumber of the poles,
> To-day they count as kindred souls ;
> They know me not, but mourn with me.

This is the progress at these spaces of time. But if we wish to test it in a better way, we should choose, not the anniversaries of death when the poet is sure to have his sorrow driven home to him, but other times when the mind is freed from so close a pressure of memory. I take now the three Christmas Days.

When the bells of the first Christmas Eve (xxviii.) ring out peace and goodwill, he remembers that he had almost wished to die in his grief before he heard them, but they control his spirit with a touch of joy; and though he scarce dare keep his Christmas Eve, so deep is regret, yet let me give, he cries, their due to ancient use and custom, though they too die. But this bitterness perishes next day. He keeps his Christmas and remembers his friend who was with him the year before. A gentler feeling creeps into his heart. The dead rest, he says, their sleep is sweet ; and then the first prophecy in the poem of the resurrection of the soul from the sorrow of loss is made, and the verse lifts to the thought :

> Our voices took a higher range ;
> Once more we sang—"They do not die
> Nor lose their mortal sympathy
> Nor change to us, although they change ;

O

> " Rapt from the fickle and the frail
>   With gather'd power, yet the same,
>   Pierces the keen seraphic flame
> From orb to orb, from veil to veil."

> Rise, happy morn, rise, holy morn,
>   Draw forth the cheerful day from night;
>   O Father, touch the east, and light
> The light that shone when Hope was born.

A year passes, another Christmas comes (lxxviii.). The snow was silent, the day was calm, and the sense of something for ever gone brooded over all Nature; but this sense of loss was no longer stormy with passion of grief but quiet like the day. They played, he says, their ancient games, but none showed one token of distress; no tears fell. "O," he cries,

> O last regret, regret can die!
>   No—mixt with all this mystic frame,
>   Her deep relations are the same,
> But with long use her tears are dry.

This is not victory, and the grief is still only personal. The poet has not escaped from himself, and the year, which has been spent in a half-intellectual analysis of doubts and the replies of the undertanding to them, has not brought peace to the life of the soul.

Everything is changed at the next Christmas (civ.–cvi.). He hears the bells again, but he has left the old home for another; and the change of place has broken, like the growth of time, the bond of dying use. He holds the night of Christmas Eve solemn to the past, but as it falls, he feels that the merely personal is no more. He sees the stars rise, and the thought of the great course of time moving on to good for all the world, of the summer of mankind that sleeps in the winter seeds, enters his heart.   The universal has come.

> No dance, no motion, save alone
> What lightens in the lucid east
>
> Of rising worlds by yonder wood.
>   Long sleeps the summer in the seed;
>   Run out your measured arcs, and lead
> The closing cycle rich in good.

The full significance of this great change of temper is seen in the next song, which celebrates the incoming of the new year :

> Ring out, wild bells, to the wild sky ;

a poem all men know.   It bids the past die, and the present and future live.   The sound of the bells is happy ; they ring out all evil, and ring in all good.   They ring out the grief that sapped his mind ; they ring out his mournful rhymes, but they ring in the fuller minstrel who sings of the world that is to be, of the Christ who comes again. The personal has wholly perished.   His heart is full of all mankind.   His own victory over sorrow has taught him the victory over sorrow that awaits the race, and the triumph of the hour sounds nobly in the noble verse.

Once more, take the coming of the three spring-tides.   There is some soothing thought in the verses that describe the spring of 1834 (xxxviii.). Six months have passed since Arthur's death, and he thinks that his friend may know that he has sung of his goodness.   Yet though he has some comfort, he has no delight :

No joy the blowing season gives,
    The herald melodies of spring,
    But in the songs I love to sing
A doubtful gleam of solace lives.

When, however, the spring of 1835 arrives (lxxxiii.), his temper is no longer retrospective. Sorrow is with him still, but he prophesies a new time, when his heart will be filled with the joy of a spiritual spring, and his soul sing of its resurrection. "O sweet new year, why dost thou linger, what trouble can live in April days?"

Bring orchis, bring the foxglove spire,
    The little speedwell's darling blue,
    Deep tulips dash'd with fiery dew,
Laburnums, dropping-wells of fire.

O thou, new-year, delaying long,
    Delayest the sorrow in my blood,
    That longs to burst a frozen bud
And flood a fresher throat with song.

And then, last of all, in the spring of 1836 (cxv., cxvi.) regret has wholly died. The re-orient life of the world is the symbol of the departure of the wintry grief that looks back to a friendship that seemed lost, and symbol also of the gain of the new friendship that is to be. His friend's face shines on him while he muses alone; the dear voice speaks to him. "O days and hours," he cries, "your work is this"—

To hold me from my proper place,
    A little while from his embrace,
For fuller gain of after bliss;

That out of distance might ensue
    Desire of nearness doubly sweet;
    And unto meeting, when we meet,
Delight a hundredfold accrue.

These contrasts are enough to mark out clearly, not only that *In Memoriam* is the history of a soul continued from point to point of change during nearly three years, but also that it is the history of a soul in progress from darkness to light, from the selfishness to the unselfishness of sorrow; from despair of God and man to faith in both; and, as a personal matter, from the thought that friendship was utterly lost in death to the thought that friendship was gained through death at a higher level of love and with a deeper union.

I will sketch this progress also. The first part of the poem is entirely personal to himself and his friend. It records the several phases of sorrow— sullen hopelessness, wild unrest, calm despair, tender tears, the woes of memory and association. The end of this period comes in the hidden hope which arises on Christmas Day, and which is followed by those lovely verses about Lazarus and Mary (xxxi., xxxii.), in which the hope of the life to come and the peace of love begin to dawn upon his heart. Then follows that transition time which interests the most those who care for intellectual analysis. It interests me therefore the least of all. It is the least poetical, the least imaginative, the least instinct with beauty and feeling. And Tennyson, while he records the various movements of his mind in it, does not himself think much of them, when he escapes from them. During this passage of thinking, which lasts about a year and a half, various arguments concerning immortality, for and against, are put, and answers attempted to them : mood after mood of the questioning soul is represented, some bright, some dark, half doubt,

half faith ; some of wonder whether the living
shall have life, others of wonder if the dead be
alive ; and, if so, of what kind is their life, and
whether it touches ours at all—a long period of
argumentative questioning, useless for any conclusion, but useful so far that the soul sees at last that
the problem of sorrow and of the future life cannot
be personally solved in the realm of argument.
Then comes the crisis, and the end of all the thought,
of all the doubt—so far as he has gone—in that
long and famous stanza (lxxxv.) beginning :

> This truth came borne with bier and pall,
>   I felt it when I sorrow'd most;
>   'Tis better to have loved and lost
> Than never to have loved at all.

It gathers together all that has past.   It establishes
his belief that his friend is alive, and that his
friend's being is working in his own ; that therefore he has now sufficient comfort to live again in
other men, to remember the mighty hopes that
make us men.   It is the beginning of a new
departure, and is followed at once by the lovely
verses, " Sweet after showers, ambrosial air," in
which all Nature leads to heavenly peace.   Then
through recalling what his friend was, he wishes to
see him as he is.   " Come back to me," he cries,
" come as thou art," and he begins to realise
that the dead belong to our life, till (xcv.) the
splendour of that truth is borne in upon him,
and Tennyson gives his full power to its expression.   This is a sun-risen piece of work—the
evening, and the summer calm upon the lawn, the
night when he is left alone, the hunger at his
heart for union, the reading of the letters, and at

last the passionate intermingling with the living
soul of the dead in waking trance; the momentary
doubt when the exaltation died, and then the
prophecy of the victory, of light and life at hand
for him in the coming of the dawn. Here is the
passage ; it is the embodiment of the second crisis
in this history of the soul :

So word by word, and line by line,
  The dead man touch'd me from the past,
  And all at once it seem'd at last
The living soul was flash'd on mine,

And mine in this was wound, and whirl'd
  About empyreal heights of thought,
  And came on that which is, and caught
The deep pulsations of the world,

Æonian music measuring out
  The steps of Time—the shocks of Chance—
  The blows of Death. At length, my trance
Was cancell'd, stricken thro' with doubt.

Vague words! but ah, how hard to frame
  In matter-moulded forms of speech,
  Or ev'n for intellect to reach
Thro' memory that which I became:

Till now the doubtful dusk reveal'd
  The knolls once more where, couch'd at ease,
  The white kine glimmer'd, and the trees
Laid their dark arms about the field:

And suck'd from out the distant gloom
  A breeze began to tremble o'er
  The large leaves of the sycamore,
And fluctuate all the still perfume,

And gathering freshlier overhead,
  Rock'd the full-foliaged elms, and swung
  The heavy-folded rose, and flung
The lilies to and fro, and said

"The dawn, the dawn " and died away;
  And East and West, without a breath,
  Mixt their dim lights, like life and death,
To broaden into boundless day.

Thus the " spectres of the mind " are laid. Indeed, these questionings of the understanding on subjects beyond its powers, and over which men and women worry themselves into a prolonged infancy of restlessness or a senility of pride, are mere phantasms which the intellect creates in its vanity with which to trouble love. There are only two ways of getting rid of them—one is the way that Tennyson pictures in his own fashion in the rest of *In Memoriam*—the way of love and of faith following on love—and all may read it there, expressed in pure art, and in a series of short poems which are as lovely in form as they are in feeling, as full of the higher human passion as they are of an exquisite sentiment for the beauty of Nature, and so closely knit together by spiritual joy that they—rising incessantly from point to point of universal love—form a single poem. It is the triumphal march of Love. It is also a triumph of art.

The other way of getting rid of these questionings of the understanding concerning those things which it never can prove is to empty the mind of them entirely, abandon all care for anything beyond this present world. It is a way many take, and it has its advantages. It sets the mind free to give itself wholly to the practical business, as it is called, of life. But it has also a disadvantage which may be excessively unpractical. It leaves the soul empty

of the ideas which carry man and his work beyond
this world, and which link all the history and end
of mankind to a wider history, and to an eternal
life. It leaves personal love forlorn, and human
love for all men in the arms of death. The history
of the universal love of man is made by it a history
of universal death.

Many persons stand that easily. It does not
trouble them, but I do not know any poet, even the
most despairing, who does not at times soar above
it or regret it. At least, Tennyson could not
endure it, and he was never satisfied till he had left
it behind him. "Power was with me," he cries,
"in the night;" and in the rush of love by which
he clasped to his spirit the living being of his dead
friend, faith in life filled his heart. "I cannot
understand," he said, "but I love." This is the
beginning of his victory; and as love creates life
and joy wheresoever it moves, all things change
now to the poet. The whole of Nature breathes
and thrills of his friend; every memory of him,
while they walked amidst her beauty, is happy.

> No gray old grange, or lonely fold,
>   Or low morass and whispering reed,
>   Or simple stile from mead to mead,
> Or sheep-walk up the windy wold;
>
> Nor hoary knoll of ash or haw
>   That hears the latest linnet trill,
>   Nor quarry trench'd along the hill,
> And haunted by the wrangling daw;
>
> Nor runlet trickling from the rock;
>   Nor pastoral rivulet that swerves
>   To left and right thro' meadowy curves,
> That feed the mothers of the flock,

But each has pleased a kindred eye,
And each reflects a kindlier day ;
And leaving these, to pass away,
I think once more he seems to die.

All humanity also opens before him, filled with hopes that will not shame themselves. It is here that " Ring out wild bells " comes into the poem, " Ring out the thousand wars of old, ring in the thousand years of peace " ; and with this universal hope, impulse to make his sorrow into love for man deepens his heart. " I will not shut me from my kind," he sings, "nor feed with sighs the passing wind." Then, that he may know how he ought to live for man, he draws, in a succession of short poems, the picture of his friend's character and of how *he* would have lived for the race. And out of it all arises this——That knowledge is needed to save the world from its outward and inward pain, but that knowledge is not enough. Wisdom, such as Arthur had, must be added to knowledge, and must rule it ; and wisdom is of things that Love knows, but that knowledge cannot know. " Come then, my friend, enter into me ; quicken me with this wisdom of thine ; let love be all in all in me. I could not find God alive, nor my friend, in the questionings of the understanding, but now I love and I have found them both—found God, and my friend in God. And with them I have found life, life for myself and life for all my brother men. I see the progress of the world as I have seen my own progress; I see the working of love in the evolution of mankind; I see ourselves labouring on, and our labour useful and lovely when it is for others ; and, lastly, I see the great labour of God's love underlying all and moving to a perfect close."

> And all, as in some piece of art,
> Is toil co-operant to an end.

And the conclusion that sums the whole is a solemn prayer to God that all the world may conquer, as he has conquered, the besieging years, and the powers of sorrow.

> O living will that shalt endure
>   When all that seems shall suffer shock,
>   Rise in the spiritual rock,
> Flow thro' our deeds and make them pure,
>
> That we may lift from out the dust
>   A voice as unto him that hears,
>   A cry above the conquer'd years
> To one that with us works, and trust,
>
> With faith that comes of self-control,
>   The truths that never can be proved
>   Until we close with all we loved,
> And all we flow from, soul in soul.

Nine years after Arthur Hallam's death, Tennyson's sister was married, and he writes her marriage song as the epilogue to his poem. We see then what was his temper of mind in 1842. Had he gone back, had he lost the fruits of the victory he had won? Love is not less, he says, but more. It is solid-set like a statue; it is moulded into calm of soul, all passion spent, and he has himself grown into something greater than before; so that his songs of dead regret seem "echoes out of weaker times." It is not that he loves his friend less, but that his friend is with him so closely, in so vivid a life and with sc

great a power—being as it were a part of God and
of the life of God in him—that only joy remains.

Even as he sits at the wedding feast, he feels
Arthur with them, wishing joy. And then, as
before, he passes from the personal, from the peace
of home and its shelter, to think of the greater
world of man, of the nobler race which God is
making out of ours. He retires when night falls,
and looks out on the skies as the moon rises.
" Touch with thy shade and splendour," he cries,
the bridal doors ; let a soul from their marriage
draw from out the vast, and strike his being into
bounds, and be a closer link betwixt us and the
crowning race, the higher humanity to be, of which
my friend (and he sweeps back, enamoured of unity
like a poet, to the first subject of *In Memoriam*)
was a noble type—the race to the making of
which God is moving forward the whole creation.
Thus he ends with the universal, with the reitera-
tion of the victory of man over pain in the eternity
of the love of God :

> That God, which ever lives and loves,
> One God, one law, one element,
> And one far-off divine event,
> To which the whole creation moves.

Seven years then passed by, during which
Tennyson still revised his poem, during which his
spirit was continually kept close to the conclusions
of faith and hope and love, and of love the
greatest of these three, to which he had come in
In Memoriam. How would he feel towards these
when so long a term of years had come to an end ?
We have an answer to that question in the

prologue to the poem written in 1849. Every conclusion he had come to is confirmed and re-expressed in that profound and religious psalm. All that he loved, hoped for, and believed, is there laid in the hands, held in the grace, and enshrined in the spirit of Him who is " Immortal Love."

CHAPTER IX

"MAUD" AND THE WAR-POEMS.

THE main point concerning Tennyson himself on which I dwelt in the last chapter was that he had freed himself in that poem from the merely personal. He has passed in *In Memoriam* from the particular to the universal. Before he had finished that poem, the pain of the world of man had flowed into his soul. He had reached full manhood in his art. From this time forth then, from 1850, when Tennyson was just over forty years of age, a vaster emotion belongs to his poetry, the solemn swell of the passion of mankind; yet the poetry does not lose, when he desires it, its happy brightness. The idyll of *The Brook*, published along with *Maud*, is as gay as it is gentle. Then, too, though his poetry has thus more than before to do with the larger life of man, he can still see Nature with the keen sight and enjoyment of youth. Moreover, he can still " follow the Gleam," still breathe with ease the ideal air, though his experience has been sad, though maturer years have led him to keep closer in his work to the facts of real life.

His poetry has certainly lost some of the animation, opulence, unconsciousness in singing, which are qualities of youth——of which qualities, however, he seemed to have less than other poets, because graver qualities, unusual in youth, balanced them ; but it has gained more character ; it knows itself better ; it has more of the wisdom of life in it——and yet it has not lost passion. Nay, that is more profound ; there is a greater general intensity of feeling on subjects worthy of deep regard. Moreover, the same width and depth of feeling with which he wrote about religion in *In Memoriam* now extended itself over the movements of the world. He is in closer sympathy with the life of England at home and abroad. The stories of the joys and sorrows of men and women which he took as subjects in 1842 (*Dora* and the rest) are now continued, but the colours in which he paints them are fuller and deeper in hue, and they are also more various. He writes of the farmer, the sailor, the city clerk, the parson and lawyer and squire. *Enoch Arden, Aylmer's Field, Sea Dreams, The Brook, The Grandmother, The Northern Farmer, The Sailor Boy*, prove with what variety and power and charm he wrought at this vein, and he loved to work in it to the very end.

But it was not only English life at home which engaged him. He followed up that life abroad. Rumours of war and war itself, after 1850, stirred his heart. The patriotic spirit which he felt so strongly all his life was now awakened, first by the threatening aspect of France, then by the death of the Duke of Wellington, and then by the Crimean war. Three short poems, written in 1852, and published in the newspapers, belong to the French menace : *Britons, Guard your Own ! The Third of*

February ! and *Hands all round; God the tyrant's cause confound !* They are sturdy, full-bodied things, and *The Third of February* maintained against our shameless alliance with the Man of December the moral censure of England on his murderous work :

> What ! have we fought for Freedom from our prime,
> At last to dodge and palter with a public crime ?

We are grateful to Tennyson for these words, though afterwards he seemed to be a partisan of the war in which the Third Napoleon became the comrade in arms of England. But we may pardon him for that, for it was his long hatred of Russia for her bloody work in Poland which was at the root of his approval of the Crimean war. This patriotism had soon a noble subject in the praise of the great Duke. Tennyson issued his Ode on the day of Wellington's burial, and republished it a year after with many notable changes. This is one of his finest poems. It was fitting that the foremost man in England, who had worn his honours with a quiet simplicity for so many years in the "fierce light" which shines on a world-wide fame, and in whom the light never found anything mean or fearful, should, after his death, receive this great and impassioned tribute. What he did in politics was always questionable. He was nothing of a statesman, as Tennyson calls him. He proved his inability when he was called to the Premiership. Then he was first arrogant, and afterwards perplexed by the mischief he wrought. Indeed, he was profoundly ignorant of England ; but, when he found out his ignorance, he had the good sense

of a great general. He knew when to retreat, and
he retreated, even though his retreat had the
appearance of a flight. He stood "four-square to
all the winds that blew," but when all the winds
became one wind, he opened the doors to it and
bade the Crown and his peers give way. This
was the wisest thing he did in his old age, and it
is somewhat characteristic of Tennyson that, except
in one line, "rich in saving common sense," he
takes no notice of it at all.

"Let all England mourn her greatest son, let all
England thank God for him, and bury him with
honour upon honour"—that is the motive of the
beginning of the poem; and it is worthy to be felt
by a poet and by a nation. Magnanimity and magnificence, great-mindedness and great-doing, are the
life-blood of a people. To celebrate them with a
lavish splendour when he who embodied them in
life is dead, is a lesson in a people's education.
Then Tennyson passes to the Duke's glory in war,
and perhaps in all commemorative odes there is
nothing finer than his imagination of Nelson waking
from his grave in St. Paul's and wondering who was
coming, with this national mourning, to lie beside
him:

> "Who is he that cometh, like an honour'd guest,
> With banner and with music, with soldier and with priest,
> With a nation weeping, and breaking on my rest?"
>
> Mighty Seaman, this is he
> Was great by land as thou by sea.
>
> *   *   *   *   *
>
> This is he that far away
> Against the myriads of Assaye
> Clash'd with his fiery few and won;

and the poet, starting from this early battle,

P

sketches with rapid and clear pencil the great wars till the day of Waterloo. I wish the division of the poem (vii.) beginning—

A people's voice! we are a people yet—

were excluded from the poem. But that would be to wish away one of Tennyson's most characteristic utterances as a patriot. Nevertheless, it is too exclusively English, too controversial, too much an attack on France, too contemptuous of the people whom he sees only as the mob; too fond of the force of great men to the exclusion of the force of the collective movements of the nation. A great artist should not overstep so much the limits of temperance; or, to put this otherwise, he should not lose his sympathy with the whole of humanity in his sympathy with his own country.

This is, however, as great a poem as the character was which it celebrated. The metrical movement rushes on where it ought to rush, delays where it ought to delay. Were the poem set by Handel, its rhythmical movements could scarcely be more fit from point to point to the things spoken off, more full of stately, happy changes. Moreover, the conduct of the piece is excellent. It swells upwards in fuller harmony and growing thought till it reaches its climax in the division (vi.) about Nelson and Wellington. Then it slowly passes downwards in solemn strains like a storm dying in the sky, and at the end closes in soft spiritual passages of ethereal sound, like the lovely clouds about the setting sun when the peace of evening has fallen on a tempestuous day. Its conduct is then the conduct of one form of the true

lyric, that whose climax is in the midst, and not at
the close.

During the years which followed this poem
Tennyson's mind was kept close to the subject of
war, though his dislike to France had to be placed
in abeyance, for these were the years of the
Crimean war.   In 1854 the news of the splendid
and foolish charge of the Light Brigade reached the
country, and set it all on fire.   When it was made,
and a petulant mistake had all but annihilated the
Brigade, we forgot the folly in the glory of those
who rode so steadily to all but certain death.
Steady obedience, cool self-sacrifice, disbelief in
the impossible, courage which rises higher the
nearer death is at hand, are some of the things
which have made England.   They made her glory
in this deed of war.   It was more the glory of
the troopers than of the leader, and Tennyson has
felt that throughout his song.   And since he felt
it, I wish that he had celebrated Inkerman rather
than this isolated and splendid blunder.   Nevertheless, it was a fine thing done in the face of the
whole world, and it has handed down so great a tradition of mortal courage and magnificence that it was
well worthy of song, and Tennyson could hardly
help taking it as a poetic theme.   He did it well ;
but the weakness inherent in the subject (" some
one had blundered ") prevented him from doing it
very well.

In after years he took another subject of the
same kind, and out of the same battle—*The Charge
of the Heavy Brigade at Balaclava*.   The poem has
its own force, but it is too like its predecessor.
It first appeared in 1882, and was published with

a prologue and epilogue in 1885. The prologue is addressed to General Hamley, and contains a charming description of the view from his Sussex home, and an allusion to the glory of the war in Egypt against Arabi. But it is the epilogue which it is right to notice in this place, for it contains his defence of his war-poems against Irene, who stands, I suppose, for Peace, but who is with all a poet's love of the personal, made into a delightful girl.

> You wrong me, passionate little friend.
> I would that wars should cease,
> I would the globe from end to end
> Might sow and reap in peace.

Yes, Tennyson loved peace, and has sung of it with grace and loveliness ; but the objection men have taken to the praise of war in *Maud* is none the less. War is held in *Maud* to be the proper cure for the evils of peace, and it is not a cure, but an additional disease. In this defence also, he still clings to the notion that Trade, " with kindly links of gold," may refrain the Powers from war, when Trade, as at present conducted, is the most fruitful cause of war. Moreover, he sees, in this defence, no way of making true peace but fighting, meeting force by force. A poet might have thought of other ways ; yet it was scarcely possible that Tennyson, with his character, should have seen those other ways. We must not expect from a man that which is beyond his nature ; and therefore we accept with gratitude his declaration in this epilogue—

> And who loves War for War's own sake
> Is fool, or crazed, or worse.

There is no one also who will not agree with the view expressed at the end of the epilogue—that it is right, even though the realm be in the wrong in the war, " to crown with song the warrior's noble deed."

> And here the Singer for his Art
> Not all in vain may plead
> " The song that nerves a nation's heart,
> Is in itself a deed."

This is truth he sings, and it makes us wish that he had written more war-lyrics on the noble gests of Englishmen. He did write two extraordinarily fine things—*The Fight of the Revenge* and *The Defence of Lucknow*, but the latter is a little too detailed, a little too historical.

The Charge of the Light Brigade was written in 1854. In the year following, *Maud* appeared. The war element continues to live in this poem, and its presence does not improve, but injures it. War presides at its conception, is inwoven with it, and directs its end. The beginning of the poem, which attacks, in the mouth of a nervous, slothful man, the evils of a world whose only god is commerce and whose goddess is competition, is written with apparently the direct purpose of holding up, at the close, war as the remedy for those evils.

> For I trust if an enemy's fleet came yonder round by the hill,
> And the rushing battle-bolt sang from the three-decker out of the foam,
> That the smooth-faced, snub-nosed rogue would leap from his counter and till,
> And strike, if he could, were it but with his cheating yard-wand, home.

This is said in the character of the spleenful hero, but yet the verse is Tennyson's own. The war waged *then* would be in defence of hearth and home—a just war. But the Crimean war was not in that category. And the poem ends with that war as the cure for the evils of peace. There is too little distinction made between war and war.

Further on, the death of Maud's brother in a duel at the hand of Maud's lover, which dissolves the love story in catastrophe, contrasts the sin of private war with the nobility of public war for a worthy cause. The madness caused by this private revenge is healed by the lover joining in the national effort to right a wrong. The social war of competition is to be also healed by the spirit of sacrifice in the nation which is aroused by a public war. The whole of this, as I have said before, is a great pity. Moreover, this part of the subject is artistically unfortunate, for the Crimean war was the most foolish, the most uncalled for, and the least deliberate of all our wars. It mixed us up with the Emperor of the French, a miserable companionship for a country which desired honour and freedom. Its management at first was a disgrace to the War Office of England. The subject, then, of the poem was radically bad so far as the war-element in it was concerned, and this acted not only on those parts of the poem which belonged to the war, but also, even without the artist's consciousness of it, disturbed the beauty of the whole, and weakened the emotional impression he desired his work to make. An element, troubling to art, underlies the handling and the conduct of the poem.

But, in spite of this, *Maud*, in its joy and
sorrow alike, is the loveliest of Tennyson's longer
poems. It does not possess much natural description. We see the landscape only in allusions, but
it is clear enough. Above is the moor-land, dark
purple ; below is the shore and the loud-resound-
ing sea, whose restless waves in storm thunder on
the pebbled beach. Between the moor and the
sea, on the low ground, are the village and
the village church, "gables and spire together" ;
and on the hillside the hall and garden where
Maud lives ; and not far off the lover's house,
a haunted place, near which is a flowery wood
and a dark red sandstone hollow in the hill.
This is the scene where so fateful a passion is
played, and there is not much of Nature in it.
But here and there throughout the poem there
are separate touches full of observation :*

"A million emeralds break from the ruby-budded lime,"

is as faithful to the colour, as this which follows is
to the sound of the thing described :

> Just now the dry-tongued laurels' pattering talk
> Seem'd her light foot along the garden walk.

He saw every year the temper of a south-coast
gale and the look of the sky :

* Nothing can be closer to truth than the line
"The scream of a madden'd beach dragg'd down by the wave ;"
but it is only true for the beach of the southern coast where the
sea-rounded pebbles of the chalk, piled in loose banks on the
shore, are rolled over and over, grating and grinding, by the
retreating wave.

> Morning arises stormy and pale,
> No sun, but a wannish glare
> In fold upon fold of hueless cloud,
> And the budded peaks of the wood are bow'd,
> Caught and cuffed by the gale:
> I had fancied it would be fair.

Contrast with this wild cloudy morning the quiet pure sky of a night in spring—fitted, as it is, to the dark calm which had followed the lover's madness:

> My mood is changed, for it fell at a time of year
> When the face of night is fair on the dewy downs,
> And the shining daffodil dies, and the Charioteer
> And starry Gemini hang like glorious crowns
> Over Orion's grave low down in the west,
> That like a silent lightning under the stars
> She seem'd to divide in a dream from a band of the blest.

These are broad sketches, but Tennyson can do the most minute and finest drawing, and no better example exists of it than the description of the tiny shell the lover finds on the beach. The shell is dead, but the poet's animating hand cannot bear that it should be lifeless ; and he images, with the finest sympathy, with ornamenting love, its last inhabitant:

> The tiny cell is forlorn,
> Void of the little living will
> That made it stir on the shore.
> Did he stand at the diamond door
> Of his house in a rainbow frill ?
> Did he push, when he was uncurl'd,
> A golden foot or a fairy horn
> Thro' his dim water-world ?

These are direct descriptions of Nature, but *Maud* is remarkable, even among the other poems, for the determined way in which Nature is charged in it

with the human passions.   The hollow where the
lover's ruined father slew himself is red, flower and
rock, to the eyes of his son.

> Its lips in the field above are dabbled with blood-red heath,
> The red-ribb'd ledges drip with a silent horror of blood.

He had lost his fortune by speculation, wherefore,
when he walked out,

> the wind like a broken worldling wail'd,
> And the flying gold of the ruin'd woodlands drove through
> the air.

When the lover first hopes for Maud's love,
every bird in the sky cries to her and calls to
her; the daisies that her foot touches are rose-
tinted by her touch.   All the world from west to
east, all the seas, blush with joy when she is on
the point of yielding.   The great cedar that sighs
for Lebanon sighs no more, for it is haunted by
her starry head, over whom

> thy darkness must have spread
> With such delight as theirs of old, thy great
> Forefathers of the thornless garden, there
> Shadowing the snow-limb'd Eve from whom she came.

The stars, feeling with his joy, go in and out on
the heavens with merry play.

> A livelier emerald twinkles on the grass,
> A purer sapphire melts into the sea.

The swell of the long waves on the shore is
enchanted ; and in that lovely song, when her
lover waits for Maud in the dawn, and the planet
of love begins

> to faint in the light that she loves
>   On a bed of daffodil sky,

he transfers all the passion of his heart to the
flowers and the flowers become part of his heart.
" The soul of the rose went into my blood." The
lilies kept awake all night with him. When she is
coming at last, the garden speaks for him :

> There has fallen a splendid tear
>   From the passion-flower at the gate.
> She is coming, my dove, my dear :
>   She is coming, my life, my fate ;
> The red rose cries—" She is near, she is near ; "
>   And the white rose weeps—" She is late ; "
> The larkspur listens—" I hear, I hear ; "
>   And the lily whispers—" I wait."

No example can be better of this method by which
Nature is made the reflection and illustration of a
human soul, except perhaps this beautiful thing—

> From the meadow your walks have left so sweet
>   That whenever a March wind sighs
> He sets the jewel-print of your feet
>   In violets blue as your eyes,
> To the woody hollows in which we meet
>   And the valleys of Paradise.

As to the upbuilding of the poem, Tennyson
called it a Monodrama. The story, though very
simple, is capable of bringing together a host
of complex feelings, and in the one character of
the hero they all clash into a drama of the soul.
Fate, too, broods over it from the beginning. Given
the characters of Maud and her lover, and the
events that preceded their love, the tragedy is
inevitable. This is a justly dramatic situation.
We expect the ruin ; and the transient happiness

of the lovers only renders it more pitiable. But
the openly dramatic part of the poem ends with
the first part where Maud's brother is slain by her
lover, and the girl dies of the double pain. The
second part is the result of this catastrophe on
the life of the hero—his flight, his madness, and
the resurrection of his manliness. The dramatic
element in this part is in the mind of the lover—
in the involution and struggle of the sane and
insane in him.

The hero is a nervous, affectionate, half-
hysterical person, often gentle, often violent from
weakness ; who lives on the edge of the
supernatural ; morbidly excited by the suicide
of his father, by his lonely life, and by brooding
in inaction on those iniquities of commerce which
ruined his father, and which he imputes to the
whole of society. The roots of his hair are
stirred when his father's corse is brought home at
night. He hears the dead moaning in his house
at noon, and his own name called in the silence.
The physical irritability transfers itself to his moral
world, and becomes a weak anger with man and
God without one effort to meet the evils at
which he screams. His first utterance in the
poem is a long shriek in a high falsetto note
against the wrongs and curses which come of
a vile peace. "Is it peace or war?" he cries ;
"better war ! loud war by land and sea."
And then he thinks of Maud, who was his play-
mate. She is coming home. "What is she
now? My dreams are bad. She may bring me a
curse." When Maud comes, his diseased pride
pictures her as cold and contemptuous, while his

heart is thrilled by her charm. Pride and first love are at variance, and he has no strength to decide between them. Now one, now the other gains the mastery. And in the strife, he breaks into fury with the world again. All men and women are slanderers and cheats, and Nature is one with rapine. " The whole little wood where I sit is a world of plunder and prey." And we are puppets in the hand of an unseen power, and degraded puppets. Nature and man and God, if there be a God, are all bad.

On this shattered character Maud dawns like the morning ; fresh, simple and young, full of gentle feeling, easily won to love; romantic, having her womanhood in a sweet purity and grace, but as yet with no character—characterless, like Miranda. And her joyousness breaks in on his gloom. He hears her singing :

> A passionate ballad gallant and gay,
> A martial song like a trumpet's call.
> Singing alone in the morning of life,
> In the happy morning of life and of May.

Singing of honour and death in battle—for now the war motive steals in—till he is ready to weep for a sordid time, and for his own base languor. From that moment their love runs on from point to point. His character forbids him to believe in her; yet he cannot but believe in her a little, for love has mastered him. Jealousy comes next, and in the turmoil within he recognises that he is not a true man. It is a man the country wants, some strong man to rule it ; it is a man he needs himself to be, and the midmost motive of the poem is in the lines :

> And ah for a man to arise in me,
> That the man I am may cease to be!

Then comes the outburst of this enfeebled character, half conscious of its possibility of madness, for the joy of love——one of the finer passionate things of Tennyson :

> O let the solid ground
>   Not fail beneath my feet
> Before my life has found
>   What some have found so sweet ;
> Then let come what come may,
> What matter if I go mad,
> I shall have had my day.

He meets Maud in the woodland places, and begins to hope, and at night he wanders round her house. And here Tennyson calls up again the special note in this lover's nature, the nervous thrill which passes into presentiment of evil even in the moment of his joyous hope, and which is awakened by so slight a thing as all the curtains of the house being drawn close. He hears no sound where he stands but the rivulet running and the dash of the waves, but he looks and sees all round the house

> The death-white curtain drawn ;
> Felt a horror over me creep,
> Prickle my skin and catch my breath,
> Knew that the death-white curtain meant but sleep,
> Yet I shudder'd and thought like a fool of the sleep of
>   death.

The same half-physical, half-imaginative horror comes on him in the very height of his delight, when Maud has promised to love him. All the beginning of the splendid ode of joy he sings to his heart is full of love's loveliest rapture:

I have led her home, my love, my only friend.

It continues rapturous to almost the close. But mortal affairs never stand for long on the topmost peak. And this man was sure to tremble into a suggestion of misery when he was most victorious in delight. "Beat, happy stars," he cries, "timing with things below,

> Beat with my heart more blest than heart can tell,
> Blest, but for some dark undercurrent woe
> That seems to draw—but it shall not be so :
> Let all be well, be well.

Another element comes into the poem when Maud's brother arrives. The lover hates him. Is he not the son of the man who cheated and ruined his father ? Yet Maud loves her brother, and Maud has loved himself. Shall he not then cease to hate ? Shall he not forgive ? May he never forget, in his hatred of the brother, all he owes to the sister ! Yes, may God make him then more wretched even than he has been. And he feels hysterically happy that he is free from hate, when, in reality, it only needs a touch to bring the hatred to the surface and to make him forget everything in the moment, except the moment. He has no strength, no steadiness, no self-control. All this is careful preparation for the catastrophe, and for the madness that follows it. The inevitableness of the end is seen in the character. And it is fine intellectual work, an excellence in this poem which is too much forgotten in the admiration we give to its beautiful love-passages—an excellence which is even greater in the descriptions of the lover's madness in the second part of the poem.

At last, these two meet in the garden, and while he waits, he sings that lovely song which all the world knows, and on which I need not dwell, but in which, through all its eager emotion, the poet does not lose his intellectual self-control, nor his steady directing of his subject. He prepares, at its very close, for one of the most forcible motives which he uses regarding the lover's madness in the second part——the motive of the living man believing that he is dead and that Maud, were she to come, would make him rise again. Here is this preparing passage, a *leitmotif* for the next part, the melody of which Wagner would introduce again and again in the second part :

> She is coming, my own, my sweet ;
>   Were it ever so airy a tread,
> My heart would hear her and beat,
>   Were it earth in an earthy bed ;
> My dust would hear her and beat,
>   Had I lain for a century dead ;
> Would start and tremble under her feet,
>   And blossom in purple and red.

She comes ; the brother finds them together ; in rage he strikes Maud's lover, answering a fierce outbreak of wrath. But even before his sweetheart this lover has no power over himself, and he strikes again. The duel follows ; the brother is slain, and Maud sees the slaughter. On the top of rapturous love comes bloody tragedy.

The second part follows. The lover has fled, Maud's wild cry in his ears, and a ghostly image of her haunting his steps. His brain is for a time on the verge of madness, and Tennyson pictures this tottering condition along with love's pathetic agony. Then a time of real madness supervenes, and this also the poet strives to paint as it would be in the character he has drawn. Both these states of mind and emotion are wrought with the most careful intellectual consideration. A study of the characteristics of madness and its approach seems to lie behind them, and to have preceded the emotional representation of the mortal sorrow and love of the hero. This scientific element is a little too prominent, at least it is so in Part v., which begins,

> Dead, long dead,
> Long dead !

in which the madness has fully come. The mind of a madman gambols from the point in hand, and Tennyson has skilfully wrought this out. But these sudden changes do not arise, as Tennyson makes them arise, from a thought or a memory suggested by what the madman is saying to himself, so much as from some physical change in himself, or from some suggestion to his senses from the world without. Here his madness is set off on a new path by the words he hears himself using. He runs away on the new images they suggest to him. And as this is the case, the whole of this Part v. falls almost into a logical order, as if at the bottom of his madness the man was not mad at all. We can trace, then, the elaborate argumentative way in which Tennyson has worked it out—a thing we cannot do, for example, in the madness of Ophelia —a similar madness of love and sorrow and death. The picture is also carefully made up of scattered impressions recorded in the first part of the poem. These are apparently huddled together in the disorder of madness, but it is not really so. They

have a connection, and the stitches which unite
them are too clear. The interspersed reflections
are also too sane—as, for instance,

> Friend, to be struck by the public foe,
> Then to strike him and lay him low,
> That were a public merit, far,
> Whatever the Quaker holds, from sin ;
> But the red life spilt for a private blow—
> I swear to you, lawful and lawless war
> Are scarcely even akin.

A madman might think a part of it, but not the
whole, and not in that way.

Even in two previous divisions (ii. and iv.)
reflections are introduced which are too exclusively
of the intellect. They lower the emotional note by
their intrusion. The verse in division ii.—

> Strange, that the mind, when fraught
> With a passion so intense
> One would think that it well
> Might drown all life in the eye—
> That it should, by being so overwrought,
> Suddenly strike on a sharper sense
> For a shell, a flower, little things
> Which else would have been past by !
> And now, I remember, I,
> When he lay dying there,
> I noticed one of his many rings
> (For he had many, poor worm) and thought
> It is his mother's hair,

is out of tune with the rest of this lovely and
pathetic poem. I wish also that the physiological
reflection in verse 8 of division iv. were out of the
poem :

> 'Tis the blot upon the brain
> That *will* show itself without.

Every now and then the science Tennyson chose

Q

to meddle with enters into his art in this distressful
way.

With these slight exceptions, the divisions ii. iii.
and iv., in which the approach of madness is drawn,
are of extraordinary loveliness.   They do not sound
the deep-sea depths of sorrow, remorse, and love,
but they are of an exquisite and pathetic gentleness, and their grief and love are as profound as
the character Tennyson has drawn was capable of
feeling.   In iv. he rises with that lonely cry at the
beginning

> O that 'twere possible
> After long grief and pain
> To find the arms of my true love
> Round me once again

into perhaps the tenderest music of sorrow in all
his poetry, half of sweet memories of the past, half
of broken misery in the present, and with one
touch of hope for the future made out of the image
of his love in heaven.   If only he had left out
these lines in the last verse,

> And I loathe the square and streets,
> And the faces that one meets,
> Hearts with no love for me,

the end would be as perfect as the beginning.

Part iii. is the resurrection of the lover, and is
dedicated to war as the redeeming power.   The
first verse is beautiful, but it is strange for a soul in
the peace of heaven to place a new hope for the
world in the Crimean war; nor do the fine passages
and river-rolling metre of the rest of the poem
excuse, in my opinion, the advocacy of war, by
means of art, as the saviour from national sin.

In conclusion, there are yet two things to say. The first regards the intellectual power revealed in the first and second parts of the poem, in due subordination to the rule of passionate imagination. There is no view so mistaken as the common view, that poets, because they deal chiefly with the emotions, are for that very reason less intellectual than men whose work lies in science, philosophy, logic, or law. On the contrary, it is in the sphere of the highest and deepest emotions, when they are so controlled by the artist's will towards the perfect representation of his idea as not to flame in violent rush but to burn with a steady core of white fire, that the loftiest efforts and successes of the intellect of man are made, and reach their keenest point of expression. Every great poem, then—and no poem can be great without intensity of feeling—is also a treasure-house of the intellectual powers, and can be studied, like a universe, from that point of view. *Maud* is not one of the least of these.

Secondly, I have made certain criticisms on *Maud*, and I am troubled by having made them. To point out imperfections, or what seem to me imperfections, in a poem I love so dearly, is like a patriot who draws attention to the imperfections of his country. But if he love her well and honestly, his country is none the worse. She is so far above him, and her beauty is so clear, and he is so conscious of it, that no one, he thinks, will imagine that he desires to lessen the world's admiration of her. And *Maud* is so beautiful a poem that the small regrets of criticism are as nothing in comparison with the large delights its poetry gives.

Moreover, the criticisms may be all wrong. When we approach a great poet's work, our proper position is humility.

But these criticisms have been all of one kind. They have objected to the intrusion of scientific analysis into a work of art, and to the direction of it to the support of a disputable moral theory—that the nation and the individual may be set free from selfishness by war. These objections are stronger against *Maud* than against a different kind of poem, because *Maud* is, of all Tennyson's longer poems, the most distinctly a piece of pure art. All the love story, both in its joy and sorrow, lies solely in the realm of imaginative and passionate art, and its loveliness is there supreme. The jarring note then which is made by intellectual analysis, and by moral purpose, pushed into this sweeter and higher realm, is more harsh and grating than it would be in a poem not so divinely beautiful. This, which is the real excuse for the criticisms, is in itself an additional homage to those lovely, unalloyed parts of the poem which are charged with personal emotion alone.

It is difficult to say anything in praise of these parts, because that which reaches a high loveliness is above all praise. It is loved of those who can love it. When they are asked *why* they love it, they answer, "I love it because I love it," and when they are asked why it is good, they answer, "Because it is good ; he that hath ears to hear let him hear." What are we to do with folk who cannot hear the soft, wild, changeful music of verse and of emotion——repeating one another in difference, each echo awakening a new melody, and beauty making all their atmosphere—of poems like

A voice by the cedar tree,

or, still more varied in interwoven changes of feeling, each change it makes with its own metrical form—that high canzone of enchanted love—

I have led her home, my love, my only friend.

But why should I say more ? It is impossible to criticise these things, to explain why they or the Garden Song are beautiful, or why the poem of the broken heart, " O that 'twere possible," reaches in simplicity those depths of sorrow where beauty sits in the garb of pity and subdues the soul.

CHAPTER X

IDYLLS OF THE KING

IN the *Idylls of the King* Tennyson has worked up into a whole the ancient story of Arthur, a story which is at least a thousand years old. How it first arose none can tell. Whether it has any historical basis, it is also impossible to decide. It is supposed that there was an historical Arthur who fought twelve great battles with the English heathen, and who had many hero-chieftains under his sway and in his devotion, but the more we look at him the more his figure recedes into the mist of legend or of myth. Even the country where he reigned, and the lands over which his wars were waged, are not known to us. Some scholars make him a warrior of Southern Britain. Others place him in the North, beyond the Border, and he fights with the Saxon chiefs from Dumbarton to the eastern coast, beating them back in twelve great battles. Out of the dim vapour of ancientry these two great figures rise, and the name of Arthur alone mingles them into one. Tennyson takes the first tradition, and it is the one that has the most prevailed in literature.

It is not, however, with an historical, but with a mythical Arthur that we have to deal, and we need not be forced to surrender the wild island of Tintagil, the mystic expanse of Lyonnesse, the rock of Glastonbury rising from its marshes, and the lovely meadows round Caerleon upon Usk. *There* is our romantic country ; there the legendary land where Arthur was born ; there the valley of Avalon where he took refuge when wounded to the death. There is not one touch of the real world in all the scenery that Tennyson invents in his poem. It belongs throughout to that country which eye hath not seen nor ear heard, but which the heart of man has imagined. It is more than invented landscape. It often breathes the atmosphere of the fairy lands, and of those dreams which open the spaceless realms beyond our senses. It seems to be born before the sight and then to die and be born in another form—changing, yet unchanged. No mortal hands have built the city of Arthur and his palace. It is no land dwelt in by bold bad men we see, when Arthur rides through the mountains and finds the diamonds ; when Geraint and Enid go through the green gloom of the wood ; when Galahad rides over the black swamp, leaping from bridge to bridge till he sail to the spiritual city ; when Lancelot drives through the storm to the enchanted towers of Carbonek seven days across the sea. Nor is the Nature actual Nature, but that which is seen

> From magic casements opening on the foam
> Of perilous seas, in fairy lands forlorn.

And when we can disburden ourselves of the ethics and allegory, the personages are still as dreamlike as the landscape, old as the seas that roll over

Lyonnesse, and yet young for ever in imagination.
In our everyday world the Arthur and Guinevere
of Romance, Lancelot and the Lady of the Lake,
Gawain and Galahad, Percivale and Elaine are unreal
shapes; yet how real they are in a better world!
The interests of the world we call real fade and die,
our children will not care for them; for half of
them, for those that are not founded on love, we do
not care ourselves; but the interests of romance are
eternal.   They blossom into a new spring year by
year, and we take more thought for the fates of
Lancelot and Guinevere than we do for what the
Swede intends or what the French.   For " fable is
Love's world," and the great myths and their figures
are the dear inhabitants of the heart of man.   Centuries have been stirred and thrilled by Arthur
and his knights.   England, France, Germany, and
Italy have awakened into creation at their Celtic
touch; and poetry, painting, sculpture, and music
have replied to their enchantment.   From Cornwall or the North the story got to Wales; from
Wales it fled to Brittany.   From Brittany it
returned to Wales and crossed the March into
England in the *Brut* of Layamon, the first English
poem of the imagination after the Conquest.
But before that time, it had got from Brittany
into France, and from France in French to
England, where prose tales in Latin and poems
in English and in Norman French sent it far and
wide.   Chaucer owned its power; Malory embodied
it ; Spenser seized it ; Milton thought of it as an
epic; Dryden considered it ; Wordsworth touched
it ; Tennyson took up its lyre again; Morris
and Swinburne and Arnold entered into its

enchanted land. But it was characteristic of Tennyson's steadiness of temper and fulness of thought that he should try to make his form of it complete and new-created. At first it moved him only as romance, and we have seen how his youth played with it in *The Lady of Shalott*, in *Sir Galahad*, and in the ride of Lancelot and Guinevere through woods of love and spring. Then in the *Morte d'Arthur* the story was fitted in 1842 by certain modern touches to modern life, yet these had to be explained by the prologue and epilogue. In that poem itself the tale was chief; it follows the old romance and breathes its air.

In 1842, when the *Morte d'Arthur* appeared, Tennyson does not seem to have thought of making the story allegorical. I do not even think that when the first four *Idylls* were published—*Geraint and Enid; Merlin and Vivien; Lancelot and Elaine; and Guinevere*—Tennyson wrote them with a set allegorical intention. They are only modernised by being made a representation of true love and false love. Vivien the harlot is set over against the tender innocence of Elaine. Enid, the true wife, is opposed to Guinevere who has been untrue. The men also represent different phases of love as modern as they are ancient. Geraint and Merlin, Lancelot and Arthur, have each their distinct lesson—beyond the story— to modern life. They have not yet become allegorical, and even the lesson, the ethical aim, is as yet subordinate to the story. True conduct, as is just in art, is indirectly, not directly taught.

But when we come to 1870—to the volume which began with *The Coming of Arthur*—the inner intention of the whole poem seems to be changed. The making of a kind of epic out of the story of Arthur, which should have an instructive but indirect relation to the moral needs of society and the individual, is placed upon the second plane. The poem is now an allegory of the soul of man warring with sense, and passing on its way through life to death, and through death to resurrection. The great rulers of the kingdom of human nature —the intellect, the conscience, the will, the imagination, the divine spirit in man, are shadowed forth in mystic personages.   The historic powers which stand outside the soul and help it to reign and work——the Church, the Law, the great Graces of God——are also embodied.   Moreover, the various conditions of human nature in its growth from brutality to an ordered kingdom, that which saves or loses true life, the general desires and tendencies of man, the temptations which beset him, the wise and unwise views of the goal of life, the love which saves, the love which ruins, the religious passion which leads aright and that which leads astray, are symbolised before us in a number of other personages, episodes and events invented by Tennyson for the sake of his allegory.

The Coming of Arthur shows this conception fully orbed in the mind of Tennyson.   Arthur is the rational soul, not the son of Uther and Ygerne, but coming mysteriously from heaven and washed into Merlin's arms by a great wave.   Merlin, who educates him is intellectual power, with all the magic of science. Arthur's kingship is opposed by the brutal and sensual powers in human nature, but the soul beats them down, and lets in light and justice over the waste places of human nature where the ape, the tiger and the bandit lurk. Guinevere is the heart, and all we mean by the term. The soul, to do its work, must be knit to the heart in noble marriage—Arthur must be wed to Guinevere. The Knights of the Round Table are the high faculties in man whom the soul builds into order round it, to do its just and reforming will. When the King is crowned and married the three great fairies that stand by are Faith, Hope, and Charity; and the Lady of the Lake, "clothed in white samite, mystic, wonderful," who gives the soul Excalibur— the sword of the Spirit—with which to do his war-work against base sense, appetite, and their dis-ordered tyranny, is the Church. In embodying these conceptions, every word, every adjective, every description is weighed by Tennyson. The sym-bolism is extended into the remotest recesses of the tale. The allegory is thus fully launched in *The Coming of Arthur*, and the *Idylls* that were published with it, and that followed it, were written to the allegory. Even those that preceded it appear to have been somewhat modified to suit its require-ments.

The question now arises, Of what kind was this allegory of Tennyson's, and how did he manage it? It differed from the allegories that preceded it. The great mediæval allegory, *The Romance of the Rose* (the type of all allegory in the Middle Ages), was nothing but an allegory. There was no story connected with it which was independent of the allegory. The series of events and adventures which brought the knight at last to the enjoyment of the Rose were allegorically invented, and each of them had its meaning. The story was obscure and the allegory was plain. But in Tennyson's poem the story existed already ; it was independent of the allegory, and it forms an important part of the poem. Neither is the allegory plain, it is hidden beneath the story.

Our next great allegory is *The Faerie Queene*. That is also plainly allegorical. The names make the meaning clear. The Red Cross Knight, Una, Duessa, Orgoglio, the Dragon, all tell their tale. But there is much more of a story in this first book of *The Faerie Queene* (and I speak of the first book alone, for it is the only one which has a clear unity) than there is in *The Romance of the Rose.* We are nearly as much interested in the knight, in Una, and in many of the minor characters, as we might be if they were real personages, and not images of truth and purity, of pride and falsehood and hypocrisy. But in Tennyson's poem the story is often greater than the allegory ; it still breathes, and moves, and interests those to whom allegory is a weariness. At other times the story is of equal weight with the allegory, and we can ignore the allegory if it please us to do so. This separates altogether the *Idylls of the King* from *The Faerie Queene.* Moreover, the names are not allegorical. We have to search for a hidden, not to follow a plain allegory. Spenser invented a story to suit his conception ; Tennyson took an old tale and inserted his conception into it. But he was forced by his allegorical end to frequently invent as well, and his inventions, though they are often of the finest quality (as in *The Holy Grail*), confuse our interest in the story as much as the story confuses their meaning. The allegory and the tale do not fit throughout. They clash and trouble one another. An allegory, to be right in art, ought to have a story entirely invented for its purpose.

The next great allegory with which we may compare that of Tennyson is the first book of *The Pilgrim's Progress*. This is the finest allegory in the English language—the ideal art-thing. It proclaims itself an allegory by the names. The city of Vanity Fair, the Delectable Mountains, tell what they are ; and yet these places seem as real as London and the Surrey hills. Christian and Pliable, Faithful and the Old Adam, Wanton and Mr. Worldly Wiseman, Great-Heart and Giant Despair, tell also who and what they are ; and yet they are all alive, they talk like living beings ; we have met them in life—yesterday in the streets ; they awaken the keenest human interest.

It is this combination of reality and allegory, of story and symbol, each of them clear, vivid, and human, and both going straight home to the experiences of the soul, which lifts *The Pilgrim's Progress* into the highest place. The story and the allegory are of almost equal weight in the imagination. The inherent fault of an allegory—want of human interest—has been overcome without any loss of the allegorical interest. This is a real triumph. Nobody else but Dante has done it, and his way was only partly allegorical. Tennyson has not done it. His poem is not plainly an allegory, nor is it plainly a story. Sometimes the men and the women are real, sometimes they are mere shadows. Sometimes the events are human and romantic,

sometimes they are metaphysical, theological ideas
in a romantic dress.   We glide from reality to
vision and from vision to reality.   The two things
are not amalgamated.   In fact, the allegory might
as well have been left out altogether, and this
statement, if it be true, condemns the allegory in
the *Idylls of the King*.   Nevertheless, there is
something more to be said.   Bunyan reached his
perfection of work in this kind of literature by
natural *naïveté*, by the unconsciousness and the
faith of a childlike imagination.   Tennyson reached
what excellence he did reach in this matter by
sheer dint of intellect.   Few things have given me
so high an idea of Tennyson's intellectual power
as separate from his imagination, as his fitting in
of the allegorical conceptions into the body of the
story.   He does not succeed in doing it well,
because it was not in art to do it well; but
the efforts his intellect makes to do it, and the
comparative success he attained, are proof of great
intellectual power.   They are failures, but they are
gigantic struggles for success.

It is almost a pity that he made these efforts
at all.   They confuse his ethical ends, and they
were not needed to attain those ends.   All he
wanted to teach he could have taught and does
teach through the acts of the men and women of
the story.   The repentance of Guinevere and the
forgiveness of Arthur are far more impressive, and
far simpler in their lesson to life, when we see
Arthur as Arthur, and Guinevere as Guinevere,
than when we see Arthur as the rational soul,
and Guinevere as the heart, in human nature.
Moreover, they are not only needless and confusing

efforts, they are also not good art. They are apart from the true realm of poetry. We are conscious that in working them out and weaving them in, elaborate thinking has taken the place of creative emotion; that art has partly abdicated her throne to the understanding. Whenever the allegory is mingled up with the story, the poetry is disturbed, the tale is weak, and we are a little wearied. This is not the case when the story is all allegorical, when it is invented by Tennyson for the allegory, as in *The Holy Grail*. Then there is no confusion, and the poem is in the highest degree poetic. What I say applies to the mixed poems, like *Merlin and Vivien*. Moreover, the artist's childlike pleasure in the tale, and his sympathy with its passionate elements, are replaced (when the allegory is too obviously intruded) by a want of naturalness, even by a kind of pride in cleverness, which that *parvenu*, the analysing intellect, always brings into poetry. I sometimes seem to detect that Tennyson really loved the work his intellect did on the allegory more than the work his imagination did upon the story; that he loved the meanings he inserted into the tale more than the noble tale itself. This was a great mistake on his part, a mistake that artists make when they are seduced by the understanding. No one, a hundred years hence, will care a straw about the allegory; but men will always care for the story, and how the poet has made the persons in it set forth their human nature on the stage of life. The humanity, not the metaphysics, is the interesting thing, and Malory's book, though Tennyson decries its morality, is more human, more moral, than the

Idylls of the King. Even the far-off mythic Arthur is more at home with us than the Arthur of the *Idylls* whenever we are forced to consider him as the rational soul.

Tennyson was led away from this simple human position, yet he loved his mistake. "Accept," he writes to the Queen, "accept this old imperfect tale":

> New-old, and shadowing Sense at war with Soul
> Rather than that gray king, whose name, a ghost,
> Streams like a cloud, man-shaped, from mountain peak,
> And cleaves to cairn and cromlech still; or him
> Of Geoffrey's book, or him of Malleor's, one
> Touch'd by the adulterous finger of a time
> That hover'd between war and wantonness,
> And crownings and dethronements.

This is to like his allegory better than the story, the work of his intellect more than the work of ancient imagination; and there are a good number of persons who will thank Tennyson for this kind of thing. They will be happy to find out all about the allegory, and when they have found it out, and labelled all the characters and explained the metaphysical relations of these shadows, will persuade themselves that they are enjoying poetry. It is, however, an enjoyment of the understanding, not one of the imagination, a pleasure in analysis, not in beauty. Let them have their way; they have their reward. But our reward will be to be able to leave, as much as possible, the allegory alone, and to be happy with that which is passionate, sensuous, human, simple and lovely in the poem, and in the ravishment the imagination has in the seeing of these things.

There is plenty of opportunity for such work, in

spite of the allegory, in the *Idylls of the King.*
The romance of the story has caught hold of the
imagination of Tennyson, and in his treatment of
it he has made many fresh and delightful inventions—not allegorical, but romantic. He has had
great pleasure in opening out and developing the
ancient characters, in clothing them with new dresses
of thought, in fitting new emotions to the old events
in which they play their parts. He has re-created
some characters altogether : and even the leading
personages are frequently quite independent of his
allegory. He has built up around his people the
image of a whole country, with its woods and
streams, hills and moors, marsh and desert, dark
oceans rolling in on iron coasts, vast wastes, ancient
records of a bygone world ; hamlets and towns and
wonderful cities, halls and great palace-courts with
all their varied architecture ; storms, and sunshine,
all kinds of weather, Nature in her moods of
beauty and brightness, of gloom and horror. And
over them he has shed a light from the ancient
time, a romantic air and sky. These things
belong to art.

Moreover, within the realm of art much might
be said of the technic of the verse. The poem
belongs—though its composition stretched over so
many years—to the central period of the blank
verse of Tennyson, before he had wrought out
(not to his or our advantage) a new kind of blank
verse for his dramas, the habitude of which stole
into the blank verse of his old-age, and made it
in undramatic poems less musical, less delightful,
even less skilful than it was of old. But here,
through this long series of poems, the blank verse

R

is of almost equal excellence throughout. It is, as a vehicle of thought and emotion, entirely at the poet's command. He can make it do exactly what he likes. It has, at his choice, ease and rapidity, or slow and stately movement, or it echoes in its sound the thought, the scene, or the thing. It is by turns loud or low, soft or rough in spirit, fluid or rigid, abrupt, delayed, smooth, continuous, weighty and light. There are also none of the changes, tricks and placing of cæsura or accent which all the artists of the past in blank verse and especially Milton have used, with which Tennyson is not acquainted, and which he does not himself use with as much science as art. Yet the result is all his own. His blank verse stands apart, original, growing out of his own character and temper, and frequently modified and specialised by the special characters whom he is describing, and by the special forms of natural scenery which he paints. Lastly, it is extraordinarily concise— almost too concise. It sometimes becomes bald ; its "tricks" are sometimes too plain and too often repeated ; it often wants a rushing movement, and it is always a little too academic. We are too conscious of its skill, of the infinite care spent on it, of a certain want of naturalness ; that is, it has the defects of its qualities. But we forget these defects when it is at its best. Then indeed it is extraordinarily noble, rolling like a full-fed river through the country of imagination. Such is it in *The Holy Grail*, in *Guinevere*, in *The Passing of Arthur*.

The Coming of Arthur, the first of these Idylls, is Tennyson's prologue to them all. The allegory and the story are both mingled in it—but in this poem the allegory is more prominent than the story. In this Induction, Tennyson, having now determined on an allegory, is forced to place its main lines before his readers.

The Idyll opens with the waste and harried kingdom of Leodogran, beast-ridden, heathen-ridden, and the weak king hiding with his daughter Guinevere in his castle. Then Leodogran calls on Arthur for help, and Arthur, riding by the castle, sees Guinevere, and loves her for his life ; and having set her father free from foes, asks in reward her hand. So stand forth the two, Arthur and Guinevere, who are to grow more and more apart as life moves on ; who, meeting in high youth and joy, are to meet for the last time in deep repentance and forgiveness on the banks of the river of Death—a whole world of failure and sin and the ruin of great hopes behind them: a common tragedy! Tennyson hews out these figures with a rough, animating chisel in this first poem. In the poems that follow they are finished. But he does all that is needed now, and does it well. Guinevere is but slightly touched, but Arthur's character is, as is fitting, more elaborately treated.

He is to be the ideal king—the ruler of men ; the bringer of law and peace and good government into his world, the redeemer of waste places and wasted lives, the knitter together into one compact body of his knights for purity of life and overthrowing of wrong.

But he is to be more than king : he is to be

the ideal man ; and for that he must love. Love
then is born in him, but it is put into connection with his kingly work. No work without
love, but no continuance of love without work ;
equal love of woman and work, but neither the
woman nor the man made more than the work.
" But were I joined with her," cries Arthur,

> " Then might we live together as one life,
> And reigning with one will in everything
> Have power on this dark land to lighten it,
> And power on this dead world to make it live."

This is the ideal of marriage laid down in *The
Princess*, and consistently supported through all
the *Idylls of the King ;* and herein is the emotional
side of Arthur.

But his spiritual side is also sketched. He has
dim dreams and visions, like the prince in *The
Princess*, during which the outward world fades
away. Strange and mystic powers from the unseen
world stand round about him. He moves in God and
in eternity while yet on earth ; and in these hours
all phenomena are mist and dream. The mighty
warrior on whom it seems to his knights the fire of
God descends in battle ; the great ruler who is
to this world's work as the glove is to the hand,
cries in the spiritual hour when this solid earth is
as a vapour, and in words worthy of a great poet—

> O ye stars that shudder over me,
> O earth that soundest hollow under me
> Vext with waste dreams !

Then the allegorical side of him is sketched. His
senses are so exalted that he sees the morning

star at noonday ; he comes from the great deep and
goes to it again ; he is made king by immortal
queens ; he is not doomed to death but to return
and live again. The sword he wields blinds the
eyes of men ; the city he lives in and the great
hall of his knights is built by the intellectual and
spiritual powers.

Half, then, of this world, half of the mysterious
world beyond, Arthur has the qualities of both, and
does his work in both with equal steadiness and
fire. As such, he smites his own spirit into those
who love him, so that, when his knights swear
allegiance, into every face there comes

> A momentary likeness of the king.

So carefully, and with such foresight for the rest
of the poem, is Arthur hewn out before us by
the poet.

But another personage needs also to be introduced : Lancelot, friend of the king, yet the lover
of the queen. He first appears with Arthur in the
battle for Arthur's rights with the rebellious kings.
They each save one another's life, and they swear
on the stricken field a deathless love :

> And Arthur said : " Man's word is God in man ;
> Let chance what will, I trust thee to the death."

Alas ! in the trust, and in the friendship, lies
hidden all the tragic fate to come ; and when
we hear that Lancelot is sent by Arthur to fetch
Guinevere, we know that the joy, splendour and
hopes of the king are already doomed. The rift
is in the lute which will make all the music dumb.
What faith has bound together, unfaith unbinds.

O tragic world and tragic life of man! Tennyson has lifted to the highest peak in this poem the early inspiration of the king and his people, that our pity may be wrought to fulness by the catastrophe. Only a hint here and there suggests the pain to come, but the hints are clear. There is admirable skill shown in the management of this.

Thus the characters are placed in preparation for the whole. The story, as story, is set afloat by the questions of Guinevere's father concerning Arthur's birth. Is he a lawful king or not? Arthur's knights tell Leodogran the old legend of Uther and Ygerne and the siege of Tintagil. Thus Tennyson keeps touch with the tale which is his basis; but after that, for the sake of his allegory, he invents, and Bellicent tells the story of Arthur's coronation, and the mighty oath by which the soul binds all the powers of man to follow him in purity to redress the wrongs of the world. In the midst there rises that fine vision of the Church as the Lady of the Lake—a splendid picture, in which every word is a symbol:

> A mist
> Of incense curl'd about her, and her face
> Well-nigh was hidden in the minster gloom;
> But there was heard among the holy hymns
> A voice as of the waters, for she dwells
> Down in a deep; calm, whatsoever storms
> May shake the world, and when the surface rolls,
> Hath power to walk the waters like our Lord.

Then, to restore the humanity of the tale, Arthur's youth with his half-sister, Bellicent, is pictured—one of Tennyson's homely pictures of domestic tenderness; and then, lifting himself

easily into more exalted thought, he invents the
magic story which signifies the coming of the
soul into this world from the high heaven and out
of the great deep.   The allegory may be let go,
but the description of Merlin and Bleys, descending
while Uther is dying to the cove below Tintagil
Castle, is a piece of noble poetry—half nature and
half legend :

>   And then the two
> Dropt to the cove and watch'd the great sea fall,
> Wave after wave, each mightier than the last,
> Till last, a ninth one, gathering half the deep
> And full of voices, slowly rose and plunged
> Roaring, and all the wave was in a flame,
> And down the wave and in the flame was borne
> A naked babe, and rode to Merlin's feet,
> Who stoopt and caught the babe, and cried " The King !
> Here is an heir for Uther ! "   And the fringe
> Of that great breaker, sweeping up the strand,
> Lash'd at the wizard as he spake the word,
> And all at once all round him rose in fire,
> So that the child and he were clothed in fire.
> And presently thereafter follow'd calm,
> Free sky and stars.

Scarcely less fine than this is the dream
of Leodogran, and the description of the great
church in the Maytime, and the stainless knights
in white robes, upon the wedding morn—with the
one touch, in which so much of tragedy is held,
of the drooped eyelids of Guinevere, in whose
heart lay Lancelot while her hand was clasped in
Arthur's.   Lastly, as a piece of glorious literature,
there is the marriage and coronation song of the
knights.   It was not in the first draft of *The
Coming of Arthur*.   It embodies the thought of
the poem, grips the whole meaning of it together.
And its sound is the sound of martial triumph,

of victorious weapons in battle, and of knights in arms. We hear in the carefully varied chorus, in the very rattle and shattering of the vowels in the words, the beating of axe on helm and shaft on shield. Rugged, clanging, clashing lines—it is a splendid effort of art. King Olaf might have sung it.

> Blow trumpet, for the world is white with May;
> Blow trumpet, the long night hath roll'd away!
> Blow thro' the living world—" Let the King reign."
>
> Shall Rome or Heathen rule in Arthur's realm?
> Flash brand and lance, fall battle-axe upon helm,
> Fall battle-axe, and flash brand! Let the King reign.
>
> *   *   *   *   *
>
> Blow, for our Sun is mighty in his May!
> Blow, for our Sun is mightier day by day!
> Clang battle-axe, and clash brand! Let the King reign.
>
> The King will follow Christ, and we the King
> In whom high God hath breathed a secret thing.
> Fall battle-axe, and flash brand! Let the King reign.

We hear its contrast in Merlin's song, as soft and flowing as the other was braying and broken, and we think with gratitude of the artist who could do both with equal ease. The graciousness of the rivulet-music and soft play of Nature is in the lines of this delicate song, and the gaiety of youth; and mingled with these the deep and favourite thought of Tennyson of the pre-existence of the soul. It is pleasant to hear it, for we have companied with the shadow of tragedy:

> Rain, rain, and sun! a rainbow in the sky!
> A young man will be wiser by and by;
> An old man's wit may wander ere he die

Rain, rain, and sun ! a rainbow on the lea !
And truth is this to me and that to thee ;
And truth or clothed or naked let it be.

Rain, sun, and rain ! and the free blossom blows ;
Sun, rain, and sun ! and where is he who knows ?
From the great deep to the great deep he goes.

In *The Coming of Arthur* the King is crowned
and married, and the land subdued to peace and
justice. The heathen and the Romans are driven
out ; the Round Table established. Arthur sits on
the judgment-seat, and there is a sketch of him in
Gareth and Lynette doing this work. Knights ride
away each day from the Court to deliver the
weak from the oppressor ; and the young men of
noble birth in the kingdom whom Arthur's character has inspired come, like Gareth, to Camelot
to join his band, seeking knighthood and high
adventure. So everywhere the Order is recruited,
the King's power grows, and into all the knights,
young and clean and eager, the King pours his
spirit :

Clear honour shining like the dewy star
Of dawn, of faith in their great King, with pure
Affection, and the light of victory,
And glory gain'd, and ever more to gain.

All is well ; and the Idyll of *Gareth and Lynette*
represents this golden time. In human affairs, in
the history of great causes, in men's lives, in their
love, there is a time of glad beginnings, such
a beginning as Nature has in spring. Gareth
is the image of this pleasant, prophetic time. He
is also the image of the Arthurian kingdom in its
youthful energy, purity, gentleness, ideality ; he is

moreover the incarnation of the vigour, courage, gaiety, and audacity of youth. Nothing seems impossible to the King and the Round Table; nothing seems impossible to Gareth. When we are young, nothing seems impossible to us. "Madam," Youth says to Mother Nature, "there is no such thing as the impossible." Then Nature smiles, for she loves the bold; nevertheless, she strikes hard. If we are gay when we are smitten, she is on our side. We get our way for a time, and do what all the world says cannot be done. But if our courage fade at her stroke, or we take it sullenly, she frowns in scorn and tramples us beneath her feet.

Gareth was one of these bold, gay creatures. He did not mind being a kitchen knave, nor the taunts of Sir Kaye, nor the mocking of Lynette; and when Lancelot's spear hurled him to the ground, he broke out into frank laughter. Nor was he one whit daunted by the magic horrors of Night and Death. Fools of pageantry he thought them, and fools they are. The soul that laughs and loves and rides for the right, has the world at his feet while he is young.

Something of this was in the mind of Tennyson when he invented and added to the story the symbolism of the knights that defended the fords of the river. The first was the Morning-Star, the second Noon-Sun, the third the Evening-Star, the fourth Night and Death. One by one they are overthrown by Gareth. His youth laughs at the attack which the temptations of youth, of middle age, of the evening of life, of death, of time itself, make on men—that long, wrathful siege of battering days.

Tennyson marks this meaning. In the carved allegory (a thing he has invented) near the hermit's cave, the rock bears five knights with the names *Phosphorus, Meridies, Hesperus, Nox,* and *Mors* sculptured beneath them, and they are running down the soul—

> A Shape that fled
> With broken wings, torn raiment, and loose hair
> For help and shelter to the hermit's cave.

It is " the war of Time," he says, " against the soul of man." But Gareth conquers all of them by audacity and gaiety. The encounters in this pageant are alike clear, varied, brief, set each in its own fair landscape, and the sound of the river accompanies them with warlike music. They are real enough, but they are also allegorical. It is easy for the faith and boldness of youth to conquer the sins and troubles of the dawn of life ; it is harder to slay those of its noonday ; it is harder still to overcome those of its late afternoon; and Tennyson's representation of the Knight of the Evening Star is full of original thought. He is old and hard ; he blows a hard and deadly note upon his horn. A storm-beaten, russet, many-stained pavilion shelters him. A grizzled damsel arms him in ancient arms. Beneath his arms a hardened skin fits close to his body. All is different from that which the commonplace imagination connects with the evening star. We see the poet's meaning by the comparison he makes to illustrate the difficulty of Gareth's battle against the Knight of the Evening Star :

> Till Gareth panted hard, and his great heart,
> Foredooming all his trouble was in vain,

> Labour'd within him, for he seem'd as one
> That all in later, sadder age begins
> To war against ill uses of a life,
> But these from all his life arise, and cry,
> " Thou hast made us lords, and canst not put us down ! "

Nor is the representation of Night and Death both of whom one champion images, less imaginative. The black horse, black banner, and black horn, the black armour painted with the white skeleton and helmed with the skull, are the ordinary thing. But the thunder gloom under which he rides, the chill of his aspect which strikes ice even into Lancelot, his huge pavilion which

> Sunders the glooming crimson on the marge,

lift the work Tennyson does beyond the ordinary. And finally we reach thought, symbol, and full imagination together, when (the skull cloven by Gareth and then the helm) there issues forth from the black terror and the deadly chill the bright face of a blooming boy, " fresh as a flower new-born." It is Tennyson's view of Death, it is also his image of what it seems to youth, to gaiety, to daring, and to faith. And the story ends with the pregnant line :

> So large mirth lived, and Gareth won the quest.

All this part of the tale is vivid with pictures, touched with happy illustrations drawn from Nature,* and steadily builds up into fulness the

---

* Here are a few of these illustrations. Gareth cannot wholly overthrow the Evening-Star, no more

> Than loud Southwesterns, rolling ridge on ridge,
> The buoy that rides at sea, and dips and springs
> For ever.

character of Gareth. But the beginning is not so well done. The scenes between Gareth and his mother, who strives to keep him under her wing, are much too long, and the mother's dulness of perception when Gareth places, in two illustrations his position before her, and her last argument, that the King may not be the true King, and therefore Gareth must stay at home, are quite out of nature. It is not till Gareth escapes, and is on his journey

This also of the honeysuckle that flies about the cave

> Good lord, how sweetly smells the honeysuckle
> In the hush'd night, as if the world were one
> Of utter peace, and love, and gentleness,

might have been said by Jessica in the night scene in Portia's garden.

Take two others. The first likens the cloth of gold which Mark sends to Arthur to

> A field of charlock in the sudden sun
> Between two showers.

That is as quick-eyed as it is simple and true. See how the poet, to make our sight of the thing more brilliant, puts in "Between two showers," just as in the next his imagination makes the plant feel its own fate.

> Wan-sallow as the plant that feels itself
> Root-bitten by white lichen.

Gareth drops his cloak, and breaks bright in arms, like those

> Dull-coated things, that making slide apart
> Their dusk wing-cases, all beneath there burns
> A jewell'd harness, ere they pass and fly.

And the shield of the Noonday—

> As if the flower,
> That blows a globe of after arrowlets,
> Ten thousand-fold had grown, flashed the fierce shield,
> All sun.

These come out of the full treasury Tennyson had collected in his mind of the precious sights of Nature.

to Lancelot, that Tennyson recovers himself.   And he does recover himself admirably in his description of Camelot, and the mystic gate, and the magic music, and the visionary impression that the city makes upon the imagination, and the meeting with Merlin.   It is fine invention, and many a line is worth a magic spell.

Lastly, the first of the types of womanhood that Tennyson draws in the *Idylls* is Lynette, a fresh and frank young person, smart and thoughtless, quick-tongued, over-rude, over-bold both with the King and with Lancelot, but honourable and pure of heart—the petulant, impatient type.   Such a woman may be charming, but Lynette's sauciness wants charm, just because too much of the masculine roughness of Tennyson speaks in her.   I do not allude to her rude scorning of Gareth as the kitchen-knave and her unsavoury mocking of him, for all that is taken directly from the original story; but to the way in which Tennyson has expressed it, especially to his attempt to give it a humorous turn.   Lynette in Malory's hands is entirely in earnest, and her character is throughout consistent. She repents of her abuse, but she has no humour, and she has no delicate sentiment.   But in Tennyson's hands we cannot quite tell whether she is in earnest or not, and what humour there is attempted is like that of an undergraduate.*

* It is curious that a poet, whose humour is so excellent in *The Northern Farmer*, and the other dialect poems, should fail so completely when he tries to be humorous in the *Idylls of the King* and in the Dramas.   When, for example, Geraint is irritated by the villagers who answer all his questions by talking of the knight who calls himself the Sparrow-hawk, he cries:

Lynette, overdone in this way, is more a study of
the saucy type of woman than a real woman.
Moreover, when Tennyson wants to improve her,
and show fineness of nature in her, he divides her
from herself.   She becomes full of sentiment, and
when she sings those charming little songs which
one by one embody the change of her view of
Gareth, they are over-delicate for her previous
character.   We cannot fit

> O trefoil, sparkling on the rainy plain,
> O rainbow with three colours after rain,
> Shine sweetly : thrice my love has smiled on me,

with a voice like this :

> Dish-washer and broach-turner, loon !—to me
> Thou smellest all of kitchen as before.

Malory does not make that mistake.   Lynette is
one woman in his hands.   In Tennyson she is
two, and the two do not agree.

> A thousand pips eat up your sparrow-hawk !
> Tits, wrens, and all wing'd nothings peck him dead !

Tennyson means him to be spleenfully humorous, and he is only
absurd.   When in the next two lines he leaves humour alone, he
is excellent.   Geraint cries out :

> Ye think the rustic cackle of your bourg
> The murmur of the world !   What is it to me ?

Then he tries to be humorous again :

> O wretched set of sparrows, one and all,
> That pipe of nothing but of sparrow-hawks !

This is ridiculous on the lips of a stately knight.   The only explanation I can make is that the solemn vehicle of heroic blank
verse, and especially of blank verse so elaborate and academic as
that of the *Idylls of the King*, is wholly unfitted for the expression
of humour.

I cannot make the same criticism with regard
to Enid, whose character fills the next two Idylls,
The Marriage of Geraint and *Geraint and Enid.*
Enid is one woman, both as girl and wife. As
Lynette is the type of petulance, so Enid is the
type of patience. She is Tennyson's Griselda.
Lynette is audacious and free of tongue. Enid is
silent in endurance of wrong. She is silent also
when she ought to speak. She is afraid to blame
Geraint for his sloth, because she knows he is
slothful from love of her. And her fear, falling in
with Geraint's suspiciousness, makes the trouble of
the piece. Patience, when it is accompanied by
fear or over-fancy, is turned from doing good to
doing wrong. But, independent of this evil side of
patience, Tennyson seems to like this kind of
womanhood. Of all his women, Enid is the most
carefully drawn, the most affectionate. She is
gracious, but she is one of those women who do a
great deal of harm to men. The defects of their
patience make in men tyranny and selfishness,
jealous overbearing and ugly suspicion. In bad
men these evils grow worse, till the man turns
into a brute. In a suspicious but noble-hearted
man as Geraint originally was, they produce, and
often with startling suddenness, detestable conditions of mind and life, out of which men like
Geraint, being good at root, are shocked back
again into self-knowledge and repentance.

This effect, however, is overdone by Tennyson.
It would be difficult to find, outside of bad men,
any one whose conduct is made more odious than
Geraint's. Tennyson could not have recognised
how far apart he wanders from what we call honour,

nor do I think that his conduct is sufficiently motived from the point of view of art. Only the *madness* of jealousy, and not mere suspicion, is enough to partly excuse all he thought and all he did. He is not even represented as having sufficient cause for his conduct. He is expressly said not to believe in Enid's loss of honour. Moreover from the very beginning he is not quite a gentleman. A few days before his marriage, he doubts Enid's affection for him ; he wishes to prove her obedience, to test whether it is love for him she has, or desire for the splendours of a Court. If she will at a word, without reason given, come in her shabby dress to Court, then he will rest, fixed in her faith.

What sort of a man is this ? He, at least, does not know what love means ; lost in himself, in vanity and suspicion. There is nothing of this suspicion in the original story. Geraint there is, like Leontes, suddenly attacked by jealousy and its special anger when he hears his wife say that he is not the man he was. And this furious jealousy motives his rude conduct. Jealousy maddens, and the Welsh writer, careful for his hero's repute, expressly says that for the time he was insane. But Tennyson does not make Geraint jealous in this way, nor put him into the madness of jealousy. He is only suspicious and angry, and his conduct to Enid, far worse than it is in the original, has not cause enough at the back of it to make it possible. The position is overdone. Nor does Tennyson's short introduction to the second part in *Geraint and Enid*—

O purblind race of miserable men,
How many among us at this very hour
Do forge a life-long trouble for ourselves
By taking true for false, or false for true—

give a sufficient reason for the meanness of Geraint. Many men, indeed, lose the use of life in that fashion, but if they are of noble nature, as Geraint is represented at first, they do not fall so low as he, they do not quite dishonour their original character, they do not lose all chivalry to a woman. Or if they do, they do it because they believe their wife to be utterly false to them. This cause is excluded by Tennyson. Geraint falls too low, and his fall has not sufficient motive. Art has failed Tennyson.

When the rumour about the Queen and Lancelot comes to Geraint's ear, he thinks that his wife may suffer taint because she is the Queen's friend, and he removes her from Court. Then he forgets all his duty and his fame in uxorious love of her. He fights no more; he lets his province fall into confusion. This is natural enough, and though he is suspicious and feeble, he has not yet altogether lost gentlehood. Men laugh at him for his weakness. His wife saddens, and, seeing her sad, his base suspicion that she is tainted deepens. He hears her murmuring one morning that she is no true wife, and leaps at once to the conclusion that she is not faithful in thought to him, bursts out into a reckless passion, and bids her ride into the wilderness with him—utterly careless of her, careful only for himself. When he meets the first three bandits, and she warns him, he cries : " If I fall, cleave to the better man "—an odious insult.

In the midst of all this wrath, he eats like a man who has no trouble, and jokes at the mowers whom he has deprived of their dinner. When Limours (Enid's old lover) comes into the inn, and, seeing Enid alone, asks leave to speak to her, Geraint answers :

> My free leave,
> Get her to speak ; she doth not speak to me.

This is partly in the original, but what follows is not. While Enid sits in the room, Limours drinks and jests and tells loose tales. Geraint is pleased, and bursts into laughter ! Then it is that he gives Limours leave to tell his wife of his love to her. What ensues is still worse. Limours is slain next morning, and Geraint (though it is Enid herself who has asked Geraint to defend her from his pursuit, though he has himself almost handed Enid over to Limours) calls Limours her lover. These vilenesses are added by Tennyson to the Geraint of the old tale. There is not a trace of the gentleman left in Geraint. Limours is twice the lover and twice the gentleman.

All this is overdone. It is impossible a gentleman could fall so low. It is also quite out of character with the days of chivalry in which the original story took its form. Moreover, as I said, the motive is not sufficient. Nor is Arthur's reproof to him sufficient punishment. His punishment ought to come in Enid's ceasing to love him. But Enid is not of that temper. She continues to love him ; but I wonder, even with her, whether in the future there was not some mild contempt mingled with her love. There would have been if Geraint fell as low as Tennyson makes him fall. Enid's love, after Geraint's conduct, is even more improbable than Griselda's.

Independent of this main criticism, the poem is well wrought and full of beauty. The story is skilfully introduced, continued, and ended. The pictorial passages, and these are brilliant, are full of many happy touches of light and colour, happy asides of sentiment, with epigrams of wisdom and thought scattered among them like jewels on a golden robe. There is no weariness as we read : the eye sees something new, the ear hears some fresh sound, the heart and brain are stimulated from line to line. The work is delightful through- out from this point of view—concise, chosen, and luminous. We wish nothing out of, and rarely anything into the descriptions. There is no modern poet who has painted his landscapes in fewer words, and yet who painted all that was needful to make the scene, as far as he chose to see it, leap out before the eyes :

> So thro' the green gloom of the wood they past,
> And issuing under open heavens beheld
> A little town with towers, upon a rock,
> And close beneath, a meadow gemlike chased
> In the brown wild, and mowers mowing in it ;
> And down a rocky pathway from the place
> There came a fair-hair'd youth.*

He has rejected every unnecessary detail. I think he has rejected too much of his original, which I give below, but he is judge.* At least, he has

* Here is the original in Lady Charlotte Guest's translation of the *Mabinogion* :—" And early in the day they left the wood, and they came to an open country, with meadows on one hand, and

carefully kept the human figures. The mowers mowing, the youth descending the path, strike forth the landscape. From 1842 onwards, indeed earlier when that brilliant apparition of Paris in *Œnone* issues from the wood, Tennyson rarely painted a landscape without humanity, and he places his figures with all the skill of a painter. He knew that Nature alone was not half as delightful as Nature and man together. Lover of Nature as he was, he avoided the crowning fault of modern poetry—the unmitigated merciless description of Nature, trickling on for fifty and a hundred lines together, without one touch of human interest. He knew the great masters—Homer, Virgil, and the rest of those who see and feel at the same moment—too well to fall into that dreary error. He was too much of a great master himself to commit it. It is from this impassioned mingling of the soul and sight of man with the soul and sight

mowers mowing the meadows. And there was a river before them and the horses bent down and drank the water. And they went up out of the water by a lofty steep, and there they met a tender stripling, with a satchel about his neck, and they saw that there was something in the satchel but they knew not what it was. And he had a small blue pitcher in his hand and a bowl on the mouth of the pitcher. And the youth saluted Geraint," &c. &c.

That this is more alive, that there is more of the witchery of representation in it than Tennyson's lines, illustrates what is elsewhere said of the loss sometimes in his natural description of charm, and especially of livingness, from too great a devotion to conciseness. The river is gone, and the horses bending to drink; and the river is the living spirit of the landscape. I am sorry also to lose my curiosity about the satchel. Above all, why have left out the eye of the picture, and in colour too? How could he leave out the blue pitcher? Tennyson had no intense love of colour. He was no Venetian. Black and white were his favourite vehicles. Few of his shadows are in colour.

of Nature that the specialised loveliness arises
which charms us, and dignifies itself, in the descriptions of Tennyson.   There is no finer example
of this than in Geraint's first sight of Enid.   We
see the castle courtyard, the ruined towers, with all
their grass and flowers and ivy, as with the naked
eye.   But in the midst we see Geraint and Yniol,
and then we hear Enid singing and the castle court
is filled with her.   Nothing can be closer to nature
than these lines, which describe the ivy climbing
the castle ; every word is alive with fact :

> And monstrous ivy-stems
> Claspt the gray walls with hairy-fibred arms,
> And suck'd the joining of the stones, and look'd
> A knot, beneath, of snakes—aloft, a grove.

Wordsworth would have given a life of its own to
that, but Tennyson draws it only as it is, leaves it,
once he has brushed it in, and passes on to fill the
ancient court with youth by Enid's voice, and to
make her voice awaken fatherly love in Yniol's
heart and passion in Geraint's.   They stand still,
enthralled, looking up, and listening.   And Enid
sings that song of fortitude in poverty, of the
mastery of the soul in good or evil fortune, which
is so finely written that it speaks the very soul of
enduring manhood and womanhood all over the
world.*   There is as much strength as there is
beauty in the whole scene ; and the two comparisons of the effect on Geraint of Enid's voice

---

* The motive comes from Dante ; but with what grace and
beauty it is varied and enhanced !   The soul of the girl is in it,
and the soul of the situation.   And it fits, enlightens,
strengthens and consoles those everywhere who are in a similar
condition.

are one of the noblest instances we can give of
that sweet keen delicacy in Tennyson which, in
contrast with his bluff power, is so pleasant a
surprise. Let me quote the passage :

> And while he waited in the castle court,
> The voice of Enid, Yniol's daughter, rang
> Clear thro' the open casement of the hall,
> Singing ; and as the sweet voice of a bird,
> Heard by the lander in a lonely isle,
> Moves him to think what kind of bird it is
> That sings so delicately clear, and make
> Conjecture of the plumage and the form ;
> So the sweet voice of Enid moved Geraint ;
> And made him like a man abroad at morn
> When first the liquid note beloved of men
> Comes flying over many a windy wave
> To Britain, and in April suddenly
> Breaks from a coppice gemm'd with green and red,*
> And he suspends his converse with a friend,
> Or it may be the labour of his hands,
> To think or say, " There is the nightingale " ;
> So fared it with Geraint, who thought and said,
> " Here, by God's grace, is the one voice for me."

To this first impression of her Enid is true
throughout. Her patience is too overwrought to
permit us to class her among the higher types of
womanhood—indeed, these very patient women
are always painted by men—and her own character
is sometimes overwhelmed by the allegorical representation of patience Tennyson makes through her.
But when we ignore this, and get down, below the
type, to her natural womanhood, Enid is full of
truth and life. When she hears that she is
loved by Geraint and lies awake all night ; when she

---

* Chaucer also saw these spring colours of the young trees—
    Some very red, and some a glad light green.

longs to be beautifully dressed to pleasure her lord
and do him credit; when she slips from her couch
into her golden dress, like the star of morn from a
bank of snow into a sunlit cloud; when time after
time she warns Geraint of his foes; when she is
left alone in the bandit hall and thinks Geraint is
dead, and sends the power of her suffering and her
nature into the rude crowd, she is always of the
same strength and gentleness, always sweet with
a sacred charm, so that we do not wonder that
Tennyson was so moved with his own creation as
to write about her some of the loveliest lines he
ever wrote of womanhood, when once more at
home in her husband's heart she rides away with
him from the savage lands:

> And never yet, since high in Paradise
> O'er the four rivers the first roses blew,
> Came purer pleasure unto mortal kind
> Than lived thro' her, who in that perilous hour
> Put hand to hand beneath her husband's heart,
> And felt him hers again: she did not weep,
> But o'er her meek eyes came a happy mist
> Like that which kept the heart of Eden green
> Before the useful trouble of the rain.

And with these lines, beautiful with a paradise of
tenderness, I leave these Idylls of Geraint and
Enid.

Balin and Balan, the Idyll next in order in
the completed book, was the last published by
Tennyson. It shows no weariness of hand or
brain, no lack of his clear conciseness, no want of
imaginative presentation either of the moods of men
or Nature. The blank verse is as skilful and robust

as ever, only a little more abrupt, less flowing than in the earlier Idylls. The subject, however, continually demands this abruptness, for Balin is the incarnation of natural violence of temper. The intellectual treatment of the story is as fine as the imaginative. If we compare the tale as it is in Malory with Tennyson's re-making of it here for the purpose of his allegory, we shall understand how acutely, skilfully, and profoundly the combining intellect has built up the skeleton of the tale before the imaginative passion put flesh upon it and sent the blood racing through it. As he painted in Geraint suspicion growing into rudeness and meanness, and in Edyrn pride, or rather arrogance—and these evil things as enemies of the soul of man—so he paints in Balin the general idea of furious anger as another enemy of the soul. Balin, for Tennyson clings at times to the theory of heredity, drew this temper from his father. He was begotten in an hour of wrath. He was banished from the Table Round for an outbreak of violence. He is restored to it by Arthur and begins to learn gentleness from Lancelot and the King. But his moods, born in his blood, leap on him like fiends, and he despairs. The gentle temper of the Court is too high for him, and he takes to the wild woods again, his rage now turned upon himself—the chained rage "which yelpt within him like a hound." Struggle after struggle he makes against himself; and well, and with a imaginative ethic, these are varied and drawn by Tennyson. The last struggle is that which he makes by keeping before his eyes the Queen's crown upon his shield. But the good this is to him is destroyed when he hears from Vivien that the Queen is false to Arthur and with Lancelot. His two ideals are overthrown. He bursts into frenzy, tramples on his shield, and Balan, his brother, mistakes his unearthly yell for the cry of the Demon of the Wood. Ignorant of their brotherhood, these two charge one another, and both fall wounded to the death. Vivien removes their helms, they recognise each other, and their farewell is one of the most pathetic things which Tennyson has written.

> " O brother," answered Balin, " woe is me !
> My madness all thy life has been thy doom,
> Thy curse, and darken'd all thy day ; and now
> The night has come. I scarce can see thee now.
> Good-night ! for we shall never bid again
> Good-morrow. Dark my doom was here, and dark
> It will be there. I see thee now no more.
> I would not mine again should darken thine.
> Good-night, true brother."
>   Balan answered low,
> " Good-night, true brother here ! Good-morrow there !
> We two were born together, and we die
> Together by one doom : " and while he spoke
> Closed his death-drowsing eyes, and slept the sleep
> With Balin, either lock'd in either's arm.*

This study of Tennyson's of Anger is quite original, and is made vivid by other characters clustered round it which exhibit different aspects of the same passion, of the means to overcome it, and of the powers opposed to it. It would be interesting to make a full comparison of it with the various Angers of Spenser—with the Wrath in the chariot

---

* Compare Mrs. Barbauld's
  Say not Good Night,—but in some brighter clime
  Bid me Good Morning.

of Pride, with the Furor of the second book of *The Faerie Queene*, with the frenzy of Pyrochles and Cymochles. In Spenser these characters are wholly allegorical. In *Balin and Balan* the human element is greater than the allegorical. The inevitableness of Balin's fate makes the pity of it. The constant love of the two brothers is drawn with as much tenderness as beauty, and the ethical lesson which is indirectly given by their story does not arise from the allegory but from their human fates, their sorrow and their love.

Again, two new elements are introduced into the general representation, directly opposed one to the other—asceticism in King Pellam, and luxury (in the old sense of the word) in Vivien. Pellam, leaving human wrongs to right themselves, retires to his castle, lichen-bearded and grayly draped with streaming grass—

A house of bats, in every tower an owl—

scarcely eats, repudiates his wife, and lets neither dame nor damsel enter his gates, lest he should be polluted. Tennyson's hatred of asceticism, of monkery, of the gloom and curse of it, is here accentuated. It has risen far beyond that which he felt when he wrote *Simeon Stylites*. He intensifies it when he represents King Pellam as taking it up from spiritual conceit and to spite King Arthur. Moreover, he attacks the chief evil which follows asceticism when he makes Garlon, King Pellam's son, into the lover of Vivien the harlot, and places his lair in a cave, so black that it is like the mouth of hell. This horror of asceticism, of all religious views which separate

men from doing the work of justice and love in
the open world, is fully developed, but in a different
way, in *The Holy Grail.*

Vivien is the other element, now for the first
time brought into the whole poem. She is
here altogether allegorical, the incarnation of that
impurity of sense which is, in Tennyson's mind,
the bitterest enemy the soul can have, which more
than all else breaks up and ruins not only States
but also the powers by which States are made
and held together—justice, knowledge, harmony,
order, truth, true love, man's energy and woman's
insight. All go down before her attack, and the
next Idyll develops her fully.

Lastly, the descriptive power of Tennyson, which
in the previous Idylls is concentrated into separate
passages, is here diffused through the whole.
When we have finished the Idyll, we see the
whole wood—great trees, dense underwood, sweet
springs, wolf-like caves, lonely castles, long
avenues of trees, green glades, shadowy demons
and hoar-headed woodmen in it. It is not separately described; it grows up, as the wood of
Arden grows before us, from notes of woodland
scattered among the action of the piece; and a
delightful example it is of an artist's work.

There is, however, one little touch of direct
description of Nature in this Idyll which enables
me, by contrasting it with Coleridge's image of the
same thing, to mark out a quality in Tennyson's
natural description. There is a spring in the
wood, and the spring makes a clear pool with a
sandy bottom. Tennyson looks into the spring,
and sees the sand leaping up under the water-

glass, impelled by the fountain jet. Balin and
Balan sit statuelike—

> To right and left the spring, that down
> From underneath a plume of lady-fern
> Sang, and the sand danced at the bottom of it.

The thing to be seen is perfectly clear, and no
poet in the world could put it into a shorter
phrase. This is Tennyson's brief, concise method,
and it has its special value. And now let us hear
Coleridge telling the same story of the spring and
the dancing sand :

> This sycamore, oft musical with bees—
> Such tents the Patriarchs loved ! O long unharmed
> May all its aged boughs o'er-canopy
> The small round basin which this jutting stone
> Keeps pure from fallen leaves! Long may the spring,
> Quietly as a sleeping infant's breath,
> Send up cold waters to the traveller
> With soft and even pulse ! Nor ever cease
> Yon tiny cone of sand its soundless dance,
> Which at the bottom, like a Fairy's page,
> As merry and no taller, dances still,
> Nor wrinkles the smooth surface of the fount,

The comparison of these, for the purpose of
saying which is the best, would not be fair,
for Tennyson, as I have said already, refrains
deliberately in these stories, lest the human interest
should be overwhelmed, from any set description of
Nature ; and Coleridge has given himself wholly to
such description. Nevertheless, the two pieces
illustrate two methods—the concise and the expanded—of describing Nature ; and Tennyson, as
he grew older, loved and used the concise method
more and more. We meet very rarely in his

later work anything like the long description of
the land around the town of Lincoln in *The
Gardener's Daughter*. It was his way, and we
are grateful for it ; but, on the whole, I love
Coleridge's way better. It is more pleasant that
the piece of Nature we have to see should be
dwelt on with curious love, coloured as well as
outlined, played with by the imagination, as when
Coleridge turns the cone of sand into a fairy's
page, as merry and no taller, dancing alone. This
pleases more, and I feel in it the life that is
in Nature more than in the other. But Tennyson is no less the artist than Coleridge, only he is
an artist of another kind. We should feel ourselves happy to have these different musicians of
Nature, whose varying harmonies fit our changing
moods ; for it is not by saying that one poet is
better than another that we shall win a good
delight for ourselves, or learn how to see or
company with beauty. It is by loving each of
them for his proper work, and by our gratitude to
them all.

There are two things which, according to
Tennyson, break up the Table Round ; which
first decay and then destroy the work of Arthur.
The first of these is the lust of the flesh, and the
second is mystic-ascetic religion. *Merlin and Vivien*
represents the first, and *The Holy Grail* the second.
Tennyson expresses in them the set of his mind
towards two recurring problems of society. He
looked, and in the direst light, on the growth of
sensuality, on the indifference to purity, on the
loosening of the marriage vow, on the unchaste

results of luxury of life, on the theory and practice of free love, as one of the worst evils, and perhaps the worst, which can afflict individual, social and national life. The sin of Lancelot and Guinevere, which he takes care to represent as induced by a love almost irresistible and as supported by unbroken faithfulness, and which does not therefore wholly destroy the noble elements in their characters, is nevertheless (though "the light that led astray seemed light from heaven," though every excuse that can be made for it is made) the primal cause of the ruin that follows. The sin of these two high-placed persons, however modified in them, initiated and licensed an unmodified guilt of a similar kind, and brought with it when it was committed by others not as noble as Lancelot or Guinevere, lightness of character, loose desire, scorn of truth and honesty in the things of love, and naturally in other matters ; and, finally, a luxurious life, in which the doing of justice and the support of good government were neglected for sensual enjoyment.

There is a difference between Lancelot, faithful all his life to one love, and Gawain who lightly flies from one to another all his life ; between Lancelot, whose love was mingled with a vast remorse, and Tristram who in the Idyll of *The Last Tournament* has, in the airy cynicism of free loving, become careless of faithfulness, and then uncourteous towards the woman whom he once loved so well. Nevertheless, it was not in Tennyson's way to finally excuse Lancelot and Guinevere because they loved faithfully. He brings all the ruin back to them. It is their guilt also which made the invasion of the Court by Vivien possible—that is, through their love, with all its faithfulness, the lust of the flesh stole in, and the whole of society was corrupted. Again and again this point is made by Tennyson. No matter how seeming fair an unlicensed love may be, no matter how faithful and how deep, it ends in opening to others the door to sensuality, which itself has no faithfulness, no depth, and no enduring beauty. Guinevere is followed by Vivien, and Lancelot by Tristram. That is his view, and I give it without comment. It is part of the ethical message Tennyson chose to set forth for our society.

But the state of things to which he finally brings Arthur's Court and realm—the state of which Vivien is the true queen—is not reached at once. There are reactions against it, and such a reaction is described in *The Holy Grail*. It was not a useful nor a permanent reaction, though it was a religious one. On the contrary, it did as much harm to the State and to Arthur's work as the sensualism. But then it would not have done so much harm had it not been for the previous existence of the sensualism. That had weakened not only individual moral power, but the collective force of righteous statesmanship, so that work for the good of the whole people no longer seemed the best and wisest thing. It was better, men who were half repenting of a sinful life began to think, to pursue after a mystic and ascetic holiness than to live naturally in the present world and strive to make it wiser and happier. It was better, or pleasanter, to seek for supernatural excitements of religious passion than to confirm the good and deliver the

oppressed and walk humbly with God in the
common duties of home, society and the State.
This is only another form of sensualism, or its probable consequence.   The unbridled life according
to the senses induces a condition both of body and
mind which cannot do without excitement.   When,
therefore, as in Arthur's realm, there is a reaction
against sensualism and folk turn to religion, they
demand a religion which replaces the sensual by a
spiritual thrill, or by the excitement of the mira-
culous ; which revels in the mystic ecstasies of
ascetic purity ; which thinks that human love
injures the love of God ; and which takes men and
women away from their nearest duties.

This, in Tennyson's mind, was a deadly misfortune, not only for the spiritual life of the individual,
but for the civic life of societies.   In making this
clear, he spoke another part of what he conceived
to be his message to his time.   How far he was
right is not the question here, but what he thought
is.   He was of the school of Maurice and Kingsley
in this matter.   He deliberately attacked in *The
Holy Grail*, but with some of a poet's tolerance and
pity, this kind of piety.   He allowed the possibility
of its truth and fitness in a few persons of the
temper of Galahad and Percivale's sister.   He
abhorred it in the generality of men and women.
Its origin was chiefly in the senses, and its end was
the dissolution of all true work for mankind.   This
is the aim of *The Holy Grail*.

Our question now is, In what manner, from the
literary point of view, has he done this double
piece of work—this attack on impurity and on
ascetic and sensational religion ?   For the work

T

is not only allegorical, it is also a story; not only symbolic but human. In what fashion, then, are wrought, first *Merlin and Vivien* and then *The Holy Grail?*

The conception of Vivien, from the allegorical point of view, is always careful and sometimes fine, and keeps close to the traditional symbolism of Luxuria. She is born of rebellion, that is, of disobedient pride. Her father dies fighting against Arthur. Her mother brings her forth on the battle-field, and, giving her birth, falls dead. She is thus cradled in bloody war, war for which there is no greater cause in all history than the lust of the flesh. She is also cradled in death: "Born from death am I," she says, "among the dead," for sin and death are woven together, warp and woof. The first of sins in the mind of the ancient Church is pride, and the second lust, and death is their child. Milton in his mighty symbolism makes Satan, immediately after his rebellion, give birth to Sin from his head, and then, burning for her beauty, beget Death upon her; and Death, in turn, unites himself in unnatural guilt to his mother Sin. This is a horror terrible enough for the Titanic imagination of Milton. Tennyson's symbolism falls far below that huge conception; but then his story interfered with his allegory, as his allegory interferes with his story.

Vivien, thus bound up with death, causes physical war and death. She also leaves behind her moral death in men's souls, and death of law and order in States.

Another symbolic touch is given when she says that she was "sown upon the wind." Perhaps

Tennyson thought of the text, " They that sow the
wind shall reap the whirlwind"; but the main thought
is the inconstancy and fierceness of the lust of the
flesh, its veering and flittering fancy, its tempest-
wrath and fury at other times ; and it is in the
yelling of the storm that Vivien has her way with
Merlin.   Then she is corrupted by Mark, king of
Cornwall, whose life and Court are set opposite to
Arthur's.   Injustice, falsehood, cruelty, are his
characteristics, and out of these are born coarse
cynicism in sensualism, and hatred of pure love.
Vivien, under his tuition, is shown the truth
betimes—

> That old true filth, and bottom of the well,
> Where Truth is hidden.

Therefore when she hears of the vows of chastity
at the Court of Arthur, she does not believe that
a single one of the knights is pure.   Absolute
unbelief in good is part of the mere lust of the
flesh.   With it is hatred of those who differ from
herself, and deep hatred makes her cruel, fearless,
and deceitful.   Then, there is nothing she does
so easily as lying, and the lying, combined with
hatred and unbelief of goodness, causes her to be
the furious slanderer, or the soft-sliding suggester
of slander.   This is Tennyson's outline of sensuality
and of its attendant sins.

This allegorical outline is filled up carefully, and
in nothing better than in Vivien's sincerity.   She
makes a bold defence of the lust of the flesh being
the proper god and king of the world.   Of this
god she is the worshipper, the priestess, and the
missionary.   There is a song of hers in *Balin*

and Balan which glorifies the fire of the appetites
and senses.   It might have been written for the
worship of Astarte, and it is splendidly imagined
by Tennyson.   It sets the sensual side of pagan
Nature-worship into the keenest contrast with the
self-control of Christianity.   The fire from heaven
she speaks of is not the holy fire of the pure
spirit ; it is the fire of that heaven which some
have conceived, and which consists in the full enjoyment of desire.   It is this blaze of desire which
she sees in all Nature as well as in man, and it
creates, she thinks, the real beauty of the world.
Tennyson got to the heart of the thing in this
exultant pagan song.   Take the two last verses :

> The fire of Heaven is on the dusty ways.
> The wayside blossoms open to the blaze.
> The whole wood-world is one full peal of praise,
> The fire of Heaven is not the flame of Hell.
>
> The fire of Heaven is lord of all things good,
> And starve not thou this fire within thy blood,
> But follow Vivien thro' the fiery flood !
> The fire of Heaven is not the flame of Hell !
>
> Then turning to her squire: "This fire of Heaven,
> This old sun-worship, boy, will rise again,
> And beat the cross to earth, and break the King
> And all his Table." *

This is Vivien as she is——honest, true, and bold,
confessing evil and rejoicing in it.   The whole
sketch of her in *Balin and Balan* is of this strain

---

* See in *The Holy Grail* what the Paynim people say to Sir
Bors :

> What other fire than he,
> Whereby the blood beats, and the blossom blows,
> And the sea rolls, and all the world is warmed?

of triumphant daring. Her tale of slander about the Queen is there delivered with a ring of conquest in it. Her mocking of her boy squire and of Balan has the bravery of a queen of sin. She laughs loud at the fools of knights who have cast away their lives when they were goodly enough to have " cropt the myriad flower of May." She has not only no pity, but active cruelty. Come, she cries to her squire, I cannot brook to look upon those wounded to the death—leave them to the wolves.

It is a fine sketch—better, I think, than anything contained in *Vivien and Merlin* itself. In that Idyll Vivien comes to the Court. She creeps and whispers through it, sowing the seeds of slander and of her own impurity. She leavens the lowest characters, as Arthur does the highest. She fixes the scandal of Lancelot and Guinevere in all men's minds ; and finally flies away with Merlin that she may destroy his use and name and fame by the spell which consigns him to a living tomb. The incarnation of the pure intellect is ruined by the lust of the flesh.

There is no need to tell the story of this Idyll. It is excessively disagreeable, but it is chiefly disagreeable because its form is ill-conceived. The main tale is as old as humanity. It is the tale of knowledge, of experience, of philosophy made foolish in old age by a woman, that she may gain the glory of a conquest at which she will laugh for a week with the young. It is so common that it has formed one of the folk-tales of the world. The most famous of these is the bridling and saddling of Aristotle by the mistress of Alexander, and her riding the philosopher up and down the garden paths in the sight of the king.   Tennyson re-invents this common tale, and his way of doing it is open to the gravest criticism.   There are noble episodes in the poem, passages of fine ethical quality, passages of creative imagination ; but as a whole, and especially in the conceptions of Merlin and Vivien, it is not only in the wrong, but unpleasantly in the wrong.

Vivien almost ceases to be allegorical, and is represented as a woman. She is endurable as long as she symbolises the Lust of the flesh. We know that in the realm of allegory the personification of Luxuria must be made devoid of any possibility of good. But when Vivien is made a woman, as in this Idyll, she is detestable. Absolute falsehood, unredeemed meanness, "motiveless malignity," are not found in sane humanity, and Vivien is all the three. She is not a woman at all. Not even the very worst of her type was ever like her. This native inhumanity makes her ways and speeches unnatural, and because unnatural, vulgar. All the art of the piece, because of this error in form by which Vivien the woman is confused with Vivien as Luxuria, is not good in art. The immense skill Tennyson bestows upon it is wasted.

The conception of Merlin is equally unnatural. The story of an old man allured to his ruin by a young woman is in itself almost too disagreeable for art to take as a subject ; but if it be taken, it ought to be kept within nature ; it ought not to be made revolting ; it ought to be excused and made piteous by a kind of madness in the man. And this is done in the original tale in Malory. Merlin there falls into a dotage; he is "assotted" by one of the Ladies of the Lake. Love in an old man, the most miserable and cruel of all the forms of passion, turns the wise magician into a fool; and the Lady of the Lake, herself quite pure, but weary to death of him, works the spell upon him and buries him under a rock. This is natural and human, and it wakens our sorrow and pity; moreover, it excuses the man and the woman. But Tennyson has chosen to work it otherwise. Merlin is not in love; he only wavers on the verge of affection. He has not lost his senses or his sense. He is as wise as ever; he sees through Vivien; he even hates her character, her slander and her foulness of soul; he suspects she wants to destroy his use and fame and name— and yet he yields. Up to the last moment he is in full possession of his good sense, and then he is swept away by the woman's importunity, by a momentary warming of his blood. He is made by this, not an object of pity, but of contempt. Had he been in love, he would have been a fool as Vivien calls him; but he would have been assotted, in a dotage from the beginning. As it is, he is not mad, not a fool, but he is suddenly self-degraded. And yet he says nothing base, which makes the art of the piece all the worse. The conditions and the position are out of Nature; or, if such a thing can be in Nature, it is too improbable for art to use as a subject, and too ugly.

Of course, to make such a conception endurable at all, the greatest intellectual skill has to be employed, and Tennyson labours at the situation

he has invented. It is done by the understanding, not by the imagination ; for the imagination would refuse to work at this false conception. The speeches Merlin and Vivien make are
concocted, not created. The worst of them are
Vivien's. Tennyson had some notion of what the
man would say, but he did not know what the
woman—and especially this type of woman—was
likely to say. His ignorance of such women does
not make his work better. Nevertheless, in the
midst of this main current of the story there are
islands of noble poetry ; and there are episodes,
apart from the story, which belong to the pure
imagination. One part, even of Vivien's representation, is admirable. It is her outburst of false
tenderness, during which she sings the song of
" Trust me not at all, or all in all," which begins :

> In love, if love be love, if love be ours,
> Faith and unfaith can ne'er be equal powers ;
> Unfaith in aught is want of faith in all.
>
> It is the little rift within the lute
> That by and by will make the music mute,
> And, ever widening, slowly silence all.

This song is excellent in its representation of
half-true, half-false sentiment, and for the subtle
way in which the false sentiment in it is made to
overtop the true. It is all the more excellent when
we contrast it with that true rendering of Vivien
by herself in the song which extols the fire of the
Pagan heaven. Merlin detects its masked untruthfulness, and sets over against it the song he once
heard sung by a young knight in the early days of
Arthur's reign, when they projected the founding

of the Round Table for love of God and men. This is a lovely, clarion-versed passage—one of the brilliantly-invented episodes which occur in this Idyll :

> Far other was the song that once I heard
> By this huge oak, sung nearly where we sit :
> For here we met, some ten or twelve of us,
> To chase a creature that was current then
> In these wild woods, the hart with golden horns.
> It was the time when first the question rose
> About the founding of a Table Round,
> That was to be, for love of God and men
> And noble deeds, the flower of all the world.
> And each incited each to noble deeds.
> And while we waited, one, the youngest of us,
> We could not keep him silent, out he flash'd,
> And into such a song, such fire for fame,
> Such trumpet-blowings in it, coming down
> To such a stern and iron-clashing close,
> That when he stopt we long'd to hurl together,
> And should have done it ; but the beauteous beast,
> Scared by the noise upstarted at our feet,
> And like a silver shadow slipt away
> Thro' the dim land ; and all day long we rode
> Thro' the dim land against a rushing wind,
> That glorious roundel echoing in our ears,
> And chased the flashes of his golden horns
> Until they vanish'd by the fairy well
> That laughs at iron.

A speech of Merlin's follows, on true love and fame, and their relation each to each, worthy of the study of all men and women, and done in Tennyson's weightiest and fullest manner. The more excellent it is in itself, the more it reveals the unnaturalness of the main conception. That Merlin should so speak, and an hour afterwards yield as he yielded, shocks both intelligence and feeling. But the speech is not only good ; it is

also personally interesting.   It tells us Tennyson's
thoughts about his fame, and his desire to have
his fame in the use that his poetry may be to the
world.   Merlin's memory of what he felt when he
looked as a young man on the second star in the
dagger of Orion, is so particular a recollection that
I cannot but imagine that Tennyson is relating a
story of himself :

> A single misty star,
> Which is the second in a line of stars
> That seem a sword beneath a belt of three—
> I never gazed upon it but I dreamt
> Of some vast charm concluded in that star
> To make fame nothing.

If this conjecture be true, we see the poet in his
youth, dreaming of fame and yet controlling his
dreams.   It is Tennyson all over, and this sober
self-control, standing guard over fervent imagination, is one of the secrets of his power.   But the
most brilliant of the episodes, happy in invention,
vivid in imaginative treatment, is the story Merlin
tells of his magic book and of the origin of the
spell by which he is finally overcome.

Moreover, in dispraising the drawing of Merlin
under Vivien's temptation we should not forget
to praise the drawing of his state of mind at the
beginning ; the melancholy for himself and the
world that fell upon him in dark and dim presentiment, and the illustrations from Nature by
which it is imaged.   Merlin before his vanishing,
and in the prophetic air of death, sees all the woe
that is to be, all the fates of Arthur's kingdom :

> Then fell on Merlin a great melancholy :
> He walk'd with dreams and darkness, and he found

A doom that ever poised itself to fall,
An ever-moaning battle in the mist,
World-war of dying flesh against the life,
Death in all life and lying in all love,
The meanest having power upon the highest,
And the high purpose broken by the worm.

This is greatly conceived and felt, and equal to it in poetic power—one of Tennyson's most subtle and splendid illustrations—is this :

So dark a forethought roll'd about his brain
As on a dull day in an ocean cave
The blind wave feeling round his long sea-hall
In silence.

The full power of human imagination is added in those lines to the business of the sea, and lifts the thing into a great nobility ; while in his next illustration of the same presentiment he describes exactly what many have seen but few observed :

O did ye never lie upon the shore,
And watch the curl'd white of the coming wave
Glass'd in the slippery sand before it breaks ?
Ev'n such a wave, but not so pleasurable,
Dark in the glass of some presageful mood,
Had I for three days seen, ready to fall.

It remains to say one word of the scenery of the piece and of its close. We are in the wild forest of Broceliande in Brittany. Great meadows, full of buttercups, fill the space between the sea and the huge wood. The wood is of ancient oaks ; in it there are glades, and sweet springs dropping from the rocky clefts, and fairy wells ; and Merlin and Vivien sit near a hollow oak, the same, perhaps, that Heine saw. There the storm overtakes them, and they refuge in the hollow tree. As the

lightning leaps and the thunder peals, Vivien flies
into Merlin's arms and has her way :

> And ever overhead
> Bellow'd the tempest, and the rotten branch
> Snapt in the rushing of the river-rain
> Above them.

It is a habit of Tennyson's, as I have said
before, to make Nature reflect the passions of
man, and the end of *Vivien* is no exception to this
common rule.

The Idyll of *Lancelot and Elaine* follows that of
Merlin and Vivien. Woven in and out of it is
the story of the development to which the love of
Lancelot and Guinevere had now attained, and this
is one of the best and most human pieces of work
in the Idylls. I will, however, keep it for a more
fitting place. The character of Elaine herself and
her story can be put with brevity, and it is not
difficult to see why Elaine follows Vivien.

Elaine is set over against Vivien in the fullest
contrast. As the root of Vivien is conscious guilt,
so the root of Elaine is unconscious innocence. As
Vivien has the boldness of Hate derived from lust,
so Elaine has the boldness of Love derived from
purity. Vivien lives in the dry, clear world of
cynicism. Not one wavering mist of fancy clouds
her cruel eyes—not one imagination of love touches
her. Elaine lives in a world of dim fantasy and all
the fantasy is born of love. She was happy, not
knowing she was happy, till she saw Sir Lancelot.
Then she loved, and loved for her death. She

is the Lady of Shalott (Shalott is Astolat) over again, but with a tender difference :

> Out flew the web and floated wide,
> The mirror crack'd from side to side,
> "The curse is come upon me," cried
> The Lady of Shalott.

Vivien lives, Elaine dies—it is the way of this world. But Elaine begins in joy. Lancelot, riding in secrecy to the jousts for the diamond, comes to Astolat, the castle of Elaine's father, and leaves his shield, since its emblazonings would reveal who he was, behind him. And Elaine, who, having seen him once, has loved him at first sight and for ever, keeps the shield in her chamber, and with the creative fancy of a maiden, weaves histories over every dint and scratch made in it, conjecturing when and where :

> This cut is fresh ;
> That ten years back ; this dealt him at Caerlyle ;
> That at Caerleon ; this at Camelot ;
> And ah, God's mercy, what a stroke was there !

" So she lived in fantasy "—and a beautiful and true picture it is of a young girl's heart ! If the dreams of young imagination, as Wordsworth sings, keep pure the heart, the pure heart of youth has lovelier imaginations than any experience of life can bring, sweeter and more varied fantasies than any genius that has sinned and sorrowed. But they are always silent. Tennyson has seen clearly this beautiful thing. In all his work there is nothing truer to womanhood than his picture of Elaine ; and true to that moment of womanhood so difficult to represent, when the girl, suddenly touched by a great love, becomes the woman. If here and there the allegorical element enters into her, it is not obtrusive, and it is a comfort to be freed from it. This is a real woman : not symbolic, but human. Her blood is eloquent upon her cheek ; she lives most keenly when she dies. Her movements are thoughts, her thoughts are passions. Her dead body speaks. She is a true creation.

Nor do I know anything in his work more tender than her character, her love, and her fate. The tenderness of Tennyson is one of his remarkable qualities—not so much in itself, for other poets have been more tender—but in combination with his rough power. We are not surprised that his rugged strength is capable of the mighty and tragic tenderness of Rizpah, but we do not think at first that he could feel and realise the exquisite tenderness of Elaine. But, no : both are in his capacity. It is a wonderful thing to have so wide a tenderness, and only a great poet can possess and use it well.

Moreover, with the power of delicate tenderness goes subtlety of treatment ; and Elaine was exceedingly difficult to do with sufficient fineness of touch. Her innocent boldness might well have become unmaidenly. She does not conceal her love ; she lets Lancelot see it ; she strives to make him hers ; finally, she confesses her love to him, she will be anything to him—if not his wife, to follow him as servant.

> Then suddenly and passionately she spoke :
> " I have gone mad. I love you ; let me die."
> " Ah, sister," answer'd Lancelot, " what is this ? "
> And innocently extending her white arms,

" Your love," she said, " your love—to be your wife."
And Lancelot answer'd : " Had I chosen to wed
I had been wedded earlier, sweet Elaine ;
But now there never will be wife of mine."
" No, no," she cried, " I care not to be wife,
But to be with you still, to see your face,
To serve you, and to follow you thro' the world."

She rises to the very verge of innocent maidenliness in passionate love, but she does not go over the verge. And to be on the verge, and not pass beyond it, is the very peak of innocent girlhood when seized by over-mastering love. It was as difficult to represent Elaine as to represent Juliet ; and Tennyson has succeeded well where Shakspere has succeeded beautifully. It is great praise, but it is well deserved. Moreover, had her love been commonplace, if true love is ever commonplace, she might have been somewhat injured in our eyes. But the greatness of Lancelot excuses her. She loves no young carpet-knight, but the noblest ; gaunt with battles without, and his face marred with fierce battles within. He wins her heart as Othello won Desdemona by telling of glorious wars, and few battle-passages are finer than Tennyson's rapid and fierce sketch on Lancelot's lips of the twelve great battles, and finally of Arthur standing after the last fight on the top of Mount Badon :

High on a heap of slain, from spur to plume
Red as the rising sun with heathen blood,
*   *   *   *   *
I never saw his like, there lives
No greater leader.

"Save your great self, fair lord," said Elaine to her heart. And next morning he rode away, wearing her favour, which her innocent daring

asked him to carry, and leaving her his shield.
When she hears of his dreadful wound—

> Through her own side she felt the sharp lance go.

It is a line of which Shakspere might be proud.
When Gawain asks for her love, she is not ashamed
to tell him she loves Lancelot. She cannot rest
at home, having heard of his wound, and begs her
father to let her go and tend on Lancelot. It is
a lovely passage, and she woos her father to her
will as sweetly as a bird sings; and then, going,
she hears in her heart:

> Being so very wilful you must die.

And her conviction that she will die of her love
excuses all her devotion to one who does not care
for her. When to the world she would seem
unwomanly, she is most womanly. Certainty of
death dissolves conventions. When she sees
Lancelot she utters

> A little tender dolorous cry;

and when he kisses her as we kiss a child, it is
more to her:

> At once she slipt like water to the floor:
> *   *   *   *   *
> And all her heart's sad secret blazed itself
> In the heart's colours on her simple face.

And, having tended him into health, she tells her
love, and he offers her all friendship and its
offices. "Of all this will I nothing," she cries,
and, swooning, is borne to her tower-room, and
Lancelot rides away. All this is beautifully, intimately conceived. Nor is her death less graciously,

less powerfully wrought. These are lovely lines
which tell of her lonely watch at night :

> Death, like a friend's voice from a distant field
> Approaching thro' the darkness, call'd: the owls
> Wailing had power upon her, and she mixt
> Her fancies with the sallow-rifted glooms
> Of evening, and the moanings of the wind.

And the song that follows, how simply wrought
it is, and yet how subtly—with the subtlety of
long passion's inter-woven thought :

> Sweet is true love tho' given in vain, in vain ;
> And sweet is death who puts an end to pain ;
> I know not which is sweeter, no, not I.
>
> Love, art thou sweet? then bitter death must be :
> Love, thou art bitter ; sweet is death to me.
> O love, if death be sweeter, let me die.
>
> Sweet love, that seems not made to fade away,
> Sweet death, that seems to make us loveless clay,
> I know not which is sweeter, no, not I.
>
> I fain would follow love, if that could be ;
> I needs must follow death, who calls for me :
> Call and I follow, I follow ! let me die.

This is almost like a piece out of the sonnets
of Shakspere, full of his to-and-fro play with
words that are thoughts ; with the same kind of
all-pervading emotion in the lines ; the same truth to
the situation and the character of the singer ; and
with Tennyson's deep-seated waters of love—which
too rarely come to the surface—welling upwards in
it. That which follows is almost at the same
level :

> High with the last line scaled her voice, and this,
> All in a fiery dawning wild with wind
> That shook her tower, her brothers heard, and thought

U

With shuddering, " Hark the Phantom of the house
That ever shrieks before a death," and call'd
The father, and all three in hurry and fear
Ran to her, and lo ! the blood-red light of dawn
Flared on her face, she shrilling, " Let me die."

Then, out of that great passion she entered into
quietude, and set forth her funeral, becoming in
her memory a little child again. For she remembers
how often she wished to pass the poplar on the
stream, and might not ; but now she will, laid in
her boat, pass beyond it, dead, and so sail with
her dying message to Lancelot into the very palace
of the King. Therefore, this being promised her,
and saying many beautiful things of trust and
honour, in innocence and cheerfulness she dies.

A fair life and a fair death ! It is sorrowful, but
she had her joy. She loved ; she loved one worthy
of her love, and her heart made him worthier still.
Of him she believed no wrong, for in herself there
was no wrong. Her innocence was more than
earth could bear, and it was well it was borne
away to heaven. None may dare to mourn her
fate ; it was as blest as the heart of Love could
make it. There are, like her, rare souls on earth
so wonderfully fortunate in their fate that our
troubled hearts cannot imagine their happiness ;
and she was one of these. Our pity is with
Lancelot, with Guinevere, with Arthur, but not
with her.

The story of the Holy Grail, the Holy Vessel,
traces its origins back to a remote antiquity. The
oldest elements of the tale were Celtic (chiefly
Irish), and their symbolism was not Christian,

but heathen. Two sets of stories, according to
Mr. Nutt, were the starting-point of the Grail
legend. In the first set a kinsman avenged a
blood-feud by means of three magic talismans—
the sword, the lance, and the vessel; in the
second set the hero visits a castle under a spell, and
finds all its indwellers fed by a magic vessel, and
living by its means a prolonged life; from which
fortune or misfortune they are freed by the hero
asking a question about the vessel. When these
two tales were mixed up with the tale of Arthur,
they were thrown together into one story. The
Grail, the sword, and the lance mingle in this one
story all the powers they have in both the series
of tales. The two castles become one castle.
But the most important amalgamating element
(which was sure to run both stories into one) was
that both the castles—that to which the avenger
goes to find lance and sword for his work, and
that to which the hero goes to set free from the
spell those who are kept immortal by the vessel—
are both symbols in the original Celtic tales of one
and the same thing—of the other world, the fairyland of eternal youth. How this single story came
to be Christianised is a question which still remains
under debate. But it is plain that when it became
Christian in Britain it had a local habitation. It
had housed itself in Glastonbury, where possibly
under Welsh rule a small heathen temple dedicated
to Bran was transformed into a Christian church.
Bran in Celtic mythology was the ruler of the
Other World and would have in his charge these
talismans; the sword, the lance, and the cup.
When the temple became the church, Bran was

turned into a saint, and his magic gear naturally
takes a Christian meaning; and the first notion of
the cup and the lance as connected with Jesus, the
feeder of His people, whose blood saved them, and
whose side was pierced by the lance, would then
arise. That is, the characteristics of Bran the
heathen god of the far-off world of eternal youth,
and the gear that he possessed, were transferred to
Jesus, and fitted to the story of the Gospel.

Then an addition to this, and a modification,
were made from the legend of Joseph of Arimathea
in the Gospel of Nicodemus, a gospel which had
a great vogue in England in early English times.
A fuller Christian import was given to the Grail
from the story of Jesus in that gospel. The Grail
is now the dish used at the Last Supper, and that
with which Joseph caught the last drop of blood
which fell from the side or the feet of Christ.
Joseph, thrown into prison, is supernaturally fed
from this sacred vessel for forty-two years.

The next step is when a British legend brings
Joseph to Britain, and the Grail is laid up at
Glastonbury. Joseph takes the place now of Bran.
After his death, the Grail is hidden from men, until
the destined knight appears who is to achieve its
Quest. Then its meaning further developed. It
became the symbol of the mightiest miracle of the
Roman Church, of the change of the body and
blood of Jesus into the substance of the bread and
wine. Thence arose the great and fruitful conception of the search for the Holy Grail as the search
for absolute union with Christ. A few, now and
again, behold it. It seems a crystal cup with rose-
red beatings as of a heart in it, and with it is often

a platter on which bread lies, into which bread a white child smites himself. It holds then the body and blood of God. When the knights of Arthur see it in the hall, it appears covered ; thunderings and lightnings attend it, and the roofs rack and rive as it passes by. The heroes leap to their feet, and swear that for a year and a day they will take up the Quest to see it uncovered. This is only one form of the manifold tales of this Holy Quest. A hundred poets took it up, and wove round it the romantic adventures of a hundred knights. The people loved it for its adventures ; the Church loved it, for it brought, by means of the tale, all the poetic enjoyment of the people into close contact with the central doctrine of the Church of Rome.

There is one more thing to say. Before the Grail embodied the full sacramental meaning it had, while it was yet half heathen and half Christian, Percivale is the hero of the Quest ; but when the notion of absolute chastity, of total division from woman as the necessity for perfect union with Christ, spread far and wide, Percivale was not pure enough to achieve the Quest, and Galahad, the virgin in body and soul, was invented. A new series of tales having Galahad as hero, and glorifying virginity, now arose. To this there was one exception. When the story of the Grail was used by Wolfram von Eschenbach in Germany, we find Percivale in his pre-eminent position ; and Tennyson, in this Idyll, reverts as it were unconsciously to the original importance of Percivale.*

* This is a remark of Mr. Nutt in his delightful book on *The Holy Grail*. I have followed his explanation of the development of the Grail story—an explanation largely, it should be noted,

It is Percivale that tells the story—we see Galahad through his eyes. Nevertheless it is the virgin Galahad alone who in the *Idylls* fully wins the Quest, who not only always sees the Grail, but finally goes with it to that spiritual city which is the Christian representative of the Welsh Avalon, and also of the Irish Tir-na-nogue, the land of undying youth.

So far Tennyson clings to the ecclesiastical form of the tale. But though he accepted the virginity of Galahad as necessary for the achieving of the Quest, the spirit of his poem is whole leagues away from the ideal of the Galahad-romances which glorified a life of complete spiritual asceticism, and which, conceiving that woman was the great plague and evil matter of the world, made this hero reject, as deadly to spiritual perfection, human love and marriage.

That was not the ideal of Wolfram in the *Parsifal*. Parsifal in Wolfram's poem is the ideal king who marries the woman he loves and completes his life in her, whose work is to stay in the world, and to make it better by noble government. Tennyson takes this line in the *Idylls*, but he is plainer than Wolfram, for Wolfram only lets us infer his view. Tennyson deliberately sets himself to make an allegory, the meaning of which shall be——That ascetic

---

hypothetical, owing to the nature of the evidence upon which the student must rely. This caution applies with especial force to that portion of the hypothesis which assumes the conversion of a heathen Bran into the Christian Bron. It may be added, however, that although considerable research has been bestowed upon the Grail legend since the appearance of Mr. Nutt's book (1888), no alternative hypothesis has been propounded that has won the acceptance of scholars.

religion, an exciting pursuit of signs and wonders, severance from home and from the common love of man and woman, and a retreat from the daily work of the world into cloistered seclusion or in pursuit of a supernatural spiritualism, are, save for a few exceptional characters, entirely evil. These things dissolve societies, injure human life, and produce the very evils they are invented to overcome. The opposite life to that, the life of Arthur, is the right life.

In this modern re-making of the legend of the Holy Grail the symbolism of the story is wheeled right round by Tennyson. The search for the Holy Grail is a mistake; an evil, not a good. The true life is to bring heaven to earth for others; the untrue, to seek, apart from earth, a heaven for one's self. Nevertheless, like the wisest poets who are not intolerant of all theories of life but their own, nor ignorant of the variousness of man, Tennyson allows that there may be a few for whom this virgin, ascetic, spiritual life is fitted, and who perform, in that life, their own special work of representing before mankind the ideal holiness, the immortal quest of perfection. And he chooses to put this point in the persons of Percivale's sister and Sir Galahad.*

* I think there is more in it than this. The image of the stainless knight, wholly apart from sex and appetite, divided from the material interests of the world, a pure spirit clothed for a time in flesh, but the flesh so refined by the spirit that it becomes archangelic matter, a terrible crystal of pure love; moving in the supernatural world, with all its powers round him, yet on earth—this image, independent altogether of ascetic theology, was one of the finest "motives" art could have; and its artistic elements were a great part of the reason why it entered the heart of the world and lodged there. Wolfram's

Percivale's sister is admirably drawn, all the main characteristics of the mystic female saint, like Catherine of Siena, are embodied in her ; and the picture is made by scattered touches given with apparent lightness through the story. She was no cold-hearted maid. The type of which she is the image has a passionate temperament :

> A holy maid—tho' never maiden glow'd,
> But that was in her earlier maidenhood,
> With such a fervent flame of human love.

This passion, rudely blunted, turned to an ardent longing for union with Christ. In that longing all that was earthly in her wasted away, till in her eyes alone shone fire, the spiritual fire of holiness that had power to awaken in others the same desire :

> And so she pray'd and fasted, till the sun
> Shone, and the wind blew, thro' her, and I thought
> She might have risen and floated when I saw her.

At last she sees the vision, and she sees it through her own high-wrought and delicate passion. It comes, attended by such music as an ethereal ear might hear—as of a silver horn far off, blown o'er the hills, a slender sound, unlike all

Parsifal drops to a lower level of art because he did not use this "motive." When Wagner imagined the *Parsifal*, he felt an artist's need of this motive, and he restored this other-world purity to Percivale. When Tennyson took up the story, he preserved this virgin, spotless ideal of Galahad, even though his view of human life and duty was opposed to the ascetic life connected with it. He could not miss the dazzling ideal of Galahad as an art-subject. The artist, as it were against the man's will, was stronger in him than the social moralist. Galahad remains Galahad. Tennyson even adds another image of the same conception in a woman, in the sister of Percivale.

earthly music. And when the Grail streams through the cell, the beam down which it steals is silver-cold, as the maiden heart that sees it ; but the Grail is rose-red ; in it are rosy beatings as of a living heart, and the white walls of the cell are dyed with rosy colours. Cold to earth, ecstatic to heaven ; it is the very vision of a mystic maiden's passionate purity. And the verses are fitted to the vision. Then, recognising a kindred soul in Galahad, she weaves a belt for him out of her hair, and speaks to him in the language of earthly love, yet there is no earth in it.

> " My knight, my love, my knight of heaven,
> O thou, my love, whose love is one with mine,
> I, maiden, round thee, maiden, bind my belt.
> Go forth, for thou shalt see what I have seen,
> And break thro' all, till one will crown thee king
> Far in the spiritual city : " and, as she spake,
> She sent the deathless passion in her eyes
> Thro' him, and made him hers, and laid her mind
> On him, and he believed in her belief.

From point to point, the representation embodies the whole type, gathering together into one personality many characteristics of separate enthusiasts.

Galahad is different. He sees the same glory, but he does not retire from the world, save in spirit. He is still the warrior. He has courage to sit in the "Perilous Seat," in which whosoever sits, loses himself. Merlin was lost in it, seating himself in it inadvertently. But Galahad, claiming loss of self as salvation——and the whole passage with Tennyson's spiritual meaning in it is his own invention——sits in it of set purpose, crying, " If I lose myself, I find myself," and sees the Holy Grail.

After that, day by day, the thing is always with him :

> Fainter by day, but always in the night
> Blood-red, and sliding down the blacken'd marsh
> Blood-red, and on the naked mountain top
> Blood-red, and in the sleeping mere below
> Blood-red.

But it companies with him, not to send him to the cloister, but to war.   " I rode," he cries,

> " Shattering all evil customs everywhere,
> And past thro' Pagan realms and made them mine,
> And clashed thro' Pagan hordes and bore them down,
> And broke thro' all, and in the strength of this
> Came victor."

His hour has now come to be crowned in the spiritual city, and he bids Percivale go with him, and see his departure.   In conception, in invention, in description of invented landscape, and in artistic work, this passing of Galahad is splendidly written. It is too long to quote in full, too knit together to be spoiled by extracts, and too poetic to criticise. It is its own best criticism.*

This great and lofty vision of the glory of the

---

* This beginning I may quote. Whoever has seen, while involved in it, a fierce thunderstorm on a mountain-top, and the pine-forests below smitten by the quick-gleaming bolt, will know with what extraordinary truth and force Tennyson has made it.

> There rose a hill that none but man could climb,
> Scarr'd with a hundred wintry watercourses—
> Storm at the top, and when we gain'd it, storm
> Round us and death ; for every moment glanced
> His silver arms and gloom'd : so quick and thick
> The lightnings here and there to left and right
> Struck, till the dry old trunks about us, dead,
> Yea, rotten with a hundred years of death,
> Sprang into fire.

pure spiritual life, refined and thrilled by heavenly holiness into full union with the world beyond the sense, and needing no death to enter into the perfect life, is done as no one has done this kind of work since Dante. It is made all the more vivid, and its unfitness for the common toil of goodness on this earth is shown, by the contrast which Tennyson immediately makes to it in the daily life of the poor monk Ambrosius, who knows nought of marvels, but is the providence of the little village near which he lives ; who does not understand these unearthly visions, but who pities the men who, having known the sweetness of love, surrender it for dreams. His head swims when he reads of ecstasies and dreams, and then " I go forth," he says, " and pass

> Down to the little thorpe that lies so close,
> And almost plaster'd like a martin's nest
> To these old walls—and mingle with our folk."

And the delightful description, which follows these lines, of the work of this small, comfortable and comforting village priest shows not only how Tennyson liked this type, but also marks the range of a poet who could, as it were in one breath, write the sublime passing of Galahad and, immediately after, this homely, loving sketch of a small monk's life in a small world.

These then, Percivale's sister and Galahad, were the two, woman and man, who might attain the vision of the perfect love through utter separation from the flesh—that is, in the Christian idea, through loss of self. But, in attaining it, they were ravished from earth and the work of earth.

All men and women were as phantoms to them. They left behind them the impression of excelling purity, and that was good ; but it was purity severed from humanity, and that was not good.

But as to the rest of the knights, who made their vow to see the vision of the Grail, the greater number failed to see, but did not fail to be useless. They "followed wandering fires," lost themselves, and were lost to men. A few saw something, but not the whole. The vision comes to each according to the soul of each. Lancelot, who has made the vow to seek the vision of pure holiness and love, while his heart loves his sin, sees the Grail covered, but sees it as holy wrath and fire, as swift and stern condemnation. That which is sweet and gentle to Galahad——the light of which is soft rose, and the colour and the music of which is as of a silver horn among far hills to the sister of Percivale——is to Lancelot a stormy glare, a heat

As from a seventimes-heated furnace,

from which he swoons, blasted, and burnt, and blinded. We hear how the others fared, according to their character. But however the vision came or did not come, the pursuit of it, as Tennyson thought, was the ruin of noble association for just government, the contradiction and not the realisation of true religion. It breaks up the Round Table. The kingdom is left without its defenders, and when the remnant return they are exhausted. Their failure to reach ideal goodness has made them reckless, and drives them into base materialism. That which was left of truth and purity in the court lessens day by day. Sensuality, in swift reaction from asceticism, has full sway, and the fall is rapid. But where then, Tennyson asks, is spirituality to be found, where pure holiness, and love which beholds the invisible kingdom? It is to be found where Arthur found it, in the midst of human life, in honest love of men, in doing our duty where God has placed us.

Arthur, who represents this view of Tennyson, has, he says, his own visions. He has more. He sees God, not as a vision, but face to face. He does not wander on the quest of the Holy Grail, but He whose sacrifice of love the Holy Grail embodied is always with him. So says the king, and Percivale, less spiritual in his ascetic solitude than Arthur, does not "know all he meant." For, and I quote the passage, it is Tennyson's summing up of all the Idyll and its allegory :

> "Some among you held, that if the King
> Had seen the sight he would have sworn the vow;
> Not easily, seeing that the King must guard
> That which he rules, and is but as the hind
> To whom a space of land is given to plow.
> Who may not wander from the allotted field
> Before his work be done; but, being done,
> Let visions of the night or of the day
> Come, as they will; and many a time they come,
> Until this earth he walks on seems not earth.
>
> *   *   *   *   *
>
> In moments when he feels he cannot die
> And knows himself no vision to himself,
> Nor the high God a vision, nor that One
> Who rose again : ye have seen what ye have seen."
>
> So spake the King; I knew not all he meant,

I turn now to the literary quality of this poem. I have written at large concerning its allegory, because this Idyll, unlike the rest, is pure allegory. It does not come under the objection I have made to the others in which the allegory and the story are mixed together to the troubling of both. In this Idyll, the story is Tennyson's own ; he has invented it for the sake of his allegory. The form then is excellent, and the excellence of the form has acted throughout upon the minor inventions within the main invention, on the verse, the metaphors, and the details. It is good from beginning to end ; the most unexceptionable piece of work that Tennyson has done in the *Idylls.* Criticism has nothing to object to ; it is lost in admiration and respect.

The framework of the tale could not be better conceived. Sir Percivale who has known the great world tells the story to Ambrosius, a simple brother of the monastery who knows nothing but his village. This invention enables Tennyson constantly to contrast the exalted with the simple type of mind, the earth-loving with the heaven-loving soul. Again we hear in the remarks of Ambrosius the same views as those which Arthur held concerning the Quest, given, not in the high words of the king, but in the simple thoughts of the uneducated monk who loved the daily life of men. This was a happy thought of the artist. It leads up to and doubles the force of Arthur's view of the matter—that is, of Tennyson's decision of the whole question.

An inner unity is also given to the story and to its various episodes, which otherwise would be too unconnected, by their being knit up into the one tale of Percivale. We never lose the image of the quiet, war-worn knight, sitting with Ambrosius in the cloister. Even the unity of place is thus preserved. The great adventures and the great adventurers, the city of Camelot, the pictured hall and the fierce vision of the Grail that went through it, the ride of Percivale, the passing of Galahad, the wild voyage of Lancelot, are all brought into the still enclosure where the two peaceful figures sit in the sun. There,

> Beneath a world-old yew-tree, darkening half
> The cloisters, on a gustful April morn
> That puff'd the swaying branches into smoke *
> Above them, ere the summer when he died,
> The monk Ambrosius question'd Percivale.

Then, step by step, every episode in order, each illustrating one another, each in its right place to advance and clinch the conclusion, the story, or rather the allegory in the story, flows on with such ease and simplicity, that it seems to grow like a tree by its own divine vitality. And each episode has the quality, character, and power of its chief personage stamped upon it and ruling its manner of representation, its invention, its wording, and even its rhythm.

I have quoted enough from the story of Percivale's sister and Sir Galahad to prove the splendour of the invention. Even when the story is not quite

---

* The stamen-bearing flowers of the yew are covered with an abundant yellow pollen, which the wind disperses. Each flower sends up its little puff of sulphur-coloured smoke. Thus the pistil-bearing flowers which, like small acorns, grow apart from the stamen-bearing ones, receive the pollen. This smoking of the yew, which belongs more to March than April, seized on Tennyson's observing fancy. He added a stanza to *In Memoriam* in order to use it in the poem. [xxxix.]

new, as in the case of Lancelot's voyage to
Carbonek, it is so entirely recast that it becomes a
fresh pleasure—recast, not only for the sake of
the allegory, but also for the joy that Tennyson,
like a child, felt in the making of high romance.
I illustrate this by three things in the poem.
The first of these is Percivale's story of his setting
forth upon the Quest. Tennyson's object is to
show that pride in one's self, and its extreme
opposite—despair of sin, which throws us back on
self—alike render the life of exalted holiness impossible, because for that we must, like Galahad,
lose self altogether.

Percivale starts full of joy in his own bravery,
but as he goes, Arthur's warning that his knights
in this Quest are following wandering fires occurs
to him, and he drops down into despair. Then
he sees a series of visions. A burning thirst
consumes him ; it is the symbol of the thirst for
union with God. " And on I rode," he cries, and
I quote this especially for its accurate description
of Nature—

> And when I thought my thirst
> Would slay me, saw deep lawns, and then a brook,
> With one sharp rapid, *where the crisping white*
> *Play'd ever back upon the sloping wave*,
> And took both ear and eye ; and o'er the brook
> Were apple trees, and apples by the brook
> Fallen, and on the lawns.

And while he drank the brook and ate the apples,
all fell into dust, and he was left alone, thirsting
still, and in a land of sand and thorns. It is
the symbol of the thirsty soul trying to find in
the beauty of Nature its true home, and failing.
Then he sees a woman spinning at the door of a

fair home, and she cries " Rest here," but she and the house fall also into dust. It is the symbol of the soul trying to find rest in domestic love, and failing.

Then he sees a yellow gleam flash along the world, and the plowman and the milkmaid fall before it ; but One, in golden armour, splendid as the sun and crowned, comes along—and he too, touched, falls into dust. It is the symbol of the soul seeking to be satisfied with the glory of the earth, chiefly to be attained in war. Then he finds a city on a hill, walled, and a great crowd that welcomes him and calls him mightiest and purest ; but when he comes near, the city is a ruined heap, and the crowd is gone. It is the symbol of the soul seeking to slake its thirst by popular applause, and especially in the fame of a ruler of men, but all is thirst and desolation as before ; and then he finds the valley of humility and of forgetfulness of his sins in the glory of God's love. It is a rich invention, and perfectly wrought.

The next illustration of this brilliant inventiveness is the description of the city of Camelot and of the hall of Arthur, and of the streets of the mediæval town when the knights depart on the Quest. The towers, the roofs, the ornaments of the town, the sculpture in the hall, the great statue of gold with its peaked wings pointing to the northern star, the glass of the twelve windows emblazoned with Arthur's wars, are all described as if the poet had seen them face to face, and with a richness which truly represents the gorgeous architecture and furniture of the old romances. Tennyson has

x

absorbed and then re-created all he has read in them. I can scarcely praise this work too highly.

Lastly, there is the story of Lancelot's half-vision of the Holy Grail and his drift over the sea to the enchanted rock of Carbonek. Its basis is to be found in the old tale ; but whoever reads it in Malory's *Morte d'Arthur* will see how imaginatively it has been re-conceived. It is full of the true romantic element ; it is close to the essence of the story of the Holy Grail ; there is nothing in all the *Idylls* more beautiful in vision and in sound ; and the art with which it is worked is as finished as the conception is majestic. I will praise it no more, but quote a part of it. To hear it is its highest praise. Lancelot, torn between his horror of his sin and his love of it, seeking the Grail that he might be free from his sin, yet knowing that he does not wish to be freed, is driven into a madness by the inward battle, " whipt into waste fields far away," and beaten down to earth by little folk, mean knights—and then " I came," he cries :

> " All in my folly to the naked shore,
> Wide flats, where nothing but coarse grasses grew ;
> But such a blast, my King, began to blow,
> So loud a blast along the shore and sea,
> Ye could not hear the waters for the blast,
> Tho' heapt in mounds and ridges all the sea
> Drove like a cataract, and all the sand
> Swept like a river, and the clouded heavens
> Were shaken with the motion and the sound."

He finds a boat, black in the sea-foam, and drives in it seven days over the deep till it shocks on the castled rock of Carbonek whose " chasm-like portals open to the sea." Then climbing the steps he passes the lions :

" And up into the sounding hall I past;
But nothing in the sounding hall I saw,
No bench nor table, painting on the wall
Or shield of knight; only the rounded moon
Thro' the tall oriel on the rolling sea.
But always in the quiet house I heard,
Clear as a lark, high o'er me as a lark,
A sweet voice singing in the topmost tower
To the eastward: up I climb'd a thousand steps
With pain : as in a dream I seem'd to climb
For ever : at the last I reach'd a door,
A light was in the crannies, and I heard,
' Glory and joy and honour to our Lord
And to the Holy Vessel of the Grail.'"

Lancelot was not only the greatest knight ; he proves here that he was the greatest singer.

The story of *Pelleas and Ettarre* as told in Malory's book is natural, simple, and common. The ground of the trouble in the tale is also simple. It is the boredom of Ettarre. She is wearied of being loved by Pelleas, for whom she feels no love. " I have no peace from him," she cries. A woman in such circumstances is naturally cruel. These are simple lines on which to move a tale ; and the Pelleas of Malory is quite an ordinary person and his Ettarre not an uncommon character of the Romances. The love-tale also has nothing out of the common, but it is interesting ; it has the romantic air, and it goes up and down between pain and pleasure in an adventurous fashion, of which it is agreeable to read in a quiet hour. I need not tell Malory's tale, for the things that happen are much the same as in Tennyson's Idyll, at least as far as that place in the tale where Pelleas leaves Ettarre and rides away. At that point, Tennyson re-casts the

story.   Pelleas, in Malory's book, departs furious
with the treachery of Gawain, and equally furious
with Ettarre, not for her unchastity, but because she
has loved another than himself.   Tortured by these
two angers, he takes to his bed to die of rage
and disappointment.   He is then found by a
Lady of the Lake who has pity on him, cures his
sickness, replaces his love of Ettarre by love of
herself; and in order to avenge Pelleas on Ettarre,
bewitches Ettarre into a hopeless love of Pelleas.
Ettarre, drawn to his bedside, beseeches for the
affection she has rejected.   Pelleas cries out,
" Begone, traitress ! " and Ettarre dies of that
sorrow.   Then Pelleas goes away gaily with the
Lady of the Lake.

There is no moral direction, nor indeed any special
purpose, in the original tale.   It is only a faithful
record of a piece of human life, quite clearly and
simply told.   But Tennyson, when he took it, had
a special aim in view, and wrote it afresh with a
moral purpose.   He wanted to represent the luxurious society which precedes the downfall of a nation,
especially after the failure of a religious revival
founded on the supernatural.   The knights have now
returned reckless from their unsuccessful effort to
achieve the Quest of the Grail ; not better but worse
than before. Religion, they feel, is useless, and an
ideal life absurd.   They had been sensual, now they
have become cynical.   Vivien, the lust of the flesh,
the enjoyment of the senses alone, is full mistress of
the world.   Ettarre represents this society ; Pelleas
represents its deadly influence on an innocent heart
that believes in love, purity and truth, and their
embodiment in the King.   He finds a world in

which the King is thought to be a fool, purity
ridiculous, love a lust, and the realm of the senses
the only realm.   Thrown suddenly and unprepared
into this society, the full force of disillusion struck
on Pelleas like a storm and sank him in the seas.
He is the later Gareth of the *Idylls*.   Frank,
faithful, loving, innocent, he steps into life ; but
where Gareth is victor, he is victim.   The conditions of society into which Gareth enters are all on
his side.   He finds life as beautiful and true as he
imagined it to be.   The conditions of society into
which Pelleas enters are all against him.   He finds
life the exact contrary of all he imagined it to be.

Gareth's history, the history of Pelleas, are
equally common stories.   When, by long neglect,
by long indulgence, a base society is made, the
souls and bodies of far more than half of the
innocent children sent into the world are murdered.
When society is just and pure, simple and loving
beautiful things, the children are destined to a noble
happiness.   Those who make a world of which the
judgment of the pessimist is true, are the worst of
criminals.   Its children, for the most part disillu-
sioned like Pelleas, are driven into madness or
cynicism.   And cynicism, or rather that recklessness
of everything but of present excitement which is the
forerunner of cynicism, is what Tennyson sketches
in *Pelleas and Ettarre*.   Ettarre and her flock of girls
laugh at the innocence and the love of Pelleas.   A
grizzled knight, they say, who knew the fashion of
the world were a better companion than this baby—
" raw, yet so stale."   Ettarre promises him her love
that he may win the prize for her and give her
fame, and when she has got her jewelled circlet,

flings his love away, flings a taunt at Guinevere, and leaves Pelleas outside her gates to cool his romance. She is the great lady of a debased society in which everything ideal is only matter of mockery. Such a society lives on the very marge of the incoming tide of weariness. It only continues to live by the fierceness of its strife to gain, hour by hour, enough of light or cruel amusement to keep that tide at bay. When Pelleas will not cease to believe in Ettarre, she is bored to death, and this turns to wrath, and wrath to hate; and when he endures all, she pushes him out of doors in bonds. When he goes, for a moment she knows herself. "He is not of my kind. He could not love me did he know me well." But the momentary touch of conscience fails when Gawain comes to see her, bringing merriment and the manners of the court with him, and she is guilty at once with him. This woman is Tennyson's ethical warning against a loose and luxury-bitten society, and, as ethics, it is well enough expressed. But to bind up these modern warnings with a mediæval tale is to render either the tale or the warnings feeble. The naturalism of the story suffers. The allegory eats it up. And the allegory suffers, for the ancient story does not carry it.

Moreover the whole Idyll is too plainly a stop-gap, a transition tale inserted to represent the kind of society which intervened between the religious excitement of *The Holy Grail* and the cynical languor of *The Last Tournament*. It does not seem to have naturally grown out of Tennyson's original conception. I conjecture this, because there is little in it of the passion of an artist. The shaping

of the poem is not fully imaginative, the work of it
seems jaded, and even the verse is inferior to that
of the other Idylls. When Tennyson attempts to
rise into passionate expression, as when Pelleas
turns and shrieks his curse at Ettarre and her harlot
towers, he becomes only violent without power.
Even the natural description suffers from the artist's
apparent want of interest in his conception. That
vivid sketch, at the beginning, of the wood and of
the bracken burning round it in the sunlight, cannot
keep up its speed and fire to the end. Either the
poet's memory of what he saw played him false, or
he did not see the thing with his usual clearness.
It is like a studio-picture, not like one painted in
the open air. Nor is there a single piece of noble
or passionate writing in the whole of it, save at the
very end, when Pelleas breaks into the hall of
Arthur, swordless, and his ruined life upon his face,
and will not speak to the Queen when she speaks
to him.

> But Pelleas lifted up an eye so fierce
> She quail'd; and he, hissing "I have no sword,"
> Sprang from the door into the dark. The Queen
> Look'd hard upon her lover, he on her;
> And each foresaw the dolorous day to be;
> And all talk died, as in a grove all song
> Beneath the shadow of some bird of prey;
> Then a long silence came upon the hall,
> And Modred thought, " The time is hard at hand."

That is finely done ; there is more of gloom and
coming woe in it than in all the cursing of Pelleas.
But it is alone ; it is the only real good piece of
art in this, the poorest of all the *Idylls*.

The Last Tournament is more a work of art than
Pelleas and Ettarre, though it is by no means up to
the level, even in form, of many of the other Idylls.
It also, like its predecessor, has the air of being
an afterthought, of something inserted to point a
moral, not to adorn the tale.　Since the whole poem
is a moral poem, we have no right to object that
this portion of it points a moral, but we have a
right to ask that it should seem a natural branch of
the whole tree.　Such a vital connection does exist
in the first part ; but the second part, the story of
Tristram, is not much more than a graft, and far too
plainly a graft.　Tristram and his story is scarcely
ever alluded to in the rest of the *Idylls :* he has
nothing to do with the Tennysonian movement of
the piece, and his story, thus foisted in at the end,
is nothing more than an illustration of adultery.
The form of the Idyll is spoiled, and we are forced
to place it on the lower plane, along with *Pelleas
and Ettarre.*

The time of the year in the preceding Idyll is full
summer, and this represents, in Tennyson's way,
the full flowering of the brutal society which he
describes.　But the season in which the last tournament is held is that of departing autumn—grey
skies, wet winds, and all the woods yellowing to
their fall.　This also is Nature's reflection of the
catastrophe in the Idyll.　Arthur knows, when the
tale is done, the guilt of Guinevere ; and Lancelot
and all his kin are finally divided from the king.
Meantime we are first shown the further degradation of the society drawn in *Pelleas and Ettarre.*
The story of this social picture is well introduced.
The tale is told of Lancelot and Arthur riding

through a mountain-pass and hearing a child wail :

> A stump of oak half-dead,
> From roots like some black coil of carven snakes,
> Clutch'd at the crag, and started thro' mid-air
> Bearing an eagle's nest : and thro' the tree
> Rush'd ever a rainy wind, and thro' the wind
> Pierced ever a child's cry.

And Lancelot climbed for the child, and round its throat lay a ruby carcanet which, when the child died, the Queen bade be tourneyed for. The purest knight, she said, should win for the purest maiden the jewels of this dead innocence. Hence the tournament is called *The Tournament of the Dead Innocence* by a court to which innocence is unknown. The prize is won by Tristram, the free-lover, and given to Isolt who abhors her husband. In this fierce contrast Tennyson strikes out on his canvas the mocking cynicism in which he involves the court. There is no innocence which is not dead, and there is no love which is innocent.

Secondly, before the jousts are held, we see how the government of the kingdom has broken down. A knight, once of the Table Round, has set up a new Round Table in the north, framed directly counter to Arthur's Table. He slays, burns, robs and maims the poor, hangs the knights of Arthur, and bids the King beware, for—

> his hour is come ;
> The heathen are upon him, his long lance
> Broken, and his Excalibur a straw.

Arthur rides away to chastise this felon, and when he returns all is ruin. But before he goes—and this is finely conceived by Tennyson—he touches those two who have destroyed his work, and leaves

an impression of himself upon them ; on Lancelot,
that which kindles remorse in him, on Guinevere,
that which awakens awe in her. She feels his
apartness, his greatness, and his spirituality.

> In her high bower the Queen,
> Working a tapestry, lifted up her head,
> Watch'd her lord pass, and knew not that she sigh'd.
> Then ran across her memory the strange rhyme
> Of bygone Merlin, "Where is he who knows?
> From the great deep to the great deep he goes."

It is the theme, the introduction theme, of the Idylls
that follow—*Guinevere, The Passing of Arthur*—
and its dim melody, brought in here, is the thought
of a true artist.

Then comes the tournament. A day of brooding
storm, low thunder, sunless skies, and then of heavy
rain, images, in Tennyson's fashion, the exhaustion,
the dull coarseness and draggle of the last days of
luxury and adultery. Lancelot, all weary, like a late
guest over a fading fire, sat umpire of the lists,
half careless, half angry with the lawlessness and
cowardice of the tourney. All its rules were
broken ; and when Tristram entered the lists no
one was brave enough to oppose him. The tournament ends in mockery and cursing, and Lancelot
cries,

> "The glory of our Round Table is no more."

When Tristram comes for the prize, Lancelot asks,
"Art thou the purest, brother?" and Tristram
scoffs, "Be happy in your fair Queen, as I in mine."
There is no trace of shame left; the nakedness of
life is openly displayed. When Tristram rides round
the lists with his prize he is discourteous to all

the women. "This day," he cries, "my Queen of Beauty is not here." So, even the glory of courtesy, that last infirmity of chivalry, is gone. Then falls thick rain, and in the wet and weariness the women mock :

> Praise the patient saints,
> Our one white day of Innocence hath past,
> Tho' somewhat draggled at the skirt. So be it.

At the revels which follow, the mirth is so loud that the Queen retires indignant, and in her bosom pain is lord. And the first part ends with a talk between Tristram and Dagonet the fool, which insists in other fashion on the ruin a general sensuality has wrought.

The second part takes up the ancient story of Tristram and Isolt, and the story is used and modified by Tennyson to represent another phase of illicit love and of its result on character. The love of Tristram and Isolt in his hands is of a very different type from that of Lancelot and Guinevere. Lancelot and the Queen have loved from the beginning, and through the golden times of the Round Table. The nobleness of the time, and the nobleness it made in them, pervaded their love, and lifted it above itself. It is always faithful, always courteous, always silent, always intense, and often repentant. But Tennyson makes Tristram and Isolt love without any nobleness. Their passion has nothing spiritual in it, nothing that lifts it into the imaginative realm. The light that leads astray is the fire of sense alone. Tristram is unfaithful, and has become uncourteous. He talks of the freedom of Love to love wherever it may please, and of their love failing when beauty fails, and when desire is cold. He speaks in this light, tossing way in the presence of the woman whom he has loved; and Isolt, though she shows indignation, suffers it at last with indifference. In the midst of this Mark comes by, and cleaves Tristram through the brain.

This sketch, not of our Tristram, but of an invented Tristram, of his lightness of character, and his random heart, of his wandering thought, of his soul led by the senses, and his conscience hushed by pleasure—and of the result of these characteristics made into a theory of life and love—is admirably done. What he is, is embodied in his song.

> Free love—free field—we love but while we may:
> The woods are hush'd, their music is no more:
> The leaf is dead, the yearning past away:
> New leaf, new life—the days of frost are o'er:
> New life, new love, to suit the newer day:
> New loves are sweet as those that went before:
> Free love—free field—we love but while we may.

The introduction of this Tristram story no doubt enhances, in another form, the whole of the ethical lesson to nations and to individuals which is contained in the first part, but I feel from the point of view of art that there are strong objections to the whole of it.

First, the old story of Tristram and Isolt is entirely changed and degraded. Tristram is not the Tristram we know, nor Isolt our Isolt; they are both vulgarised. All the romance is taken out of them; their great and inevitable love is turned into a common intrigue. Their mighty sorrow, which has drawn the heart of the world to it, which so many poems have made into a purification of the soul, and to which Wagner gave all his strength, is left untouched by Tennyson. Nay, their characters, as he draws them, are incapable of such a sorrow. No one has a right to alter out of recognition two characters in one of the great poetic stories of the world, and to blacken them. Tennyson ought to have had more reverence for a great tale, and more intuition. What he does is all the worse because portions of the ancient story are kept and dwelt on, so that we are forced to think back over the whole tale we know, and to see through this travesty the noble things which have been travestied. To make a great tale in this fashion the stalking-horse of morality, to use it for a passing shot at adultery, to degrade characters which are not degraded, is an iniquity in art. If Tennyson wanted to do this kind of thing for the sake of a moral end, he ought to have left the beautiful romance alone, and to have invented a quite new story for his purpose.

Moreover, this piece about Tristram and Isolt was quite unnecessary. The story told of them may, as I said, enhance by a fresh example the ethical aim of the first part ; but it is weaker than the first part, and the lesson is as strong without it. The additional weight given by it is not worth the artistic mistake the poet makes in introducing it. The reader, made angry by the degradation of Tristram and Isolt, becomes angry also with the moralities of the beginning of the Idyll. The first part says all that was necessary to say, and says it well.

Thirdly, to shove in at the end, and into a corner, an immense story of human passion, covering as many years and as many events as the story of Lancelot himself, was a complete mistake.

Tristram introduced as the victor in the jousts is
well enough, and we may even endure his soulless
talk, though it falsifies his ancient character ; but to
attempt to force a story, which is like a great sea,
into this narrow pool, is beyond endurance, especially when the first event (that of the love-drink)
which, by making the love of these two inevitable,
raises the tale into fatefulness, is deliberately left
out.   It would have, by excusing them, spoilt the
ethical use which Tennyson makes of their story.
This is too bad of him.

Moreover, Tristram and Isolt take us away from
the main contention. At the very moment when
the whole conception of Tennyson should have been
concentrated into white light, in which everything
else should be lost, around Arthur and Lancelot and
Guinevere, we are carried away to Tintagil, and
forced to remember at that distant place the whole
of the Tristram story. It would have been far better
to have omitted it altogether, and to have told, for
the second part of this Idyll, the history of the last
meeting of Lancelot and Guinevere, of the treachery
of Modred, and of the flight of Guinevere, which at
present is told in the Idyll of *Guinevere*.   These
belong to this Idyll properly, for when Arthur
returns from his expedition to the north, he finds
Guinevere gone.   Then too, the expedition to the
north could be told in its proper place.   Tennyson
would not have been obliged to drag it in, like a
belated recollection, in the middle of Tristram's ride
through the forest. These, then, are the unfortunate
things into which the ethical direction of a work of
art, when it is primary and not secondary, forces
an artist.

The description of Arthur's expedition is the one excellent thing in this Idyll. It has the keenest sight of the things described, and it sets Arthur forth, as he ought to be at this time, in heroic proportions. We see him, the unstained, the majestic king, midst of a stained and degraded world, faithful alone among the faithless. We see also the wild northern land near the sea, the black and lonely tower among the marshes ; and they are painted with undiminished vividness and strength.

> He dream'd ; but Arthur with a hundred spears
> Rode far, till o'er the illimitable reed,
> And many a glancing plash and sallowy isle,
> The wide-wing'd sunset of the misty marsh
> Glared on a huge machicolated tower
> That stood with open doors, whereout was roll'd
> A roar of riot.

One of the knights of the Round Table has been hung near the gate on a dead tree, and beside him hangs a horn. And Arthur blew the horn—

> Then at the dry harsh roar of the great horn,
> That sent the face of all the marsh aloft
> An ever upward-rushing storm and cloud
> Of shriek and plume—

a splendid description of the host of water-birds rising startled from the marsh—the felon knight comes forth, and before the mighty presence of the king, not a blow stricken, fell—

> as the crest of some slow-arching wave,
> Heard in dead night along that table-shore,
> Drops flat, and after the great waters break
> Whitening for half a league, and thin themselves,
> Far over sands marbled with moon and cloud
> From less and less to nothing ; thus he fell.

This, with the illimitable reed and the wide-winged sunset over glancing plash and sallowy isle, is a magnificent description of Nature. Every adjective in it is superbly chosen ; but not less magnificent is the last vision of the flaming tower reddening all the meres and the sea beyond :

> Which half that autumn night, like the live North,
> Red-pulsing up thro' Alioth and Alcor,
> Made all above it, and a hundred meres
> About it, as the water Moab saw
> Come round by the east, and out beyond them flush'd
> The long low dune and lazy-plunging sea.

Lancelot, of all the male characters in the *Idylls of the King*, is the least troubled by the allegory. He is so un-allegorical that when he is present with the other characters, at those times when they are allegorical, he confuses their symbolism, or materialises them into real personages. He often seems like a man among ghosts. His tale is modernised, but not so flagrantly modernised as that of the rest. We might sometimes mistake him for the Lancelot of Malory.

But though not allegorical, he is ethical, and, in this sphere, he is entirely modernised. The moral teaching embodied in him and his relation to Guinevere and Arthur, gathers round the question of faithfulness and unfaithfulness in love and marriage. Of the three, Lancelot is again the most actual, if I may use that word in this manner. But he is actual as a gentleman of our own time, not as the romance knights of the thirteenth century, or of the book of Malory They had a totally different code of

honour in their love-matters from that which rules
our social conscience.

It is quite allowable in art to re-create the characters of an old tale, provided this re-creation
ennobles the men and women as much as the original
treatment, or awakens as much sympathy for them.
The old story gathers our affections in one fashion
round Arthur, Guinevere and Lancelot. Tennyson
does it in another way altogether—in the ethical, not
in the romantic way. He was justified in this if his
form was good. But he keeps so much of the romantic story that he forces us to mix up his Lancelot
with the ancient Lancelot, and the two clash in our
minds. Again and again their unfittedness each to
each, the irreconcilability of their atmospheres,
disturbs the reader of the *Idylls*. It is difficult to
keep them apart, yet to read the poem with justice
to Tennyson we must do this difficult thing. We
must ignore the Lancelot of the Romances, when at
the same time we are continually reminded of him.

Outside of this criticism which has only to do
with the form of the tale, Tennyson's conception
and drawing of Lancelot are full of power. He
is Arthur's earliest and dearest friend. He and
Arthur swear undying fealty to one another on the
field of battle. On Lancelot's steadiness in this, since
he is the greatest of the knights and has the largest
clan, depend half the strength and enduringness
of the Round Table. He has himself an unbroken
admiration for the King, and pays him undiminished
honour and affection from the beginning to the end.
He never wavers in this faithfulness, which is the
root of his character. So he is represented in the
old story, and so Tennyson represents him.

But at one point, not in romantic eyes but in ours, he is unfaithful to Arthur. He loves Guinevere and takes away her love from the King. There is a certain inevitableness in this love, for which Tennyson allows, while he condemns the love. And there is an absolute faithfulness in it on both sides which keeps the characters noble, while the thing itself is represented as not noble. Lancelot, the lover, is as constant to Guinevere, as Lancelot, the friend, is to the King. But it is in this double faithfulness that the pain and the punishment of life inhere—faithful to Arthur, but unfaithful at the dearest point ; faithful to Guinevere, but making her unfaithful at that central point of life in which the fate of her husband, of his work, and of his kingdom is contained.

This is a tragic position. It cannot be called tragic in the Romances, for in the chivalric circles of the romantic centuries Lancelot's love of the Queen did not altogether clash, in men's minds, with his fidelity to Arthur. But Tennyson, making the first element in the situation Lancelot's profound constancy (he cannot love the King less, he cannot love the Queen less), wraps Lancelot up in the moral atmosphere which, in our century as in others, surrounds the marriage tie, and the situation is at once ethically tragic. Lancelot's fidelity to the King jars with his fidelity to Guinevere, and his life is rent to pieces between the two. Both are the deepest things in him, and both are at war in his heart ; and the best piece of character-work in the *Idylls* is the slow delineation of this intimate and tormented strife. He is true to the King and true to the Queen, but his truth to the King makes him shrink

from the Queen, and his truth to the Queen makes
him shrink from the King. Tennyson puts this
terrible position—terrible to the character he represents Lancelot to be—in the two well-known
lines—

> His honour rooted in dishonour stood,
> And faith unfaithful kept him falsely true.

The battle in his soul comes to a crisis in the Idyll
of *Lancelot and Elaine*. Arthur asks Lancelot if he
will come to the jousts for the Diamond. " No," he
replies, for he thinks the Queen wishes him to stay
with her. " To blame, my Lord Lancelot," the
Queen says, when Arthur is gone. " You must go ;
our knights and the crowd will murmur if you stay."
" Are you so wise, my Queen ? " answers Lancelot,
vext that he must seem to have lied to the King,
" once it was not so." But he obeys, and on his
way to the jousts he meets Elaine, who loves him,
and who, being unloved by him, dies of her love.
The Queen is jealous, and her suspicion makes
Lancelot realise the restlessness and misery of a
life which absolute trust between him and Guinevere can alone make endurable. Moreover, he is
wronged by her jealousy, and to be thus wronged in
love by one we love, while it deepens love, makes
it seem for the time contemptible. He is thought
to be untrue when he is conscious he is most true.
And he disdains love, life and all things.

Then the King is sorry that his knight is unable
to love—why could he not love this maiden ? And
the unsuspiciousness of the King makes Lancelot
conscious of friendship failed and of honour lost.
He is thought to be true when he knows he is most

untrue. This is a double torture, and it is finely wrought out by Tennyson. It comes to a point ot self-knowledge and self-abasement in his soliloquy, when, leaving the Queen wrathful, and Arthur sorrowing and surprised, and the girl who loved and died for him in her grave, he sits thinking by the river, and wishes that his life had never been. The lines in which he analyses his inmost soul are equally plain and subtle, full of that curious truth with which a man, embittered for the moment, views himself; and as concentrated as if they had been done by Milton's intellectual force. Indeed, some of them are entirely in Milton's manner :

> For what am I? What profits it my name
> Of greatest knight? I fought for it and have it;
> Pleasure to have it, none; to lose it, pain;
> Now grown a part of me: but what use in it?
> To make men worse by making my sin known?
> Or sin seem less, the sinner seeming great?
> Alas for Arthur's greatest knight, a man
> Not after Arthur's heart! I needs must break
> These bonds that so defame me: not without
> She wills it: would I, if she will'd it? nay,
> Who knows? but if I would not, then may God,
> I pray him, send a sudden Angel down
> To seize me by the hair and bear me far,
> And fling me deep in that forgotten mere,
> Among the tumbled fragments of the hills.

It is the commonest cry of weakness in the unhappy hours of passion to ask the gods to work a miracle. But what the will does not will to do the gods leave alone.

And now remorse, envenomed by love's vexation, grew in the man ; and when the quest of the Holy Grail arose, Lancelot, thinking he might get rid of his sin, thinking the miracle had come—his love less dear to him for the moment, because the Queen had been unjust to him—said to himself : " If I can but see this Holy Thing, my sin may be plucked out of my heart." But while he strove, his love awoke again, for not from without but from within is passion quelled ; and the strife so deepened that madness came upon him,

> And whipt him into waste fields far away.

Afterwards, when he half saw the Holy Grail, it knew that his wrong love was dearer than his desire to be right, and it smote him down. Yet nobleness lived in him, and might have come to flower had he but willed to surrender his love. But how could he surrender it when the surrender meant misery to Guinevere ? Was he not bound to be faithful to her, even if he perished for it eternally ? And in that thought, which was of course half made up by his own desire, the personal wrong to Arthur, the still greater wrong to the kingdom and to society which his love was slowly accomplishing, became like vapours in the sun. He ceased to desire freedom from his guilt. And as in all the heat of his feeble remorse and of his search for the Grail, he had never willed, but only wished for righteousness, the failure of the spiritual excitement left him weaker than before, but less repentant. In *Pelleas and Ettarre*, the Idyll which succeeds the Holy Grail, he has wholly lost his remorse. He is at peace, and has given himself wholly to his love. These are the lines from *Pelleas and Ettarre*, in which we see the quiet content of accepted guilt :

> Not long thereafter from the city gates
> Issued Sir Lancelot riding airily,
> Warm with a gracious parting from the Queen,
> Peace at his heart, and gazing at a star
> And marvelling what it was.

But this peaceful pleasure in wrong, when all effort to overcome it is over, does not endure. Love in unrighteousness loses animation at last, and the pleasure of it passes into languor. In the Idyll of *The Last Tournament* Lancelot presides in Arthur's seat instead of the King, and all the world seems to him lifeless. He has lost all care, even for the laws of chivalry:

> Sighing weariedly, as one
> Who sits and gazes on a faded fire,
> When all the goodlier guests are past away,
> Sat their great umpire, looking o'er the lists.
> He saw the laws that ruled the tournament
> Broken, but spake not.

Nevertheless, long love, in spite of languor, holds him by a thousand ties to the Queen, till she herself, fearful of discovery, bids him go. But to the very close he is loveloyal, courteous, obedient to the woman whom he loved; and when he leaves her he repents and dies. His faithfulness even in false love is reckoned to him for righteousness, or rather, when he ceases to violate his conscience, becomes a root of righteousness in him. This is Tennyson's ethical picture of this tragic situation, and it is done with great poetic insight into the human heart. Moreover (though it is charged throughout with a moral lesson) the artistic representation is, on the whole, the foremost thing.

I may say the same, though not so strongly, of
the representation of Guinevere. It is said that
Tennyson intended her, in his allegory, to image
forth the Heart (or what we mean by that term) in
human nature. She certainly does not represent
the infinite variety of the human affections.. However, by falling short of the allegorical aim of the
poet, she gains as a real person. She is a living
woman, not an abstraction. But at the same time
she is not an interesting woman. She represents
a somewhat common type. Her intelligence is of
the slightest, and her character has little variety.
We infer that she had charm, but it does not appear
in the *Idylls of the King*, save once when she talks
with Gareth on the hillside. She is stately
and lovely, courteous, eager to please, capable of
a great passion, and, in this Idyll, of a great repentance; but this is nothing extraordinary. Such
a woman may be found anywhere. There is
nothing especially creative in Tennyson's conception. She is a Queen, but not a queen in
poetry.

Young, she threw herself recklessly into her love.
In after years she loved on, but with a prudence
for which Lancelot half reproaches her. She
admires her husband, but the reasons for which she
admires him are, she thinks, reasons why she should
not love him ; and she is cool and still enough—in
an hour when passion is in abeyance—to contrast
him in Lancelot's presence with Lancelot ; and to
analyse why she came to love Lancelot more than
Arthur, as if it were an intellectual inquiry. This,
too, is essentially usual, and her passion has little
to separate her from the rest of her sex into an

individual interest, such as Browning could not have failed to give to her. The central passage of her delineation is in *Lancelot and Elaine*. Tennyson marks it as important, for he quotes a thought from it in the last speech of Guinevere after her parting from the King—that phrase about light and colour. Lancelot asks if Arthur has said aught.

> She broke into a little scornful laugh:
> "Arthur, my lord, Arthur, the faultless King,
> That passionate perfection, my good lord—
> But who can gaze upon the sun in heaven?
> He never spake word of reproach to me,
> He never had a glimpse of mine untruth,
> He cares not for me: only here to-day
> There gleam'd a vague suspicion in his eyes:
> Some meddling rogue has tamper'd with him—else
> Rapt in this fancy of his Table Round,
> And swearing men to vows impossible,
> To make them like himself: but, friend, to me
> He is all fault who hath no fault at all:
> For who loves me must have a touch of earth;
> The low sun makes the colour: I am yours,
> Not Arthur's, as ye know, save by the bond.'

She stands forth then—settled down in wrong, and thinking herself right. In the same Idyll jealousy comes upon her. In her jealousy she is still the ordinary woman. It is true that a woman does not show, while she is jealous, variety of character. Jealousy eats up all other feelings and interests. But if she be a woman of intellect, power, or variety, what she says in her jealousy —since it is said in the very hell of passion— will at least display shreds of these qualities. Guinevere is without them. That which Tennyson makes her say in the passage beginning

> It may be, I am quicker of belief
> Than you believe me, Lancelot of the Lake,

has not sufficient strength for the situation. It may be that Tennyson desired to run the character on very simple lines, but, if so, the simplicity should have been either forcible or pathetic. It is neither : it is somewhat commonplace. It may be, he thought that to keep her the great lady he was bound to subdue her to this moderated tone, under which she is supposed to veil her wrath. But the passion does not appear under the phrases—the tongues of flame do not lick upwards through the crust. It is worth while to read the scene between Cleopatra and the messenger who tells her that Antony is married to Octavia, and contrast it with this passage of Tennyson's. Cleopatra is furious with jealousy ; she is the passion itself, but in the very heat of it ; what imagination, what power, what intellect dazzle from her like lightnings ! The myriad variety of the woman emerges through the dominant passion.

After this jealousy—being convinced that it was baseless—she, like Lancelot, settles down into the pleasant peacefulness of accepted wrong; but as this peacefulness does not last with Lancelot, so it does not last with Guinevere, and Tennyson tells, and excellently, of the waking of her conscience. When the moral conduct of life, when the great sanctions of morality are to be represented, Tennyson impassionates them and lifts them into poetry. This is one of his greatest powers. He cannot draw the passions themselves or their working with the excellence of the great masters, but he does draw with a level power the moral exaltation which follows on noble passions nobly felt, or the moral depression which follows when they begin to feel themselves ignoble. Henceforth

> the Powers that tend the soul,
> To help it from the death that cannot die,
> And save it even in extremes, began
> To vex and plague her.

Grim faces and vague spiritual fears beset her as she lies awake at night beside the sleeping King. Or, if she sleep, she dreams

> An awful dream ; for then she seem'd to stand
> On some vast plain before a setting sun,
> And from the sun there swiftly made at her
> A ghastly something, and its shadow flew
> Before it, till it touch'd her, and she turn'd—
> When lo ! her own, that broadening from her feet,
> And blackening, swallow'd all the land, and in it
> Far cities burnt, and with a cry she woke.

And all this trouble grew, till she could bear no more, and bade Lancelot go. On the eve of their parting all is known. The shame outbreaks, and fills the Court and land. Weeping, they ride away and sever, he to his castle, she to the convent of Almesbury, and all night long as she rode the spirits of the waste and weald moaned round her, and the raven, flying high

> Croak'd, and she thought, " He spies a field of death "—

for what her dream presaged was nigh at hand.

All this is told in the beginning of the Idyll of Guinevere, the story of which properly opens at her coming to Almesbury, where she lives, no one knowing who she is, and is waited on by a young and innocent novice. She is alone with her past love and with her sin, and sometimes the soft memory of the one is with her, and sometimes the grim presence of the other. Her repentance is not full as yet. She still regrets. The little novice talks of the wicked Queen, and urges that the King's grief is the greatest in all the land. "May I not grieve," Guinevere says, "with the grief of the whole realm?" "Yes," replies the little maid, "all women must grieve that it was a woman who wrought this confusion in the Table Round." "O maiden," answers the Queen, "what dost thou know of the great world?" And when the maid speaks further of Lancelot himself and his disloyalty, she can bear it no more. Lancelot is first with her still, and she breaks forth in sudden flush of wrathful heat, thinking that the child has been set on to do this by the Abbess. "Spy and traitress," she cries, "get thee hence!"

Then she is sorry for her anger. "'Tis my own guilt," she says, "that betrays itself;" whereat (in a subtle passage of self-deceiving) she argues whether she repents, and does the very thing the not doing of which she thinks is a proof of repentance—thinks again of Lancelot :

> " But help me, heaven, for surely I repent.
> For what is true repentance but in thought—
> Not ev'n in inmost thought to think again
> The sins that made the past so pleasant to us :
> And I have sworn never to see him more,
> To see him more ! "
>   And ev'n in saying this,
> Her memory from old habit of the mind
> Went slipping back upon the golden days
> In which she saw him first.

She paints that happy time in a beautiful recalling, her long ride with Lancelot to meet the King, then the meeting with Arthur, and how she

> sigh'd to find
> Her journey done, glanced at him, thought him cold,
> High, self-contain'd, and passionless, not like him,
> " Not like my Lancelot ! "

This is not repentance. It is the cherishing of ancient joy. " She grew half-guilty in her thoughts again." At this very moment of crisis in the inward life the King rides to the convent door.

It is well conceived by Tennyson ; and Guinevere, hearing the King's step, falls prostrate on the floor, and a voice speaks to her :

> Monotonous and hollow like a ghost's
> Denouncing judgment, but, tho' changed, the King's.

We know that speech of Arthur's, spoken by one who was going to his death, and having to the woman's ears the weight and truth of dying words. It tells her of her sin and the destruction she has wrought, and sternly :

> The children born of thee are sword and fire,
> Red ruin, and the breaking up of laws,
> The craft of kindred and the godless hosts
> Of heathen swarming o'er the Northern Sea.

But it also tells her that he loves her still, that he will urge her crimes no more, that he forgives as Eternal God forgives. He will not touch her here on earth, but in the world where all are pure she will understand at last, and claim him, not Lancelot, as her true love. Farewell, he says, and he bends to bless her.

And this breaks down the woman's long love for another, and at last she loves Arthur! When she loves him she repents, but not till then. Guinevere is the ordinary woman. A strong-hearted woman, in whom either conscience or intellect was powerful, would have repented without loving Arthur, or not repented at all ; but this type of woman does not really repent of a sin of this kind till she loses love for one, and finds herself loving another. Guinevere at last loves Arthur, and then she has a horror of herself—but, since she loves afresh, she is upborne on this new delight, and, forgetting the past, looks forward to be Arthur's mate in heaven. That also is characteristic of this ordinary type. Her love saves her, and she passes into good deeds and ministrant power, and in the end, being Abbess as she has been Queen, she died and went—

To where beyond these voices there is peace.

Passing from Guinevere to the poem itself, it is necessary to repeat that it is entirely modern in form, feeling, and thought. There is not a trace in the Romances of its moralities, of its view of the relations between Arthur and Guinevere and Lancelot, of Arthur's feeling in the matter ; of its strict sense of sin and of repentance, of its careful insistance on the results of Guinevere's wrong on her inner life, of a single one of the motives used by Arthur in his last address to Guinevere.* If we wish then to live in this poem,

---

* It is true that, in Malory's book, Arthur in his fury condemns Guinevere to the stake, and would "shamefully slay" Sir Lancelot; but it is more because their crime was treason than immorality. Arthur is miserable, not because Guinevere has

to feel and understand Tennyson's work, we must put ourselves out of the romantic society and into the social and ethical position that he occupies. To find the power and beauty of any poem, we must breathe for the time the air the poet breathes.

Some, however, attack this poem because of this ethical direction ; and there are places, certainly, where the ethical aim is made too prominent. But, after all, the artistic direction is here the dominant direction, and the ethical issues, though clear, are subordinate. It is not just to say that they override

---

been false, but because he has lost Sir Lancelot, the support of his Round Table. He regrets that he was told of the matter. He goes to war with Lancelot, not so much to wreak his private wrong as to satisfy Sir Gawaine whose brothers Lancelot has slain. "Alas," he cries, "that ever this war was begun." He bursts into tears of sorrow, thinking on Lancelot's great courtesy, when Lancelot horses him in a battle. He falls sick with sorrow. "My lord King Arthur," says one of his knights, "would love Sir Lancelot, but Sir Gawaine will not suffer him." There is nothing in the original story of Arthur's moral indignation in the *Idylls*. That passage in Tennyson where Arthur says that he holds the man the worst of public foes who lets the wife he knows to be false abide with him and rule his house, is utterly at variance with the sentiment of the original. Arthur is there anxious to have Guinevere back, and does receive her back with honour. Moreover society and the Church in the story differ altogether from Tennyson on this point. When the Pope hears of the war—"he considering the great goodness of King Arthur and Sir Lancelot, the most noble Knight of the world, called to him a noble clerk that at that time was there present, which was the Bishop of Rochester. And the Pope gave him bulls, under seal, charging him, upon pain of interdicting all England, that he take his Queen, dame Guinevere, to him again, and accord with Sir Lancelot"—which Arthur gladly does, receiving Guinevere from the hands of Lancelot ; but is driven by Gawaine to banish Lancelot, to his great sorrow. So the Head of the Church and an English bishop—and all society agrees with them—intervene to do that very thing which Tennyson's Arthur declares is deadly to public morality.

this Idyll ; and it seems to me that the real things these objectors dislike is his view of the relation between man and wife. To criticise the poem from the ground of that dislike has no weight as art-criticism. Moreover, Tennyson really felt passion-ately on this matter, and this strong emotion of his lifts the poem out of ethics into art. We feel all the strength and intensity of his nature in it ; personal feeling burns in it. There are places where the poem fails to keep its full power, not from any original want of deep feeling, but from spinning out the emotion into too fine a thread. But on the whole the poem preserves a steady level of moral passion which is almost unique in English poetry. Nevertheless, the ethical aim, by its very nature, and in spite of the poet, tries to get the upper hand, and when it succeeds in this, the poem instantly becomes troubled, and its power and beauty lose weight and fineness. It intrudes, for instance, into the most important passage of *Guinevere*, and injures the intensity and the effect of the last speech of the King. Tennyson makes Arthur, at a time when personal feeling should be supreme, turn aside to give a lecture on the subject of national purity, and of Guinevere's destruction of his work as a King. The King should have been dropped alto-gether and the man alone have spoken. I wish, if it be not impertinent to do so, that the whole of that passage beginning so like a sermon,

Bear with me for the last time while I show

and ending with

The mockery of my people and their bane.

were, with the exception of a few lines, left out,
and I wish also that the other passage, beginning

> O golden hair, with which I used to play
> Not knowing:

and ending,

> So far, that my doom is, I love thee still,

were also expunged. It is too literal; it may be
thought, but not expressed. I do not believe that
the imagination would have permitted it, if it had
not been half-blinded by the sermon that precedes
it. Both passages are outside the situation; the
first is too much in the cold, the second too much
in the flesh.

As to literary criticism, this Idyll is one of the
best in the book. I think its form, as I have already
said, would have been better if all the beginning of
it, which explains the reason of Guinevere's flight to
Almesbury, had made part of the previous Idyll. We
should then be wholly at Almesbury with the Queen,
and there would be a clearer unity of place for the repose of the imagination. But, putting that aside, this
Idyll makes a full unity of impression. We are
wholly involved in the fate of Guinevere from the beginning to the end. Moreover we are carried back by
two episodes which concern her, one of which is told
to her by the maiden, to her earlier and happier days.
These do not confuse the impression of her sorrowful fate and presence. They heighten it by contrast.
They bring her whole life into the narrow convent
room and lay it at the feet of her pain, and our pity
for the woman, and the moral impression of her
story, are both deepened.

These episodes are wrought out with great beauty; clearly invented, full of colour, life, and movement, imagined in the air of old Romance, and relieving the pity and sorrow of the piece with the charm of youthful love, and with the gaiety of the elfin world. We see through Guinevere's soft, regretful memory her ride with Lancelot from her father's castle in the sinless Maytime,

> under groves that look'd a paradise
> Of blossom, over sheets of hyacinth
> That seem'd the heavens upbreaking thro' the earth—

and we think of Tennyson's earlier poem when as yet nothing but the thoughtless delight of their youth and love engaged his mind. The next moment we are borne from this glad beginning to the tragic end, and the Queen hears the step of Arthur on the stair. The same sharp contrast is made by the story the little maid tells of the elfin rapture of the land and all its throng of life, on the news of Guinevere's marriage with Arthur. This is a lovely tale of fairy gaiety, as youthful, as much enchanted in imagination, as if its writer were only five-and-twenty. The novice tells what her father saw.

> He said
> That as he rode, an hour or maybe twain
> After the sunset, down the coast, he heard
> Strange music, and he paused, and turning—there
> All down the lonely coast of Lyonnesse,
> Each with a beacon-star upon his head,
> And with a wild sea-light about his feet,
> He saw them—headland after headland flame
> Far on into the rich heart of the west :
> And in the light the white mermaiden swam,
> And strong man-breasted things stood from the sea,

Z

And sent a deep sea-voice thro' all the land,
To which the little elves of chasm and cleft
Made answer, sounding like a distant horn.

There is much more, and of equal life and charm
and strength ; and then, right over against this
delightful flashing of fairyland in a conscience-less
joy, is set the gloom and sorrow of the present, and
the sympathy of Nature with it. The whole of
Britain is covered with a pall of mist, the earth is
cold and dark beneath it.

The white mist, like a face-cloth to the face,
Clung to the dead earth, and the land was still.

Thus, while this happy story is told within, the
vapour creeps on without, the symbol of the overwhelming of Arthur's work and life, and of the guilt
of Guinevere. As Nature fitted herself to the
rapture of the beginning, so she fits herself to
the tragic end.

Moreover this is done by the poet in preparation for the next Idyll, for the last dim battle
in the west which is to be fought in the death-
white vapour beside the moaning sea. Arthur is
already folded in that mist ; his work is drowned
in it ; and he fades away like a gray shadow, no
man knowing whether he be dead or alive. Therefore in this Idyll we see the King through
Guinevere's eyes make his departure in the mist—a
noble picture, exalting the image of the King as
warrior and as lord, and vividly drawn, as if by
Rembrandt, in the torches at the convent door.

And lo, he sat on horseback at the door !
And near him the sad nuns with each a light
Stood, and he gave them charge about the Queen,

To guard and foster her for evermore.
And while he spake to these his helm was lower d,
To which for crest the golden dragon clung
Of Britain; so she did not see the face,
Which then was as an angel's, but she saw,
Wet with the mists and smitten by the lights,
The Dragon of the great Pendragonship
Blaze, making all the night a steam of fire.
 And even then he turn'd; and more and more
The moony vapour rolling round the King,
Who seem'd the phantom of a giant in it,
Enwound him fold by fold, and made him gray
And grayer, till himself became as mist
Before her, moving ghostlike to his doom.

That doom is told in *The Passing of Arthur*, but
that he is already enwound by its misty pall, and
himself a ghost in it, is nobly conceived, and as
splendidly expressed.

 The Passing of Arthur is set over against *The
Coming of Arthur*, the epilogue over against the
prologue. These two are not Idylls in Tennyson's
idea. They are the framework in which the
Idylls are contained, the coming and going of the
great King whose character and life make the
existence of all the other characters in the book;
whose fate, from its beginning to its end, makes the
unity and the diversity of the book. In every
Idyll, save two, Arthur is the master of the action
of the piece or the final judge of what has been
done; or if not master or judge, the dominant
figure to accomplish whose destiny the doings in
the Idyll have occurred. Even in *Merlin and Vivien*
and in *Pelleas and Ettarre*, he broods like a shadow
over the events. We are forced to ask in the first

what will happen to him and his work when he is
deprived of his great councillor, the only one who
knew his inmost soul ; and Tennyson, with great
skill, drives us into asking that question. In
Pelleas and Ettarre enough is said of him to force
us to realise the dreadful fate which overhangs his
work. We see him there, like Abdiel among the rebel
host, the only one who still loves the great Virtues
and the pursuit of perfect duty in a world which
loves vice as he loves virtue, and which worships
the material as he worships the ideal life. He
scarcely enters into the action of the piece, but he
is, nevertheless, vividly present, standing in the
background alone, wrapt in his fate as in a cloak.

This dominance of one central figure towards
whom converges all the action as well as all the
personages of the poem, is that which gives it
unity, and supplies it with whatever epic character
it has. The *Idylls of the King*, as a whole, borders
on the epic ; it is not an epic. Its form forbids
us to call it by that name, and I suppose that
Tennyson, feeling that, gave it the name of the
Idylls of the King. Nevertheless, the idea of its
becoming an epic was originally in his mind, and
influenced his later work upon the whole poem.
He hovered, that is, between two forms of his
art, and this apparent changing, here and there as
he wrote, of the class of poetry in which the work
was placed, vaguely troubles the reader. That unity
of specialised impression which should at once tell
a reader to what kind of poetry the poem belongs,
is not here.

Again, the proper end of an epic is the moral
triumph of the hero over fate, over the attack of

time, and over pain. He may be beaten into the
dust, all but ruined by life; but his soul is not subdued. He emerges clear, like Arcturus after a
night of storm, purified, almost equal in calm to the
immortal Gods. Conquered without, he is conqueror within. Even Fate retires, saying : " This
man is greater than I." Even the Furies become
the Eumenides. In the true epic this is always the
position of the hero at the close. It is the position
of Adam, it is that of Dante, of Æneas, of Achilles.
It is not altogether, only partly, the position of
Arthur. He passes away, it is true, into the land
beyond, tended by the Queens. There is a vague
rumour that he will return, but no one knows.
Ignorance, doubt, dimly lit at rare times by faith,
enshroud his fate. His kingdom, he thinks, will
reel back into the beast. This is not the true end,
nor the feeling, of an epic hero.

Arthur's work has failed. Love, friendship,
his ideal—have also broken down. That fate
might belong to the epic hero, but that which could
not, in an epic, belong to him, is the breaking down of
Arthur's soul. He has no clear faith in moral
victory, or in the Gods being, beyond our follies
and our pain, the masters of right and love.
Such was the faith of Œdipus at Colonus, in
that Trilogy which is so near an epic in feeling.
Such is the faith of Achilles, of Æneas, of Adam,
in the great epics. The epic hero always issues
forth from Hell, *a riveder le stelle;* and from his
Purgatory, *puro e disposto a salire alle stelle.*

This faith does not pervade or close the Idylls.
The steady belief of *In Memoriam* in the certainty
of the end being good, and of the value, therefore,

of all human effort, is gone from the *Idylls of the King*. I suppose that the sceptical trouble of the confused and wavering time during which the *Idylls* were written had now stolen into Tennyson. He did not become, judging from this poem alone, altogether a pessimist. He was too much of a prophet to be altogether that lifeless personage. But he drifted frequently towards that position, and then drifted back again. And the *Idylls of the King* represent this wavering between hope and despondency, between faith and unfaith in either God or man. Their writer, if we judge from this poem alone, and from the fate he allots allegorically to Arthur, did not know at this time where he was, nor what he believed, nor what he disbelieved, but, on the whole, flung himself at last on prayer. Even that conclusion belongs to the earlier poem. The beginning of *The Passing of Arthur* places Arthur in a condition which is best expressed by one line in *In Memoriam:*

And vaguely trust the larger hope.

I give the passage:

> I found Him in the shining of the stars.
> I mark'd Him in the flowering of His fields,
> But in His ways with men I find Him not.
> I waged His wars, and now I pass and die.
> O me! for why is all around us here
> As if some lesser god had made the world,
> But had not force to shape it as he would,
> Till the High God behold it from beyond,　·
> And enter it, and make it beautiful?
> Or else as if the world were wholly fair,
> But that these eyes of men are dense and dim,
> And have not power to see it as it is:
> Perchance, because we see not to the close;—

> For I, being simple, thought to work His will,
> And have but stricken with the sword in vain;
> And all whereon I lean'd in wife and friend
> Is traitor to my peace, and all my realm
> Reels back into the beast and is no more.
> My God, Thou has forgotten me in my death:
> Nay—God my Christ—I pass but shall not die.

Doubt, and all its trouble! Unable to affirm or deny anything! No clear belief, no triumph of the soul! And the last battle is fought in a death-white mist, not one ray of sunlight to illumine it! Men know not friend from foe; old ghosts look in on the fight; every man who fought in it fought with his heart cold

> With formless fear; and ev'n on Arthur fell
> Confusion, since he saw not whom he fought.

I remember the years in which these lines were written, and the temper of society, and they describe that temper with a great imagination. It was a time when every belief was challenged, when society had almost ceased to hope or believe in the future even of man on the earth, and when political and social ideas which prophesied the advent of a more unselfish world were laughed at as unpractical. Moreover those ideas were then only to be found in a vague form among the working classes, of whose life and hopes and struggle Tennyson knew nothing. Few then kept their faith, whether in God and Man, or in Man alone; few were bold enough to believe that the confusion was not the prelude to decay but the turmoil that precedes a new birth, and Tennyson was not one of these. He was in one part of his nature, and judging from his poetry alone, too much the product of

the Universities, too much in the society which is
called cultured, too apart from the surgings of the
people, too much in harbour——to be able in the
midst of the confusion to see the great order, in
the midst of the battle to be sure of the victory.
At other times, and in another part of his nature,
whenever he yielded himself wholly to the pure
Muse within him, and did not bring his impulse
to the tribunal of the understanding for criticism,
he escapes into that land of faith where the sun
shines on the glory which shall be, and, doubting
no more, prophesies clear good; but this, which
is true of the time when he wrote *In Memoriam*,
and also of his old age when the epic of his life
closed in a hero's victory, is not true of the period
when he wrote the beginning of *The Passing of
Arthur*, nor indeed, as I think, of the whole of
the period of the composition of the *Idylls of the
King*. These were the days of his dim battle in
the mist. And perhaps this trouble was all the
worse for him, because the audacities, the reckless
hopes, the faiths which believe without seeing, the
keen contempt for any society which says "All is
wrong or going wrong," or, "I cannot tell whether all
is wrong or right," were not his dowry as a poet.
Even when Arthur is carried away over the mere to
Avalon, and when he cries back to Bedivere—in the
part of the poem which was published in 1842—that
prayer has power with God, he says :

> For all my mind is clouded with a doubt.

I do not press that line, however, into my statement,
for it may be merely a suggestion of the vague-
ness of Arthur's fate, of which we are left ignorant

in the Romances ; but it, with all the rest, fits in to
prove the point with which I began and to which
I now return, that Arthur is not an epic hero, and
that this poem cannot be called an epic. Tennyson
did not call it so, but others have. The epic
hero must have a clear moral victory and be
purified into clearness, and this is not the case
with Arthur.

I turn now to Arthur himself as conceived by
Tennyson. First, it must be understood that
Tennyson's Arthur has even less to do with the
Arthur of the Romances than his Lancelot has with
the romantic Lancelot. The moral or even the social
atmosphere of the Arthur of chivalry is not the
atmosphere which Tennyson's Arthur breathes.
Again I recur to the primal fault of form, which
belongs to the whole poem. The Arthur in Tennyson's mind, and the Arthur of the romantic era, are
linked together by an unnatural tie, and the two often
quarrel. Most of the objections made against Arthur
have their real root in this. They are objections
rather against the form than against the poem. But,
on the whole, Arthur as the modern gentleman, as
the modern ruler of men, such a ruler as one of
our Indian heroes on the frontier, is the main
thing in Tennyson's mind, and his conception of
such a man contains his ethical lesson to his
countrymen.

As to Arthur the King, he is a man who has the
power of sending his own soul into the soul of his
followers, and making them his own—images of
himself—and this is the power of a born ruler
of men. It is the one-man power, that power of
which Carlyle as well as Tennyson made too

much—because the secret of the progress of mankind, a secret the true ruler should understand, does not lie in one great individuality devouring all other individualities and making them into his pattern, but in his so sacrificing his natural mastery as to develop into vividness the individual forces of all the characters he governs.   Carlyle never saw that truth, nor Ruskin, nor Tennyson.   But Tennyson, though he often preached this one-man theory, does not hold it fast.   It seems to have crept into his mind—wavering hither and thither on many subjects during the years in which he wrote the *Idylls*—that this theory did not hold water in practice.   For, though Arthur imposes his character at first on all his knights, they all glide away from him.   Their separate individualities assert themselves, and assert themselves in reaction from the foreign, overmastering, and exalted personality of Arthur.   In fact, Tennyson represents in the *Idylls*, whether consciously or not, the complete breaking down in practice of the theory of the heaven-born ruler who makes every one into his own pattern.   I do not think he meant to give us this good democratic lesson, but he has given it.

Another part of the conception of Arthur as ruler, is that with which all the ethical writers, whether of history or fiction, have, during the last fifty years, made us familiar ; and which many Englishmen, sent to our far dependencies, have illustrated by their lives.   Arthur is the clearer of the waste places of the earth, the driver forth of the cruel beast and the lawless man, he who lets in the light and air, the doer of stern justice, the deliverer of the oppressed, the organiser of law and order,

the welder together of all the forces of the kingdom
into a compact body for right and against wrong,
the builder of great cities and noble architecture,
the teacher of agriculture, the maker of roads and
water-ways, the Culture Hero, as the Folklorists
would call him ; and, finally, the great warrior who,
though he does not excel the rest of his men in
courage, excels them all as leader of the battle. On
all this there is nothing particular to say. It is the
general, the well-known conception.

The rest of the conception of Arthur as King is
as the moral lawgiver, and chiefly as the demander
of chastity. It is on the breaking of the law of
purity that he most insists to Guinevere as the cause
of the ruin of his aims and of his Order. His
knights may love—nay, nothing so well makes a
man as the maiden passion for a maid. His knights
may marry : life finds its crown in a true marriage.
But only one maiden is to be loved, and wedded
man and woman must live only for each other.
And we have seen that this is Tennyson's opinion.
All his poetry is full of it.

Yet, he makes the whole effort utterly break
down, and I do not comprehend his position. I
sometimes think that the hopelessness of the years
in which he wrote the *Idylls* seized upon him, and he
ceased for a time to believe in the victory of good.
For it is not only the partial failure of purity of life
which he represents in the *Idylls;* it is its complete
overthrow. Every one, with the exception of Arthur,
Percivale, his sister, and Sir Bors, becomes unchaste.
I sometimes think that he wished to illustrate the
truth that vows imposed from without were not only
useless, when the character remained unchanged,

but that they drove men and women into their opposites ; and perhaps that his hatred of monkery influenced him further in this direction ; but the astonishing result to which he comes is more than these motives should produce. Not a soul keeps the vows, except Arthur and those who have left the world for the cloister. I do not understand why he works out a result which seems not only to contradict the possibility of his rule of chastity being observed, but which makes that rule issue in a wholly shameless society. It is as if he despaired of purity. The thing he most insists on is made by him to be the impossible thing. This is an excessively curious conclusion for Tennyson to come to.

Every one in the *Idylls*, save the few I have mentioned, thinks this vow too much for mortal man. Merlin says that no one can keep it. Vivien and Mark, of course, laugh it to scorn. Guinevere declares it to be impossible, and Lancelot knows it. Gawain openly adopts unchastity. Pelleas says that the King has made his knights fools and liars ; Tristram, that he himself had sworn but by the shell, that the strict vow snaps itself, that flesh and blood were sure to violate it.

> Bind me to one ? The wide world laughs at it.

Why does Tennyson, we wonder, make almost all his characters think chastity impossible ?

Then, he even goes further. The condition of society in the court and country set forth in *Pelleas and Ettarre* and in *The Last Tournament* is incredibly bad. Every woman is unchaste and every man. Ettarre is as immoral as Tristram, and both far more so than they are in the original tales. Rome in its decadence, France under the Regent, were not so wholly evil as Arthur's court, with the sole exception of Arthur. The poet proves too much. Arthur's effort is too ghastly a failure. And the representation of this result—unless we fall back on the needs of the allegory for an explanation—is not in the interests of morality. Tennyson does not really—in this working out of his moral aim— strengthen the will to be chaste, but weakens it. The chief thing that appears is that chastity is an impossibility. Tennyson cannot, of course, have meant this; but his art ought to have saved him from the possibility of its inference. Had he been less ethical and less allegorical, he would not have fallen into this artistic error.

There are better things to say when we think of Tennyson's conception of Arthur as a man—as the "very perfect knight." We have a part of the character he meant to represent in the dedication to the *Idylls of the King*, where he compares his Arthur to Prince Albert.

> And indeed he seems to me
> Scarce other than my King's ideal knight,
> "Who reverenced his conscience as his king;
> Whose glory was, redressing human wrong;
> Who spake no slander, no, nor listen'd to it;
> Who loved one only and who clave to her——"

But Arthur is more than that. He is not only faithful to his wife, he is as faithful in friendship as in love. Affection of any kind once given is always given. His chastity is as perfect as Galahad's, within the bounds of marriage. His honour is unstained, and no passion of whatever force has power to make him waver from its call. His word, once passed, is passed for ever. He is so true that he cannot believe in untruthfulness, so faithful that he is unsuspicious of unfaithfulness. What is right and just to do he does, though all the world fall to ruin round him. His moral courage is as great as his physical courage. He can rise into a white heat of wrath or love; but he is not led away by false or fleeting heats of feeling into folly or intemperance. Add to this absolute courtesy, gentleness, pity, forgiveness for the fallen, unselfish joy in the fame and glory of others, and we see the perfect knight of Tennyson. It is confessedly an ideal, but an ideal to which the poet desired us to aspire, and to gain which he thought possible. This ideal has been the object of many critical attacks, or, to put it more justly, Arthur has been depreciated as a man with various mockeries. I need not particularise them. They have been about us for a long time in reviews, in society, among men and women who call them-selves emancipated, and the question is : " Is there any truth at the bottom of this irritation against the character of Arthur ? "

If the irritation be directed against those parts of his character on which I have now dwelt, against this ideal of a knight, then it is not only a false irritation, but it also speaks ill for the society which is afflicted by it. Tennyson has drawn in Arthur that which every man ought to wish to be. The qualities of Arthur would, when vital in our lives, make our society noble and loving, magnanimous and magnificent. The whole world ought to be better for this picture of a man, and the future will be grateful to Tennyson for it. On this side of the matter these critics are not to be trusted.

But is there no side on which Arthur fails, on which he makes a not quite human impression, a part of the picture in decrying which the critics have some reason ? Yes, there is—but they have no cause to boast themselves of their acumen. What they say is not original. Tennyson himself has said it by the mouth of Guinevere, and it appears in the sayings of even the knights of Arthur—of Gawain and Tristram, much more in the sayings of Vivien and of Mark. There is scarcely a single attack made by the critics on Arthur which has not been made by Tennyson himself. In fact, Arthur is a little superhuman, a little too out of the world, a little too easily deceived, a little too good for human nature's daily food. Tennyson made him so, and deliberately. "Why ? " we ask ; "there was no need. He would have had even more force as an ideal character, even more influence on us, if he had shared more in our humanity. Why did Tennyson superhumanise him ? "

The real reason lay in the necessities of that allegory which Tennyson chose to infiltrate into his poem. He represents Arthur as a man, and when he does so, even when he makes him ideal in conduct and aim, the character is just and clear and human. But he is forced by his allegory to paint him also as the rational soul, as an abstract idea, and whenever he does this Arthur steps outside of humanity, and that is naturally resented. At all the points where Arthur represents the soul alone, Guinevere and the critics are right. He does want colour and warmth, he is too much outside of the world; he is under-passioned, if I may coin a word; and the demands of his perfection do not sufficiently consider the weakness of human nature. He loses life, and becomes, in his allegorical form, the image only of a man. But because Tennyson was unfortunate enough as an artist to trouble his poem by making his chief character not only a man but an allegorical symbol, we have no right to transfer our impatience with the characteristics of the unhuman symbol to the ideal character of the man. Let us keep them separate. Nevertheless the artist ought not to have given us this trouble— ought not to have mixed up the man with the general notion of the soul of man. Arthur ought either to have been one thing or the other—either the rational Soul alone, or the man alone; not some- times one and sometimes the other. And in this *Passing of Arthur* he is so much the man and so little of the Soul that he pleases more than else- where in the book. Even in the great speech to Guinevere in the last Idyll, the portions of it which are spoken by the King as the Soul in man con- tending with sense, lessen the humanity of those parts of it which are spoken from the man to the woman.

But here in this *Passing of Arthur* he is alto- gether the man, and he is dear to us throughout. He feels his failure in the great work he desired to do with the same self-pitifulness that many a high reformer has felt in the hour of his death. I have already quoted the lines. They are full of humanity. They are not the voice of an abstract soul. And their wild cry at the end:

My God, Thou hast forgotten me in my death!

is changed suddenly, as many a prophet's has been changed, into a cry of trust concerning his personal fate.

> Nay—God my Christ—I pass but shall not die.

Then, like many another leader of men, he dreams on the day before he dies——and the ghost of Gawain, blown

> Along a wandering wind, and past his ear
> Went shrilling, "Hollow, hollow, all delight!
> Hail, King! to-morrow thou shalt pass away.
> Farewell! there is an isle of rest for thee."

And the shrill voice fades away, likened in a noble simile to

> wild birds that change
> Their season in the night and wail their way
> From cloud to cloud;

and is imaginatively mingled with dim cries as of a city sacked at night, and Arthur wakes and thinks, like a poet, that all the Faery things that haunt the waste and wild mourn: for, when he goes, they too will go.

This also is human to the core, and when, mournfully saying that to fight against his people is to fight against himself, and that their death is a death-stroke to him, he feels the love of his youth recur and its late misery darken the whole world, so that the mist in which he moves is made less by Nature than by his own sorrow for Guinevere:

> This blind haze,
> * *   *   *
>   which ever since I saw
> One lying in the dust at Almesbury,
> Hath folded in the passes of the world,

2 A

he is still more one with whom we can feel as man to man. Then comes that noble passage of the fight in the dead mist upon the ocean-shore, on the sunset bound of Lyonnesse—in which the allegory recurs, but splendidly recurs, in veiled words which describe the whole battle of desperate humanity for life and faith and hope in the midst of its chill mystery—till with the falling night the North wind rose and the tide; the mist dissolved, and Arthur saw none alive around him but Bedivere and the traitor Modred. A great voice then shakes the world —a noble imagination of Tennyson—and seems to waste the realm, and to beat confusion into Arthur's heart :

> I know not what I am,
> Nor whence I am, nor whether I be King.
> Behold, I seem but King among the dead.

This, too, may be allegory, but the human element in it is stronger than the allegorical, and it goes home to the heart of the situation. Afterwards, in one last act of kinghood, when he slays the traitorous cause of all the woe, he passes for a moment out of his confusion into the full sense of his kinghood, of who he is, and whence he has come, and whither he is going. This is the fate of a man and the heart of a man, and after all our ethics and allegory, it is sweet and true to company with it.

And then we enter into the old and beloved piece of poetry which we know so well—into the *Morte d'Arthur*, which we read first in 1842. It is led up to so well that we feel that the hand and heart that wrote it so many years ago have not failed in skill and the power to charm, that time has not robbed the poet of his lyre-playing. But when, being led up to it, we suddenly find ourselves in it, as in a land which of old we found lovely and rejoice to see again, we are full of our earlier happiness.

When first we read it, it seemed as if Romance, sitting ever young by her wild forest stream, were stretching out her arms, and bidding us leave this weary world for her delights. And when we read it again the ancient charm returns. For here, in this chivalric work, we are close throughout to the ancient tale. No allegory, no ethics, no rational Soul, no preaching symbolism, enter here, to dim, confuse or spoil the story. Nothing is added which does not justly exalt the tale, and what is added is chiefly a greater fulness and breadth of humanity, a more lovely and supreme Nature, arranged at every point to enhance into keener life the human feelings of Arthur and his knight, to lift the ultimate hour of sorrow and of death into nobility. Arthur is borne to a chapel nigh the field—

> A broken chancel with a broken cross,
> That stood on a dark strait of barren land;
> On one side lay the Ocean, and on one
> Lay a great water, and the moon was full.

What a noble framework—and with what noble conciseness it is drawn! And Arthur bids Bedivere take Excalibur, and throw it into the mere. Twice he leaves the King to throw it, and twice he hides it, thinking it shame to deprive the world of so glorious a sword. All the landscape—than which nothing better has been invented by any English poet—lives from point to point as if Nature herself had created it; but even more alive than the landscape are the two human figures in it—Sir

Bedivere standing by the great water, and Arthur
lying wounded near the chapel, waiting for his
knight.   Take one passage, which to hear is to see
the thing :

> So saying, from the ruin'd shrine he stept,
> And in the moon athwart the place of tombs,
> Where lay the mighty bones of ancient men,
> Old knights, and over them the sea-wind sang
> Shrill, chill, with flakes of foam.   He, stepping down
> By zigzag paths, and juts of pointed rock,
> Came on the shining levels of the lake.

Twice he hides the sword, and when Arthur asks:
"What hast thou seen, what heard ?" Bedivere
answers : *

> I heard the ripple washing in the reeds,
> And the wild water lapping on the crag,

—lines so steeped in the loneliness of mountain tarns
that I never stand in solitude beside their waters
but I hear the verses in my heart.   At the last he
throws it.   The great brand

> Made lightnings in the splendour of the moon,
> And flashing round and round, and whirl'd in an arch,
> Shot like a streamer of the northern morn,
> Seen where the moving isles of winter shock
> By night, with noises of the Northern Sea.

" So flashed and fell the brand Excalibur," and

***

* The second answer is changed—

> I heard the water lapping on the crag,
> And the long ripple washing in the reeds.

Both of them have the modern note, especially in the adjectives ;
but though they lose simplicity, they gain splendour.   The words
in Malory are : " Syr, he sayd, I sawe no thynge but the waters
wappe and wawes wanne,"

never yet in poetry did any sword, flung in the air,
flash so superbly.

The rest of the natural description is equally
alive, and the passage where the sound echoes the
sense, and Bedivere, carrying Arthur, clangs as he
moves among the icy rocks, is as clear a piece of
ringing, smiting, clashing sound as any to be found
in Tennyson :

> Dry clash'd his harness in the icy caves
> And barren chasms, and all to left and right
> The bare black cliff clang'd round him, as he based
> His feet on juts of slippery crag that rang
> Sharp-smitten with the dint of armed heels.

We hear all the changes on the vowel *a*—every sound
of it used to give the impression—and then, in a
moment, the verse runs into breadth, smoothness
and vastness : for Bedivere comes to the shore and
sees the great water :

> And on a sudden, lo ! the level lake
> And the long glories of the winter moon,

in which the vowel *o* in its changes is used as the
vowel *a* has been used before.

The questions and replies of Arthur and Bedivere, the reproaches of the King, the excuses
of the knight, the sorrow and the final wrath of
Arthur, are worthy of the landscape in which the
poet has enshrined them.   They are greater than the
landscape, as they ought to be ; and the dominance
of the human element in the scene is a piece of
noble artist-work.   Arthur is royal to the close, and
when he passes away with the weeping Queens
across the mere, unlike the star of the tournament

he was of old, he is still the King. Sir Bedivere,
left alone on the freezing shore, hears the King
give his last message to the world.   It is a modern
Christian who speaks, but the phrases do not sound
out of harmony with that which might be in
Romance.   Moreover, the end of the saying is of
Avilion or Avalon—of the old heathen Celtic place
where the wounded are healed and the old made
young.

Only then—with this recurrence to the ancient
stories of the Irish land of youth, of the City of
God to which Galahad went, and of the joy of the
land where Ogier voyaged when the wars of earth
were over—only then, and with enough dimness not
to jar, the allegory steals back again.   Arthur is
again the Soul of Man that seeks the fair country
whence it came.   Sir Bedivere cries out :

> "The King is gone."
> And therewithal came on him the weird rhyme,
> " From the great deep to the great deep he goes."
>   *   *   *   *   *   *
> Then from the dawn it seem'd there came, but faint
> As from beyond the limit of the world,
> Like the last echo born of a great cry,
> Sounds, as if some fair city were one voice
> Around a king returning from his wars.

CHAPTER XI.

ENOCH ARDEN AND THE SEA-POETRY.

ENOCH ARDEN is one of a series of narrative poems by Tennyson, which have to do with ordinary human life in a simple and quiet manner. Some, like *Enoch Arden*, deal with the whole life-story of a few persons. Some, like *Aylmer's Field* and *The Gardener's Daughter*, tell the story of events in the midst of human life which lead to the misery or happiness of those involved in them. Some, like *The Brook* or *Love and Duty*, tell the events of a day in which lovers are reconciled, or part for ever; and some, like *Sea Dreams*, tell of a sudden crisis coming on the life of men and women and making a crisis in the life of their soul. There are others, like *The Sisters*, but they may all be grouped as narrative poems written in blank verse, and we may call them idylls of daily life.

They stand apart by their form from the lyric poems which treat of the same human matters, but which naturally confine themselves to moments of life made intense by the passions. Their blank verse is of a special kind. It has a natural freedom and simplicity which is not permissible in heroic blank verse such as the poet used in the *Idylls of the King* or in the classical poems. Tennyson, who knew his art, is exceedingly strict about this difference. The blank verse of *Enoch Arden* is quite distinct, for example, from that used in *The Passing of Arthur*. A great deal might be said on this matter, but it belongs to a minuter criticism than is aimed at here, and, after all, his readers can hear the difference for themselves, if they possess an ear for poetry. If they do not, no explanation will do them any good.

This narrative poem of simple life is different from that class of poems of which Tennyson may be said to have been the inventor—short dialogues or narration of dialogues in blank verse between three or four well-bred persons on topics of social interest, such as *Audley Court, Walking to the Mail*, or *The Golden Year*—sometimes delightful, sometimes too pedestrian, half-serious, half-humorous things, but the humour coarse-grained ; slowly-moving clouds of conversation touched here and there with the crimson of love. These things were wholly his own, and new ; but the narrative poem of daily life among the poor, like *Enoch Arden*, was not new. We have it in the tales of Crabbe, and very plainly in that class of Wordsworth's poems of which *Michael* is the best representative. After Wordsworth, none of the greater poets took up this special subject or used its form of poetry. It is not made by Walter Scott, by Byron, Shelley or Keats. Tennyson, who had a great deal of Wordsworth's simplicity and ruggedness, and also his power of seeing the deep things of human nature in the common life of man, saw the capabilities of this kind of subject, restored it to poetry, and enlarged its range and its variety in a way of which Wordsworth had no conception.

He invented at least half a dozen new forms of it, but the form of which I now write is that in which *Enoch Arden* is written. It resembles that which Wordsworth used in *Michael*, but Tennyson began this class of poetry with *Dora*.

Dora seems absolutely simple, but it is not really so simple as *Michael*. It is, perhaps, a little too elaborately simple. When I say that Wordsworth's poems of this type are more simple than *Dora*, I mean that the style Wordsworth uses is more in harmony with the homespun matter. The style of *Michael* does not draw attention to itself and away from the subject. The style of *Dora*, in relation to its subject, is concise to a fault— so concise that it forces us to think of it as much as of the story. We are driven, in perhaps too critical a mood, to say: "The man who wrote this was not so full of the emotion of his tale as not to consider, somewhat too much, how briefly, with justice to poetry, he could put it. So far, he was losing emotion, and so far he has caused us, by compelling us to think of his conciseness, to lose emotion also."

Moreover, this extreme brevity of representation is quite unlike the way in which life is conducted by the class of which he writes. The men and women of this class live a delayed life. When their doings and sayings are so condensely given as they are in *Dora*, we are taken out of their atmosphere. Passion, it is true, at its height is brief, but the whole of life is not spent in passion; and there ought in poems of this kind to be something which should draw the movement out, and fill up the time between the outbursts of strong emotion. The slowness in such

lives of the ebb and flow of circumstance ought to
be impressed upon us.   Even in the rapid rush of
the *Iliad*, and even in heroic life, Homer takes care
that there should be some delay.   Though the similes
he uses are so connected with the main movement
by their fitness to the things they illustrate that
swiftness is not lost, yet they also give us the sense
that there is time to spare.   They enable us to linger
a little, even in the full tide of battle, as life lingers.
Wordsworth hums along in *Michael*, as Michael
himself and his wife hummed slowly on in life.
And though the lover of conciseness, when he reads
Michael, becomes somewhat indignant with Wordsworth, and though the poet himself seems sometimes dull, yet the story is deliberately told in this
way by the artist in order that we may be kept
in the mental climate of the shepherd-class of
which he writes.   Nor, indeed, at the end does
he fail in the impression he wants to give.   *Michael*
remains a far more impressive thing than *Dora*.
Wordsworth moves more closely in the life of
which he speaks, and has lost himself in it, more than
Tennyson.   The question of style does not occur
to him.   The style of *Michael* is formed by the subject itself.   I think that Tennyson felt something
of what I have said, for it is plain that *Enoch
Arden* is written in quite a different manner from
Dora.   It is concise, of course ; Tennyson was
always concise; but *Enoch Arden* is not over-concise.
The action of the piece, and the movement of the
feelings of the persons in it, are delayed.   There is
repetition, there is enough talking over events to
make us understand that years and years pass by.
The atmosphere of a remote seaside hamlet, and

of its life from day to day, is fully preserved and felt. We do not think, as we do when we read *Dora*, of the style at all. It has come ; it is exactly right ; it has grown naturally out of the artist's profound feeling of his subject. Moreover, the verse is plain in sound, and takes pains to be like the talk of daily common life. It never rises into the heroic march save twice, once in the description of the tropic isle by day and night ; and again, when Enoch looks in at the window and sees his home in which he has no share. Even the similes (in which a poet is allowed to soar a little) are restrained into simplicity. The things used in illustration belong to the same level of life to which the rest of the poem belongs. I quote two of them to show what I mean. Annie, wrapt in sorrow for Enoch's going, does not know of what he speaks :

> Heard and not heard him ; as the village girl,
> Who sets her pitcher underneath the spring,
> Musing on him who used to fill it for her,
> Hears and not hears, and lets it overflow.

That is one—a rustic picture and a rustic heart fixed in four lines ; and this is another—born out of a sailor's life, and fitted in grave simplicity to the mighty relief of death :

> For sure no gladlier does the stranded wreck
> See thro' the gray skirts of a lifting squall
> The boat that bears the hope of life approach
> To save the life despair'd of, than he saw
> Death dawning on him, and the close of all.

Such is the atmosphere.

There is not much of natural description in the

poem. But Tennyson sets the scenery of the action in the first nine lines—

Long lines of cliff breaking have left a chasm; &c.

They cannot be called a description of Nature. They make, as it were, the scenic background before which a drama is to be played, and this is all the poet intends them to represent. Two other scenes are laid, one where the wood feathers down to the hollow filled with hazels, where both Enoch and Philip tell their love to Annie; and the other, the room in the cottage where we see Philip and Enoch's wife, and the garden without in the dark, whence Enoch looks through the window with a breaking heart. One other scene is set in the tropic isle where Enoch sits among the palms, gazing on the separating sea. This is the one distinct description of Nature in the poem, and, though it is good, it is not as good as another poet who sympathised more with that type of Nature would have made it. Tennyson, I have said, was out of his element when he was away from England. And this description, with which he seems to have taken great pains, is not fused together by any feeling for the Nature described; there is no colour in it but scarlet; and the one line in it which is first-rate might have been written in Cornwall from sight:

The league-long roller thundering on the reef.

It is instructive to compare its emotionless *

* When I call these lines emotionless, I only mean that they are not thrilled with any affection for the scenery itself. They are full of another kind of emotion—of Enoch's misery, of his

verses to those that follow, when Enoch in his hungry-hearted reverie sees in vision his native town, his native land. These are full of the very breath and passion of England :

> The climbing street, the mill, the leafy lanes,
> The peacock-yewtree and the lonely Hall,
> The horse he drove, the boat he sold, the chill
> November dawns and dewy-glooming downs,
> The gentle shower, the smell of dying leaves,
> And the low moan of leaden-colour'd seas.

Nor can I omit the exquisite sentiment which sighs through Enoch's first sight of England, when all the quintessence of his native land and of her natural scenery is wafted from the dim coast to the returning ship. In these visions of his country—for surely Tennyson himself is speaking here—he is unequalled in English poetry.

> His fancy fled before the lazy wind
> Returning, till beneath a clouded moon
> He like a lover down thro' all his blood
> Drew in the dewy meadowy morning-breath
> Of England, blown across her ghostly wall.

As to the humanity of the poem, he that runs may read it. It also is kept at a quiet level, but it is none the less impressive. It never breaks into sensation ; not even when Enoch returns to see his wife married to another, and his children with another father. Nor has Tennyson any

hatred for the incessant and foreign beauty of the land and sea. And it may be that the faint praise I give them ought to be, in another aspect, the fullest praise possible. Perhaps the poet made them cold that he might express the weary anger of Enoch's heart.

special ethical aim in what he writes. His work
springs straight out of the situation. Enoch, Philip,
Annie could not have acted otherwise—once we
see their character. How easy it seems, as we
read it, to do this well! How supremely difficult it
is except for an artist who has loved his art for
years!

It is with an art charged with humanity that the
introduction to the poem prophesies the whole
action of the poem by the play of the children
on the beach. In the narrow cave the children
keep house. Enoch was host one day, Philip the
next, while Annie still was mistress. " This is my
house, and this my little wife," cries Enoch.
" Mine too," said Philip, " turn and turn about."
And when they quarrelled,

> The little wife would weep for company,
> And pray them not to quarrel for her sake,
> And say she would be little wife to both.

The childhood's play contains the fate of the
men and the woman. This is well-shaped, skilful
composition.

Step by step, on these simple lines, the story
grows. The passage where Philip sees Enoch speak
to Annie, and slips aside like a wounded life into
the hollows of the wood, is beautiful, alike for the
joy and the sorrow described in it, and for its simple
gravity of style. Yet it is only one of many
passages full of that quiet strength of emotion which
belongs to lowly English life, and especially to those
who live on the sea-board. We do not feel, at first
reading of the poem—owing to its careful lowness
of note—the force with which Tennyson has grasped

the humanity of his subject, but we do feel a vague impression of it. Afterwards the vague impression becomes a conviction of extraordinary power. But of course the full humanity of the poem gathers round the return of Enoch to find his wife Philip's wife, and his own children Philip's children. And Tennyson, without transgressing his peaceful limit, is steadily equal to the central emotion of the tale.

As Enoch draws homeward to meet his tragedy, nature sympathises with him. The sea-haze shrouds the world in gray, the holt is withered, the robin pipes disconsolate. Thicker the drizzle grew, deeper the gloom. At last the town "flares on him in a mist-blotted light." He heard at the inn the doom which had happened to him, and stole out to look at his home in the sad November dark. And while he stood without the cottage, clothed in the gloom, he saw wife and children and friends happy in the genial light. It was difficult to describe the passion in the lonely man ; it was still more difficult to keep him true to the highest in his character, to his staid and sacred sense of duty resting on love, in this terrible hour ; but Tennyson does it with concentrated power. The poet is as nobly self-controlled as the character he draws.

> Now when the dead man come to life beheld
> His wife his wife no more, and saw the babe
> Hers, yet not his, upon the father's knee,
> And all the warmth, the peace, the happiness,
> And his own children tall and beautiful,
> And him, that other, reigning in his place,
> Lord of his rights and of his children's love,—
> Then he, tho' Miriam Lane had told him all,
> Because things seen are mightier than things heard,
> Stagger'd and shook, holding the branch, and fear'd

> To send abroad a shrill and terrible cry,
> Which in one moment, like the blast of doom,
> Would shatter all the happiness of the hearth.

The last three lines lift the description into the lofty tragic note. Nor is the close less nobly conceived. Enoch might have died a miserable man, shattered by his fate, and our pity for him been charged with a sorrowful contempt for human nature. But this is not in the bond. Like the epic hero, he conquers fate. The soul triumphs. He is more of the hero than Arthur :

> He was not all unhappy. His resolve
> Upbore him, and firm faith, and evermore
> Prayer from a living source within the will,
> And beating up thro' all the bitter world,
> Like fountains of sweet water in the sea,
> Kept him a living soul.

The whole of his self-sacrifice is accomplished, and at the end the poet uses splendidly a common legend of the sea-coast. He brings all the mighty Ocean into Enoch's chamber at the hour of death to glorify him with its sympathy. On the third night after he left his message for his people,

> There came so loud a calling of the sea,

that he awoke and died.

This is Tennyson's one long poem about the poor, for Enoch is always a poor man. And it is characteristic of him that he chooses for his hero among the working-classes one who belongs to the sea rather than the land, a fisherman and then a merchant sailor ; for, next to his own sweet, soft English southern land, he loved the sea. He saw it day by day for a great part of his life

from his home in the Isle of Wight. It dwelt in
his observing imagination, and he knew, all along
the coast, its moods and fantasies, its steadiness and
its changes, its ways of thinking and feeling and
acting, as a man knows his wife. But he loved it,
not only for itself, but for the sake of the English
folk that sailed upon it, whose audacity and
constancy had made England the mistress of the
Deep. He loved it also as a part of England and her
Empire. Wherever over all the oceans Tennyson's
imagination bore him, he felt that there, from tropic
to pole and from pole to tropic, he was in England.
His love of country and his love of the sea were
fused into one passion :

> Thine the myriad-rolling ocean, light and shadow
>   illimitable,
> Thine the lands of lasting summer, many-blossoming
>   Paradises,
> Thine the North and thine the South and thine the
>   battle-thunder of God.

So chanted the prophetesses in *Boadicea* concerning
a future England with which they had but little
national concern, but in reality Tennyson is singing
in these splendid lines his own English folk
and their glory ; and I cannot finish this chapter
better than by gathering together the greater part
of what he says about English seamen and the
English sea. It forms a special element in his
work.

Enoch—to speak first of him—is the type of
the " able seamen " of England, nourished in
the fishing-smack, and then passing from land to
land through the wonders of the waves in the
merchant-vessel ; and then, when wars arise, the

2 B

mainstay of our navies—a type which has lasted
more than a thousand years. Arden's godfearing-
ness is not uncommon in English seamen, but his
slow-established sense of duty is common ; and so
are also his sturdy endurance, his settled self-sacrifice for those ideas that his soul approves, his courage
unconscious of itself, his silent love of his country
—a careful, loving, and faithful picture, for which
we have to honour the poet. Nowhere has he
shown more convincingly the noblest side of his
patriotism.

We have another type in Sir Richard Grenville,
painted in that ringing and high-angered ballad—
the fight of *The Revenge.* The soul of the
Elizabethan age and of its great adventures, its
hatred of Spain, its bold sea-captains who laughed
the impossible to scorn, even the very ballad-music
of the time, inform that ballad, which dashes along
like the racing billows of the sea. Nor is the
mystic element of the sea and ships absent from it
in the end. *The Revenge* herself is alive, and does
not desire to live when she has an alien crew.

And away she sail'd with her loss *and longed for her own,*

is a line of pure imagination. And the great ocean
and the sky feel with the ship—they, too, are English ;
no English boat, they think, shall belong to Spain—
and they bury *The Revenge* in the fathomless main
by the island crags. This is a noble close to a
ballad which, while the sea endures, the sea-wolves
of England will love to hear.

The Sailor Boy enshrines another type ; nay
rather, it is a concentration into a short poem of
the temper of all seamen in lands where the sea

is loved. It holds in it the sailor's sense of the dangers of the deep, of the woes and weariness of his life, of his wonder that he can endure them, of his wish to stay on land, of his superstitious terror, of his lonely death in the homeless waves or on the cruel shore; and, as we read, we hear the long cry which began with the first poetry of England; and which Tennyson also placed on the lips of the Greeks who were almost as eager seamen as the English:

> Most weary seem'd the sea, weary the oar,
> Weary the wandering fields of barren foam.
> * * * * *
> We have had enough of action, and of motion we,
> Roll'd to starboard, roll'd to larboard, when the surge
> was seething free,
> Where the wallowing monster spouted his foam-fountains
> in the sea.
> * * * * * *
> Surely, surely, slumber is more sweet than toil, the shore
> Than labour in the deep mid-ocean, wind and wave and oar:
> Oh rest ye, brother mariners, we will not wander more.

But there is also in *The Sailor Boy* that fierce and keen attraction, that Siren-singing of the sea, as of beauty hiding horror in it, which, pulling at the hearts of English sailors, dragged them forth from their quiet hamlets under the cliff; whose voice drew Drake round the Horn and Frobisher to the Arctics, and a million hardy souls into every recess of the wide ocean, to live and die in adventure and in trading, in treasure-hunting and battle-hunting, in discovery, and in undying imagination. This also comes down to us from poetry more than a thousand years ago. Those who will read *The Seafarer*, a Northumbrian poem of the eighth or

ninth century, will hear, through its strangely
modern note, this double music of the sea, its two
cries of repulsion and attraction which may perhaps
mingle into one voice in that allurement of danger,
which is more felt, I think, by seamen than by any
other class of men. *The Sailor Boy* embodies all
these elements of feeling. I refer my readers to
it. To quote a part of it would spoil it ; to quote
the whole of it would not be fair.

Again and again this wild attraction of the
Unknown in the deep sea is expressed by Tennyson.
It breathes underneath the *Ulysses*. I have suffered
greatly, cries Ulysses, and enjoyed greatly, on shore,
and when

> Thro' scudding drifts the rainy Hyades
> Vext the dim sea——
> *   *   *   *   *   *
> Push off, and sitting well in order smite
> The sounding furrows ; for my purpose holds
> To sail beyond the sunset and the baths
> Of all the western stars, until I die.

It lives in *The Voyage*, that delightful poem, with
its double meaning, half of the life on the sea and
half of the life of the soul, and wholly of those who,
like seamen, have no care for business and science
and the real world ; who race after the undiscovered
shore, who follow the gleam, who live for ideas, not
for things. The same desire is at the root of the
invention of Tennyson concerning the passing
away of Galahad, who seeks the sacred and golden
city, not on land, as in the original, but by sailing
over the untravelled seas ; and, finally, the full
yearning of the seaman for the discovery of new
lands after patient sailing on the huge wastes of

ocean, and his rapture in the first sight of them, break forth in the true extravagance of the only entirely noble lines in the *Columbus:*

> Who push'd his prows into the setting sun,
> And made west east, and sail'd the Dragon's mouth,
> And came upon the Mountain of the World,
> And saw the rivers roll from Paradise.

As to the great creature herself, the Woman of our universe—the soft, cruel, reckless, restless, delightful and terrible mistress of the land— she lives in a changeful variety through the poetry of Tennyson, but she lives only on the coast. With his turn for truth, for writing only of what he had observed, he does not take us into the deep ocean, save in one stanza of *In Memoriam*, in *The Voyage*, and in a few scattered lines.* He rarely goes beyond the edge of the cliff or the margent of the beach. But he describes there the manners of the great waters with far more accuracy than any other of the bygone poets. His whole eyes were given to see truly and vividly, and all his imagination to record with joy, the doings of the billows on the land. It may be well to bring some of these together. Most of them are of the waves racing in upon the coast, and breaking on the cliffs or up the beach. The first of these I choose is in *The Lover's Tale*, and the manner of it is already Tennyson's own :

* Here is one noble passage of wave-tossing in fierce wind on the outer sea:

> As a wild wave in the wide North Sea
> Green-glimmering toward the summit, bears, with all
> Its stormy crests that smoke against the skies, &c.

> The slowly ridging rollers on the cliffs
> Clash'd, calling to each other.

"Deep calleth unto deep" saith the Psalm. This ridging of the billows is a favourite image, and he generally mingles it with the breaking down of the ridges into cataracts—a word he uses to suggest the roar and whiteness of the waters as they fall:

> Tho' heapt in mounds and ridges all the sea
> Drove like a cataract, and all the sand
> Swept like a river.   *The Holy Grail.*

>   *   *   *   *   *

> And the hollow ocean-ridges roaring into cataracts.
>   *Locksley Hall.*

Those who have walked on the Lido near Venice, when a tempest was blowing, know what Tennyson meant by the sweeping river of the sand. The dry grains stream past in a continuous cloud, as thick as torrent rain. Another time he sees a different effect of wind over wet sand:

> Crisp foam-flakes scud along the level sand
> Torn from the fringe of spray.

He hears "the shingle grinding in the surge," and "the scream of a maddened beach dragged down by the wave;" but sees, with equal truth, the soft upcoming of the peaceful swell on the smooth, flat sand—"dappled dimplings of the wave;" or

> the crisping ripples on the beach
> And tender curving lines of creamy spray.

Or with the sad creatures in *Despair*, waits

> Till the points of the foam in the dusk came playing about
> our feet.

He looks on a nobler, larger aspect of the waters
outspreading over distant, shallow sands—when
from " the lazy-plunging sea "

> the great waters break
> Whitening for half a league, and thin themselves
> Far over sands marbled with moon and cloud.

Or, once more, he lies on the shore to watch

> the curl'd white of the coming wave
> Glass'd in the slippery sand before it breaks.

He has seen with no less force the wave breaking
on the cliffs, and heard its roar with a no less
attentive ear. Into the cove at Tintagil comes a
ninth wave, which,

> gathering half the deep
> And full of voices, slowly rose and plunged
> Roaring, and all the wave was in a flame.

> * * * * * *

> And the fringe
> Of that great breaker, sweeping up the strand
> Lash'd at the wizard as he spake the word,
> And all at once all round him rose in fire.

This splendid piece of phosphoric sea is matched
by the tidal-wave in *Sea Dreams* scaling the cliffs
and exploding in the caves. When a wave fills a
cave the compressed air bursts out like a clap of
thunder :

> But while the two were sleeping, a full tide
> Rose with ground-swell, which, on the foremost rocks
> Touching, upjetted in spirts of wild sea-smoke,
> And scaled in sheets of wasteful foam, and fell
> In vast sea-cataracts—ever and anon
> Dead claps of thunder from within the cliffs
> Heard thro' the living roar.

A similar thunder is recorded in *The Palace of Art*, where the billows

> roar rock-thwarted under bellowing caves
> Beneath the windy wall.

Then he describes not only the noise, but the still advance of the windless swell into and through the cavern :

> As on a dull day in an ocean cave
> The blind wave feeling round his long sea-hall
> In silence.

He does not often speak of the great calm. There are the tropic lines in *Maud*:

> Half-lost in the liquid azure bloom of a crescent of sea,
> The silent, sapphire-spangled, marriage-ring of the land.

There is that passage in *Enoch Arden* where the Pacific lies outspread and blazing in the sun, but even that is made alive by

> The league-long roller thundering on the reef.

There are the lines in the *Princess*, where the Prince sees in vision

> A full sea glazed with muffled moonlight, swell
> On some dark shore just seen that it was rich.

This is the only calm sea-moonlight I remember in the poems. That lovely metaphor in *Maud*:

> If a hand as white
> As ocean-foam in the moon,

borders upon storm ; and so does the only other moonlighted sea I can recall—a very jewel of truth and imagination :

A still salt pool, lock'd in with bars of sand,
  Left on the shore ; that hears all night
The plunging seas draw backward from the land
  Their moon-led waters white.

And once at least we see in a lovely verse of the
poem to F. D. Maurice, the Channel and the ships :

Where, if below the milky steep
Some ship of battle slowly creep,
  And on thro' zones of light and shadow
Glimmer away to the lonely deep.

One other sea-piece, amid all these collected
aspects of observant truth, I myself saw realised. I
used to think that the phrase "wrinkled sea," in the
fragment called *The Eagle*, was too bold. But one
day I stood on the edge of the cliff below Slieve
League in Donegal. The cliff from which I looked
down on the Atlantic was nine hundred feet in height.
Beside me the giant slope of Slieve League plunged
down from its summit for more than eighteen hundred
feet. As I gazed down on the sea below which was
calm in the shelter, for the wind blew off the land,
the varying puffs that eddied in and out among the
hollows and juttings of the cliffs covered the quiet
surface with an infinite network of involved ripples.
It was exactly Tennyson's wrinkled sea. Then, by
huge good fortune, an eagle which built on one of
the ledges of Slieve League, flew out of his eyrie
and poised, barking, on his wings ; but in a
moment fell precipitate, as their manner is, straight
down a thousand feet to the sea. And I could not
help crying out :

The wrinkled sea beneath him crawls ;
He watches from his mountain walls,
And like a thunderbolt he falls.

CHAPTER XII

AYLMER'S FIELD, SEA DREAMS, THE BROOK

*A*YLMER'S FIELD seems from one point of view to have been written as a contrast to *Enoch Arden*. *Enoch Arden* was a tale of humble life and of a fisherman's self-sacrifice. *Aylmer's Field* is a tale of a life on a higher social level, and of the other than self-sacrifices hag-ridden persons in it sometimes make. Enoch sacrificed himself for the sake of those he loved. Sir Aylmer sacrificed his daughter and his friend for the sake of his sickly pride. Enoch dies, Sir Aylmer dies, but the one leaves tenderness and happiness behind him and the other bitterness and desolation. The law of Love with its sanctions is embodied in these two quiet tales; is gathered round simple circumstances, and is woven in and out with common human passions made mean or exalted in various characters. The stories are set in carefully painted scenery, and are lit and warmed by a steadily burning fire of imagination.

But though this doctrine of love arises from both poems (in one of which its fulfilment is shown and in the other its negation) the poems themselves cannot be accused of a conscious ethical aim. Their driving-power is not morality, but the love of human nature and the desire to make beautiful its outgoings. Moreover, if Tennyson had aimed at the truth that self-forgetfulness is the mother of Life and self-remembrance the mother of Death, he would still have done his work within an artist's sphere. For that truth is spiritual, not moral. Its doings belong to impulses of love arising freely from within, not to laws of conduct imposed from without. As such, it is a subject fitted for art, and the fact is that the impression made by both these poems is first and foremost an art-impression.

The next thing to say is that *Aylmer's Field* is not so good a piece of art as *Enoch Arden*. It is not so much at unity with itself. It ranges too quickly from simplicity to sensationalism, and the sensational elements become more and more sensational. And Tennyson was entirely out of his element in this realm of writing. The sensational was not native to his character, and when an artist steps outside of his character into a kind of art for which he is naturally unfitted, he is sure to over-strain the effort he makes. The art of a flamboyant writer has its native limits, its native rules. When a writer who has nothing flamboyant (and I apologise for this term) in his nature, attempts that kind of literary architecture, he exceeds its limits and he breaks its rules. This is the case in *Aylmer's Field*. The dagger business is too like a novel. The wrath of Sir Aylmer when he drives out Leolin is more violent than even the weakness of his character permits. The sermon, though just possible, is quite improbable. The scene in the church is more than the poetic stage on which the tale is written is capable of bearing. The suicide is feebler than

the hero, feeble as he is. In fact, the hero is too
light a person to choose for a poem of this kind,
but if he be chosen, he ought to be made more
worthy of manhood, and of the girl he loves. He
should have at least one parenthesis of strength
in his life. It is not that the characters are out
of nature, their conduct is fully possible. But
from the point of view of art, they just overstep
the edge of the natural—a little too violent, a little
too solemn, a little too weak for their characters as
drawn at the beginning, a little more extreme
than the motives permit.

In *Enoch Arden* a strong character dominates the
piece, and the prevalent overshadowing of this one
character (even during his ten years of absence)
binds the whole poem into unity. In *Aylmer's
Field*, no character is dominant, and only circumstances connect the personages. The girl alone,
and she passes through the action almost like a
painted dream, leaves much impression on the
heart. But separately, the portraiture is effective.
Since the characters do not weave themselves
together, we are the more forced to look at them
apart from one another, like pictures on a wall.
From that point of view they are full of interest,
worthy of study, and realised here and there in
single lines with a master's pencil. When it is
said of Edith that she was—

> bounteously made,
> And yet so finely that a troublous touch
> Thinn'd, or would seem to thin her in a day,

we are made, in a word, to feel the girl through and
through. Not less subtle and clean-edged are the

portraits of Sir Aylmer, of his wife, of the Indian cousin who flashes in and out of the hall, of Leolin himself in his petulant love, his foaming wrath and his shrill suicide, of the parson prophesying against the world to relieve his own indignant misery, and of the parents smitten at last to the quick of their pride, and staggering home to die. These are admirable, but they would have been more admirable had they all been wrought together.

And the result, the emotional impression left behind by this work of art, is not of humanity rising above the fates of life by dint of love, but of humanity crushed by the fates of life because of self-thought. The impression we receive is one of human weakness and nothing else, and it belongs to every one of the characters. No doubt, an artist can feel such a subject, but is it worth his while to take it ? It does not purify the imagination from fear of life, from contempt of humanity, or from petty anger with the common destinies of man. It does not set free high emotion. We are left in the common not the exalted world, in the sphere of social ethics, not in the spiritual sphere of art.

I cannot help thinking that Tennyson was half-conscious of this, that he was not content with his piece, but did not like to surrender it, and therefore that he laboured on it, in order to use it, for a long time. There is an extraordinary excellence of workmanship in many parts of this poem, as if he had toiled by exquisiteness of technic to redeem its general failure. The description of Edith at the beginning, and that which Averill makes of her in

his sermon at the close touches her as if with a
pencil of delicate sunshine.

> For her fresh and innocent eyes
> Had such a star of morning in their blue,
> That all neglected places of the field
> Broke into nature's music when they saw her.

And the rest is almost equal to that. Moreover,
Tennyson has enshrined the story in lovely English
scenery.

> A land of hops and poppy-mingled corn,
> Little about it stirring save a brook!

are lines not to be forgotten by Kentish men who
love their county. This description also which
follows is scarcely bettered in all his work, full as
it is of long and meditative love of the cottages of
England seen from the outside, garlanded with
flowers, sleeping like sheep upon the green road-
side—

> For out beyond her lodges, where the brook
> Vocal, with here and there a silence, ran
> By sallowy rims, arose the labourers' homes,
>
> *   *   *   *   *   *
>
> Her art, her hand, her counsel all had wrought
> About them : here was one that, summer-blanch'd,
> Was parcel-bearded with the traveller's joy
> In autumn, parcel ivy-clad ; and here
> The warm-blue breathings of a hidden hearth
> Broke from a bower of vine and honeysuckle:
> One look'd all rose-tree, and another wore
> A close-set robe of jasmine sown with stars :
> This had a rosy sea of gillyflowers
> About it ; this, a milky-way on earth,
> Like visions in the Northern dreamer's heavens,
> A lily-avenue climbing to the doors ;
> One, almost to the martin-haunted eaves
> A summer burial deep in hollyhocks ;
> Each, its own charm ; and Edith's everywhere.

This picture, so careful in thought and sight, so skilful in words, and so full of light and flower-opulence, is worthy of the closest study ; but even that, and the piteous and beautiful lines in which the agony of two young hearts and the wild weeping of the storm are woven together, do not redeem the whole.

> So they talk'd,
> Poor children, for their comfort : the wind blew ;
> The rain of heaven, and their own bitter tears,
> Tears, and the careless rain of heaven, mixt
> Upon their faces, as they kiss'd each other
> In darkness, and above them roar'd the pine.

Even these, and the last six lines of the poem, full of the life of Nature which lived the more when Aylmer's field was desolate of all the Aylmers, are not, lovely and true as they are, more than purple patches on a robe ill-woven.

I have also sometimes thought that Tennyson did not quite relish making an attack on the things he loved so well ; on long descent and pictured ancestry, on that pride of name and lands and fitting wedlock, which the squires of England cherish. These things he loved, when they were not inhuman. When they made men and women inhuman, he denounced them as heartily as any Republican, for he was a poet, and Love with him was first. But when a man denounces the extremes of what he likes, he is liable to represent those extremes too darkly, to make them worse than they are, lest he should be thought to attack the real thing. And in this poem the representation is greatly exaggerated. What Sir Aylmer does is iniquitous, more because of the circumstances than

because of his pride of birth and wealth. I do not
believe that the Squire in the prologue of the
Princess — "the great broad-shouldered genial
Englishman"—would have yielded Lilia to the
Parson's brother, with any patience, if she were
his only daughter and the heiress of his lands.
But Lilia's father would not have been a spy on his
daughter, nor thought that she was his chattel; and
he would have behaved like a gentleman, even when
he dismissed Leolin. But he would have been as
proud as Sir Aylmer, only in a more sensible way.
It is not really pride of birth which Tennyson
attacks, but things in the man which do not belong
to a gentleman—ill-bred and dishonourable ways
of acting—things which pride of ancestry would
forbid another man to do. Tennyson's attack is
not really levelled against the class or its qualities,
but against a discreditable member of the class;
not against rank and privilege or pride in them,
but against the inhumanity, the meanness, the
narrow conventions, which the diseased extreme
of pride of birth produces and supports. It is not,
to take another instance, Lady Clara Vere de Vere's
pride of rank to which he objects, but the inhuman
ways of her pride. Moreover, as a poet—whose
heart, always moved by pure and lovely maidenhood, kept with great beauty and devotion his
youthful ideal of womanhood untouched and un-
reproved, and who shaped it in many sweet and
lovely maids with a delicate tenderness never to be
forgotten—Tennyson hated the tyranny of parents
who sold their daughters, and *Aylmer's Field* and
many another poem record his steady indignation
with this iniquity.

Sea-Dreams (which in the volume of 1864 follows *Aylmer's Field*) is not a narrative of years and of many characters, but of a single day in the life of a man and his wife, and of a crisis in their soul. The man is a city clerk who has been cheated of all his savings by a hypocrite ; and who visits the seaside with his wife and infant after the loss has fallen upon him. They wander on the shore, and at evening the tide rises with a huge swell and thunder. The mighty sound flows through their sleep, and, with their circumstances, makes their dreams. The dreams stir their hearts—his to added bitterness, hers to solemn thought—and she asks her husband to forgive the injurer. " No," he cries. " No ? " she answers ; " yet the robber died to-day. I would you had forgiven." " Why," he replies, " because he is dead, should I forgive ? Yet, for the child sleeps sweetly, and that you may happily sleep, I do forgive."

That is the little tale, but few poems in the work of Tennyson are done with a finer art, or built up with a nobler imagination. Moreover the humanity, in both the senses of the word, is varied, vivid, wise and tender. The city clerk, gently born and bred ; his wife, than whom Tennyson has scarcely drawn a more gracious woman— her grace the grace of Jesus Christ—the heated preacher who proclaims the overthrow of Babylon ; the pious cheat, " so false he partly took himself for true," and the happy little child whose cradle rocks to the tune of a song that motherhood herself might have written—are all here, five distinct images of humanity. Each of them is touched by a poet's wisdom of love. When the hypocrite is

met and challenged in the street, the clerk looks
after him and

> Among the honest shoulders of the crowd,
> Read rascal in the motions of his back,
> And scoundrel in the supple-sliding knee.*

But, scoundrel as he is, the heavenly pity of the
woman leads us to pity him at the end.

Not less clear and delicate, in another kind, is
this lovely picture where husband, wife, and child
are woven together into one love in the silence of
the night.

> Saying this,
> The woman half turn'd round from him she loved,
> Left him one hand, and reaching thro' the night
> Her other, found (for it was close beside)
> And half-embraced the basket cradle-head
> With one soft arm, which, like the pliant bough
> That moving moves the nest and nestling, sway'd
> The cradle, while she sang this baby song—

The wisdom of love in the forgiveness of injury
belongs to the other sense of the word humanity,
and this humanity pleading for gentleness to wrong-
doing is the one motive which makes the poetic
unity of this poem.   It swells into fulness, like the
tide, from the beginning to the end of *Sea Dreams*.
It is in the heart of the woman ; its contrast is seen
in the cruel preacher, its need in the death of the

---

* Mr. Woolner, talking one day about this poem, told me that
when he was making his bust of Carlyle, a man well known on
'Change came in, and that, after he had gone away, Carlyle said,
" That man is a rascal ; I read it in the motions of his back—a
scoundrel ; did you see his supple-sliding knee ? " Woolner told
this story to Tennyson, and Tennyson reproduced it in this
happy way. Carlyle was right ; the man, a few years afterwards,
was guilty of felony.

hypocrite, its victory in the forgiveness which the
injured man bestows at last, its closing peace in the
sweet sleep of husband, wife, and child. Correlative
with this, and binding the poem into unity by its
all-pervading presence from without, as forgiveness
by its presence from within, is the fulness of the
sea which everywhere inundates the poem, first seen
by them as they walked

> Lingering about the thymy promontories,
> Till all the sails were darken'd in the west
> And rosed in the east ;

then heard, and waking them from sleep, when the
full tide rose, breaking on the cliffs and thundering
in the caves ; and lastly, seen in imagination, full-
watered, underneath the quiet stars. But before
they had awakened, its solemn noise had entered
the debateable land between slumber and waking,
and made their dreams. The dreams are woven
out of their story and the problem of life that
belonged to it, but the sea is their creator and their
explainer. Thus, from without, the Ocean Presence
makes also the unity of the poem. The man
dreams of life and honest work and of his speculation, in a beautiful invention through which the
sea breathes and flows. But the wife, since her
soul was in a higher land, dreamed a nobler dream,
in which the vast tide, swelling with a spheric
music, surges wave after wave on cliffs that in
the vision take the form of huge cathedral fronts
of every age, and breaks them down. Underneath,
among their ruins, men and women wrangled ; but
their " wildest wailings " (and this is a conception
equally noble and beautiful) " were never out of

tune" with the sweet low note which swelled and
died and swelled again in the belt of luminous
vapour, whence the billows rolled ashore to
sweep the cathedral fronts away. Thus, below the
wrangle of creeds, eternal Love abides, even in the
hearts of unloving men. At last, only the Virgin
and Child remain; and though they totter, they,
like the love they represent, are not seen to fall.
That dream, quaintly wrought as by the imagination working without the will, in sleep, is of the
Ocean, worthy of the Ocean's soul, and worded like
the Ocean's voice.

The passage is too long to quote, but there
are few finer things in the literature of visions of
the sea, save perhaps the dream of Wordsworth
recorded in the fifth book of *The Prelude*. It
would almost seem as if Tennyson had built his
dream in rivalry of Wordsworth's; but sublime as
it is, Wordsworth's is more sublime; and well
composed as it is, Wordsworth's is better composed.
The sea is also mighty in Wordsworth's vision,
and the barren sands on which he fell asleep are
changed into the great desert, over which the tide
encroaches to overwhelm the world. The Arab
rider in it is born out of Don Quixote, whose adventures the poet was reading, and the stone and the
shell the Arab holds in his hand are two books,
two great universes of human power, for both of
which Wordsworth had the highest reverence—the
universe of geometric truth, and the universe of
poetry—

> The one that held acquaintance with the stars,
> And wedded soul to soul in purest bond
> Of reason, undisturbed by space or time;

The other that was a god, yea many gods,
Had voices more than all the winds, with power
To exhilarate the spirit, and to soothe
Through every clime, the heart of human kind.

Meanwhile, as the Arab rode to save these two
books from the drowning of the world, and the
poet kept pace with him, his countenance grew
more disturbed——

And, looking backwards when he looked, mine eye
Saw, over half the wilderness diffused,
A bed of glittering light: I asked the cause:
"It is," said he, "the waters of the deep
Gathering upon us"; quickening then the pace
Of the unwieldy creature he bestrode,
He left me: I called after him aloud;
He heeded not; but, with his twofold charge
Still in his grasp, before me, full in view,
Went hurrying o'er the illimitable waste,
With the fleet waters of a drowning world
In chase of him; whereat I waked in terror,
And saw the sea before me, and the book,
In which I had been reading, at my side.

Both dreams are raised into sublimity by the
thoughts they represent, and both illustrate the
powers of Wordsworth and Tennyson when they
are writing at a high pitch of imaginative insight.
There are two other great sea-dreams in English
poetry. One is the vision of Clarence, far the
most splendid and passionate as poetry; the other
is the vision of the bottom of the great deep in the
Prometheus Unbound—a magnificent enlargement
of the dream of Clarence. But by weight of thought
and height of aim, thrilled, as both of them are,
by sympathy with the wants of mankind, the sea-
dreams of Wordsworth and Tennyson are greater
than Shelley's, and may even stand side by side

with Shakspere's, not by their poetic, but by their intellectual fire.

To return to Tennyson : this poem illustrates the range of his power. He passes easily from this large vision of the great deep of Eternal Love, destroying those impermanent forms of religion over which men quarrel, to the small and quiet picture, at the close, of the cradled infant and the mother. Few would dare to set them together, still fewer would have had the power to write both so perfectly.

We have a much fuller example of this variety of range in the poem of *The Brook*. It also is knit together into its brief space with delightful skill. Lawrence Aylmer, after twenty years of absence, returning from the East to see his native place, stays his steps at a stile, beside the babbling brook which joins the river near old Philip's farm. There, he remembers his younger brother, the poet who died, but who sang the rhyme of the brook he now recalls. There, too, he remembers Katie Willows, Philip's daughter, for whose petitioning grace of sweet seventeen he endured old Philip's chatter for many hours, that she might have time to make up her quarrel with her lover James—till, returning, worn with talk, he found

> the sun of sweet content
> Re-risen in Katie's eyes, and all things well.

And then he thinks how all are gone—Philip dead ; his brother dead ; Katie and James away in Australia—and bows his head over the brook.

The story is thus happily and easily wrought, but the end shows even greater skill. He lifts his

eyes and sees Katie over again come to him along
the path, and all the twenty years fade away.
Amazed, and like one who half waking feels a
glimmering strangeness in his dream, he cries—

> "Too happy, fresh and fair,
> Too fresh and fair in our sad world's best bloom,
> To be the ghost of one who bore your name
> About these meadows, twenty years ago."
>
> "Have you not heard?" said Katie, "we came back,
> We bought the farm we tenanted before.
> Am I so like her? so they said on board."

And the daughter brings him in to be welcomed by
the mother in the ancient farm. So does the poet
bring the past and present into one, and leave the
solitary man among old friends. It is an end
imagined with much grace, and it brings the whole
into a pretty unity. Moreover, as the sea, swelling
through *Sea Dreams*, binds that poem, from without,
into unity by its universal presence, so here the
brook, glancing, glimmering and singing everywhere,
runs through the poem and harmonises it and all
the twenty years into one happy thing.

The form of the poem is built on one of those
pleasant motives taken from simple things in the
far past, the charm of which we do not feel at
the time, but which, having been full of humanity,
are enchanting to remembrance. We recall them,
and are young again ; the years of monotonous
struggle glide away, and we love what we did, and
what we were. And if by chance we recollect these
events amid the same landscape in which they took
place, the illusion, and all the emotion that attends it,
are deepened—for Nature has not changed, and we

seem for the moment as unchanged as Nature. So Lawrence Aylmer felt, seeing the same flowers as of old, hearing the brook make the same music. Again Katie tells him her story ; again he sees James wading through the meadow ; again he hears old Philip chattering in his ear ; again he bids his brother farewell. Twenty years have vanished! How fair, how delightful life was long ago !

This is a frequent way of Tennyson's ; tales told years after the events, and veiled in the dewy glimmer of memory. It was so he made *The Gardener's Daughter*, and *The Miller's Daughter*. It was so he sang *The Grandmother*. It was so he made one of the tenderest of his smaller poems, revisiting a place where he had known his friend, and weaving into his recollection, as in *The Brook*, the voice and the swiftness, the beauty and the colour of the waters of the earth. Who does not remember *In the Valley of Cauteretz*, with its rhythm that flows with the flowing of the river ?

> All along the valley, stream that flashest white,
> Deepening thy voice with the deepening of the night,
> All along the valley, where thy waters flow,
> I walk'd with one I loved two and thirty years ago.
> All along the valley while I walk'd to-day,
> The two and thirty years were a mist that rolls away ;
> For all along the valley, down thy rocky bed,
> Thy living voice to me was as the voice of the dead,
> And all along the valley, by rock and cave and tree,
> The voice of the dead was a living voice to me.

There is yet a word to say about the grace of this poem, but I must not forget its portraiture. Here the portraits are all woven together by the feeling of the man who makes them. Lawrence Aylmer sees them all through his own character,

and his individual emotion secures them into unity.
But they could scarcely be better done. The young
poet, his brother—who thought money a dead thing,

> Yet himself could make
> The thing that is not as the thing that is ;

who had only begun to feel his life, like that time
which goes before the leaf,

> When all the wood stands in a mist of green,
> And nothing perfect ;

whose " primrose fancies " made the rippling song
of the brook—could not be more briefly or more
clearly sketched. Then we see Katie Willows, who
never ran, but moved—

> A little flutter'd, with her eyelids down,
> Fresh apple-blossom, blushing for a boon.
> *   *   *   *   *
> Straight, but as lissome as a hazel wand ;
> Her eyes a bashful azure, and her hair
> In gloss and hue the chestnut, when the shell
> Divides threefold to show the fruit within.

And with them both stands forth the English
farmer, of whom Tennyson paints so many types.
We hear with our very ears old Philip babbling of
his stock, his dogs, of Sir Arthur's deer that in
Darnley Chase

> in copse and fern
> Twinkled the innumerable ear and tail ;

of his colt and all its pedigree ; of his bargain with
the bailiff who in a line or two is flashed into life
before us as clearly as the farmer. Then one final
picture of Katie's daughter, coming with a low breath
of tender air that makes tremble in the hedge

> The fragile bindweed-bells and briony rings,

fills the frame with youthful freshness and re-creates
the love-story at the beginning of the tale. All
different, all excellent, these many portraits adorn
and make alive this little poem.

Finally, no poem of this class is more graceful.
It also is in a new style. I remember nothing like
it. Only a double-natured man like Tennyson,
delicate and rugged, could have written it. The
farmer is done by the farmer in Tennyson; but
when we lay him aside, all the rest is as graceful as
the scenery. The music of the brook is everywhere. The music of pleasant human love is also
everywhere. The poet-boy fills it with unworldli-
ness. The girl is happy in it, and her youth and
love make it like a summer day. And even were
these gracious, pretty, light emotions gone, we could
not resist the charm of the brook, that, coming from
the tarn far away amongst the hills, and singing all
the way, passes by Philip's farm to join the brimming
river. We follow it, as if we walked with it from
its fountains, by streets and town and bridge, by
field and fallow ; and the gay rhythm of the song
dances with its chatter and glitters with its sun and
shade. Nor does it want a momentary thought
to give it some sympathy with humanity, some
remembrance of us who company its waters with
our fleeting joy and with our steady sorrow—

> For men may come and men may go,
> But I go on for ever.

For, indeed, with all its sunny grace, there is
also a little air of human sorrow, which, like a
delicate mist, faintly sleeps above the poem, and
softening its outlines, harmonises all.

CHAPTER XIII

THE DRAMATIC MONOLOGUES

TENNYSON calls his *Locksley Hall, or Sixty Years After*, a " dramatic monologue," and it is a good name to give to a whole series of his poems, the " trick " of which I do not quite say he invented, but which he wrought into forms so specially his own, that they stand apart from work of a similar kind in other poets. Browning also made monologues of this kind. They, too, had their own qualities and manner, and were exceedingly various in metre. Browning's mind was filled with so great a crowd of various men and women, and of so many different times and countries, that he was forced, in order to realise their differences, into many different metrical movements. Tennyson, on the contrary, not conceiving so many types as Browning, is satisfied, on the whole, with one long, six-accented metre, with many trisyllables.

The dramatic monologues of Browning are sometimes lyrical, sometimes narrative, sometimes reflective, sometimes heroic, poetry. The poetic form in which Tennyson composed his monologues scarcely varies at all. It is an excellent manner for his purpose, and having found it, he clung to it. One man or woman speaks, telling a tale of the past or of the present. Another person—and here the dramatic element enters—is supposed to be near at hand, but we only know what he says by the speaker repeating a part of what he has heard and replying to it; and we only know of his presence by all that is said being addressed to him. The poor woman in *Rizpah* speaks to her visitor; the *Northern Farmer* to his servant.

This is Tennyson's form of the dramatic monologue, and it is wrought out with great skill and effectiveness. It is an easy form to work in, the easiest of all; and it is characteristic of Tennyson's love of the simple that he should choose the easiest. The form being easy to write in, the work inevitably tends to become, in inartistic hands, slovenly, long-winded, and unforceful. In Tennyson's hands, on the contrary, it is of the most robust, careful, concentrated kind. It is extremely rare when anything weak intrudes, or when the edge of the meaning is not quite sharp and clear. Any failure in excellence is more due to certain elements in the subject, chiefly controversial, and which were better excluded, than to the work itself.

It must, however, be remembered that the power of writing a good dramatic monologue does not include the power of writing a good drama. I doubt very much whether even Shakspere could have written a good dramatic monologue. He could not have kept to the single character. The pull in his soul towards the creation of more men and women would have been too much for him. On the other hand, the creator of a good dramatic monologue is not likely to be a good dramatist. Of course, he may have that power, but I remember no case of it. The habit of mind by which a poet creates, as in a dramatic monologue, one vivid personality out of himself is so totally different from the habit of creating a number of personalities, all of whom the dramatist conceives as apart from himself, that it is not probable one man will have both habits of mind. Moreover, the power of drawing one man in one set of circumstances is very different from the power of drawing a number of characters clashing together in circumstances which are continually changing. The writer of the dramatic monologue is likely to keep to his habit if he take to the drama, and all his characters will tend to express themselves in monologue. Changing circumstances will not modify their speech or their action as much as they ought to do. At root, all the characters will be the poet ; we shall detect him everywhere ; nor will there be enough distinction between the characters to make the play interesting, the action dramatic, the personages alive enough, or the catastrophe a necessity. This is true of all Tennyson's, and, in a lesser degree, of Browning's dramas. The Northern Farmer, the Northern Cobbler, the second Northern Farmer, the village wife in *The Entail*, are all keenly alive. But I do not believe that Tennyson could have brought these four into a drama, and driven them, by their characters hurtling together, to a necessary con-clusion ; or invented, with excellence, the mutual play which should lead to that conclusion. In this, the highest of all the creative forms of poetry, he would have broken down ; and he always did break down when he tried. The fact is that, for drama, his own personality was too much with him ; he could not get rid of it. But the great dramatist can divest himself of his personality. His personages have their own characters, not his. He has lost himself in making them. I might even say that his will does not order their action ; it is rather the meeting of the various characters, undei the circumstances, which makes the conclusion inevitable. He invents, it is true, the circumstances, but his personages do not act as he would act ; they follow their separate bents ; independent, as it were, of his will. And so apart from him are they, so little is he in them as a character, that I can conceive, to put it paradoxically, that he might be unaware of what they are going to do. The true dramatist sits outside of his characters.

This is the highest kind of creation. Such a creator is the true Prometheus. He makes men and women who are not himself. But this is not the kind of work Tennyson or Browning could do. We hear the individuality of their maker in all that the personages of their dramas say. We see the aims of their maker, his tricks of mental attitude, his theories of life, in all they do. The untrue dramatist sits inside of all his characters. Both Browning and Tennyson ought to have kept to dramatic monologue, or to such a variation of dramatic monologue as *Pippa Passes*, which no one can call a drama. All the same, it is necessary to say, though not here to dwell on, that Browning has made a far more successful attempt at drama than Tennyson.

Once more, in a drama the characters speak no more when the conclusion arrives. The dramatist therefore always looks to the future. He is anxious that his characters should play together towards a far-off end ; that every one of them should minister his own part to the end ; that each man's part should illuminate the parts of all the others. All his interests look forward. But in the dramatic monologue there is no forward look ; nothing has to be made for a distant end or fitted to it. What has been in the past or what is actually doing in the present is described, and to write of the past or the present is, of course, much easier than to compose a changing succession of events and varying emotions towards a close in the future. It needs twice the genius to write a good drama that it takes to write a good dramatic monologue ; but, unfortunately, those who have so much of the dramatic instinct as to be able to write a dramatic monologue persuade themselves with great rapidity that they can write a drama. It thoroughly disturbs me when I think what a series of little masterpieces of dramatic monologue we might have had if Tennyson had not spent so many years in writing dramas.

The " dramatic monologues," a few examples of which I select—since it is not possible to write of them all—belong directly to the tragedy and to the comedy of life. *Rizpah, Despair, The First Quarrel,* are examples of the first. All the dialect poems are examples of the second. There is another class which can scarcely be called tragedy or comedy, the speaker in which reviews the whole of his life, or one event in it, and with a certain social or ethical direction. Of these *Locksley Hall, or Sixty Years After,* is one example, and *The Wreck* is another. Each of them also reveals and explains a typical character, but the individual is not lost in the generalisation. Tennyson's speakers are specialised enough to separate them from other persons of the same kind. The Northern Farmer, though he represents a class, is his own delightful self. When he died, he left no one behind who was exactly he, though he left a number of men who were like him. The general lines of the Northern Cobbler's position are the same as those of many reformed drinkers, but no one but himself could have set up the bottle in the window, or declared that he would take it with him after death, like a Norse warrior his sword, before the throne. We possess the type in these poems of Tennyson, but we have also the individual.

It would be wrong also not to speak of the variety and range of the characters represented. We pass from the aged squire, whose youth was full of fire and whose age is full of the ashes of that fire, to the woman who has forsaken husband and child and found a love which satisfied her soul, but whose love and life are wrecked. We stand on the sea-shore with the working man who has been driven by misery and false creeds into suicide, and sit by the bedside of the mother whose son was hanged, and whose awful love gathered and buried his bones. The seaman's wife, the bandit's bride, the Irish girl, the hospital nurse, the ruined girl and her merciful rival, the farmer, the cobbler, the sick child, the village gossip, are all created. Almost every class of society is laid under contribution in stories which range from the black tragedy of *Rizpah* to the light comedy of *The Spinster's Sweet-arts*.

The first of these I choose is *Locksley Hall, or Sixty Years After*, and I connect it with the *Locksley*

Hall which appeared in 1842. That poem stirred the whole of England into a new sensation. We can scarcely call it a "dramatic monologue," but it held this form of poetry within it, and went to its verge. We might even say that a dramatic movement is played in the hero's soul, in which three or four aspects of his nature take personality one after another, the lover, the betrayed lover, the curser of his time, the man who reacts with anger from his disillusion and his cursing, and the one man who is looking back on all the phases through which he has passed. In whatever aspect we see him, he is the young man. Youth flames throughout the poem ; youth wandering on the shore, clinging to the present, dipping into the future, while he

Saw the Vision of the world, and all the wonder that
would be ;

youth breaking with the spring into love and into lovely imagining of love ; youth raging at his sweetheart's falseness, at her husband, at society ; youth remembering its "wild pulsation" before it entered into life ; youth exaggerating its sorrow, yearning to burst away from convention ; youth ashamed of its bluster, and emerging from it into resolution ; youth flinging love to the winds and taking to science; youth bidding good-bye to the past, and devoting it to desolation and to tempest in a new rush of wrath ; and finally going fiercely into the sea of manhood—with the roaring wind. For so it ends :

Howsoever these things be, a long farewell to Locksley
Hall!
Now for me the woods may wither, now for me the roof-
tree fall.

2 D

Comes a vapour from the margin, blackening over heath
    and holt,
Cramming all the blast before it, in its breast a thunder-
    bolt.

Let it fall on Locksley Hall, with rain or hail, or fire or
    snow;
For the mighty wind arises, roaring seaward, and I go.

Was there ever anything more youthful? It
touched everything that was young in England and
gave it voice. The very scenery is full of the
things which charm the young—the stars, the
copses ringing with the birds, the colours deepening
on their breast in spring; the curlew's cry; the
stately ships going by on the sea; the roaring
cataracts of the ocean ridges thundering on the
sands; the vision of the tropics. Take the stars—
a new, clear voice, unheard before, echoes in these
lines—

Many a night from yonder ivied casement, ere I went to
    rest,
Did I look on great Orion sloping slowly to the West.

Many a night I saw the Pleiads, rising thro' the mellow
    shade,
Glitter like a swarm of fire-flies tangled in a silver braid.

And yet, with all this efflorescence of youth, which
in its very exaggeration makes the central excellence of the poem, a curious steadiness of thought
and a restrained force of wording, such as belong
to established manhood, pervade it also. There are
many lines which have become household words,
which, while young in their expression, have also
the fulness of maturity,—and to write these and to
know that one had written them along with all
the youthful verse, must have given Tennyson the

supreme consciousness that he was a poet who had a whole world before him ; and he told England this in a single line—

> Yearning for the large excitement that the coming years
> would yield.

Sixty years pass by, and the young man is old, and Tennyson tells in a true dramatic monologue what the youth has become. It is a marvellous study to be written by a man over eighty years of age. He had now come to such years as " the many-wintered crow that leads the clanging rookery home " ; but the poetic force in this poem has a constant volume. The rhythm is as fine as in the days long past. Here is one example—

> Robed in universal harvest up to either pole she smiles,
> Universal Ocean softly washing all her warless Isles.

The poem is somewhat too long, but even that may have been the poet's intention. He had to represent age, and age is garrulous. And the image of old age is as clear and true in this *Locksley Hall* as the image of youth is in its predecessor. We might work out from the poem all the characteristics of an old man—from babbling anger to soft forgiveness, from many-passioned memory to pathetic expectation of the world to come. All is age, and an age which, even in its petulance and prejudice, is to be loved and honoured. The more I read the poem, the more I think it worthy of respect as a work of art.

Many, like myself, will dislike its views about man and the future of man. They are the views of a half-pessimist tempered by belief in immortality. But no one has at all the right to say that they are the views of Tennyson. He had created a certain type of character in the young man of the poem of 1842, and though he himself enters into this young man, it is only when he is expressing the general joy and impulsiveness of youth. The real representative of Tennyson in 1842 is the *Ulysses*, and Ulysses is wholly different from the old or the young man in both the *Locksley Halls*. Tennyson shows in the later poem into what the special character of the hero of the earlier poem was likely to grow after sixty years had fled away. It would not be just to affirm that he is painting himself, as some have said; the subject infers that he is creating another man.

The young man took to science to relieve his mind of love's disillusion. It is no wonder then that, given his temperament, he found himself in a sea of disappointment. He has not taken to work for man save on his estate; he has isolated himself with a wife and in his country-house, and he has continued to brood over the ills of the world at a distance from them. He remains as much locked up in himself as he was before. Had he had more sympathy with the movement of the world, he might have seen some good, even in the revolutionists and the jabberers. He himself, exactly as in his youth, does not refrain from noise as loud as that made by those whom he denounces. He cries, like Carlyle, against mere speech, and sins, like Carlyle, by an overflow of language; sickening at the lawless din, unaware that his own din is even more lawless, and overwhelming his grandson with " Chaos, Cosmos! Cosmos, Chaos," and with all the wailing and screaming of the pessimists—a noise a thousand-fold worse for mankind, or for a man to make, than the noise of all the mob-orators of the world. It is precisely what the young fellow of the first *Locksley Hall* would grow into, if he lived apart from men and kept an edge of poetry in him— enough to make him shudder at all the evil of which he hears, but not enough to drive him into actual contention with it. This is tempered, as I said, by belief in immortality, and in evolution. The immortality will set the poor wretches of this cruel universe right in the world to come, but it holds out no present hope for this world. And evolution? Evolution has moved us into higher life with such an infinite slowness in the past that we can only expect a better world on earth, if we can dare to expect it at all, when æon after æon has passed away. At last, out of this crying of despair, mingled with the pathetic forgiveness and the pathetic memories of personal life, arises a hidden hope, at which, if he had wrought, he would not have come to so sorrowful an age— "Love will conquer at the last," and the poem ends with an excellent morality. But the man, we feel, will yet need to reverse himself in the world to come. It is a masterly study—a wonderful thing for Tennyson to have written at an age when most men are somewhat too inactive in mind to be able to pass out of themselves, and for a time to enter into the soul of another.

The final question one asks about it is: Was it worth doing at all? Was it worth a poet's while to flood the world with all this wailing music, to depress mankind who is depressed enough, to picture so much ill and so little good, to fall into a commonplace realism, to seem to make the querulous hopelessness of the character he draws the measure of the future of mankind? It was not worth a poet's while; and I wish, in spite of the excellence of the work, that he had not taken the subject at all.

The next of these dramatic monologues I select as an example is *The Northern Farmer*. It is a vivid piece out of the great comedy of man, not of its mere mirth, but of that elemental humorousness of things which belongs to the lives of the brutes as well as to ourselves, that steady quaintness of the ancient earth and all who are born of her, which first made men smile, and which has enabled us to bear our pain better, and to love one another more, than might appear possible in a world where Nature generally seems to be doing her best to hurt us first, and then to kill us. This kind of elemental humour rarely emerges in the educated classes, except when we have scraped off all their conventions and got down to the rough grain of humanity, but is continually met in the peasant and farmer class; and, curiously enough, it was the only kind of true humour that Tennyson possessed. There was always in him, behind his delicate grace and educated charm, a piece of rugged, wild, uncultured human nature, such as might belong to a peasant——a portion of man just as he emerged from being a part of wild Nature—— which often gave an extraordinary depth and force to the lovelier parts of his poetry, but which also enabled him to write these dialect poems in a way no other poet has approached.

The Northern Farmer is the finest of them all.

There never was a more superbly hewn piece of rough and vital sculpture. What Michael Angelo did for the Prophet Amos into whose writings entered the herdsman, Tennyson has done for this farmer, with a chisel as vivid and as bold. He is the very genius of ancient agriculture, and seems born out of the fruitful bosom of Mother Earth. He breathes and smells of the earth, and the earth speaks by his voice. When he tells how he stubbed Thurnaby waste and rumbled out of it the boggle and the stones together, and made grass of the bracken and whin, it is the lover of the Earth who tells us how she desires to be handled. When he says that God Almighty scarcely knows what He is doing when He takes him away, it is the rude Teuton tiller of the land who speaks, who ploughed the land with one hand and fought the Roman with the other, and who worshipped Thor, the farmer's friend. His first duty is to the land and then to the squire who owns it, and, that done, what has he to do with parsons? God Almighty knows that he has done, and none better, what he ought to do. He belongs to the ancient nobility of the plough and the spade, and he sickens to think of that base-born plutocrat, machinery, putting his nose into the blessed fields. What has been, ought to be for ever, and what has been is as old as the world. Men ought to cling to the ancient courses. Every night for forty year he's had his ale, and he will have it now, though he die. This is a primæval creature, and he is drawn, as a giant, who happened to be a poet, might have drawn him before the Flood. It is a mighty piece of work.

I pass over the others, and take the *Rizpah*. This brings us into noble tragedy—noble, not by its story which is not of heroes, but noble by two things : by its dreadful pathos and by its infinite motherhood.

> Flesh of my flesh was gone, but bone of my bone was left—
> I stole them all from the lawyers—and you,—will you call
> it a theft ?—
> My baby, the bones that had suck'd me, the bones that
> had laughed and cried—
> Theirs ? O no ! They are mine—not theirs—they had
> moved in my side.

This is a cry out of the heart of all the mothers of the world of man from the beginning, nay, the cry of all the mother-beasts and birds before man was known on earth. All the tragedy of motherhood which has loved and lost is pressed into that verse, maddens and wails and loves through the whole poem. To find anything like the dark horror and untameable woe of *Rizpah*, we must go back to the wild Elizabethan dramatists, and to one higher than they. When I read the lines of Tennyson which bring together the passion of bereaved motherhood and the thin wailing of her boy's voice on the wind, the raging of the storm and the naked gibbet shrieking in the night, I think of Lear in the storm, when the coming madness of the old king, and the imitative madness of Edgar, and the elemental folly of the fool raised into a wildness of nature by the madness of the rest, are all matched and heightened by the roaring and flashing of the tempest over the barren moor.

> Wailing, wailing, wailing, the wind over land and sea—
> And Willy's voice in the wind, "O mother, come out to me."

Why should he call me to-night, when he knows that I
    cannot go?
For the downs are as bright as day, and the full moon stares
    at the snow.

We should be seen, my dear; they would spy us out of the
    town.
The loud black nights for us, and the storm rushing over
    the down,
When I cannot see my own hand, but am led by the creak
    of the chain,
And grovel and grope for my son till I find myself drenched
    with the rain.

This is the tragedy of Nature wedded to the
tragedy of a mother. Her only son is hanged in
chains and eaten by the ravens. The horror and
the shame, like ravens, eat her heart. Hung on
the coast, so high

That all the ships of the world could stare at him, passing by.

And the dreadful shame, struck into that splendid
line, and her unspeakable misery of love drove her
to madness. But when she was let out from her
cell "stupid and still," her mother's love was
always sane; and as the bones fell, she "gathered
her baby together":

Do you think I was scared by the bones? I kiss'd 'em, I
    buried 'em all—
I can't dig deep, I am old—in the night by the churchyard
    wall,
My Willy 'ill rise up whole when the trumpet of judgment
    'ill sound,
But I charge you never to say that I laid him in holy ground.

And now she is come to die, and the "Lord who has
been with her in the dark" will make her happy
with her son—and a vast cry, the cry of her

son's love, comes to her, shaking the walls, out of
eternity :

> But I cannot hear what you say for my Willy's voice in the
> wind—
> The snow and the sky so bright—he used but to call in the
> dark,
> And he calls to me now from the church and not from the
> gibbet—for hark !
> Nay—you can hear it yourself—it is coming—shaking the
> walls—
> Willy—the moon's in a cloud——Good-night.   I am going.
> He calls.

It was but a common hanging ; a common thief, and
an old wife mad with grief, an every-day thing!
But a great poet came by, and we have this——the
depths of sorrow, the depths of love, infinite pity,
infinite motherhood, a world on a world.

CHAPTER XIV

SPECULATIVE THEOLOGY

THE later poems of Tennyson are full of speculative theology, and of an interesting kind; that kind which not only reveals character, but also opens out those more uncommon regions of the mind where life and character combining have produced strange gardens of thought. The poet does not move here in the moral world, or as the emotional imager of life, or as the builder of tales by the harp of imagination; but in the world beyond the senses, where things are felt and thought, not seen and proved; in the great deeps of passionate conjecture. And what he thinks there, and how he feels in that spaceless and timeless country, unveil to us some of the secret places of his character.

I have used the word "passionate" above, because, unless such speculations are warmed by fire from the heart, they are not fit subjects for poetry. Tennyson's speculative subjects—such as Where was the soul before its birth?—take their rise always from the cries of love within him for satisfaction, and, since they come from that source, their treatment by him is always poetical. I have also used the word "conjecture" above, in order to distinguish these subjects from others which he did not regard

as matters of speculation, but of faith. Tennyson
believed in God and that God cared for men; and
he naturally wrote with glowing warmth about One
in whom he thus believed. I might quote many
passages to prove this, but I quote only one. It is
his great hymn, a solemn anthem rather, into which
he drew all the thoughts and their attendant emotions which during his life and in his poems he had
conceived, felt, and expressed concerning the Father
of men :

I.

Hallowed be Thy name—Halleluiah!
Infinite Ideality !
Immeasurable Reality !
Infinite Personality !
Hallowed be Thy name—Halleluiah !

II.

We feel we are nothing—for all is Thou and in Thee ;
We feel we are something—that also has come from Thee ;
We feel we are nothing—but Thou wilt help us to be.
Hallowed be Thy name—Halleluiah !

This, then, is not matter of speculation to
Tennyson ; but, in what special ways, independent
of an outward revelation, this mighty Spirit com-
municated Himself to the individual soul ; and
how He was connected with the universe of Nature
—these were matters of conjecture, and the poet
made many speculations concerning them. Then
again, immortality (that is the continuous consciousness of one's own personality after death)
was a matter of faith to Tennyson. It was fully
set forth in *In Memoriam*. It became troubled
after that poem, as I have said ; but his faith in it
fought like a hero against armies of doubt. It

finally settled down into absolute conviction. But, in what way we were immortal ; whether we were instantly alive and active after dissolution or slept for a time; whether we were still in connection with those we loved on earth; whether we moved onward in that new world as slowly as on earth ; what our relation to the universe was after death ; whether we returned in a new life to earth, losing memory but retaining our essential personality ; whether we existed before we were born into this world, and if so, of what kind was that existence ;— these and many others were matters of speculation.

The first of these is his conjecture with regard to the origin of the soul, that is, according to him, that essential part of infinite Being which, joined to the infant, becomes personal on earth. He assumes its existence ; and he held, as a speculation, that it was in God before it took form on earth. Whether he adopted the further view that it was conscious then of a separate life, I cannot make out with any clearness from his poems. Sometimes it seems as if he did think this, but chiefly not. The soul was a part of God's life, but in that general life it had no self-consciousness. When a man was to be born, a part, a spark of the divine essence, was taken forth, as it were, out of the vast Deep of Spirit, and for the time of life on earth was enfolded in that which we call matter, with all its relative limitations, in order that this piece of immortal essence, the soul, might develop and realise a separate personality, understanding that he was himself, and always to be himself :

> Eternal form shall still divide
> The eternal soul from all beside.

The new being learnt slowly the Me and the Not-me, learnt his personal apartness. The baby does not think that this is I :

> But as he grows he gathers much,
> And learns the use of "I" and "Me";
> And finds, "I am not what I see,
> And other than the things I touch."
>
> So rounds he to a separate mind
> From whence clear memory many begin,
> As thro' the frame that binds him in
> His isolation grows defined.

The "use of blood and breath" is to outline personality. When the man dies, he has secured for ever a distinct being. The other faith—That we shall remerge ourselves in the general soul, is faith, he says, as vague as it is unsweet. The soul comes, then, out of the vast Deep of God and returns to it again.* It comes impersonal ; it returns to it a personality. This is his view. It is a common view, but in a great poet's hands it

---

* In *The Two Voices*, a poem of 1833, this speculation of pre-existence has already occupied his mind. The dark vague voice suggests that beginning implies ending. How do I know, the other voice within answers, that the first time I was, I was human, or that my life now is in truth my beginning? Life cycles round, and I may have been in another world before I came here, though I remember nothing of it. I may have been in nobler place, or in lower lives, and have forgotten all I was. Or I may have floated free as naked essence (and to this theory Tennyson finally clung), and then of course I should remember nothing of it. Whatever I may have been, there is something

> That touches me with mystic gleams,
> Like glimpses of forgotten dreams—
> Of something felt, like something here ;
> Of something done, I know not where;
> Such as no language may declare.

is expressed so imaginatively that it ceases to be common. In the epilogue to *In Memoriam*, when he is thinking about the child who will be born of the marriage he then celebrates in song, he says:

> A soul shall draw from out the vast,
> And strike his being into bounds.

In the *Idylls of the King*, Arthur is born, according to the body, of Uther and Ygerne, but the coming of the soul into him (and this is made more forcible by the allegory which makes Arthur symbolise the rational soul) is mystically represented by the babe who descends from heaven with the divine ship into the sea, and is washed to Merlin's feet by the wave. The two wizards, standing in Tintagil Cove,

> Beheld, so high upon the dreary deeps
> It seem'd in heaven, a ship, the shape thereof
> A dragon wing'd, and all from stem to stern
> Bright with a shining people on the decks,
> And gone as soon as seen.

A noble piece of symbolism! When Merlin afterwards is asked about

> The shining dragon and the naked child,
> Descending in the glory of the seas,

he answers, laughing, in riddling triplets, the last lines of which are these—lines quoted again and again at every crisis of Arthur's life, and at his death:

> Sun, rain, and sun! *and where is he that knows?*
> *From the great deep to the great deep he goes.*

We know what Tennyson in this passage meant

by the Great Deep from his poem *De Profundis,*
written on the birth of his eldest son, and far the
finest of his speculative poems.   Its stately and
mystic sublimity is warmed by the profound emotion
of his fatherhood.   It is divided into two parts—
two greetings.   Here is the beginning of it—and
since Milton no more dignified lines have been
written :

> Out of the deep, my child, out of the deep,
> Where all that was to be, in all that was,
> Whirl'd for a million æons thro' the vast
> Waste dawn of multitudinous-eddying light—
> Out of the deep, my child, out of the deep,
> Thro' all this changing world of changeless law,
> And every phase of ever-heightening life,
> And nine long months of antenatal gloom,
> With this last moon, this crescent—her dark orb
> Touch'd with earth's light—thou comest, darling boy;

and then he prophesies the boy's life and the
man's, till he joins the great deep again.   The
second greeting speaks first of the great deep
itself.

> Out of the deep, my child, out of the deep,
> From that great deep, before our world begins,
> Whereon the Spirit of God moves as He will—
> Out of the deep, my child, out of the deep,
> From that true world within the world we see,*

* Of this great deep of Spirit, knowledge but stirs the surface-
shadow.   It does not pierce into its depths :

> The Abysm of all Abysms, beneath, within
> The blue of sky and sea, the green of earth,
> And in the million millionth of a grain,
> Which cleft and cleft again for ever more,
> And ever vanishing, never vanishes,
> To me, my son, more mystic than myself,
> Or even than the Nameless is to me.
>
> *The Ancient Sage.*

> Whereof our world is but the bounding shore—
> Out of the deep, Spirit, out of the deep,
> With this ninth moon, that sends the hidden sun
> Down yon dark sea, thou comest, darling boy.

And the Spirit is half-lost in its body which is its shadow, and yet is the sign and the cause of its becoming personal. It wails on entering the world, for it is banished; it knows mystery and doubt and pain and time and space, in its progress to self-consciousness. Yet that it might become a person was the intention of the Infinite One who sent it out of Himself—

> Who made thee unconceivably Thyself
> Out of His whole World-self and all in all.

And the chief miracle is this, that the child grows into a separate will and character, knowing himself to be himself, and known by others to be himself—for ever different from all other souls—

> With power on thine own act and on the world.

This is the main speculation. Within it arose two other questions which have always pervaded inquiry concerning the origin of the soul. The first is—Does the soul live over and over again in other forms on this earth, and, not carrying with it full memory of the past lives, yet carry with it the progress it has gained, or the retrogression it has made? There are two lines in this *De Profundis* which seem to suggest that this was a thought of Tennyson's:

> and still depart
> From death to death thro' life and life, and find
> Nearer and ever nearer Him.

2 E

And it was certainly his view that the spirit moved onwards hereafter ;

From state to state the spirit walks.

But this does not say that the spirit returns to earth in another form. On the contrary, many passages appear to assert that personality, established here, moves onward, self-conscious, and with full memory, in the world to come, returning no more to earth. Tennyson did not, then, hold the Oriental or the Platonic view, which has been modified by a thousand speculators into a thousand forms.

The second question is—Has the soul, while shadowed and limited by sense, vague remembrances, as Plato or Wordsworth thought, of the diviner land whence it came, touches of what it was of old in God—at which touches the sensible world fades away, and man, suddenly swept into the supersensuous life, knows again his being in the Being of the infinite Spirit ? The quotation already given from *The Two Voices* proves that Tennyson did suggest this in his youth, but in the later poems it was plainly stated. As age grew upon him, this speculation became more dear; and the passage in *The Ancient Sage* which best enshrines it is full of a personal interest. It records Tennyson's youthful experience, and looking back on this from his old age, he explains what he believes the experience meant.

The young man who is with the ancient Sage represents unbelief in any life beyond the material, and his song cries out concerning man :

> O worms and maggots of to-day
> Without their hope of wings !
> Tho' some have gleams or so they say
> Of more than mortal things.

And the Sage answers, " To-day ? "　Worms of
the present perhaps, for indeed a man may make
himself a very maggot,—" but what of yesterday ? "
Has a man no remembrance, no vague suggestion of
a past in which he had life before he was on earth ?
And here we have Tennyson's own experience ·

> For oft
> On me, when boy, there came what then I call'd,
> Who knew no books and no philosophies,
> In my boy-phrase, "The Passion of the Past."
> The first gray streak of earliest summer dawn,
> The last long stripe of waning crimson gloom,
> As if the late and early were but one—
> A height, a broken grange, a grove, a flower
> Had murmurs, " Lost and gone and lost and gone ! "
> A breath, a whisper—some divine farewell—
> Desolate sweetness—far and far away—
> What had he loved, what had he lost, the boy ?
> I know not, and I speak of what has been.

This common feeling, this mystic suggestion of
the dreaming soul, has never been more beautifully
given.

> Some divine farewell,
> Desolate sweetness, far and far away,

is perfect in truth and pathos.　The same thought
is put, almost as beautifully, in a song published
four years after *The Ancient Sage*, and the motive
of it is taken from the lingering sweetness of the
words—" far and far away "—upon his ear.　Here
also Tennyson recalls the boy's celestial dreams of
a land known in the dawn of life.　I should like to

quote it all, but I select only the three verses which
bear on the question:

> What vague world-whisper, mystic pain or joy,
> Thro' those three words would haunt him when a boy,
> > Far—far—away ?
>
> A whisper from his dawn of life? a breath
> From some fair dawn beyond the doors of death
> > Far—far—away ?
>
> Far, far, how far ? from o'er the gates of Birth,
> The faint horizons, all the bounds of earth,
> > Far—far—away ?

This, felt as a boy, brings about, in such a
temperament, and when it recurs in a different way
in manhood, the apparent dissolution of all the world
of sense, unconsciousness of the body and existence
apart from it. We have heard of this already in
the *Sir Galahad*. Transports mightier than love
lift him above the world of sense. His spirit
beats her mortal bars. His very body ceases to
be matter :

> And, stricken by an angel's hand,
> This mortal armour that I wear,
> This weight and size, this heart and eyes,
> Are touch'd, are turn'd to finest air.

The weird seizures of the Prince in *The Princess*,
in which he knew not the shadow from the substance ; the visions of Arthur, in which the earth
seems not earth, the light and air not light and air,
his very hand and foot a dream, lead us up to
Tennyson's full and personal expression of this
experience in *The Ancient Sage :*

> And more, my son ! for more than once when I
> Sat all alone, revolving in myself

> The word that is the symbol of myself,
> The mortal limit of the Self was loosed,
> And past into the Nameless, as a cloud
> Melts into heaven.   I touch'd my limbs, the limbs
> Were strange not mine—and yet no shade of doubt,
> But utter clearness, and thro' loss of Self
> The gain of such large life as match'd with ours
> Were Sun to spark—unshadowable in words,
> Themselves but shadows of a shadow-world.

It is the vision, vouchsafed to earth, of what the soul will be when it returns out of the shadow of sense into the substance whence it came :

> If what we call
> The Spirit flash not all at once from out
> This shadow into substance.

" This world," said Novalis, " is not a dream, but it ought to become one, and perhaps it will." And the misery, hardness and folly of earth are, Tennyson thinks, in the dream, and not in the reality.   We misshape through the senses the actual world.   " My God," he cries in *The Sisters*, speaking in the mouth of their father, " I would not live,"

> Save that I think this gross hard-seeming world
> Is our misshaping vision of the Powers
> Behind the world, that make our griefs our gains.

Death then is the flashing of the soul, out of a life in which all reality is distorted, into the luminous straight life out of which it came ; the passing from illusion into reality.

Yet another speculation is connected with this theory of the soul, and concerns its power of acting independently of the body.   This speculation asks three questions.   First, can the soul of one living in

the other world speak to the soul of one living on
earth, not by voice, but by intensity of thought,
driven by intensity of feeling, smiting through space
on the thought and feeling of a soul on earth?
Secondly, can those on earth communicate in this
way with those that have passed away? Thirdly,
can two persons both on earth touch one another in
this fashion—one soul vibrating, as if through the
ether, its message to another soul—across any
distance whatever? To all these three questions
Tennyson answers yes. *In Memoriam* is full of
passages which either maintain or suggest the two
first. "The dead shall look me through and
through," he cries. "If the grave divide us not,
be with me now!"

> And he, the Spirit himself, may come
> When all the nerve of sense is dumb
> Spirit to Spirit, Ghost to Ghost.

The soul of his friend in heaven answers his cry
for love,

> I watch thee from the quiet shore;
> Thy spirit up to mine may reach;
> But in dear words of human speech
> We two communicate no more.

And most of all this is laid down in that full-
versed passage, when, rapt by reading the letters of
his friend from all the world of sense, the two souls
meet, and he is swept into the infinite world:

> Till all at once it seem'd at last
> The living soul was flash'd on mine,*

---

* This is a casual experience on earth, but it will·be the normal
experience of souls in the world to come. There is a verse in the
poem entitled, *Happy*, which expresses this:

> And mine in this was wound, and whirl'd
> About empyreal heights of thought
> And came on that which is, and caught
> The deep pulsations of the world.

Many other instances occur in the poems. The mother in *Rizpah* hears her son's voice on the wind, calling to her. In the hour of her death he calls so loud that she dies in bliss after her awful sorrow. In *The Ring*, the dead mother makes her child conscious of her presence ; the child sees her face ; and the husband feels his dead wife impress her will upon him—

> The Ghost in Man, the Ghost that once was Man,
> But cannot wholly free itself from Man,
> Are calling to each other thro' a dawn
> Stranger than earth has ever seen ; the veil
> Is rending, and the Voices of the day
> Are heard across the Voices of the dark.

In *The Sisters*, the mystic bond which unites them is not dissolved by death. The love and sorrow of the dead overwhelm the life of the living sister ; and the man who loved them both feels them, from the far world, moving always with him. It is the one lovely passage of a poem which is not a great success.

> Now in this quiet of declining life
> Thro' dreams by night and trances of the day,

> This wall of solid flesh that comes between your soul and mine
> Will vanish and give place to the beauty that endures,

> The beauty that endures on the Spiritual height,
> When we shall stand transfigured, like Christ on Hermon hill,
> And moving each to music, soul in soul and light in light,
> Shall flash thro' one another in a moment as we will.

> The sisters glide about me hand in hand,
> Both beautiful alike, nor can I tell
> One from the other, no, nor care to tell
> One from the other, only know they come,
> They smile upon me, till, remembering all
> The love they both have borne me, and the love
> I bore them both—divided as I am
> From either by the stillness of the grave—
> I know not which of these I love the most.

The third question asks whether two souls while still on earth may not, in high-wrought states of intense feeling, also touch each other, sometimes clearly, sometimes obscurely. Tennyson thought it possible. In *Enoch Arden*, when Philip asks Annie to marry him, she answers that it is borne in on her that Enoch lives. When she was wed, a footstep seemed to fall on her path, whispers on her ear ; she could not bear to be alone, she thought when she lifted the latch to enter her house, she might see Enoch by the fire—and these mysterious instincts only passed away when she had a child by Philip. They were the passionate thoughts of Enoch from his far-off isle striking on her heart. And on the day of her marriage, Enoch himself heard

> Though faintly, merrily, far and far away,

the pealing of his parish bells, and started up, shuddering, for then the tragedy of his life was wrought. In fuller statement, *Aylmer's Field* records this belief of Tennyson's. When Edith dies, calling on her lover's name, he hears the cry in London and knows that she is gone :

> Star to star vibrates light ; may soul to soul
> Strike thro' a finer element of her own ?

So speaks the poet, marking the very question which the scientific men in the Psychical Society ask themselves,—Are these touches done through the finer forms of matter, or is that matter spirit ?

These were some of Tennyson's speculations concerning the soul. But they all assumed the existence of a great Spirit, and of our souls as a part of Him. As Tennyson grew old, these assumptions were more and more challenged from the side of philosophy and science, and the world in which he lived grew more and more careless of belief in them. One result of this was an assertion of materialism in which God and the soul were alike denied. He met the materialism in a Drama, *The Promise of May*, for which I have no admiration. It seems to make the altogether false assumption that materialism necessarily ends in immorality.

He is more interesting, and says nearly all he wants to say, in the poem of *The Ancient Sage* —a later *Two Voices*—which contains a great number of speculative answers to the assertions of materialism. Their speculative character induces me to call attention to a few of them in this chapter.

The young man who walks with the Sage declares that there is nothing but what the senses tell us. God has never been seen.

" In yourself," the Sage replies, " the Nameless speaks, and you see Him when you send your soul through the boundless heaven." This is Kant's famous phrase put into verse. "If the Spirit," he adds, " should withdraw from all you see and hear, the whole world of sense would vanish."

" Since God never came among us, He cannot be proved."

"No," answers the Sage, "nothing can be proved. You cannot prove the existence of the world, or of the body or the soul, or of yourself, or of me that speak with you—nor can you disprove these things. Therefore, since you can neither affirm nor deny by reason, cleave to the sunnier side of faith in a Power who makes the summer out of the winter!"

"What Power? The real power is Time, that brings all things to decay."

"There is no such thing as Time. It is relative, not absolute. You cannot argue from its effects. They exist to us, but not to God; and the earth-life and its perishing precede the true life; their darkness is in us, not in reality. It is like the yolk in the egg which breaks out into a new being."

"Ah!" sings the young man, "we are each but as one ripple in a boundless deep. Live, then, only to enjoy, and forget the darkness to which we hasten."

"Yes, but the ripple feels the boundlessness of the deep, and feels itself as at one with its boundless motion. It knows itself alive, and knows that there is a chance, even in the judgment of the understanding, that utter darkness does not close the day. The clouds you see are themselves children of the sun. The light and shadow that you say rule below are mere names. Both are only relative. The Absolute is beyond them both. And, at least, the conclusion to be drawn from our gloom is different from yours—'Eat and drink, for to-morrow we die.' Day and night are only counter-terms like border races always at war. You may talk for ever

in battle about them.   One thing, at the end of all
speculation, is plain.   There is night enough in your
city which you can make into light.   Do it, and
then, before you die, you may see

> The high-heaven dawn of more than mortal day
> Strike on the Mount of Vision."

Thus the Sage ends his speculations, and we see,
in this last advice, the practical moralist emerging
from the metaphysical poet who thinks that Time
and Space do not really exist ; that our life here
is illusion in comparison with the true life which
underlies the illusive ; and that the world of matter
in which we move is only what we, in a distorted
fashion, perceive of Spirit.

The poem is interesting to compare with *The Two
Voices*.   It knits together the views of his old age
and of his youth, the thoughts of 1842 with those
of 1885.   But we see in its constant reference to the
night and decay which beset mankind how strongly
the trouble of the world and of the individual man
had now affected him.   And he asked himself—
If there be a Spirit of whom we form a part and
who loves us, if our real self is the soul, and it comes
from God and goes to God; if it is thus necessarily
immortal—why are we in such trouble ?   The
speculative answer he gives arose out of his reading
of Darwin.   It is—That our body comes from the
brute, and carries the brute with it ; that in the
body, the soul met with the brute, and had to conquer the brute.   In that admixture, the worry and
the battle, the confusion and torment of it all, were
contained.   This battle, repeated in every individual,
is repeated also in the whole race.   It ended quickly

enough for the individual, for he was transferred to a higher world, beyond the brutal elements ; but it was to reach an end for the whole race with as infinite a slowness as it had been conducted in the past. Æon after æon was to pass before man, as a whole, would reach his perfection. I think that this latter view, of which I have elsewhere spoken, was a pity ; but how is a poet to avoid trouble in his art when he allows himself to be influenced by scientific theories ? He is sure to disturb the clearness of his fountain. He ought to keep out of science altogether.

As to the individual, it was different. Why did God link a piece of divine being to a brutal matter ? What could be the use of it ? In *In Memoriam*, in many poems before and after it, the problem is stated and speculations are made upon it. It was partly done, as we have already seen, that the soul might realise its personality ; might, having lived in the body, learn that it had distinct being ; and indeed, so far as we know, there is no other way of learning it. But there was something more. This was done in order that the soul might conquer the brute, and having conquered, might know that it could live for ever on a higher plane. When the beast was worked out, then the soul knew itself to be of God, and from God, and belonging to God, for ever. This is put most clearly in that poem entitled, *By an Evolutionist*, where we find Tennyson, at the age of eighty years, telling us not only what he thought, but also to what he had attained. Its personal record is of a profound interest. We hear one of our greatest men, in whom imagination burned to the close of life, revealing what he believed God had done for him, and had given him power to do.

> If my body come from brutes, tho' somewhat finer than their
>   own,
> I am heir, and this my kingdom.   Shall the royal voice
>   be mute?
> No, but if the rebel subject seek to drag me from the throne,
>   Hold the sceptre, Human Soul, and rule thy Province of
>   the brute.
>
> I have climb'd to the snows of Age, and I gaze at a field in
>   the Past,
>   Where I sank with the body at times in the sloughs of a
>   low desire,
> But I hear no yelp of the beast, and the Man is quiet at last
>   As he stands on the heights of his life with a glimpse of a
>   height that is higher.

So it was with the poet at the close of his long contention ; and when it comes to that, speculation is no more, and certainty is hard at hand.   The certainty is expressed even in this very volume of 1885.   Yet his well-loved speculation of the Soul coming out of the Deep and returning to it again asked once more for recognition, and attained it.

> Sunset and evening star,
>   And one clear call for me !
> And may there be no moaning of the bar,
>   When I put out to sea,
>
> But such a tide as moving seems asleep,
>   Too full for sound and foam,
> When that which drew from out the boundless deep
>   Turns again home.

Twilight & evening bell
and after that the dark
and may there be no sadness of farewell
When I embark.

For though from out this bourne of time & space
The flood may bear me far
I trust to see my Pilot face to face
When I have crossed the Bar.

CHAPTER XV

THE NATURE POETRY

" THE love of Nature," the meaning of which
term we understand without explanation,
has reached its greatest and most various development in the nineteenth century. It had always
been a part of an artist's soul among the Aryan
families of the earth, but in these last hundred
years Nature has risen almost into an equality
with humanity as a subject of art. In our own
country, Turner, during a long life, shaped into
thousands of pictures, drawings and studies, the
impressions he received from solitary Nature, and
with a passion, which, changing its methods year
by year, never changed its intensity. And he
was only the greatest of a host of painters who
have, in solitary love of Nature for her own sake
recorded her doings and her feelings with an inti-
macy, affection and joy which has been as eager
and as productive in France as in England. The
musicians were not apart from this movement.
We know from their letters and books that they
composed a great number of pieces for the express
purpose of recording all they felt in the presence
of Nature, and when alone with her. The prose-
writers of fiction and fancy gave themselves up

almost too much to natural description; and many
books exist which are nothing more than emotional
statements of the profound love of their writers for
Nature in her solitudes. The poets were not, of
course, behindhand. England, France, Germany,
Italy, Spain, but chiefly the three first, were driven
to express this love of Nature when they were
isolated with her as a bridegroom with a bride.

Wordsworth was the first to lift this love of
Nature for her own sake into a worship ; and it
passed on, receiving no less incense, to Walter
Scott and Byron, to Shelley and Keats. It exists,
undiminished, in Browning, in Swinburne, and
Morris, and in a host of other poets whose names
we need not here recall. Each of these had his
own special way of feeling the beauty of the natural
world, and his own manner of representing it, but
the lonely love they all felt was the steady element
underneath their individual forms of expression.
Tennyson had his own method, and it was different
from that of all the others. It differed curiously,
and the results to which we are led, when we consider it, are curious.

Mainly speaking, that difference consists in the
absence from his mind of any belief or conception
of a life in Nature. He described Nature, on the
whole, as she was to his senses, as she appeared
on the outside. He did it with extraordinary skill,
observation, accuracy and magnificence ; and we
are full of delight with this work of his. I have
dwelt on it from poem to poem, and I hope I have
succeeded in making clear my full admiration of its
power, beauty, variety and range. But when we
have done all this, and think less of particular

descriptions, and more of the whole impression made by his work on Nature, we are surprised to find that our interest in Tennyson's poetry of natural description is more intellectual than emotional. We ask why, and the answer is—He did not conceive of Nature as alive. He did not love her as a living Being.

Again, when we read his natural descriptions, we find them drenched with humanity. It is impossible, save very rarely, to get away in them from the sorrows, or the joys of man. But when we do not meet with humanity in his landscape, the landscape by itself is cold. It rarely has any sentiment of its own. The sentiment in it is imposed upon it by the human soul; so that, at last, we are driven to say : " On the whole, this poet did not care much to be alone with Nature, and did not love her dearly for her own sake. And this is strange ; it is unlike any other great poet of this century."

These are the two curious wants in his poetry of Nature, and I believe I can make most clear how he differed from the other poets by describing their position towards Nature in contrast with his own.

I take Wordsworth first. I need not say too much about his view of Nature. I have written of it elsewhere, and many others have also dwelt upon it. But, largely speaking, he believed within his poetic self that Nature was alive in every vein of her; thought, loved, felt, and enjoyed in her own way, not in a way the same as we, but in a similar way, so similar that we could communicate with her and she with us, as one spirit can communicate with another. There is a sympathy between us ; but there is this difference, that, with few exceptions, she is the giver and we the receiver. Then, what is true of the whole of Nature is true of the parts. Every flower, cloud, bird and beast, every mountain, wood and every tree, every stream, the great sky and the mighty being of the ocean, shared in the life of the whole, and made it, in themselves, a particular life. Each of them enjoyed, felt, loved, thought, in its own fashion and in a different fashion from the rest. Each of them could send its own special life to us men, as well as to one another; could give us sympathy and receive our gratitude. This was no mere dream, it was a reality to Wordsworth. It is not the fancy of a lover of his, gathered from poetic phrases in his work, nor is it an impossible philosophy. No one can say that it may not be true. It cannot be proved, indeed, but it cannot be disproved. He lays it down in clear form at the end of *The Recluse* as a theory which is at the base of all his poetry of Nature and Man. There is a pre-arranged harmony, he says, between man's mind and the natural world which fits them to one another, which enables them to wed one another ; and the philosophic ground of this theory is that both Nature and Man, being alike from God, and existing together in God, are capable, when separated from one another in this phenomenal world, of coming together again, and finding themselves to be consciously in a union, one with another, of mutual joy and consolation. This was the philosophic conception in the realm of which he always lived. Imagination took it up, and clothed it with glory and honour, and put into it an eager heart of life, so that Nature was his dearest friend, and all its motions in all things his passionate delight. Wherever he went, he had perfect companions, and each of them had something new to say. Wherever he went, he saw all things in an intercommunion, the love of which being given and received, made the majesty, beauty and harmony of the universe ; and the sight filled him with incommunicable rapture. And this intercommunion was of life with life. In one word, every distinct thing in Nature had a soul of its own. He seems to have gone even further. Every place—with all the separate lives which belonged to its flowers, clouds, stones, lakes, streams, and trees—had, over and above these lives, a collective life of its own. Hence such phrases as "the souls of lonely places." And, finally, all the souls of these separate places and of all their separate objects, together ran up into the Spirit of the Earth, and then into the One Spirit of the Universe.

Shelley (without Wordsworth's quasi-philosophic ground for his belief) held at root the same idea that Wordsworth held—that all the universe was alive, and that every part of it had its own particular life in the whole. He represented this vast Being in the *Asia* of the *Prometheus Unbound.* " Life of life," he calls her, in the Hymn of all her nymphs. She is the vital Love which makes the life of the Universe. She pervades every part of the animate and the so-called inanimate creation, making in everything a living spirit which lives its own life and loves in its own way ; so that every invisible molecule of vapour sucked by the sun from ocean or the forest-pool has its own delightful indweller. Practically speaking, this is a view of Nature equivalent to Wordsworth's, only that which Wordsworth conceived as Thought evoiving in life, Shelley conceived as Love evolving in life.

> The love whose smile kindles the universe,
> The beauty in which all things live and move.

Shelley then sets man, if he would escape from the darkness of sense, face to face with a living world, whose joy he might see, whose sympathy he might claim, whose life he might share, and whose life was love.

Had Tennyson any conception of this kind held, with certain differences, by these two poets with regard to Nature? Did he conceive of an active life in the natural world and its parts? Does his Nature breathe, enjoy, and love? Can we feel a personal affection for it, or believe that it gives some affection back to us, or that it is, with us, a vital part of a universal love, or a universal thought? I do not think, save in a few indefinite touches of fancy, or in an isolated poem like the song of *The Brook*, that we find any principle of this kind conceived by Tennyson, or embodied in his Nature-poetry. His natural world is not of itself alive; nor has it anything to do with us of its own accord. It is beautiful and sublime; we can feel for it admiration or awe; but it sends nothing of itself to us. It is the world of the imaginative scientific man, who has an eye for beauty, and a heart to feel it. Matter is matter to Tennyson, though no doubt he often thought of it as having no absolute existence. But he saw it, when he described it, in its existence to us, and in that relative existence he felt no conscious life in it.

There is, then, in his poetry of Nature an entire absence of that happy union of heart to heart which we feel established between us and Nature when we read the poetry of Wordsworth or Shelley. Tennyson, so far as Nature is concerned, is not our beloved companion in the lonely places of the hills, in the woods, beside the stream, near the great sea, or when we watch the moving sky. We can read him in these places with pleasure, if we read him for his records of humanity, for their pathos or their joy; but we do not read him if we wish to escape from humanity and to live with Nature alone. There is no warmth, no life, no love in his Nature. His descriptions of what he sees of the outside of the world are luminous and true, but he does not pierce below the surface of phenomena to a living soul in the universe that enjoys its own life, and can send that life to meet our own.

"So much the better," many persons will say. "There is no living soul in Nature. These are the dreams of a certain class of poets, and we welcome Tennyson, who describes things as they are with beauty and with clearness." Well, I have no quarrel with these persons. It is delightful to read Tennyson's natural descriptions, and I have shown in this book that I enjoy, admire, and honour them. I can even endure to be told that he took care, as in that description of the cove at Tintagil, that everything he said wondrously of the waves was yet scientifically true—as if that mattered

in poetry.   All I desire to say is, that this way of
looking at and feeling Nature is not the way of
the other poets of this century, whose dreams were
to them realities, and who loved Nature, not as a
picture, which was Tennyson's way, but as a living
being.

Again, when we take Coleridge, we are also in
contact with a theory which gave a life to Nature,
so that we could feel in it a spirit which answered
to our own.   Nature was not, in his poetry,
separate from us, as Wordsworth and Shelley
held ; Nature *was* ourselves.   The apparent world
was but the image of our own thoughts.   But
those thoughts, and therefore the apparent world,
were part of the life of the great Spirit.   In Him
we and the universe were both alive.

> O the one life within us and abroad
> Which meets all motion and becomes its soul!

We give, that is, its life to the universe.   What
answers from it to us is life, but it is our own.
When we are dull and dead of heart we get
nothing back :

> I may not hope from outward forms to win
> The passion and the life, whose fountains are within.

And then occurs this famous passage in which
what he thinks is so clear that to read it is to
understand :

> O Lady ! we receive but what we give,
> And in our life alone does Nature live ;
> Ours is her wedding garment, ours her shroud !
>   And would we aught behold, of higher worth,

Than that inanimate cold world allowed
To the poor loveless, ever-anxious crowd,
　　Ah! from the soul itself must issue forth
A light, a glory, a fair luminous cloud
　　Enveloping the Earth—
And from the soul itself must there be sent
　　A sweet and potent voice, of its own birth,
Of all sweet sounds the life and element!

　　　　*　　　*　　　*　　　*　　　*

Joy is the sweet voice, Joy the luminous cloud—
　　We in ourselves rejoice!
And thence flows all that charms or ear or sight,
　　All melodies the echoes of that voice,
All colours a suffusion from that light.

It is plain from these lines that Nature lived to Coleridge because he lived. The universe breathed with our being, and we loved in it the Life of God which was in ourselves. Coleridge never, then, describes Nature from the outside, as if it were a mere picture.

Had Tennyson any notion of this kind with regard to the natural world? Now and again he seems to approach it, but he does not grasp it as a faith. In his poem, *The Higher Pantheism*, he thinks of the universe as a Vision. But the vision is distorted, imperfect, and out of gear, because we are distorted, imperfect, out of gear. If we could get right and straight, that which we perceive would seem perfect, as it really is. For " That vision—is it not He? " This dim, distorted theory — as contorted in itself as it makes the universe of Nature be to us—might be brought into some relation to the theory of Coleridge, but it is better to pass it by, as Tennyson practically did. It had no direct influence over his natural description. It leaves his Nature lifeless.

This theory would not, perhaps, have left Nature lifeless to him, if he could have fully believed it. But he left it as a suggestion. It was a question he addressed to us and the universe—" This vision —is it not He ?" and to this question he had no clear answer to give. There *is* something, he thought, below the appearance of Nature, but what it is we can only guess ; and it may be something absolutely different from what we perceive the universe to be, or what we imagine to underlie our perception of it. He believes that the life of God is there, but what we see and feel in Nature tells us nothing true about that life. We only see that distorted image of it which is mirrored by our imperfection. Hence, even when Tennyson wrote about Nature within this quasi-pantheistic theory, he could not feel any love for her, nor attribute any life to her, because she was only a false picture of the true world. But he could describe what he perceived ; and he chose out of all he perceived that which he thought beautiful, and drew it as it was to the senses, not to the soul; as lifeless matter, not as living spirit.

There is another little poem concerning this supersensuous, unattainable secret which is hidden below phenomena, and which is contained in full in every separate part of the whole :

> Flower in the crannied wall,
> I pluck you out of the crannies,
> I hold you here, root and all, in my hand,
> Little flower—but *if* I could understand
> What you are, root and all, and all in all,
> I should know what God and man is.

Yes, I daresay ; but this sceptical position of

mind towards Nature, this demand to understand, prevented him, as a poet, from feeling any soul in the universe. He spoke of things only as he saw them. He said, I repeat, exactly what the scientific man, with an eye for beauty, would wish to be said about Nature. The descriptions then are vivid, accurate, lovely on the outside, but cold. They have no voice of love or comfort for the heart of man. When I say this, I apply it only to his descriptions of Nature apart from humanity, of Nature by herself. When he mingles up human life with Nature, then his descriptions of her seem warm. But it is the human sentiment transferred to Nature which warms her. By herself, in the poetry of Tennyson, she remains without any sympathy of her own for us.

I turn now to Walter Scott and Byron, and contrast them as Nature-poets with Tennyson. Neither of them had any of these half-philosophic views of Nature, but they had a lively delight in the natural world for its own sake, and in isolation from humanity. They could spend hour after hour alone in the wild land, thankful that man did not intrude upon them, and satisfied to the heart with the beauty of solitary Nature. In the midst of his story of *The Lady of the Lake* or of *Rokeby*, Scott rejoices to sever himself from his human tale, and to describe for his own special pleasure the islands of Loch Katrine and the narrow pass which led to them, or the glens of the Greta and the Tees, as if there was nothing else in all the world for which he cared.

Byron has the same solitary pleasure in Nature, the same love of her for her own sake, apart from

man.   It is the only joy left to Manfred, who spends
hours alone among the icy splendours of the Alps,
and loves to talk with the witch of the torrent when
he most hates to talk with man.   Byron rejoices
everywhere in his poetry to lose humanity in
Nature.   The verse I quote from *Childe Harold*
paints this part of his poetic life :

> To sit on rocks, to muse o'er flood and fell,
>   To slowly trace the forest's shady scene,
> Where things that own not man's dominion dwell,
>   And mortal foot hath ne'er or rarely been ;
>   To climb the trackless mountain all unseen,
> With the wild flock that never needs a fold ;
>   Alone o'er steeps and foaming falls to lean—
> This is not solitude, 'tis but to hold
> Converse with Nature's charms, and view her stores
>   unroll'd.

There is none of this lonely joy in Nature in the
poetry of Tennyson.   Man—other men, or himself—
always intrudes.   Some friend steps in, some
human event that has been in the place, some
human passion which the scene illustrates. Tennyson
must have his man.   He is half afraid to be with
Nature alone ; at least he has no satisfaction till he
can people his solitude.   I scarcely remember a
single description of Nature for her own sake, and
alone, in Tennyson ; and this also divides him from
all the other poets of this century.   We lose, then,
in him that which we still love—solitary communion
with Nature away from humanity.   That deliver-
ance from our trouble, and the world's, is not supplied to us by our poet.   We are kept close to the
weariness of being always with mankind.   I do not
say it is not good for us ; no doubt it is.   But for
all that, we, who desire a holiday at times from the

vast disorder and sorrow of human life, fall back with
a sigh of pleasure on Wordsworth or Scott, on
Shelley, or even on Byron ; and live alone with
Nature.

As to Keats, he has no theory of one universal
Thought or Love pervading Nature with life, like
Wordsworth or Shelley, but he does delight (and
especially in his first poems before *Endymion*) in
Nature for her own solitary sake, like Scott or
Byron. He sits down in a lonely place and paints
it piece by piece with the most observant joy, and
neither his own humanity nor that of others disturbs
the scene. But he also has a view with regard
to Nature which goes beyond that of Byron or
Walter Scott, and which, though it is quite unlike
that of Wordsworth or Shelley, has this in common
with their view——that it bestows an actual life on
Nature. He borrows his belief from the Greek
mythology. The Greek did not say that the stream
was alive, or the tree—but he did say that a living
being, Naiad or Nymph, lived in the stream or in
the tree, and was bound up with them. This was
re-introduced into English poetry by Keats, and it
lifted his Nature out of death into life. The
whole material world, at every part of it, was
peopled by living beings who spoke to us out of
the waves of the sea, and the trees of the wood,
and the flowers of the hills, out of the mountains
and the streams. The beauty and glory of the
universe was the beauty and glory of life. Hence
he had a more intimate sense of loveliness in
Nature than either Scott or Byron, and a simpler
sense of her life than either Shelley or Wordsworth. And this life was sympathetic with our

life. These living beings could communicate with
us ; they had something of humanity in them ; but
without our sense of sin, and without our weariness.
Even of this kind of life in Nature Tennyson has
nothing. He does not even deviate into it in
the classical poems. He has not even Plato's
tolerance for these pretty myths, nor his appre-
ciation of their charm. A tree is a tree to him,
a flower a flower, and nothing more. They are
so and so, he says, and he describes them as
lovely forms of matter, or of what seems so to us.
He tells beautifully how they seem to his eyes, with
great and delightful power, but that is all he does ;
and we desire something more, something which
will leave us "less forlorn" in Nature. We want
to touch life and feel it replying to our life,

> Have sight of Proteus rising from the sea,
> Or hear old Triton blow his wreathèd horn.

This is the main statement, and it seems to me
true. Individual lines or short passages might be
brought forward from which we might infer that he
now and then touched some view which thought of a
living Nature. But this is only momentary, and
he drifts within a few pages into another view, and
then into another view. Wordsworth, Coleridge,
Scott, Keats, Shelley had each of them one clear
conception of Nature ; and all the natural description of each was influenced and ruled by the
special view held by each of them. Tennyson
wavered from view to view. Sometimes he seems
to hold that God is full master of the universe.
Then he slips in another place into the view that
Nature may be partly in the hands of an evil power

and its cruel will. Sometimes he seems to think that Nature is the image our distorted perceptions make of a divine order and beauty which may be spiritual, or may be material; sometimes that she is the form Thought takes to us, and therefore immaterial; sometimes that she is nothing but matter, nothing more than the scientific materialist declares her to be. But none of these views are fixed; no single one of them is chosen and believed. They run in and out of one another. He wavers incessantly, like the pure sceptic, and the result is that all he says about Nature by herself makes no unity of impression upon thought.

What *is* fixed, what is clear, what does emerge in his poetry, after all these philosophic views have been played with, is Nature as she appears to the senses, the material world in all its variety, beauty and sublimity, seen as it is on the outside. "Let me tell," he thinks, "beautifully and truly the facts. I see nothing certainly but forms, and these I will describe." And these he does describe, with an accuracy unparalleled by any other English poet, and with a wonderful beauty and finish of words.

This is the influence of his scientific reading upon him, or rather of the scientific trend of thought during the years in which he wrote his chief poems. His Nature-poetry was materialised; it never suggests a life in Nature; and it is probably owing to his not feeling anything in Nature which spoke to him—soul to soul—that he did not, after his earlier poems, ever appear to love Nature for her own sake, or care to live with her alone. By herself, she was not sufficient for him. In fact, I do not think that I am exaggerating when I say

that the Nature-poetry of this century, which was
founded either on the conception of a life in
Nature, or on enjoyment of her beauty and
sublimity for her own sake alone, without any admixture of humanity, is not at all represented in
Tennyson. Its decay in him makes his position
in the history of the modern poetry of Nature of
great interest. Moreover, that he naturally took a
line on this matter of Nature which was new, and
which on the whole harmonised with a time given
up to the scientific view of the outward world,
marks out, not only his keen individuality, but his
original genius.

Of course this says that there is no sentiment
in Tennyson's description of Nature—and this is
true when he is describing Nature alone, as she is in
herself. It is not true when he introduces humanity
into the scene. Then he groups Nature round the
feelings of men and women, and the human sentiment is reflected on the physical world. Or he
takes Nature up into the life and heart of man, and,
in illustrating man by nature, colours Nature by
human feeling ; or he composes a Nature in
harmony with his own moods and those of his
personages, and this composed Nature is really
humanity. In all these ways Nature is made full
of sentiment. And the work he has thus done on
her is most lovely, far lovelier than his painting,
beautiful as it is, of natural things by themselves in
lucid words and with exquisite care. But the whole
body of sentiment which then flows through the
natural world is human, and only human. It is
associated with the landscape. It does not come
out of Nature herself—as it would have done in

the writings of Wordsworth or Scott, of Byron or Shelley or Keats.

That distinctiveness, however, makes us only the more eager to feel the humanised Nature of Tennyson, and to get from it the pleasure that it gives. It is a different kind of pleasure from that given to us by the other poets in regard of Nature; or rather, the kind of beauty which gives that pleasure was more fully wrought out by Tennyson than by any of the others. We are charmed, then, by his Nature-poetry when it is humanised, or when we wish to remember ourselves in the midst of Nature. But when we wish to get rid of humanity and to get rid of self-consciousness, to touch a Soul in Nature, to feel her life beat on our life, to love her for herself alone, in her solitudes—we find nothing in Tennyson to help us. We are forced back by his Nature-poetry either into human life, or into the world of mere phenomena.

CHAPTER XVI

THE LATER POEMS

IT is not an infrequent habit of an artist to try over again in old age the kinds of work which pleased his youth. This is his way of re-living the days when he was young. Other men do this in the silence of memory. The artist does it in work; and I may gather within this simple framework the greater number of those later poems of Tennyson which reach a high excellence, or have a special quality. He reverted to his classical, romantic and theological interests. He felt over again the poetic sentiment of friendship which was a characteristic mark of his youthful poetry, but he felt it with a natural difference. He felt over again in memory, and reproduced, also with the natural difference, the imaginative ardour of a youth for Nature and love,

> When all the secret of the Spring
> Moves in the chambers of the blood;

And, lastly, he returned, and with extraordinary force, in *Merlin and the Gleam*, to that pursuit of the ideal perfection, of the undiscovered land, which in ancient times he had expressed in the *Ulysses*.

First, then, with regard to his interest in classic subjects and the classical poets, he felt again the impulse which long ago produced *Œnone* and *Tithonus*, and shaped it now into *The Death of Œnone*, and, perhaps, into *Demeter and Persephone*. I have already treated of those poems, and need not touch them again. But something yet remains to be said, in general terms, about his imitations and translations of the classic poets, and of the affection and the praise he gave them. These great masters of idea and form, that is, of intellect and beauty, were his daily companions.

The elements derived from this life-long association with the Greek and Roman poets appear in his earliest poems and move like leaven through the whole of his work. They add to the dignity of his poetry; they bring to it a clear, reflective grace; often an old-world charm, as when some pure classic phrase carries with it suddenly into an English poem a breath, an odour of Pagan loveliness. He derives from them a sculpturesque manner in verse which often reminds me of the limbs and of the drapery of the figures in the Elgin marbles; and to their influence are due his desire and his power to see clearly and to describe with lucid accuracy things as they appear, both in human life and in nature, and to trust to this for his effects, rather than to any pathetic fallacies. These, and other qualities naturally accordant with them, were not created in him by the classics, but were educated, even awakened, in him by them. The curious thing which I seem to detect in his writings, and which is quite in harmony with his unmixed English nature, is that he is much more in sympathy with Latin than with Greek poets, much more at one with the genius of Rome than of Athens.

That tendency to over-conciseness, which in his dramas often reaches baldness, may have its root in an admiration of the Latin brevity of phrase. But the Latin language, as a vehicle of expression, did not lose soft grace or suggestion of ornament in the concise phrase. The English language, on the contrary, owing probably to the loss of its inflections, demands more expansion than the Latin, and when its poetic phrases are pared down to the brevity of Latin, they tend to become too austere, too abrupt, too squat, for poetry. Such conciseness does not afford room enough for pleasurable and fitting ornament; the imagination cannot indulge in delightful play or colour. Beauty does not live and change from point to point of the compressed verse, nor thrill along its movement.

Tennyson indeed was not without these sweet graces. His early work, as well as *In Memoriam, Maud, The Princess*, and his lyrics, are rich with tender ornament. I only wish to say that he tended to reduce his ornament too much, as other poets tend to increase it too much. And he sometimes grew cold and naked, so that on the whole we may say of him that he has less of ornament and imaginative play and soft changes than the other poets of this century. Nearly all his dramatic work, for example, has this rigidity, this want of versatility and phantasy and self-delight.

When Tennyson wrote in this fashion, his verse resembles Norman architecture in a village church. It has power, it often fits the subject well, and there is a certain beauty in it; but it would have had as much power, as much fitness, and far more beauty, had it resembled the Gothic of the thirteenth century,

2 G

and been more interesting from verse to verse with lovely ornament, with freer and more gracious invention of detail.   This tendency to austerity, to a certain rudeness or a certain over-fineness, (the two things often go together,) to wide spaces devoid of ornament, is partly due, I think, to his fondness for Latin forms.   The Greeks did not suffer from this over-polish, this beating down of impulse, this educated severity, and necessarily this want of freedom.   Tennyson would have been at all points an even greater poet than he was if he had loved Greece more and Rome less.   The natural liberty, the bold invention, the swift follow-ing of native impulse within well-defined but wide limits of law, the fearlessness which felt that beauty was always right, all of which marked Greek poetry, were not as fully Tennyson's as they might have been.   He frequently pulled too hard at the reins he fitted on Pegasus, and that soaring creature was a little too much subdued to the *manège*.   His art was more Roman than Greek.

The influence of Homer is felt throughout his heroic poetry, but he missed the rush of Homer's verse, its easy strength and freedom.   He gained in his poetry a great deal of the Homeric simplicity, sonorousness, and tenderness, but he did not gain all he might of the variety, naturalness, and the constant entertainment which Homer brings to us from line to line.   Moreover, that extraordinary flexibility to the world of man which belonged to Homer, a flexibility to every type of humanity as great as that of the air to the varied surface of the earth, was only partly possessed by Tennyson. In fact, the time in which he lived had too much

of culture and too little of nature to enable him
to attain this excellence fully.

He twice tried to translate Homer—two celebrated passages in the *Iliad*—and both seem to
me to prove the un-Homeric nature of his art.
They resemble failures more than successes, and
are even less good than might have been made by
poets very much his inferiors. Perhaps a great
poet is specially ill-fitted (owing to his naturally
strong individuality) for translating another great
poet. But even granting that, these translations
are overcarefully wrought, their art is too self-
conscious, they have no gallop in them, and the
sentiment of the original has evaporated. So
strong is the Tennysonian style, that Homer is
changed into Tennyson. Some of this failure
is owing to the vehicle he chose. Of all forms
of possible English verse, blank verse is the least
fitted to represent the Homeric hexameter. It
wants especially that shout of the long syllable
of the final dactyl which above everything else
gives its leap and cry and force to the Homeric
line, and sends it rushing to its close like the
steeds of Achilles to battle.

These Homeric translations were the only translations he ever published. But he did try to
reproduce some of the classic metres in English,
and succeeded as well as others, so far as the
metres are concerned, and better than others, so far
as the usage of words is concerned. The poem
written in alcaics to Milton is a beautiful, brilliant,
sound-changing, and harmonic thing. But it is
English in note. Tennyson never imitated; in all
he did he was English and himself. Though he

loved, as I said, the Latin conciseness, he never wrote in the manner of the Latin poets. The literary movement of *Lucretius*, though the poem is Roman in feeling to the backbone, is English, as it ought to be, not Lucretian.

Again, Virgil had more influence over him than Homer; we feel the power and the delicacy of this master in Tennyson's poetry, not in imitation, but as a controlling influence towards soft precision of phrase; but had he tried to translate Virgil he would have entirely failed. There was a rude Anglo-Saxon element in him which Virgil could not have endured, and which would have, in spite of every care, burst out of his character into such a a translation, and lowered the Virgilian grace. It may have been owing to that native roughness that he admired Virgil so much. In these later poems he wrote the praise of Virgil for the Mantuans, a homage he did not pay to Homer. Old age had increased his enjoyment of a poet he had loved when a boy. The varied kinds of Virgil's work, his subtle excellences, even his twofold relation to humanity, are expressed with a beauty and truth the critics might envy.

> All the charm of all the Muses
> often flowering in a lonely word

fully enshrines what the happy fanatic of Virgil rejoices to have said for him. " I that loved thee," he cries, " since my day began

> Wielder of the stateliest measure
> ever moulded by the lips of man.

" Stateliest measure," says, it seems, too much, and

so does "ocean-roll of rhythm." Virgil's verse is not
the stateliest, and the roll of ocean is stronger than
his rhythm ; but if the phrases suggest that Tennyson lost some of his judgment in admiration, we
like him the more because of that. The praise
also that he gives is expressed with that full mouth
of song which is so rare in an old man's work. A
line like this that I quote is like summer itself in
the golden age—

> Summers of the snakeless meadow,
> unlaborious earth and oarless sea ;

Nor are these lines less noble which tell of the
everlasting power of Virgil, whose imperial verse
shall live when empires are like the phantoms
through whom Æneas went, bearing the branch of
gold :

> Light among the vanish'd ages ;
> star that gildest yet this phantom shore ;
> Golden branch amid the shadows,
> kings and realms that pass to rise no more.

Then, too, Catullus, as well as Virgil, engaged
his heart. He had endeavoured in time past after
the metre Catullus used to the despair of his peers
—" so fantastical is the dainty metre." But now,
in his old age, he passed from the metre to the spirit
of that poet, and felt over again, and with his own
tenderness, and in the lovely place where the Latin
singer sometimes dwelt, the softly-raining tenderness of Catullus for those he loved. *Frater Ave
atque Vale*, he cried among the olive terraces of
Sirmione. For these, then, for Virgil, Catullus,
even for Lucretius, he was more fit comrade than
for Homer. Art cultivated into that which is a little

more over-refined than Nature was more to him than the art which itself is Nature.

Next, Tennyson not only reverted to these classical subjects, he also reclaimed his pleasure in Romance. Old age, though it cannot act romance, lives all the more fully with it in the chambers of the heart. Its stories, its sentiment, far outside of the daily world with which the sage has long been weary, enchant the soul even more than in early youth. It is one of the worst misfortunes of an artist's old age, that his hand can no more express in sculpture or in painting, and his brain no more shape in music or in poetry, all the beauty which he feels. It were better perhaps that he left the shaping aside, and were content with thoughts alone and their emotions. But it is hard not to try, and Tennyson tried in *The Falcon* a tale of Boccaccio, and in *The Foresters* the woodland legend of Robin Hood. Both dramas are quite unworthy of his hand ; and when Oberon, Titania and their fairies enter the groves we hear how sadly they have deteriorated since the days of Theseus. Shakespeare's Oberon and Titania are royal personages, and, though Mustard, Pease-blossom and the rest make their own jokes on Bottom, they would have sooner died than have called Oberon "Ob.," or Titania " Tit." This is the humour of *The Spinster's Sweet-arts* imposed on Fairyland, and it is incredibly clumsy.

Driven by the same feeling for Romance, he had already written in the volume of 1880 on an Irish tale, seeking all too late that plenteous fountain of imaginative work. *The Voyage of Maeldune* is a fine piece of scenic power, written with extraordinary vigour and in racing rhythm, but it has no soul, and is stripped clean of the Celtic charm and of the Celtic pathos. Tennyson loses all the sentiment of the original by imposing on the voyagers his own conception of the Irish character. The warriors who sail boast loudly of their descent; the slightest thing flusters them with anger; they shout, and hate, and wallow in flowers and tear them up in a blind passion, and gorge, and madden, and chant the glories of Finn, and fight with one another, and slay, till only a tithe of them return. This is the English form which he gave to the story—the English pleasure in rough-and-tumble killing for amusement, the Anglo-Saxon *brutalité* imposed upon the Irish nature. Did it seem to him quite impossible that sixty comrades should sail together and be excited by various adventures, without falling out furiously with one another? There is not a trace of this in the original. All are faithful, loving, and tender comrades. Not one of them acts like a drunken sailor at a Portsmouth fair. There is no boasting, no fighting and no slaying. They all return in safety, save three, who did not belong to the band. A gentle air of half-religious, half-romantic sentiment fills the tale : and a little indignation, mixed with a little amusement, belongs to the reader who finds the sorrowful romance of the story lost in the English rudeness.

Indeed, all his life long, Tennyson, though he did love the Welsh tale of Arthur, never felt, or was capable of feeling, the Celtic spirit. He felt something which he thought was it, but it was not. The Celtic magic which Arnold traced in

English poetry was in another world than Tennyson's. Other poets have the Celtic strain in their blood, and it passes into their song, but Tennyson is the unmixed English type. He is the poetic flowering of pure Anglo-Saxonism, the very best it could do alone; and a noble, fair, and splendid flower it is. But he would have climbed to a higher ledge of Parnassus if he had been baptised in the Celtic waters. As it was, he was only English, and the statement accounts for many things, both good and bad, in his poetry, on which I need not dwell. It accounts, among the rest, for the Anglicising of Arthur's character and of his tale. A man with a grain of the Celtic nature in him could never have written the *Idylls of the King* as Tennyson has written it.

Again, he reverted to his old theological interests. I have already shown how full he became of the question of Immortality. The nobly composed poem of *Vastness* is written to enforce a conclusion of the truth of that doctrine. *Despair*, the terrible pathos of which he need not have lessened by an intrusion of his own personal wrath with those who believed in everlasting death or in everlasting hell, is a powerful plea for the immortality a God of Love would naturally secure for man. His poems to friends, and on the death of friends, are all touched with eternal hopes, with his constant cry— Life and Love are not worth living and loving unless they continue, and only in their continuance is the problem of earth's trouble solved. *The Ancient Sage*, as we have seen, took up again this question, and others related to it—the questions of *The Two Voices*, of *In Memoriam*.

Another poem of his, *St. Telemachus*, recurred to
the same theological motive which he treated in his
attack on asceticism in the *Idylls of the King* and
St. Simeon Stylites.   Let the anchorite, it says, no
longer live his deedless life.   Better be stoned to
death in the Forum, and slay a vile custom, than pray
and fast, with life, in the wilderness! Fine things are
in it—Rome flaring lurid, in the hermit's imagination,
at every western sunset, and calling him forth to
act ; the description of the crowd pressing to the
Coliseum, and of Telemachus borne along by that
full stream of men,

> Like some old wreck on some indrawing wave.

I do not know if this poem belong truly to his
old age, but it has not the mighty grip with which
Tennyson would have seized on such a subject in
his youth and manhood.

In the very last volume, this return to his early
theological interests continues. *Akbar's Dream*
records how, in the poet's mind, all religious
differences were merged into one religion of goodness and love ; nor does the poem want phrases of
force and breadth.   A gentle air, a kindly quiet, as
of one who already felt the soft sunlight of a higher
peace than ours, broods over all the late religious
poems.

There is yet another matter in which an old
man reverts to his youth; and this is the emotional
sentiment of friendship.   Mature manhood has not
less of friendship than youth, but it has little time
to cherish its sentiment.   In youth it is different.
We have then time to hover over a friendship, to
prophesy about it, to take it with us for inward

pleasure, or, if we have lost our friend, for sorrow of contemplation. *In Memoriam* is full of that contemplative emotion, and Tennyson was young when he began to write it. The poem entitled *To J. S.*, beautiful throughout with a soft steadiness of chastened thought, and loveliest at its close, is also written in the air of this youthful sentiment, but it is mingled with a wisdom rare in youth.

A later kind of friendship, that of a man who has realised life and finds his affection deepen for his friend, not through imaginative feeling, but through interchange of character with him, and through their interest in humanity, breathes in the poem *To the Rev. F. D. Maurice;* as good in its gay contented way as Milton's sonnets to Lawrence and to Cyriack Skinner, the note of which, in a different form of verse, it emulates. But the earlier sentiment still lives at times. It is not spread now over the whole of life, but arises for a brief period in lonely hours, and only for the dead. There are two poems—*In the Garden at Swainston* and *In the Valley of Cauteretz*—which touch the depths of manhood's friendship in regret.

When age comes, there is a further change. The sentiment of friendship is now like that felt in youth, but the waters from which it arises are different, and its horizon is also different. The work of life is over, and emotion, as in the days of youth, has again time to feel itself. Moreover, the sadness of decay, though it be not allowed to master the soul, yet brings an autumn mist over the landscape of life, in which all thoughts are mellowed, and lays on all its woods a lovely colouring, with the beauty of which the old man is

charmed, with which he plays, but which he knows
is beauty that is departing. What we thus feel for
ourselves, we feel also for our friends who have
grown old with us. They, too, are in their Indian
summer, and year by year the final frost, touching
one or another of them, warns us of our own death.
We cannot look forward to an enjoyment of their
friendship as we did when we were young ; but
those who believe, like Tennyson, in a life to come,
think of friendship renewed in a world where life
is winterless.

These various emotions are a new source of
poetic impulse which, in regard of friendship, is
almost more productive of poetry than its sentiment in youth. Thousands of poems have been
written in their atmosphere, and a collection of
them—for they have a special quality and a unity
of emotion—would be of abiding interest and
pleasure. Some recover a little of the gaiety of
youth ; others have a trembling pleasure, such as a
tree all gold and crimson might have in its own
loveliness, with the knowledge in its pleasure that
the coming night may send the storm to strip it
bare. But if the poet be a person of an equal
mind, such poems have a courageous air, a kindly
tolerance, a wisdom inwoven with love, a gratitude
to life for all its joy, even for the strength of its
sorrows ; and often a delightful brightness as of
a veteran who has kept his shield in all his battles,
and who waits peacefully for the last calling of the
roll.

Many such poems, chiefly of Dedication, occur in
the later volumes of Tennyson. They ought to be
read together when we desire to feel his grace

and power in this special kind of poetry, which no one, I think, has ever done so well. They are revelations of character, and of a character made braver and kindlier by old age. No trace of cynicism deforms them, and their little sadness is balanced by a soft and sunny clearness, by tenderness in memory and magnanimity of hope. Each of them is also tinged with the individuality of the person to whom it was written. The poems to Edward Fitzgerald, to his brother, to Mary Boyle, to Lord Dufferin, possess these qualities, and are drenched, as it were, with the dew of this delicate sentiment peculiar to old age. They look backward, therefore, but they also look forward; and not only friends on earth, but those who have found their life in death, enter into their hour of prospect and of retrospect.

> When the dumb Hour, clothed in black,
> Brings the Dreams about my bed,
> Call me not so often back,
> Silent Voices of the dead,
> Toward the lowland ways behind me,
> And the sunlight that is gone!
> Call me rather, silent voices,
> Forward to the starry track
> Glimmering up the heights beyond me
>   On, and always on!
>
> *The Silent Voices.*

Again, correlative with the sentiment which inspires these poems, there is another kind of poetry which is naturally written in old age, and recurs to those motives of youth which arise out of the happiness of the world and of the poet in the awakening of life in Spring. This poetry is born out of the memories of that early joy, and is also touched with a distinctive sentiment, native only to old age, delicately clear, having a breath of the colour and warmth of youth, and flushed with the hope of its re-awakening. Its poems are like those February days which enter from time to time into the wintry world, so genial in their misty sunlight that the earth seems then to breathe like a sleeping woman and her bosom to heave with a dream of coming pleasure. They recall the past, and prophesy the immortal, Spring. Old age often feels this sentiment, but is rarely able to shape it; but when, by good fortune, it can be shaped, the poem has a unique charm. Of such poems *The Throstle* is one, and *Early Spring* is another. They may have been originally conceived, or even written, in earlier days, but I am sure that they were rewritten in old age, and in its evening air.

Lastly, there are the poems and those portions of poems which are inflamed with the spirit that pursues after the perfection of beauty. Of these *Merlin and the Gleam* is the best. It is this spirit in his work, as it is in the work of all great artists, which gives Tennyson his greatest power over the heart of humanity; and, though I have dwelt on it at the beginning of this book, I cannot do better than dwell upon it at the end, but in a closer connection with his poetry. To quote all the passages which illustrate this temper of his would occupy too large a space; but a long selection might be made of them, until we come to the later poems in which this enkindling aspiration burns with as clear a flame as in the days of his youth. It is even more ethereal, of a more subtle spirit.

Tennyson was never content with the visible

and the material, never enslaved by that which our world calls the practical. He never believed that the things of sense were other than illusions, which dimly represented or distorted the true substance of beauty that lay beyond the senses. His life, like every faithful artist's life, was, therefore, incessant pursuit. The true device of the artist, as it is of the religious man in religion, is this : "While we look not at the things which are seen and temporal, but at the things which are not seen and eternal ; " and what the visible world said or offered to Tennyson, however now and then he was disturbed by the temporary and material, was in reality nothing to him. It had no influence upon his work. "Brothers, I count not myself to have attained, but I press forward," is also as much a device of the artist as it is of the saint. Both, in their several spheres, write that motto on their soul. And Tennyson never found finality in his art, never had any satisfaction, save for the moment of completion, in the outward form he gave to his subject.

It is the Idea after which the artist runs. The moment one form of it is realised, it opens out something more to be pursued, and when that is seized, it discloses, in its turn, another island on the far horizon to which he is bound to sail :

> Gleams that untravell'd world whose margin fades
> For ever and for ever when I move.

To linger in the attainable is the death of art. "Be perfect in love," said Jesus, "as your Father in heaven is perfect in love." Be perfect in beauty, he would say to the artist, as your Father

in heaven is perfect in beauty. And indeed, in a
wider world than ours, the two sayings are one,
for Beauty is the form of Love. At this point,
that word of Blake's is true : " Christianity is Art,
and Art is Christianity." Nor in this view is
humanity neglected, for whom the poet writes and
the painter paints. For, since to love beauty is as
ultimate an end for man as to love goodness and
to love truth, the life of the artist is necessarily
lived for mankind. There is no higher life in all
the world, nor one more difficult and tempted. But
the greatness of the strife is tempered by the beauty
and glory of the ideal world in which the Maker
lives, the light of which is not of the sun or moon
or stars, but of the central source,

> pure ethereal stream,
> Whose fountain who shall tell!

Tennyson had long since embodied his view of
this world beyond the world we see, in which
thought and feeling follow the ineffable and infinite, in his poem entitled *The Voice and the Peak*.
All night the voices of the ocean and the waters of
the earth cried to the silent peak ; and the poet
asks, " Hast thou no voice, O Peak ? " All the
voices, it answers, rise and die, and I, too, shall
fall and pass ; and the earth below me feels the
desire of the deep and falls into it, and is no more.
The outward world vanishes away. Then the poet
replies : There is another world above the senses
that dies not, the world of the invisible thought of
man—

> The Peak is high and flush'd
>   At his highest with sunrise fire ;
> The Peak is high, and the stars are high,
>   And the thought of a man is higher,

> A deep below the deep,
>   And a height beyond the height !
> Our hearing is not hearing
>   And our seeing is not sight.

What is one to do who lives in this world above the visible, where he sees the uncreated light ? What but to leave all the material, and follow the far-off vision ? Some there are, said Tennyson in *The Two Voices* fifty years ago :

> Who, rowing hard against the stream,
> Saw distant gates of Eden gleam,
> And did not dream it was a dream.

Later on, he threw the passion of this spiritual pursuit into a different form in *The Voyage ;* painting this aspiration in those that feel it with too much lightness of character, as if it were only a gay love of youth ; but yet who never turn aside from it—the happy tribe who know not the unremitting strife, the serious passion, or the awful vision of the unapproachable loveliness, which are the badge and the burden of the greater artists.

> For one fair Vision ever fled
>   Down the waste waters day and night,
> And still we follow'd where she led,
>   In hope to gain upon her flight.
> Her face was evermore unseen,
>   And fixt upon the far sea-line ;
> And each man murmur'd, ' O my Queen,
>   I follow till I make thee mine.'

But with Tennyson it was a far graver matter. He was, even to his death, the follower of the mightier vision, of the supernal gleam. This is the subject of a poem which appears in these volumes of his old age—*Merlin and the Gleam ;*

as lovely in form and rhythm and imagination as
it is noble in thought and emotion. It speaks to
all poetic hearts in England ; it tells them of his
coming death. It then recalls his past, his youth,
his manhood ; his early poems, his critics, his central
labour on Arthur's tale ; and we see through its
verse clear into the inmost chamber of his heart.
What sits there upon the throne ; what has always
sat thereon ? It is the undying longing and search
after the ideal light, the mother-passion of all the
supreme artists of the world. " I am Merlin, who
follow The Gleam."

I know no poem of Tennyson's which more takes
my heart with magic and beauty ; but that is a
personal feeling, not a critical judgment. Yet how
lovely, how pathetic, and how noble on the old
man's lips is the beginning :

> O young Mariner,
> You from the haven
> Under the sea-cliff,
> You that are watching
> The gray Magician
> With eyes of wonder,
> *I* am Merlin,
> And *I* am dying,
> *I* am Merlin
> Who follow The Gleam.

Verse by verse we company with the poet flying
forward to the Gleam. To pursue it is the love of
life ; to die in its pursuit is joy, for beyond death
its glory shines. Therefore now, on the verge of
death, he gives his last message to the young,
calling on them to follow, as he has done, the light
that was never reached, but never failed ;

And so to the land's
Last limit I came—
And can no longer,
But die rejoicing,
For thro' the Magic
Of Him the Mighty,
Who taught me in childhood,
There on the border
Of boundless Ocean,
And all but in Heaven
Hovers The Gleam.

IX.

Not of the sunlight,
Not of moonlight,
Not of the starlight !
O young Mariner,
Down to the haven,
Call your companions,
Launch your vessel,
And crowd your canvas,
And, ere it vanishes
Over the margin,
After it, follow it,
Follow The Gleam.

Who would not wish to have written that ? Who would not wish to have so lived as to be able to leave that last impulse to the young, to cry in death that prophet-cry ? It is a cry all the more forcible on his lips because, with all this passion for the ideal, he kept so close to the actual life of men, clinging as intimately to the common thoughts and feelings of his time, so far as his range permitted, as the grass to the varied surface of the earth. But dear as the real was to him, the ideal was dearer still.

These then are the things I have tried to say of his work in old age. And now, having walked so long with a great poet, it is hard to part from him. We have lived in a large and varied world, with its own landscape and its own indwellers; no transient world, reflecting as in a bubble of air the passions and follies, the tendencies and the knowledge of the hour, but a solid sphere built slowly during a lifetime into form. Forty years of creation were given to make this new country of the imagination, which men will visit, and in which they will wander with pleasure, while humanity endures. Every one who in the centuries to come shall spend therein his leisure will leave it and return to his daily work, consoled and cheered, more wise and more loving, less weary and heavy-laden, nearer to beauty and to righteousness, more inspired and more exalted. The permanence of the work of Tennyson is secure. Few are his failures, many his successes; and I trust that this study of him will make men who love him love him more, and those who do not yet love him find that constant pleasure.

INDEX

OF PASSAGES RELATING TO THE POEMS

*The principal references are indicated by the use of
larger figures*